The first thing the Goddess Culdra created was a book.

In the book, she mapped out the size and shape of the universe, and from her design, the universe grew forth.

Culdra also described in it the vast array of Gods and living things to inhabit her newborn world.

This is how the Goddess Culdra created life and the universe--through the magical words she wrote in her book, the Culdcept, the Book of Crea

IGNIS

SYMP ATHIA

ANTI

SYMP AT

550 543 847

I

uldcept

カルド セプト

VOLUME 1

by

Shinya Kankeo

Editorial Supervison:
Omiya Soft

TOKYOPOP

Los Angeles • Tokyo • London • Hamburg

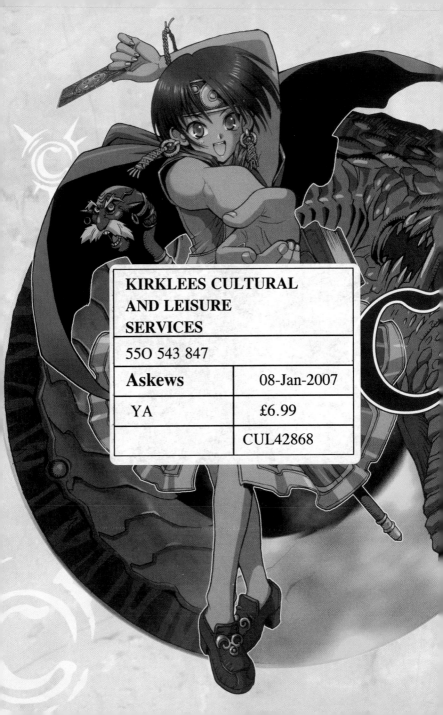

KIRKLEES CULTURAL AND LEISURE SERVICES

55O 543 847	
Askews	08-Jan-2007
YA	£6.99
	CUL42868

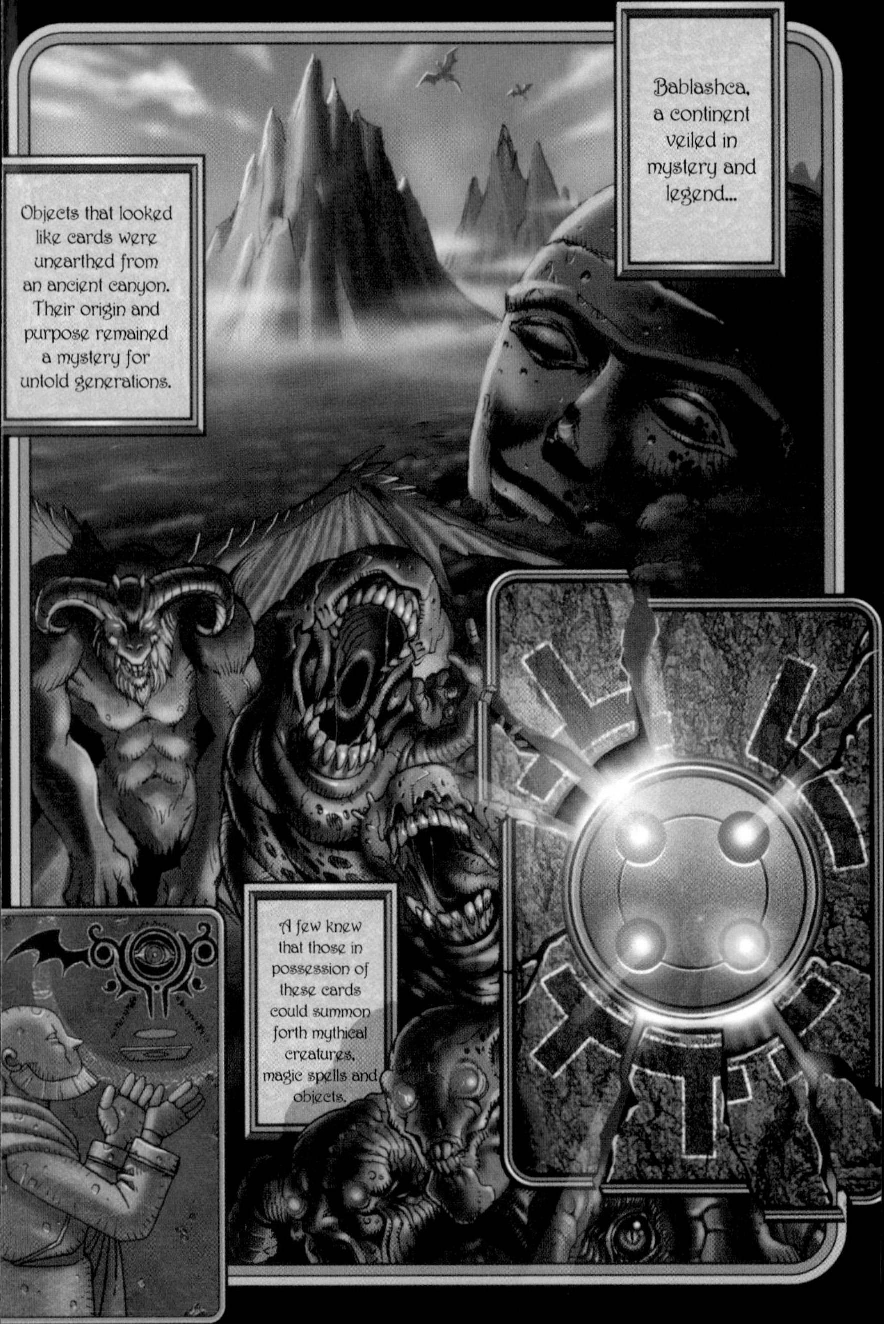
Bablashca, a continent veiled in mystery and legend...
Objects that looked like cards were unearthed from an ancient canyon. Their origin and purpose remained a mystery for untold generations.
A few knew that those in possession of these cards could summon forth mythical creatures, magic spells and objects.

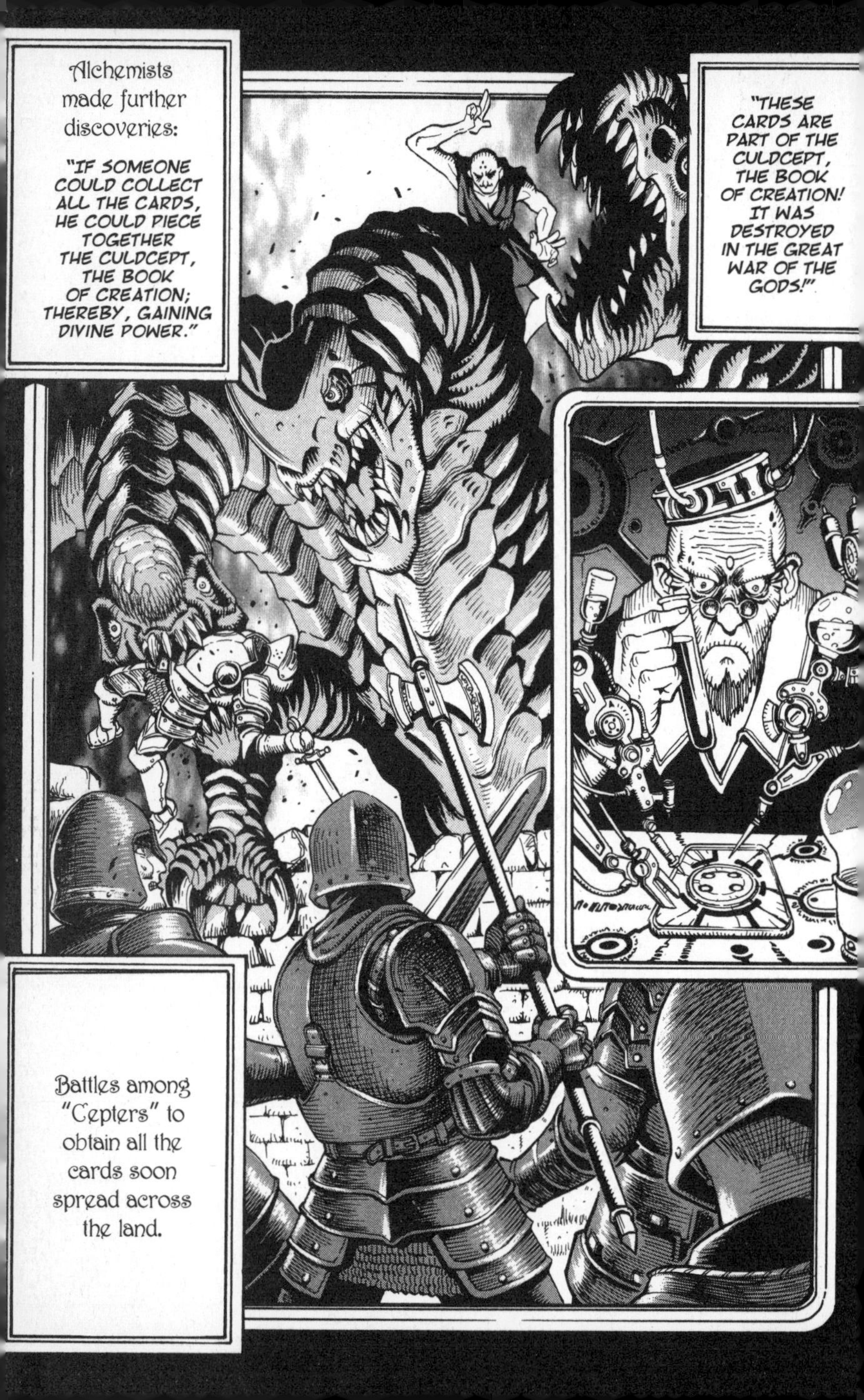
"THESE CARDS ARE PART OF THE CULDCEPT, THE BOOK OF CREATION! IT WAS DESTROYED IN THE GREAT WAR OF THE GODS!"
Alchemists made further discoveries:
"IF SOMEONE COULD COLLECT ALL THE CARDS, HE COULD PIECE TOGETHER THE CULDCEPT, THE BOOK OF CREATION; THEREBY, GAINING DIVINE POWER."
Battles among "Cepters" to obtain all the cards soon spread across the land.

CONTENTS

Culdcept

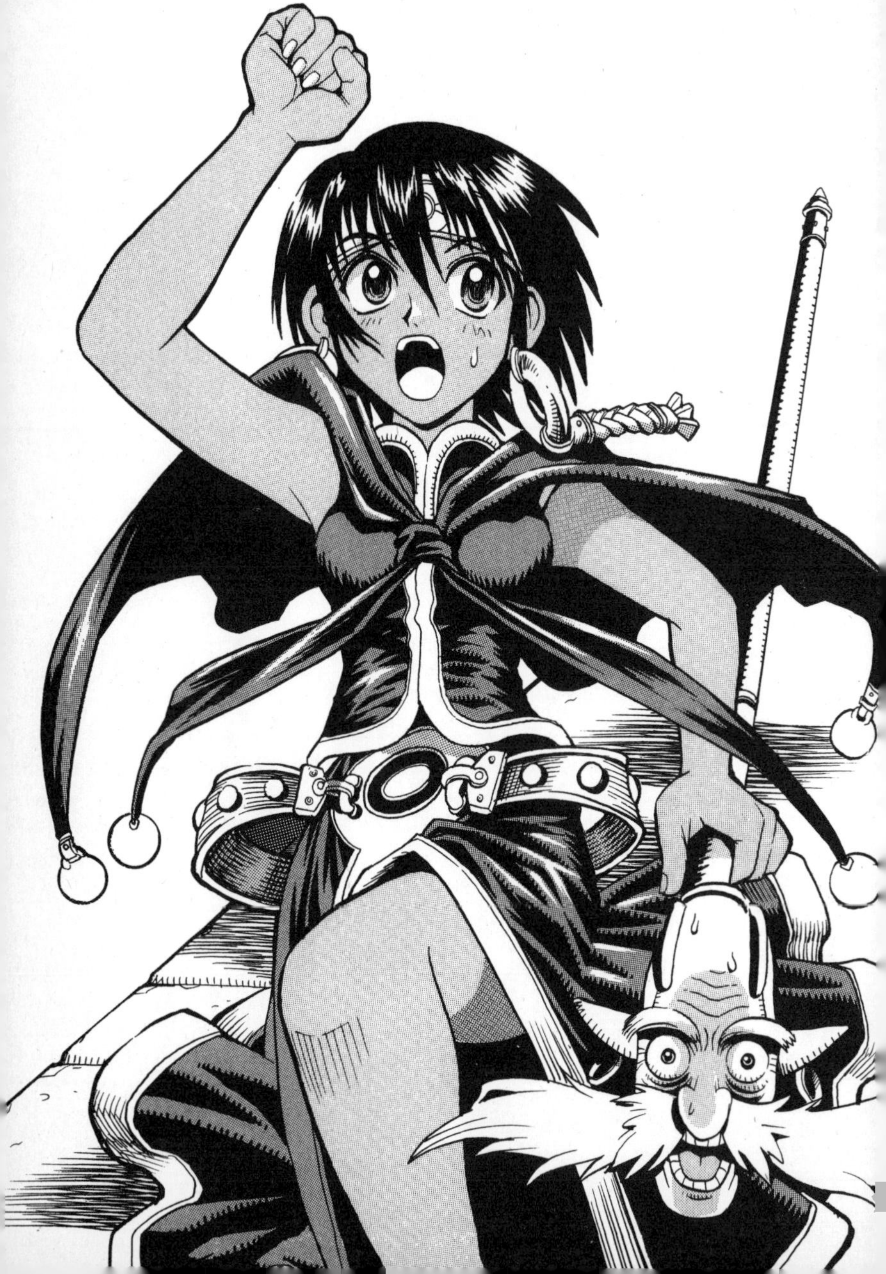

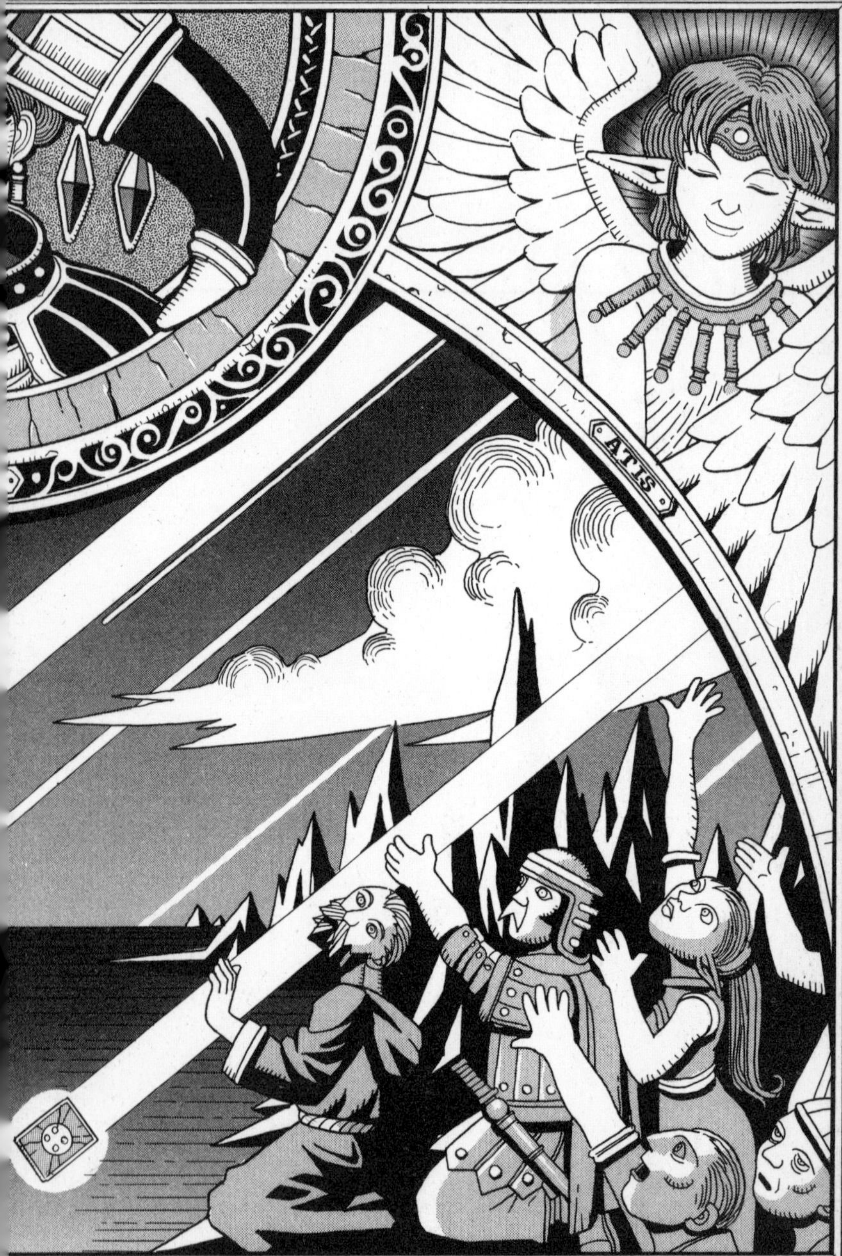
ATIS

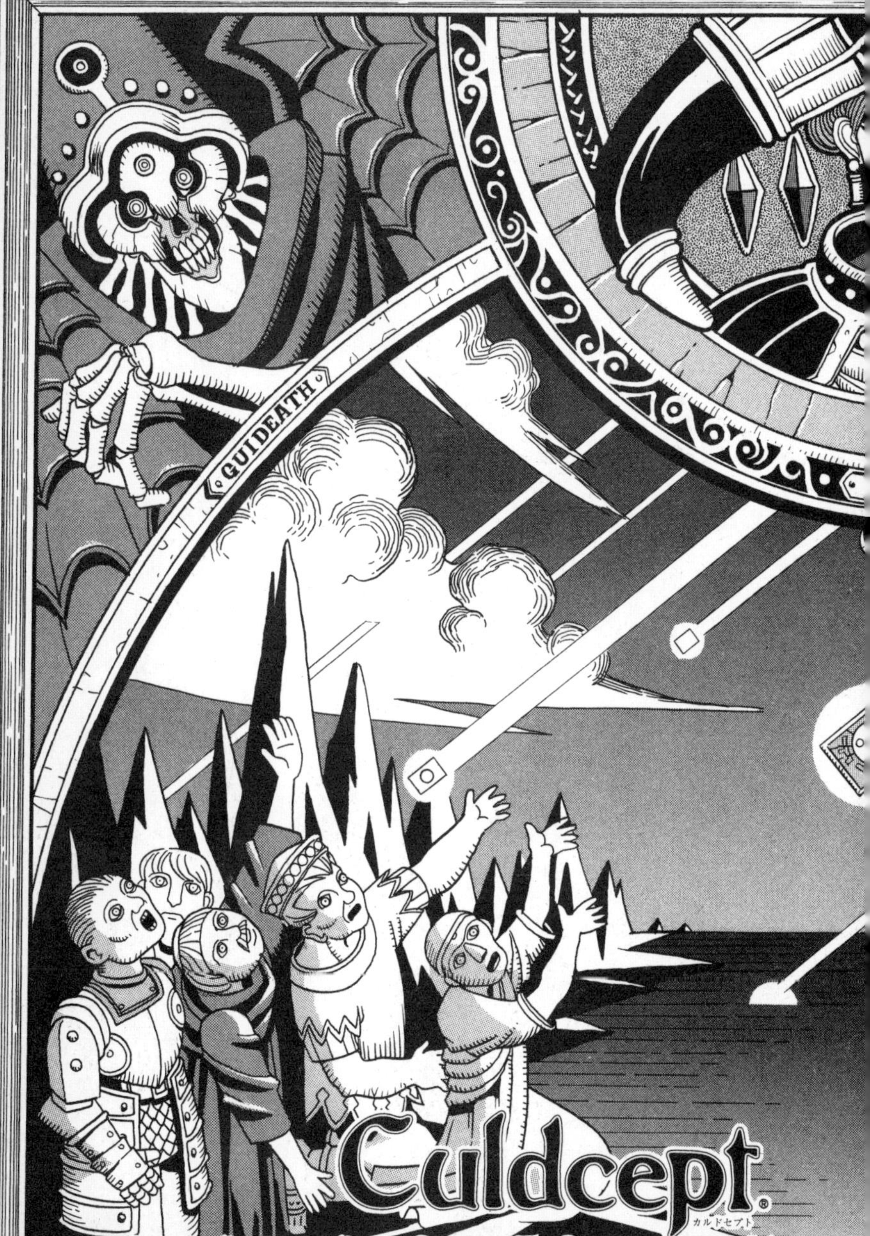
GUIDEATH
Culdcept®
カルドセプト
Round 1 Najaran, a Novice Cepter – The Beginning of Her Adventure

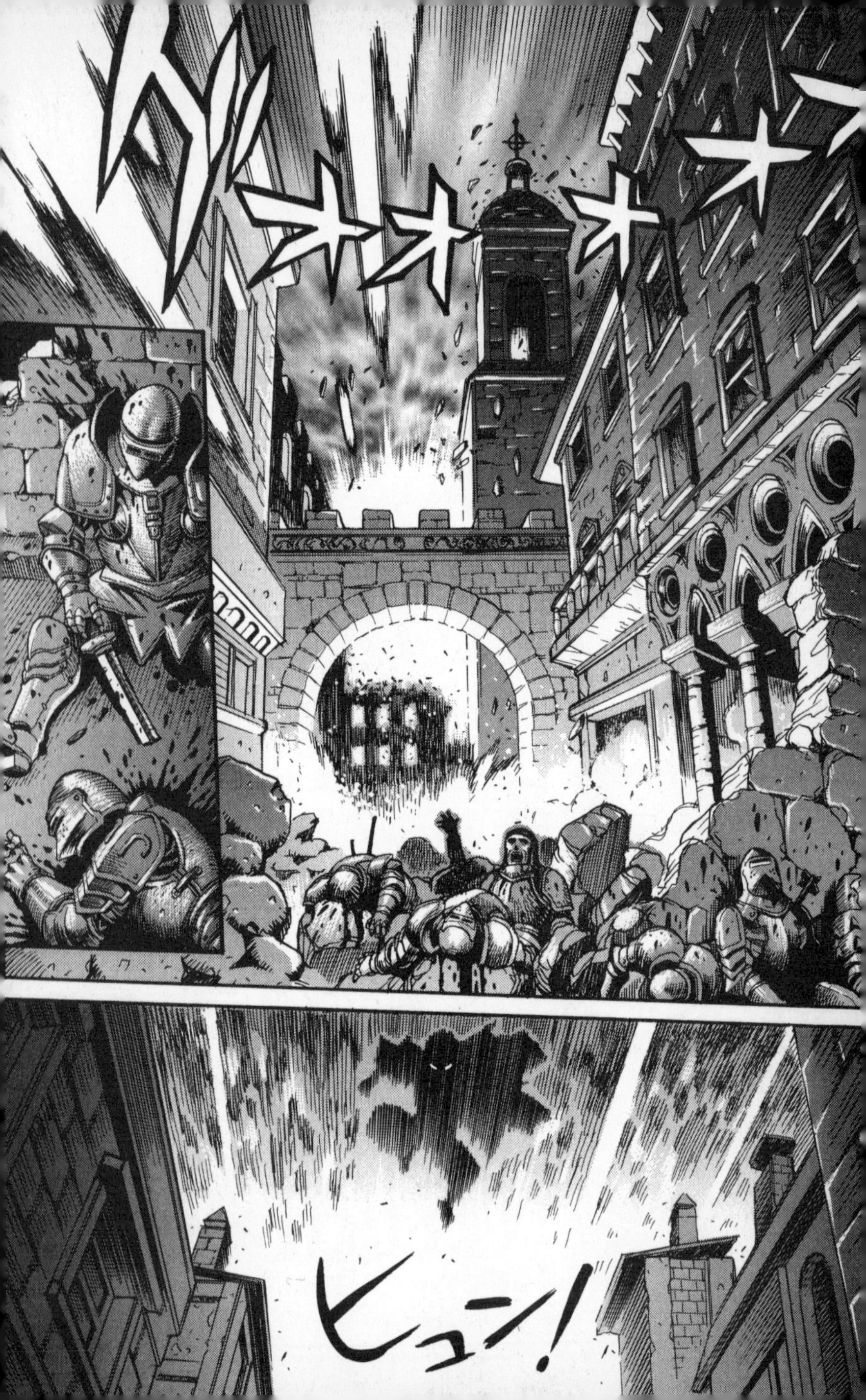
ゴォォォォ
ヒュン!

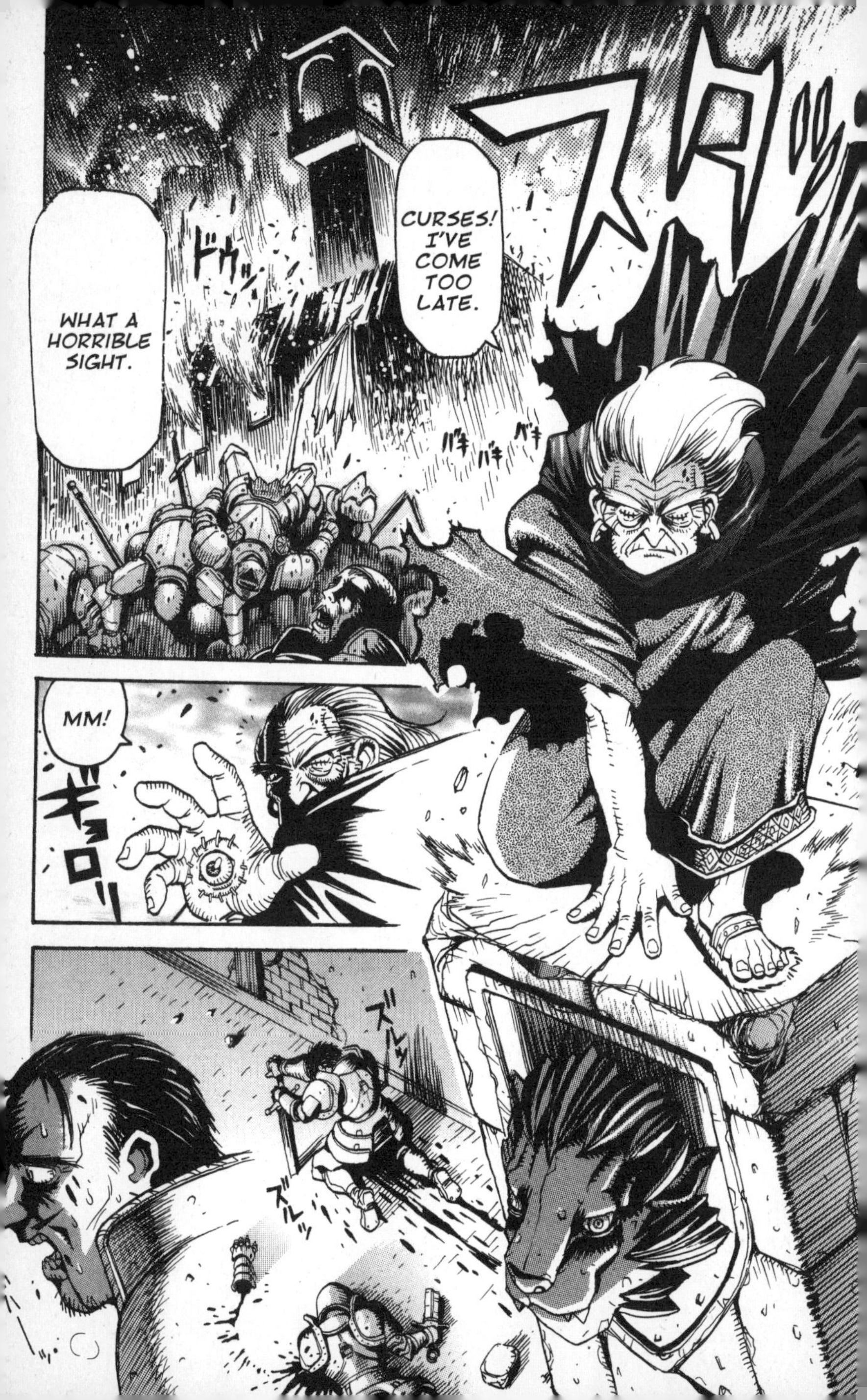
CURSES! I'VE COME TOO LATE.
WHAT A HORRIBLE SIGHT.
MM!

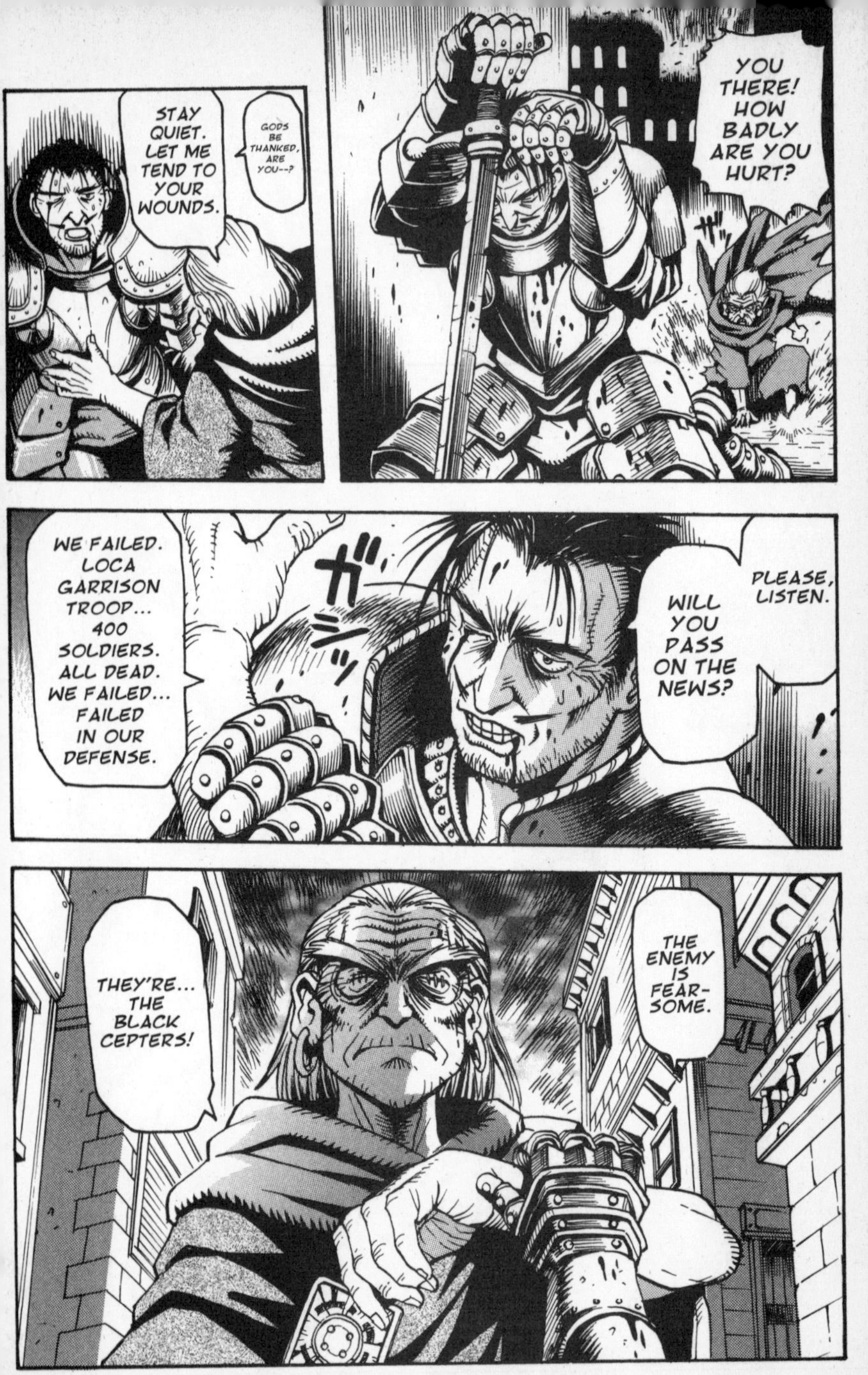
YOU THERE! HOW BADLY ARE YOU HURT?
GODS BE THANKED, ARE YOU--?
STAY QUIET. LET ME TEND TO YOUR WOUNDS.
PLEASE, LISTEN.
WILL YOU PASS ON THE NEWS?
WE FAILED. LOCA GARRISON TROOP... 400 SOLDIERS. ALL DEAD. WE FAILED... FAILED IN OUR DEFENSE.
THE ENEMY IS FEAR-SOME.
THEY'RE... THE BLACK CEPTERS!

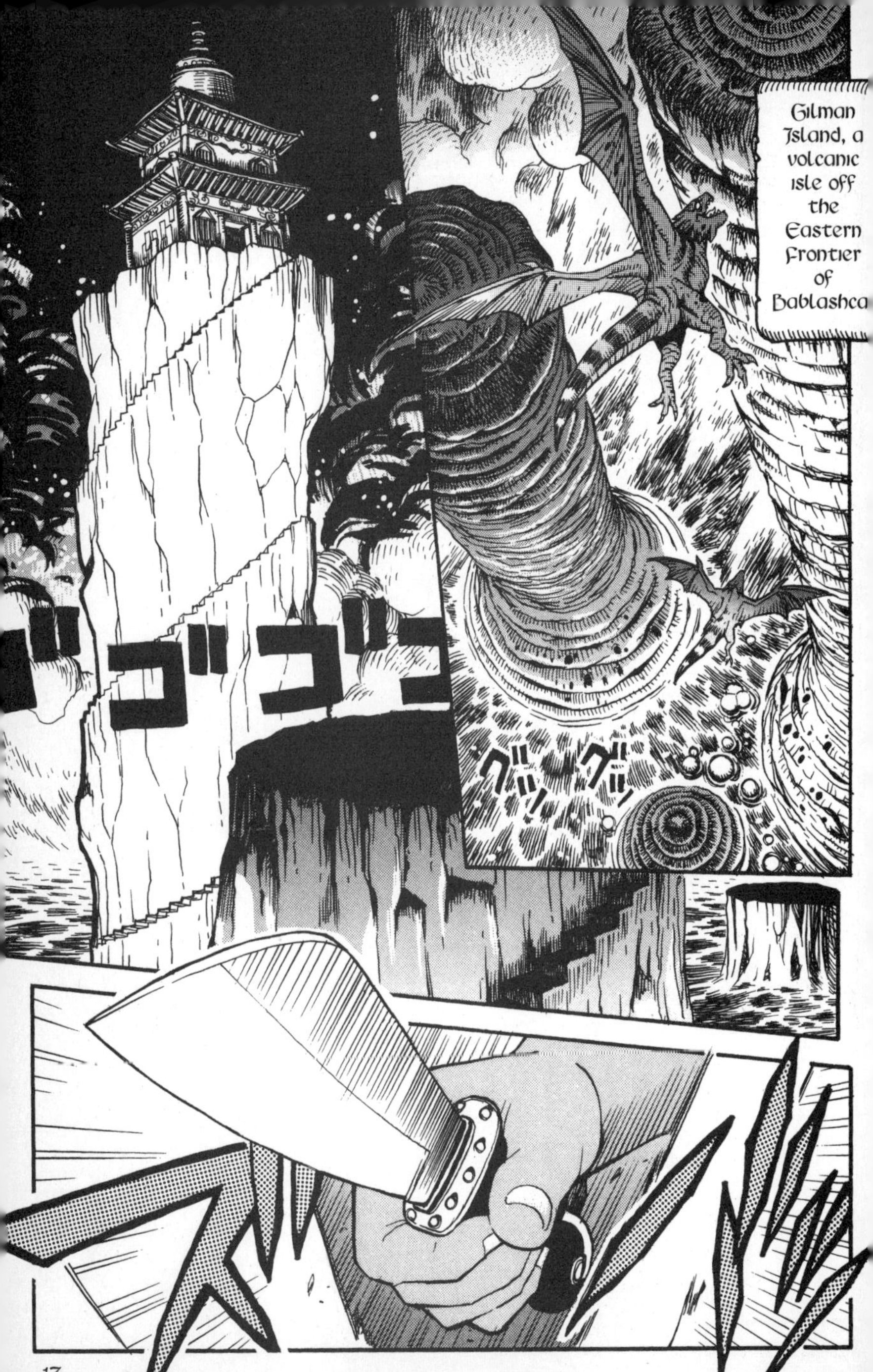
Gilman Island, a volcanic isle off the Eastern Frontier of Bablashea

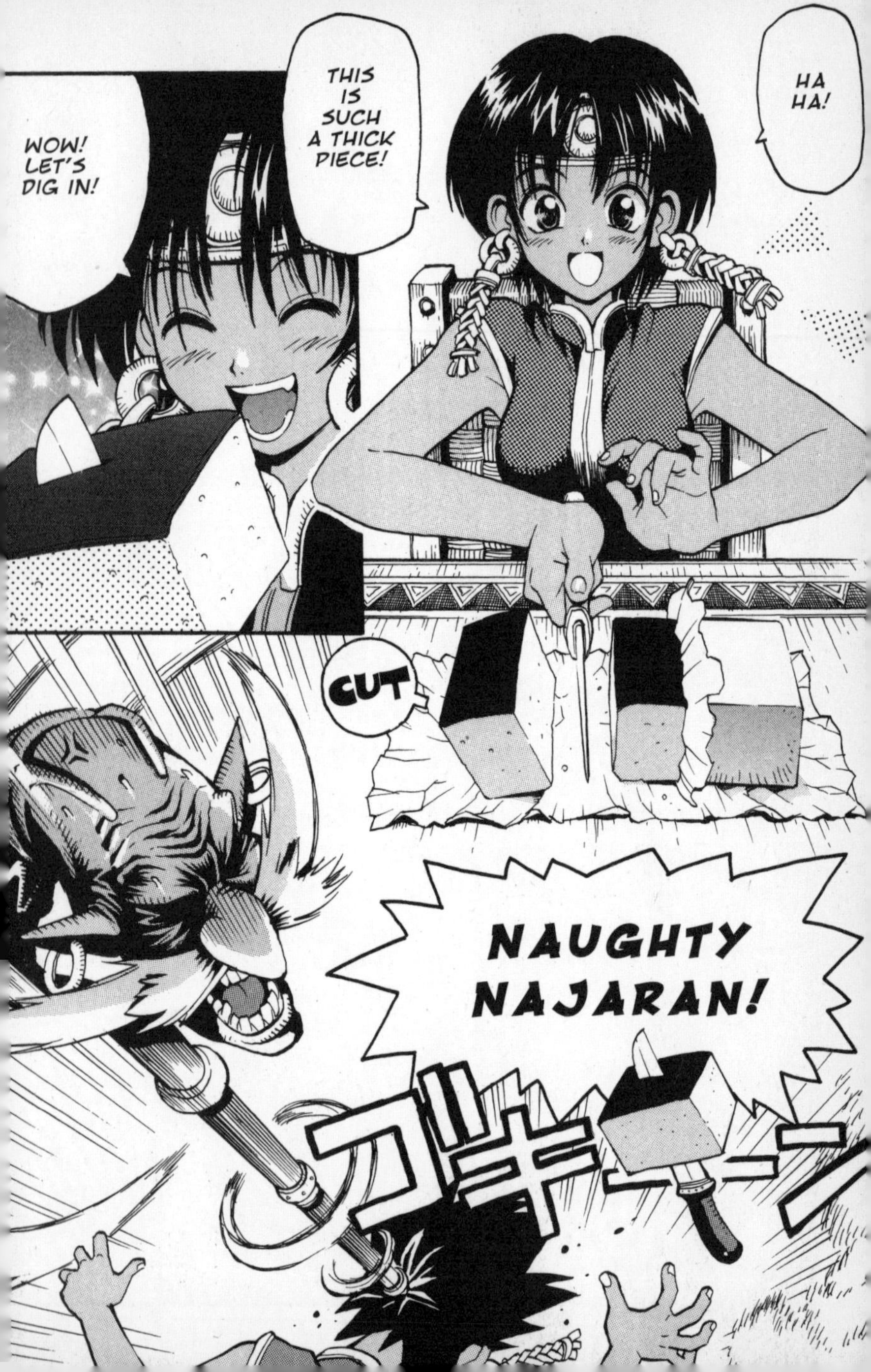
HA HA!
THIS IS SUCH A THICK PIECE!
WOW! LET'S DIG IN!
CUT
NAUGHTY NAJARAN!
ゴキーーン

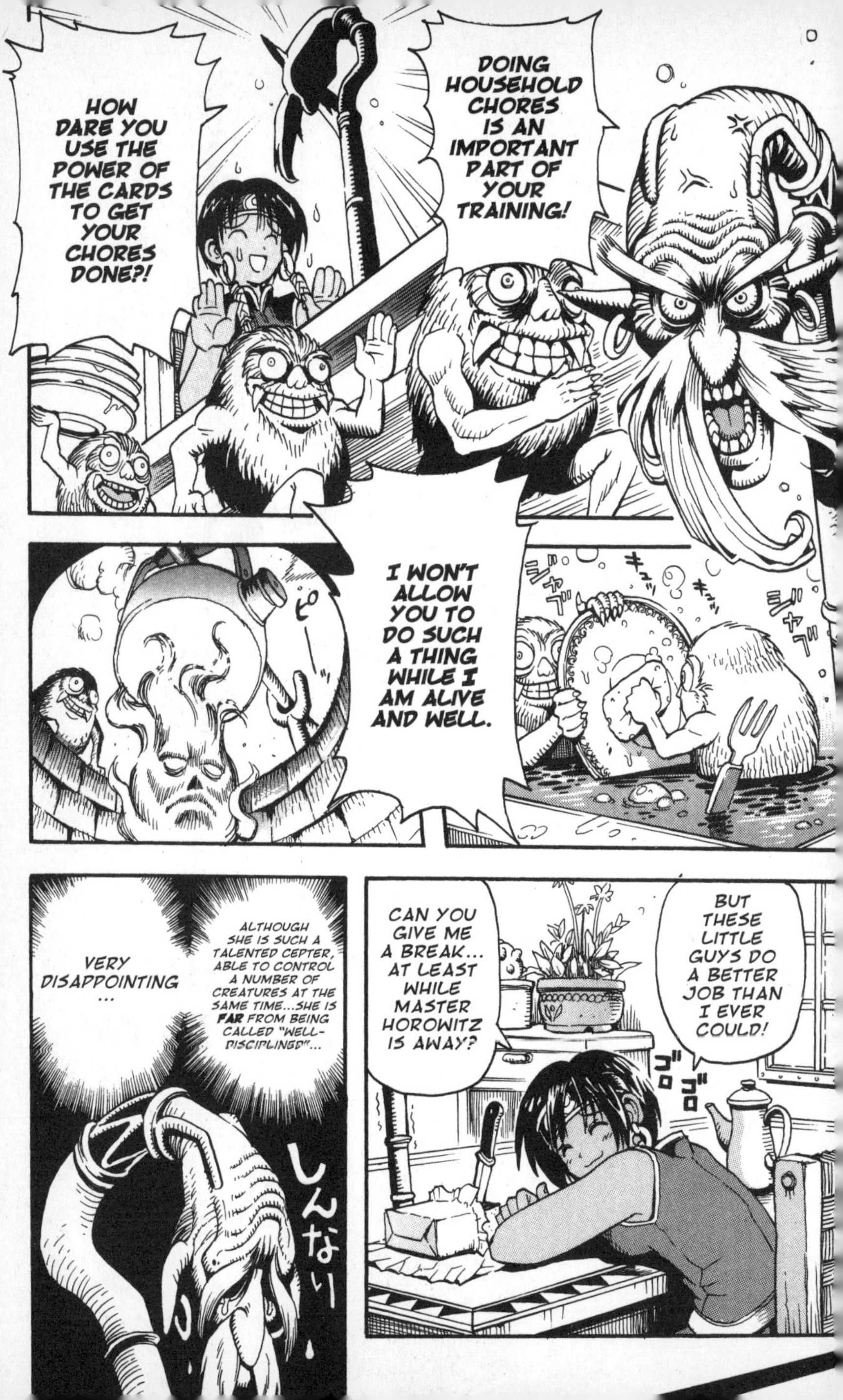
DOING HOUSEHOLD CHORES IS AN IMPORTANT PART OF YOUR TRAINING!
HOW DARE YOU USE THE POWER OF THE CARDS TO GET YOUR CHORES DONE?!
ジャブ
キュッ
キュッ
ジャブ
I WON'T ALLOW YOU TO DO SUCH A THING WHILE I AM ALIVE AND WELL.
ピー
BUT THESE LITTLE GUYS DO A BETTER JOB THAN I EVER COULD!
CAN YOU GIVE ME A BREAK... AT LEAST WHILE MASTER HOROWITZ IS AWAY?
ゴロゴロ
ALTHOUGH SHE IS SUCH A TALENTED CEPTER, ABLE TO CONTROL A NUMBER OF CREATURES AT THE SAME TIME...SHE IS FAR FROM BEING CALLED "WELL-DISCIPLINED"...
VERY DISAPPOINTING...
しんなり

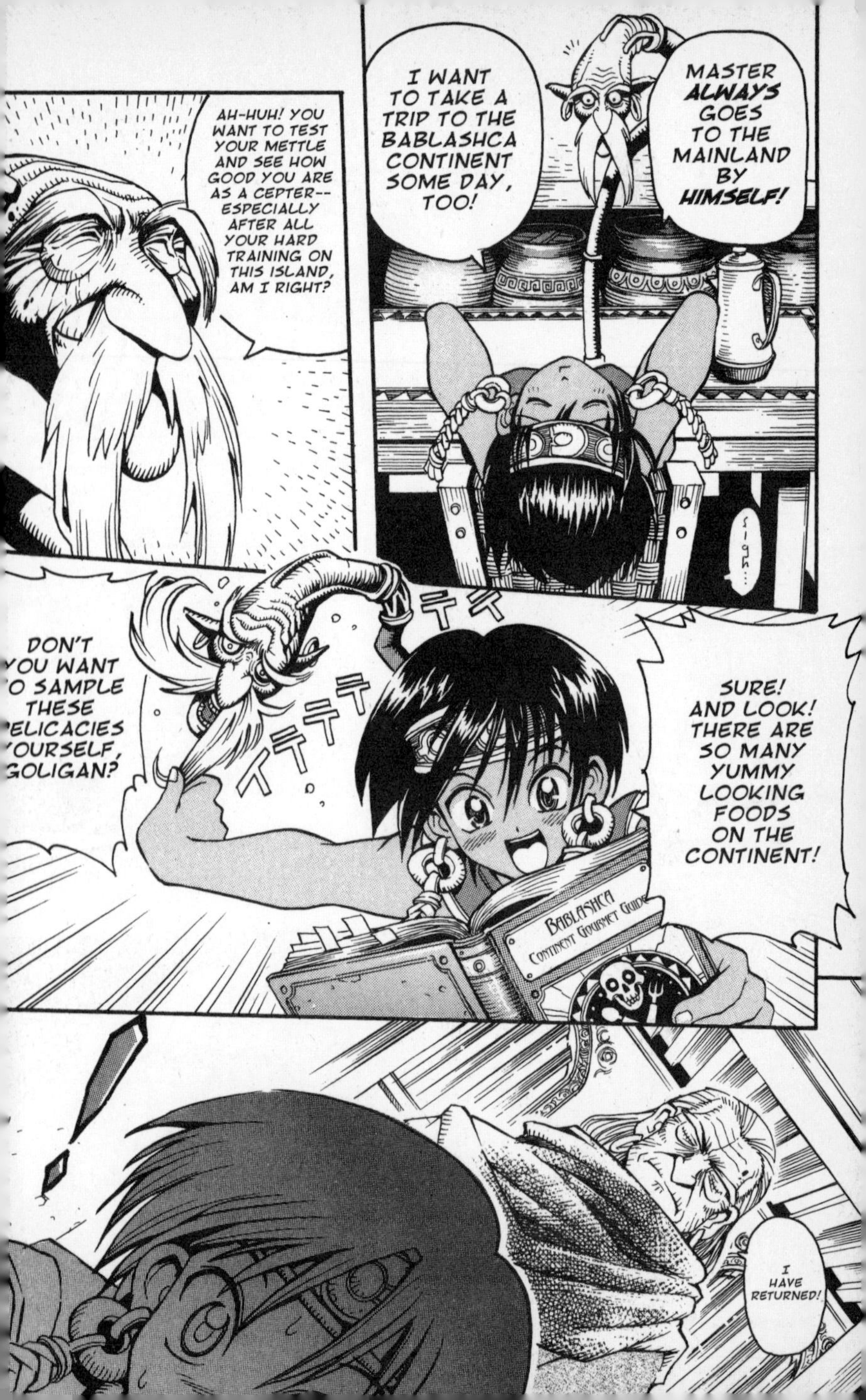
MASTER ALWAYS GOES TO THE MAINLAND BY HIMSELF!
I WANT TO TAKE A TRIP TO THE BABLASHCA CONTINENT SOME DAY, TOO!
sigh...
AH-HUH! YOU WANT TO TEST YOUR METTLE AND SEE HOW GOOD YOU ARE AS A CEPTER--ESPECIALLY AFTER ALL YOUR HARD TRAINING ON THIS ISLAND, AM I RIGHT?
SURE! AND LOOK! THERE ARE SO MANY YUMMY LOOKING FOODS ON THE CONTINENT!
テテ
イテテテ
BABLASHCA CONTINENT GOURMET GUIDE
DON'T YOU WANT TO SAMPLE THESE DELICACIES YOURSELF, GOLIGAN?
I HAVE RETURNED!

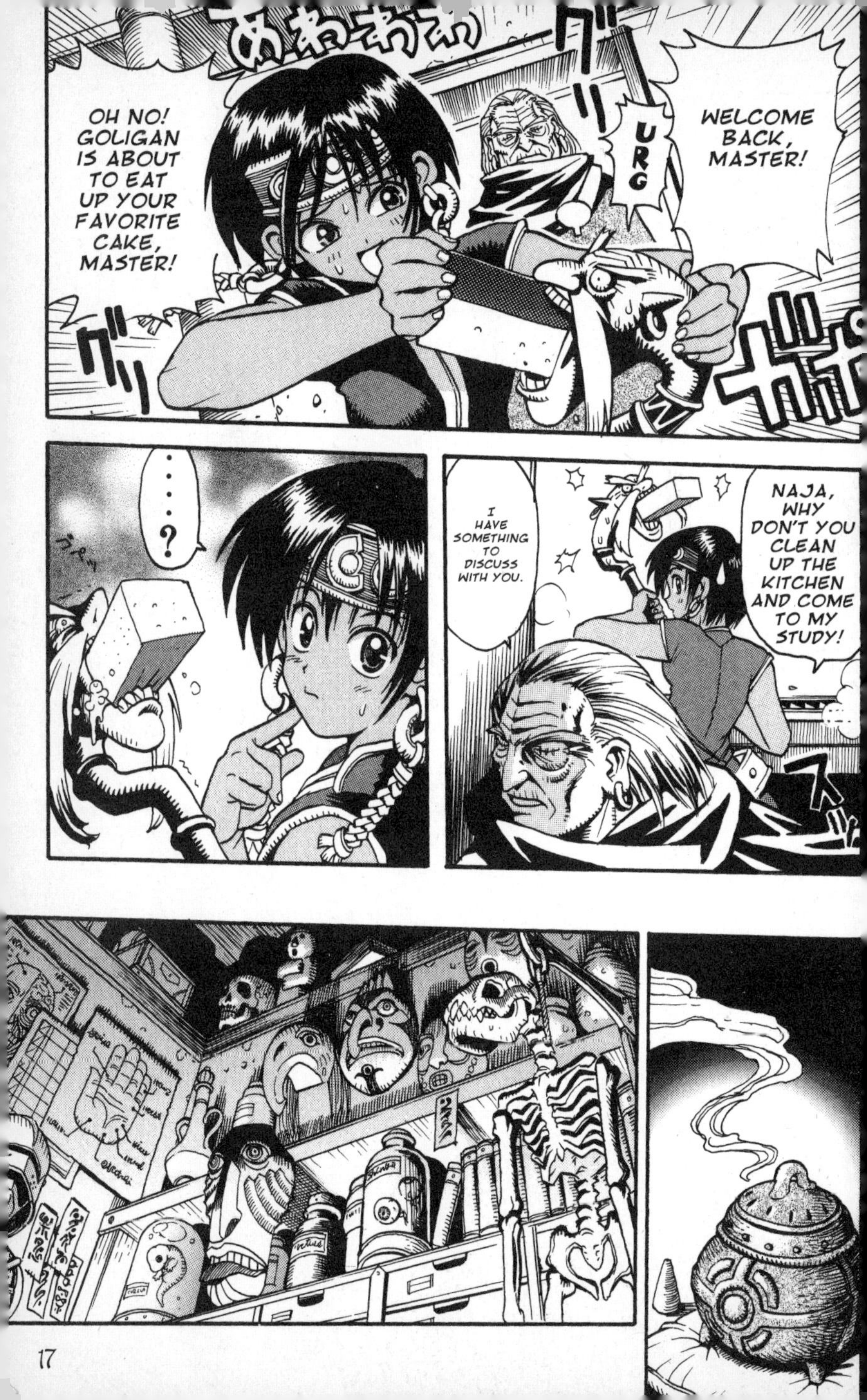
WELCOME BACK, MASTER!
URG
OH NO! GOLIGAN IS ABOUT TO EAT UP YOUR FAVORITE CAKE, MASTER!
NAJA, WHY DON'T YOU CLEAN UP THE KITCHEN AND COME TO MY STUDY!
I HAVE SOMETHING TO DISCUSS WITH YOU.
....?

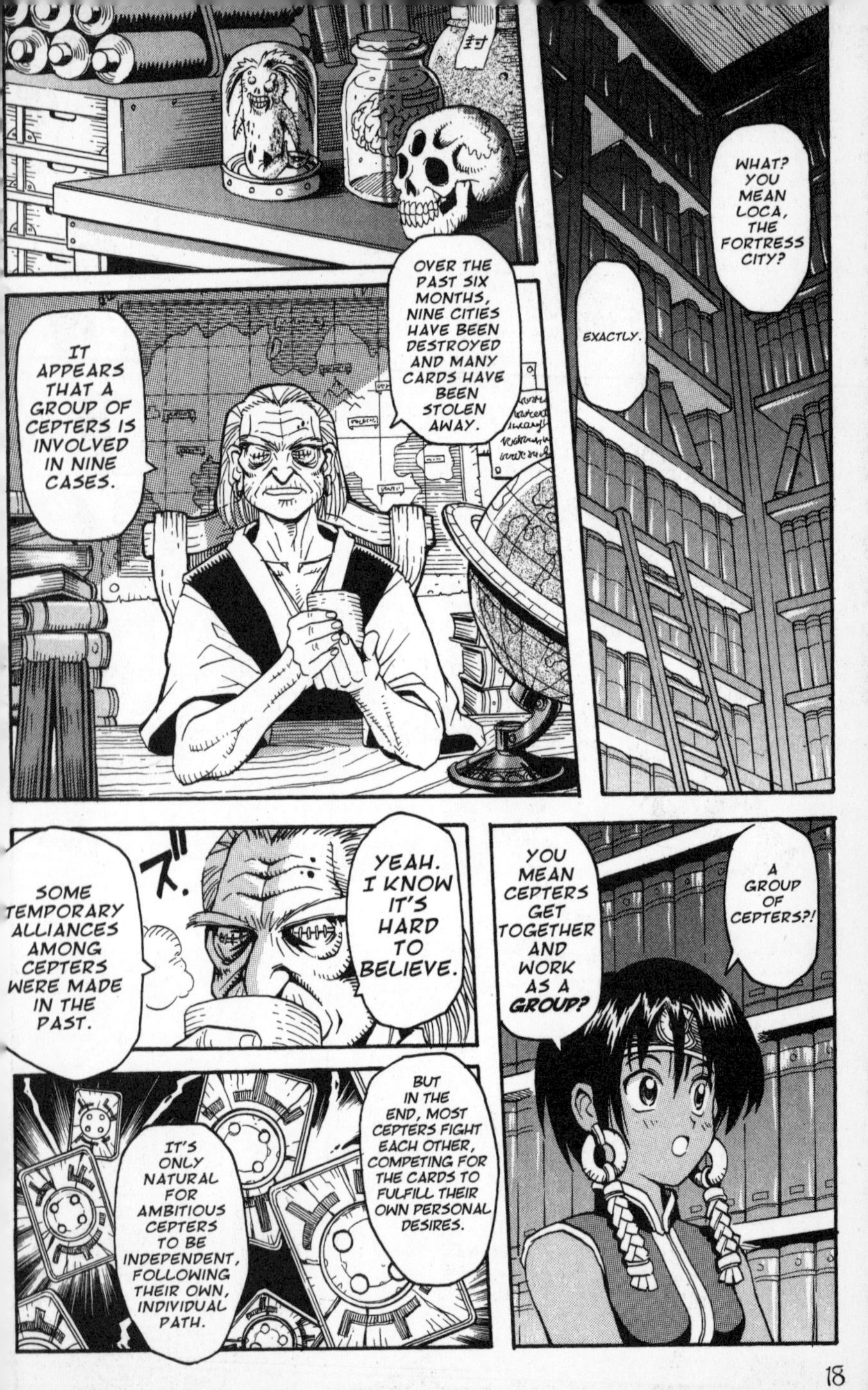
WHAT? YOU MEAN LOCA, THE FORTRESS CITY?
EXACTLY.
OVER THE PAST SIX MONTHS, NINE CITIES HAVE BEEN DESTROYED AND MANY CARDS HAVE BEEN STOLEN AWAY.
IT APPEARS THAT A GROUP OF CEPTERS IS INVOLVED IN NINE CASES.
A GROUP OF CEPTERS?!
YOU MEAN CEPTERS GET TOGETHER AND WORK AS A *GROUP?*
YEAH. I KNOW IT'S HARD TO BELIEVE.
ズ...
SOME TEMPORARY ALLIANCES AMONG CEPTERS WERE MADE IN THE PAST.
BUT IN THE END, MOST CEPTERS FIGHT EACH OTHER, COMPETING FOR THE CARDS TO FULFILL THEIR OWN PERSONAL DESIRES.
IT'S ONLY NATURAL FOR AMBITIOUS CEPTERS TO BE INDEPENDENT, FOLLOWING THEIR OWN, INDIVIDUAL PATH.

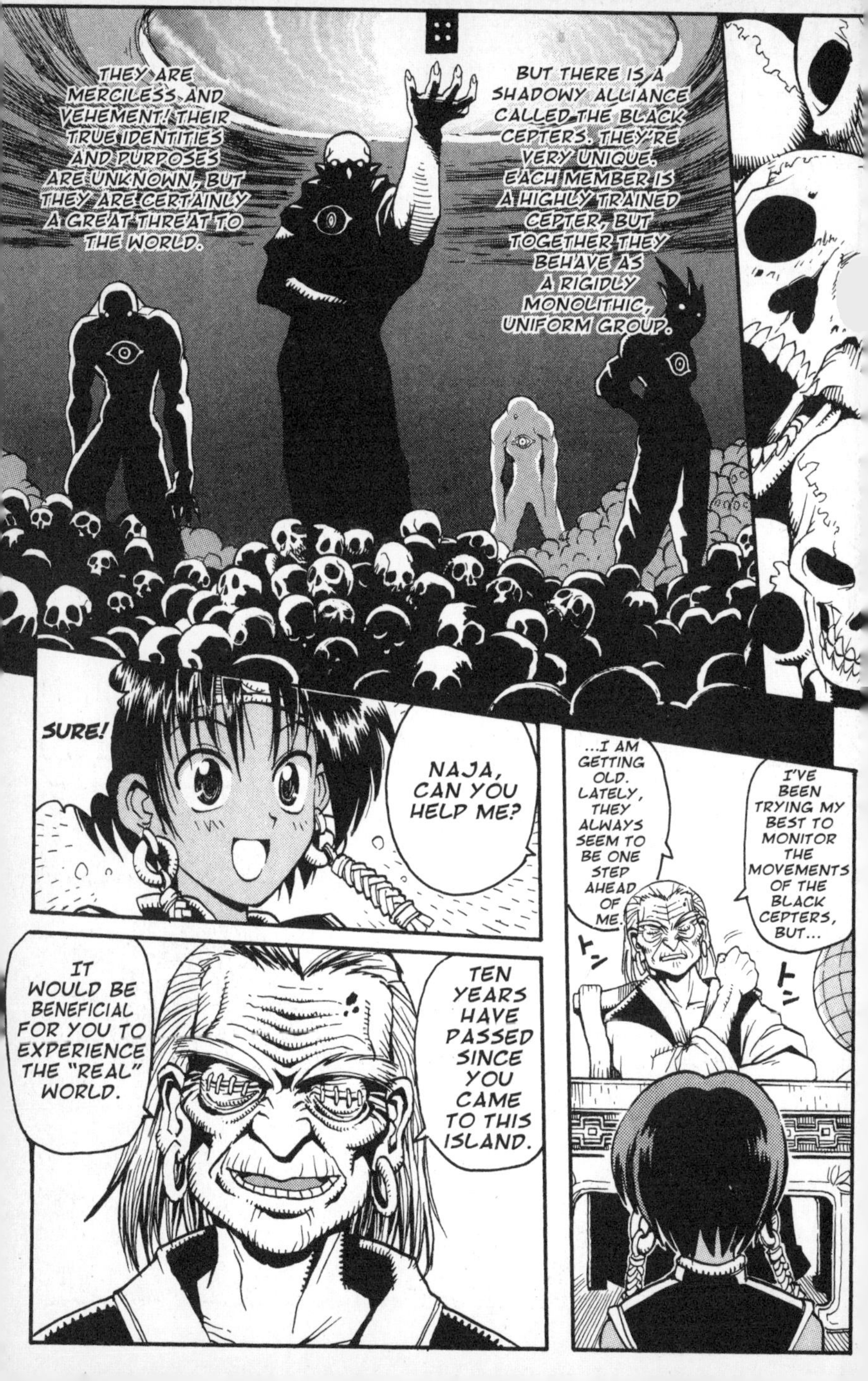
BUT THERE IS A SHADOWY ALLIANCE CALLED THE BLACK CEPTERS. THEY'RE VERY UNIQUE. EACH MEMBER IS A HIGHLY TRAINED CEPTER, BUT TOGETHER THEY BEHAVE AS A RIGIDLY MONOLITHIC, UNIFORM GROUP.
THEY ARE MERCILESS AND VEHEMENT! THEIR TRUE IDENTITIES AND PURPOSES ARE UNKNOWN, BUT THEY ARE CERTAINLY A GREAT THREAT TO THE WORLD.
I'VE BEEN TRYING MY BEST TO MONITOR THE MOVEMENTS OF THE BLACK CEPTERS, BUT...
トン
...I AM GETTING OLD. LATELY, THEY ALWAYS SEEM TO BE ONE STEP AHEAD OF ME.
トン
NAJA, CAN YOU HELP ME?
SURE!
TEN YEARS HAVE PASSED SINCE YOU CAME TO THIS ISLAND.
IT WOULD BE BENEFICIAL FOR YOU TO EXPERIENCE THE "REAL" WORLD.

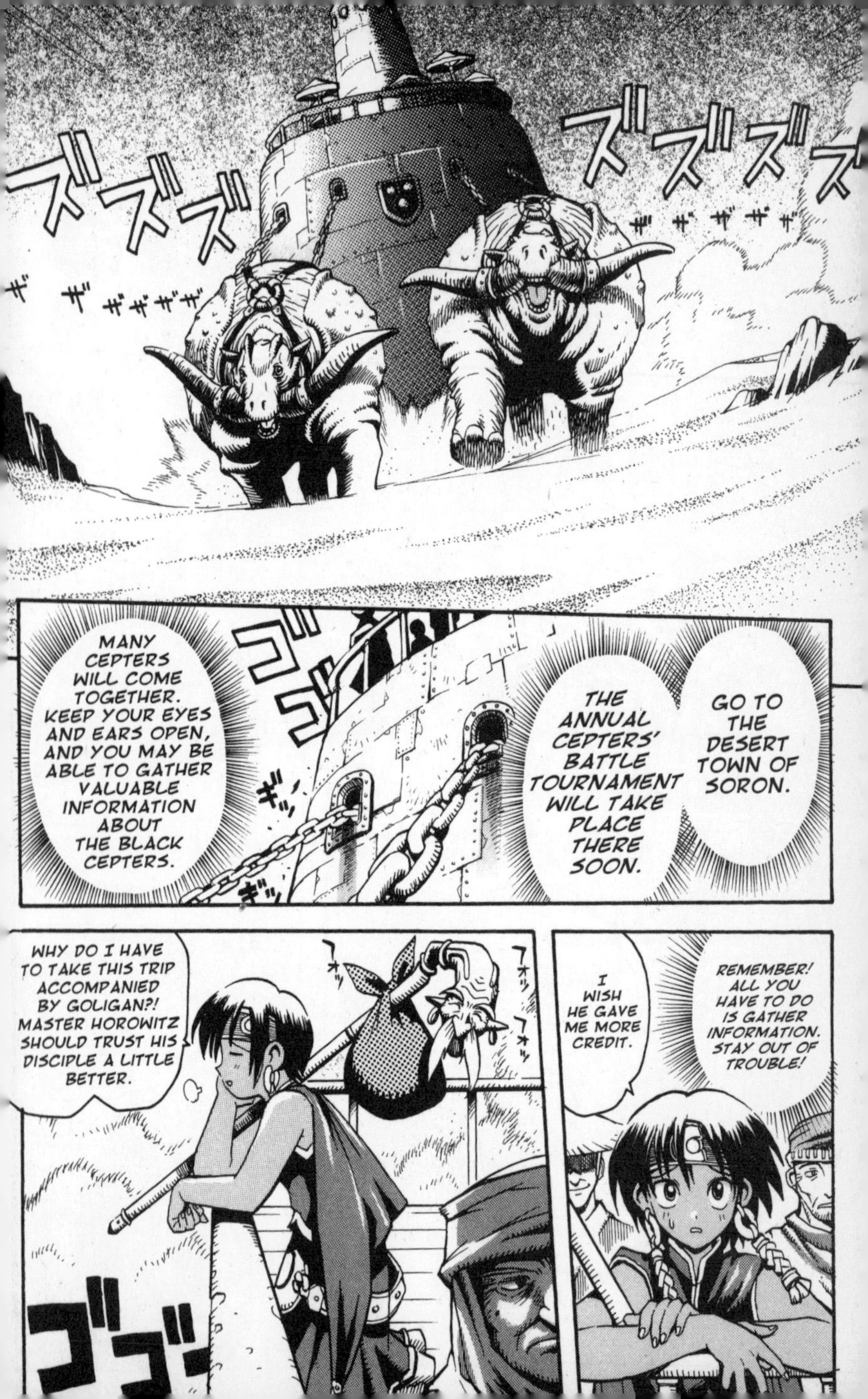

ズズズズ
ザザザザ
ズズズ
ザザザザザ
GO TO THE DESERT TOWN OF SORON.
THE ANNUAL CEPTERS' BATTLE TOURNAMENT WILL TAKE PLACE THERE SOON.
MANY CEPTERS WILL COME TOGETHER. KEEP YOUR EYES AND EARS OPEN, AND YOU MAY BE ABLE TO GATHER VALUABLE INFORMATION ABOUT THE BLACK CEPTERS.
REMEMBER! ALL YOU HAVE TO DO IS GATHER INFORMATION. STAY OUT OF TROUBLE!
I WISH HE GAVE ME MORE CREDIT.
WHY DO I HAVE TO TAKE THIS TRIP ACCOMPANIED BY GOLIGAN?! MASTER HOROWITZ SHOULD TRUST HIS DISCIPLE A LITTLE BETTER.

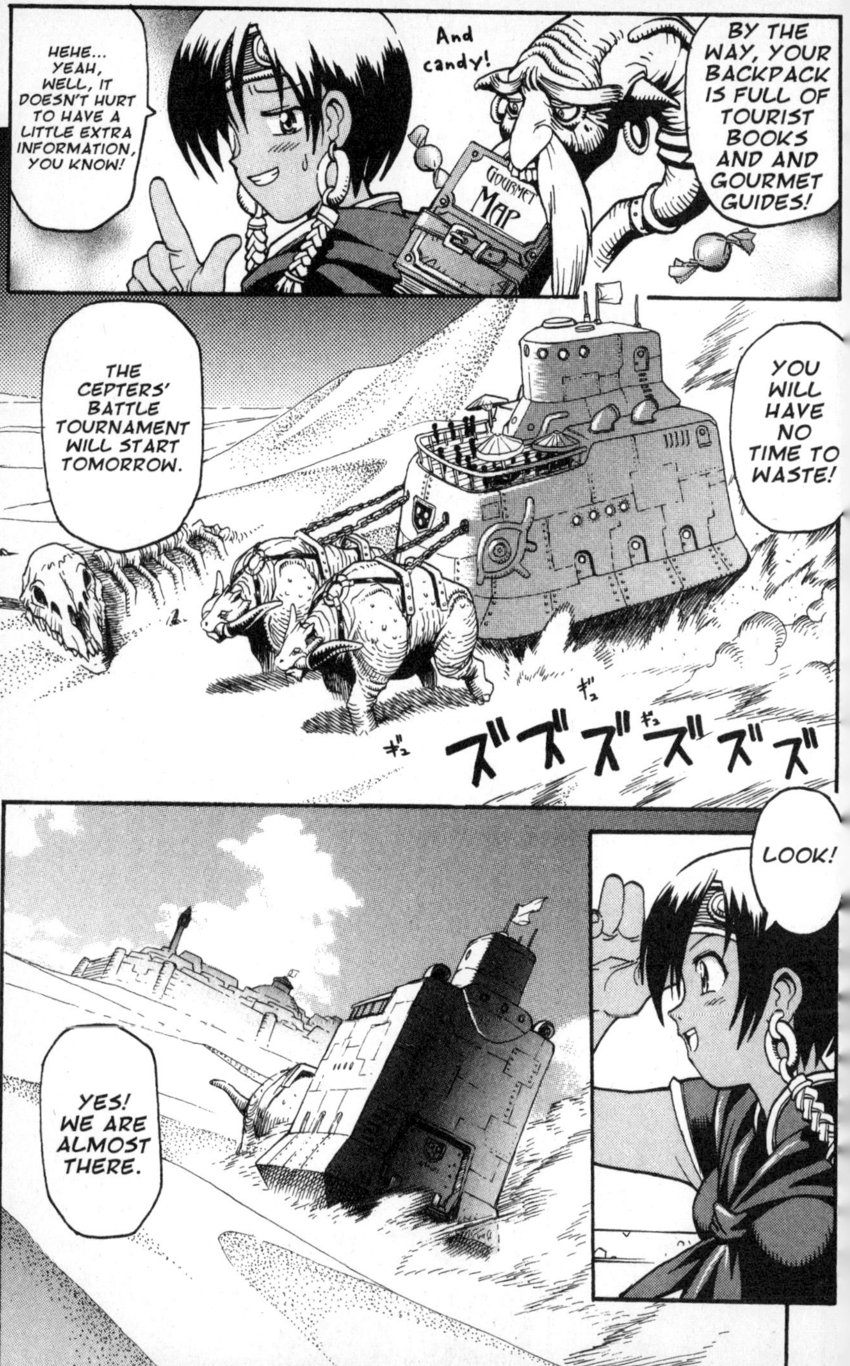
BY THE WAY, YOUR BACKPACK IS FULL OF TOURIST BOOKS AND AND GOURMET GUIDES!
And candy!
GOURMET MAP
HEHE... YEAH, WELL, IT DOESN'T HURT TO HAVE A LITTLE EXTRA INFORMATION, YOU KNOW!
YOU WILL HAVE NO TIME TO WASTE!
THE CEPTERS' BATTLE TOURNAMENT WILL START TOMORROW.
ギュ ギュ ギュ
ズズズズズズ
LOOK!
YES! WE ARE ALMOST THERE.

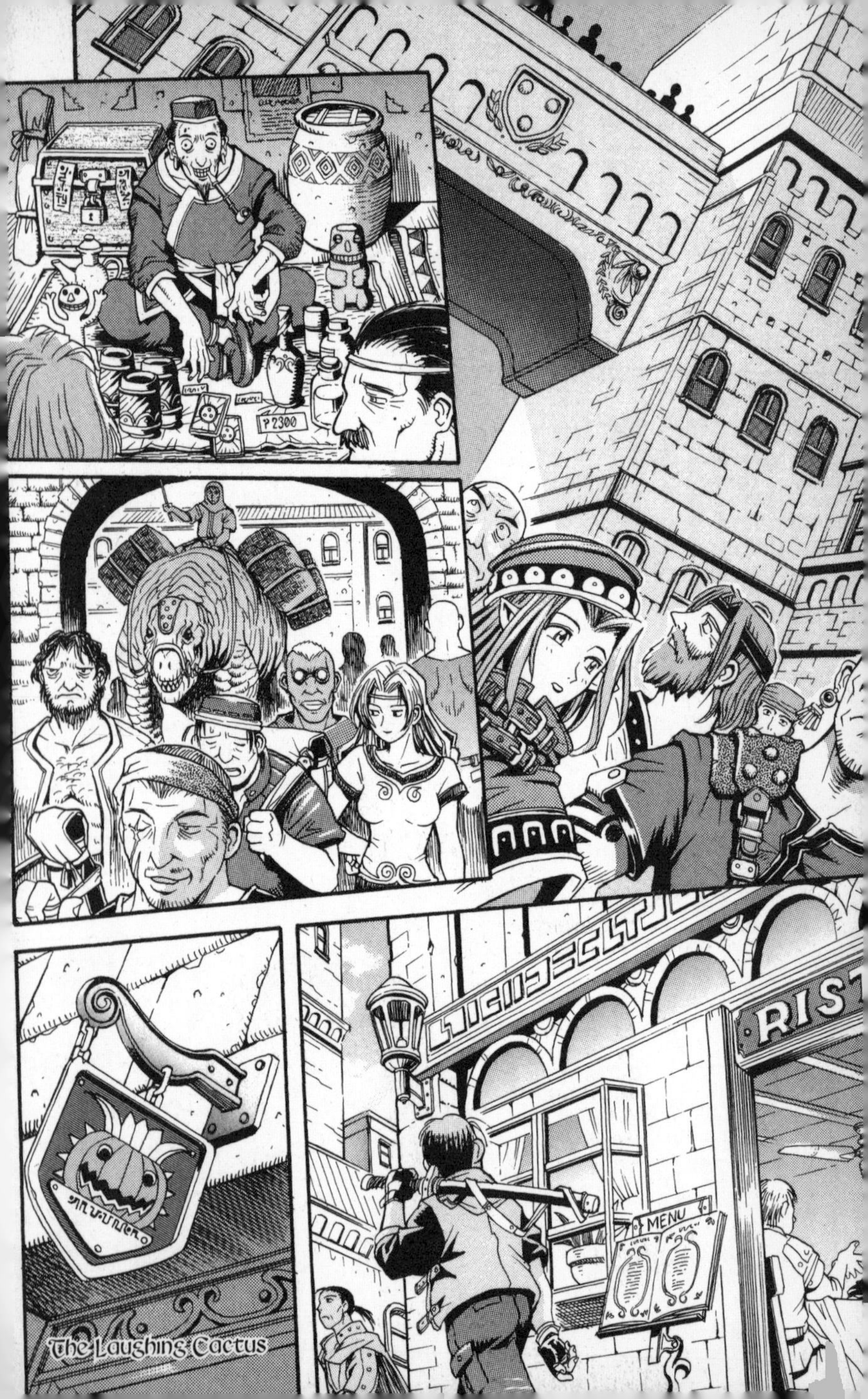
P2300
RIS
MENU
The Laughing Cactus

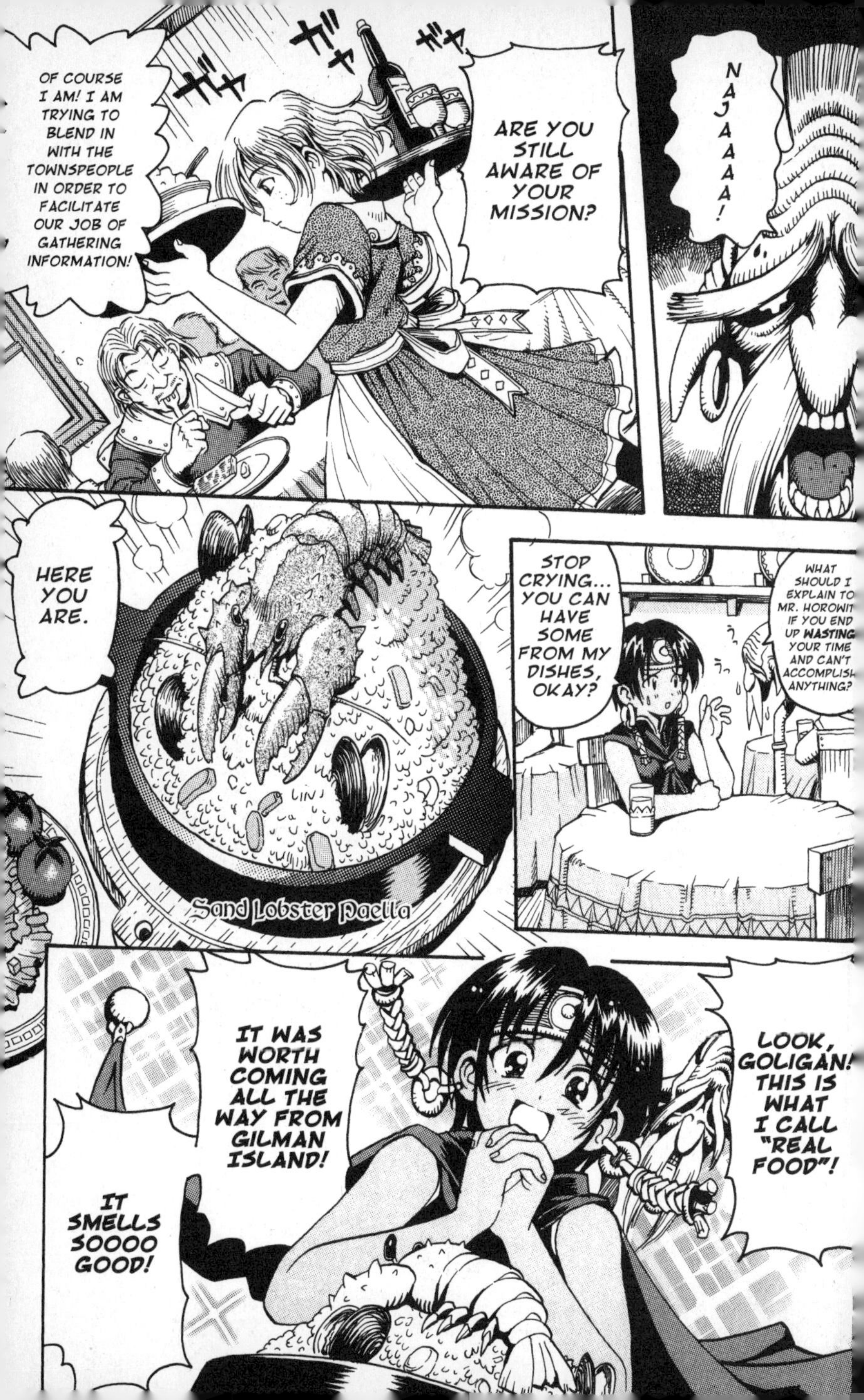
NAJAAAAA!
ARE YOU STILL AWARE OF YOUR MISSION?
OF COURSE I AM! I AM TRYING TO BLEND IN WITH THE TOWNSPEOPLE IN ORDER TO FACILITATE OUR JOB OF GATHERING INFORMATION!
WHAT SHOULD I EXPLAIN TO MR. HOROWIT IF YOU END UP WASTING YOUR TIME AND CAN'T ACCOMPLISH ANYTHING?
STOP CRYING... YOU CAN HAVE SOME FROM MY DISHES, OKAY?
HERE YOU ARE.
Sand Lobster Paella
LOOK, GOLIGAN! THIS IS WHAT I CALL "REAL FOOD"!
IT WAS WORTH COMING ALL THE WAY FROM GILMAN ISLAND!
IT SMELLS SOOOO GOOD!

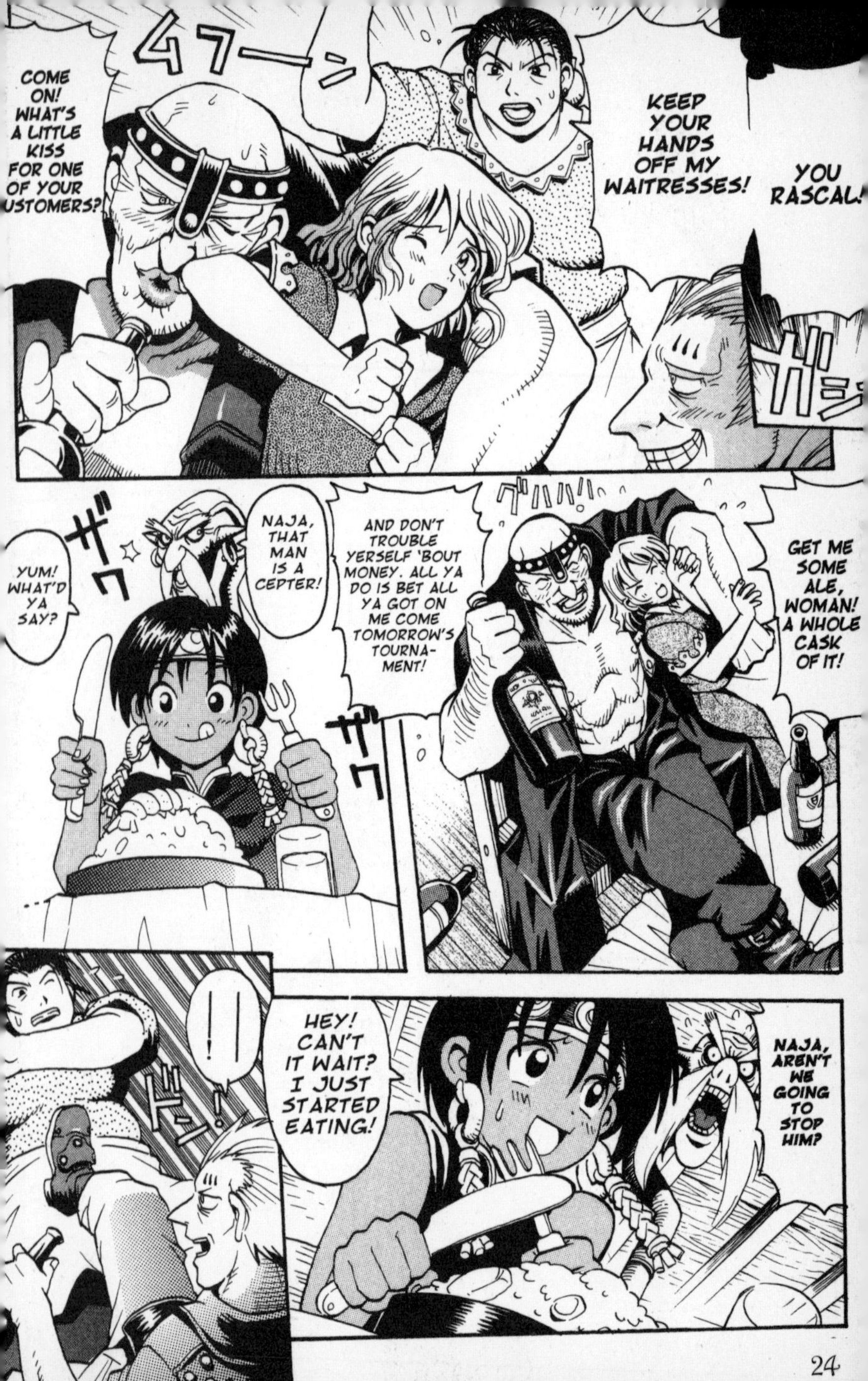
YOU RASCAL!
KEEP YOUR HANDS OFF MY WAITRESSES!
ムフーン
COME ON! WHAT'S A LITTLE KISS FOR ONE OF YOUR USTOMERS?
GET ME SOME ALE, WOMAN! A WHOLE CASK OF IT!
AND DON'T TROUBLE YERSELF 'BOUT MONEY. ALL YA DO IS BET ALL YA GOT ON ME COME TOMORROW'S TOURNA-MENT!
NAJA, THAT MAN IS A CEPTER!
YUM! WHAT'D YA SAY?
NAJA, AREN'T WE GOING TO STOP HIM?
HEY! CAN'T IT WAIT? I JUST STARTED EATING!
!!

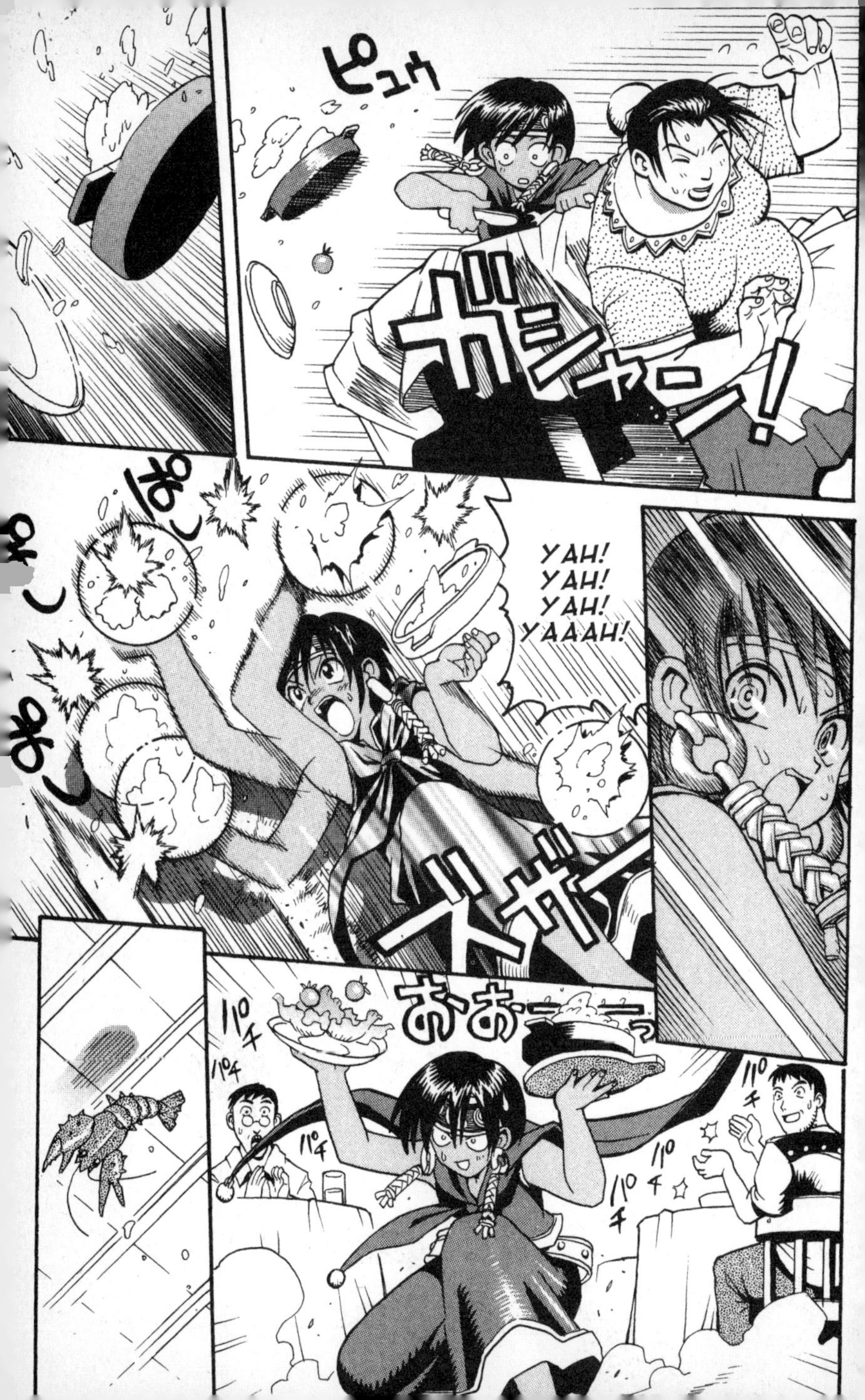

ピュウ
ガシャーン！
YAH! YAH! YAH! YAAAH!
ぽこ
ぽこ
ぽこ
ズザ
おおーっ
パチ
パチ
パチ
パチ
パチ
パチ

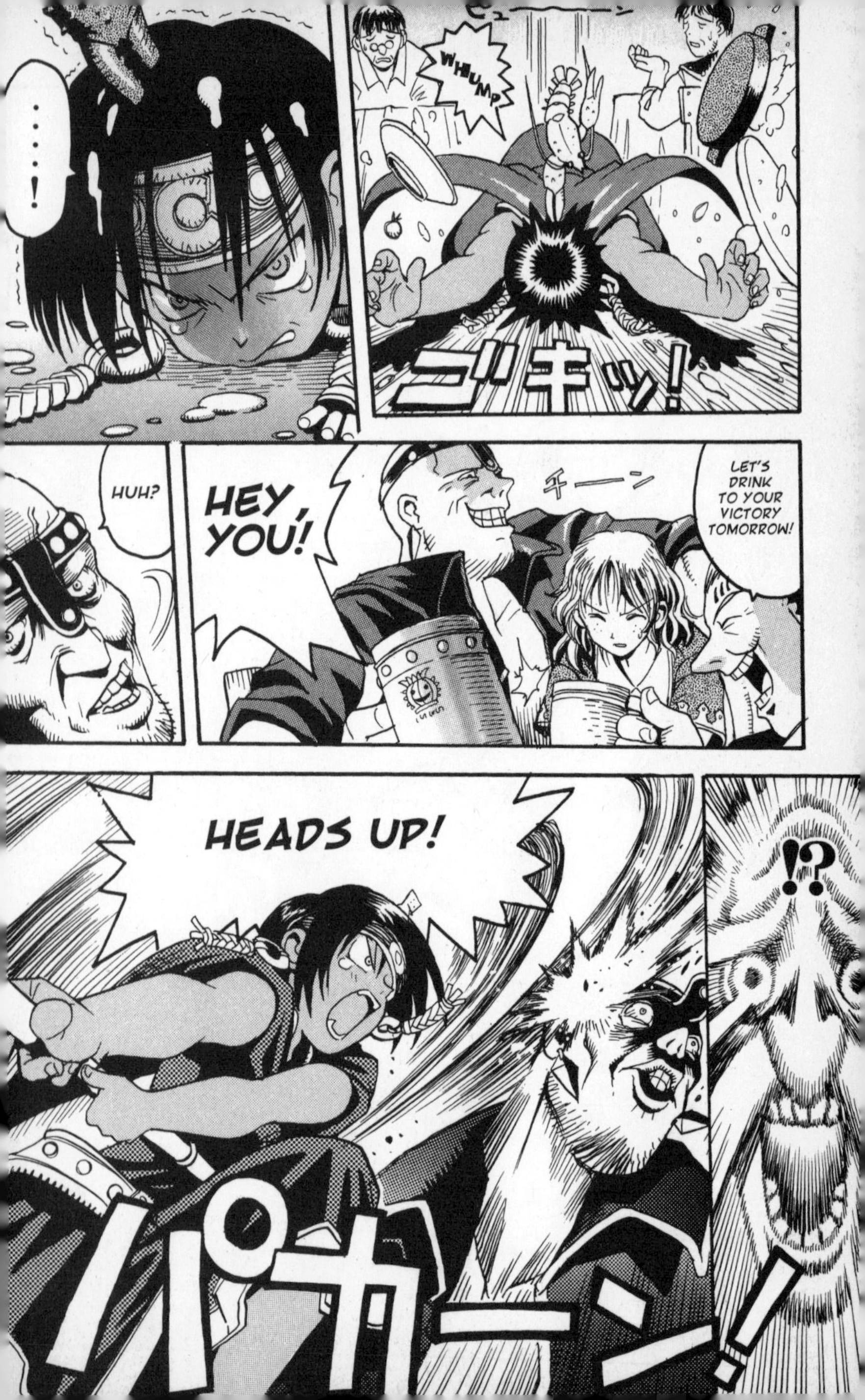
WHUMP
ゴキッ!
……!
LET'S DRINK TO YOUR VICTORY TOMORROW!
チーン
HEY YOU!
HUH?
!?
HEADS UP!
パカーン!

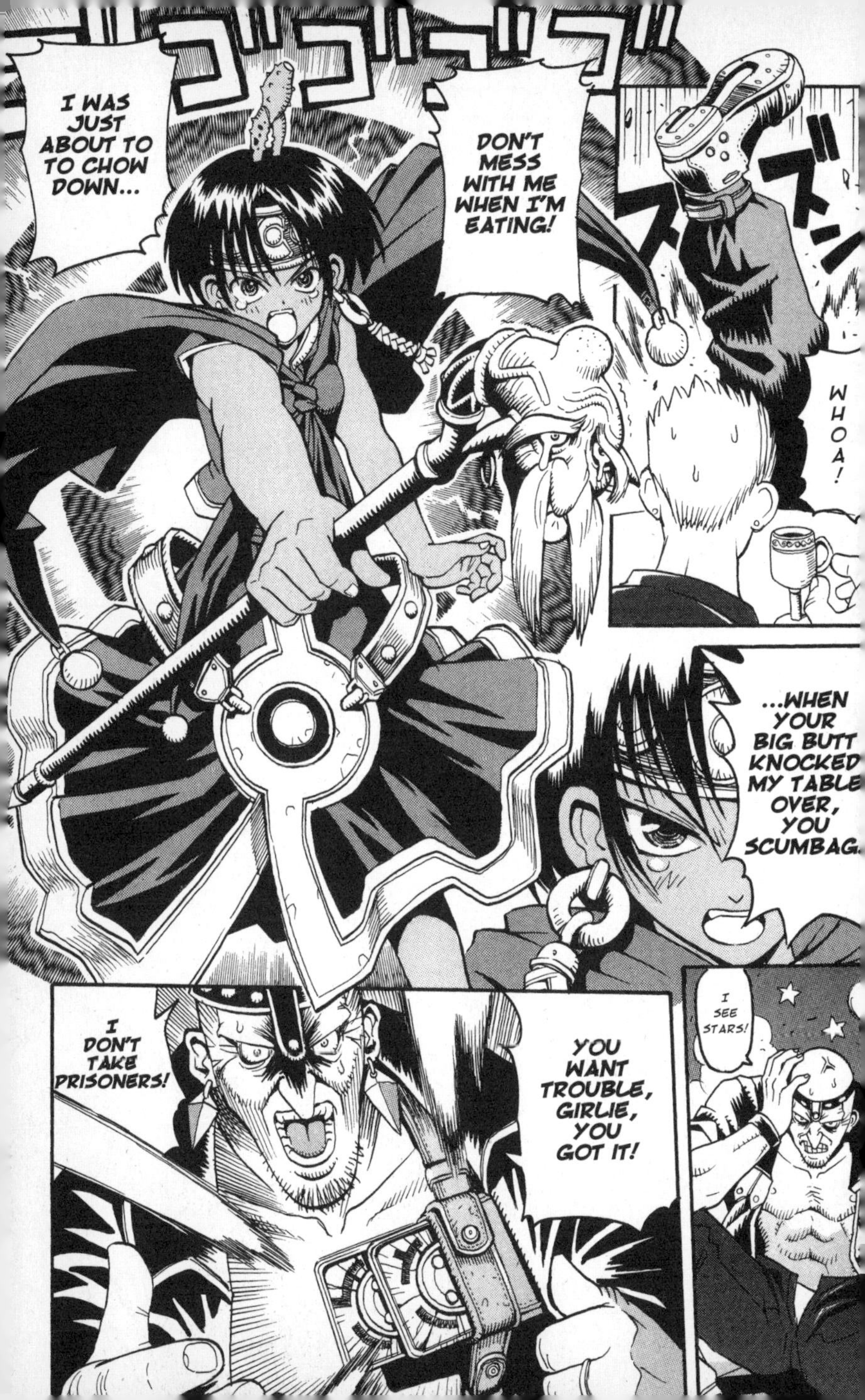

DON'T MESS WITH ME WHEN I'M EATING!
I WAS JUST ABOUT TO TO CHOW DOWN...
WHOA!
...WHEN YOUR BIG BUTT KNOCKED MY TABLE OVER, YOU SCUMBAG.
I SEE STARS!
YOU WANT TROUBLE, GIRLIE, YOU GOT IT!
I DON'T TAKE PRISONERS!

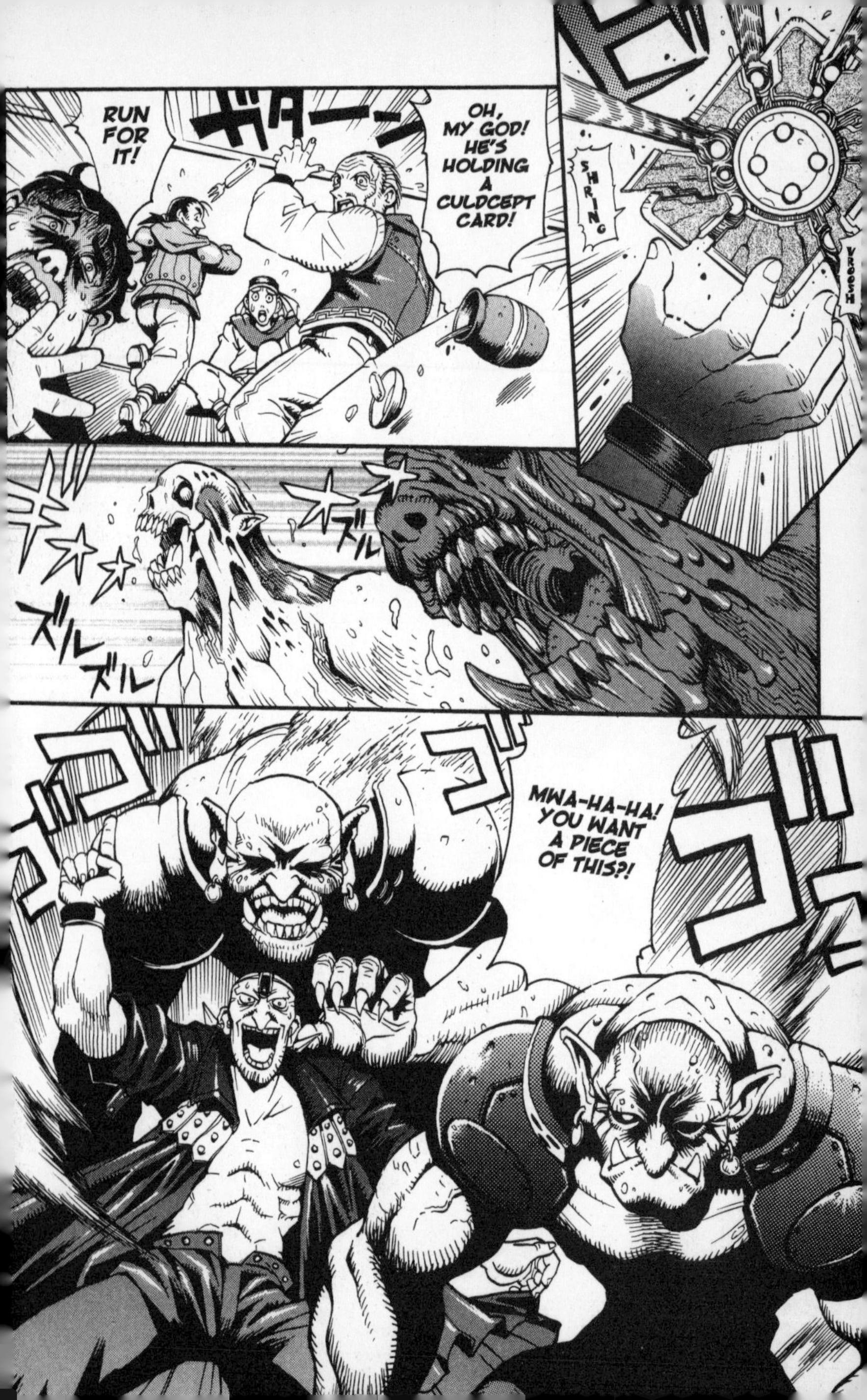
SHRING
VROOSH
OH, MY GOD! HE'S HOLDING A CULDCEPT CARD!
RUN FOR IT!
MWA-HA-HA! YOU WANT A PIECE OF THIS?!

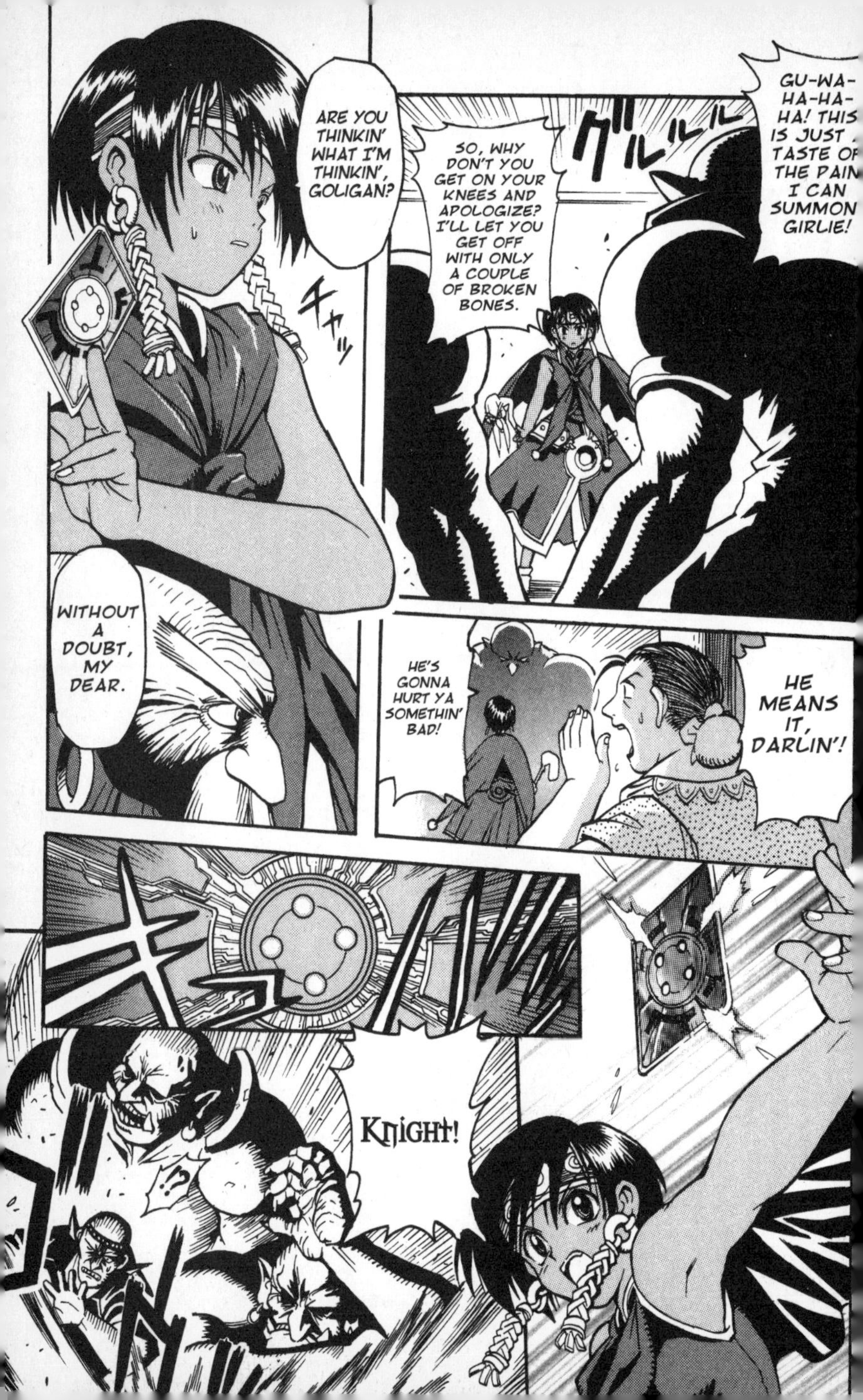

GU-WA-HA-HA-HA! THIS IS JUST TASTE OF THE PAIN I CAN SUMMON GIRLIE!
グルルル
SO, WHY DON'T YOU GET ON YOUR KNEES AND APOLOGIZE? I'LL LET YOU GET OFF WITH ONLY A COUPLE OF BROKEN BONES.
HE MEANS IT, DARLIN'!
HE'S GONNA HURT YA SOMETHIN' BAD!
ARE YOU THINKIN' WHAT I'M THINKIN', GOLIGAN?
チャッ
WITHOUT A DOUBT, MY DEAR.
KNIGHT!

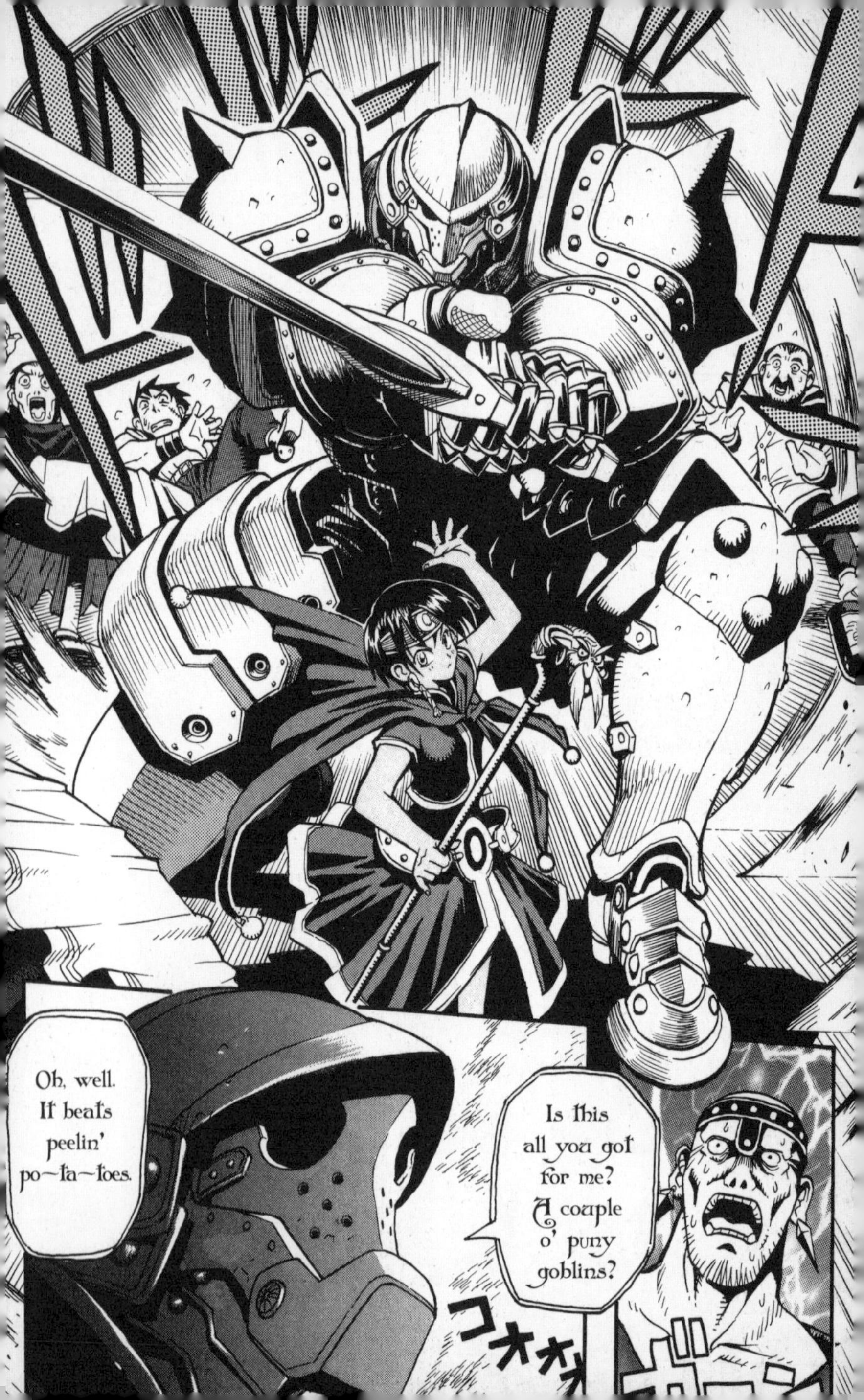
Is this all you got for me? A couple o' puny goblins?
コオオオ
Oh, well. It beats peelin' po~ta~toes.

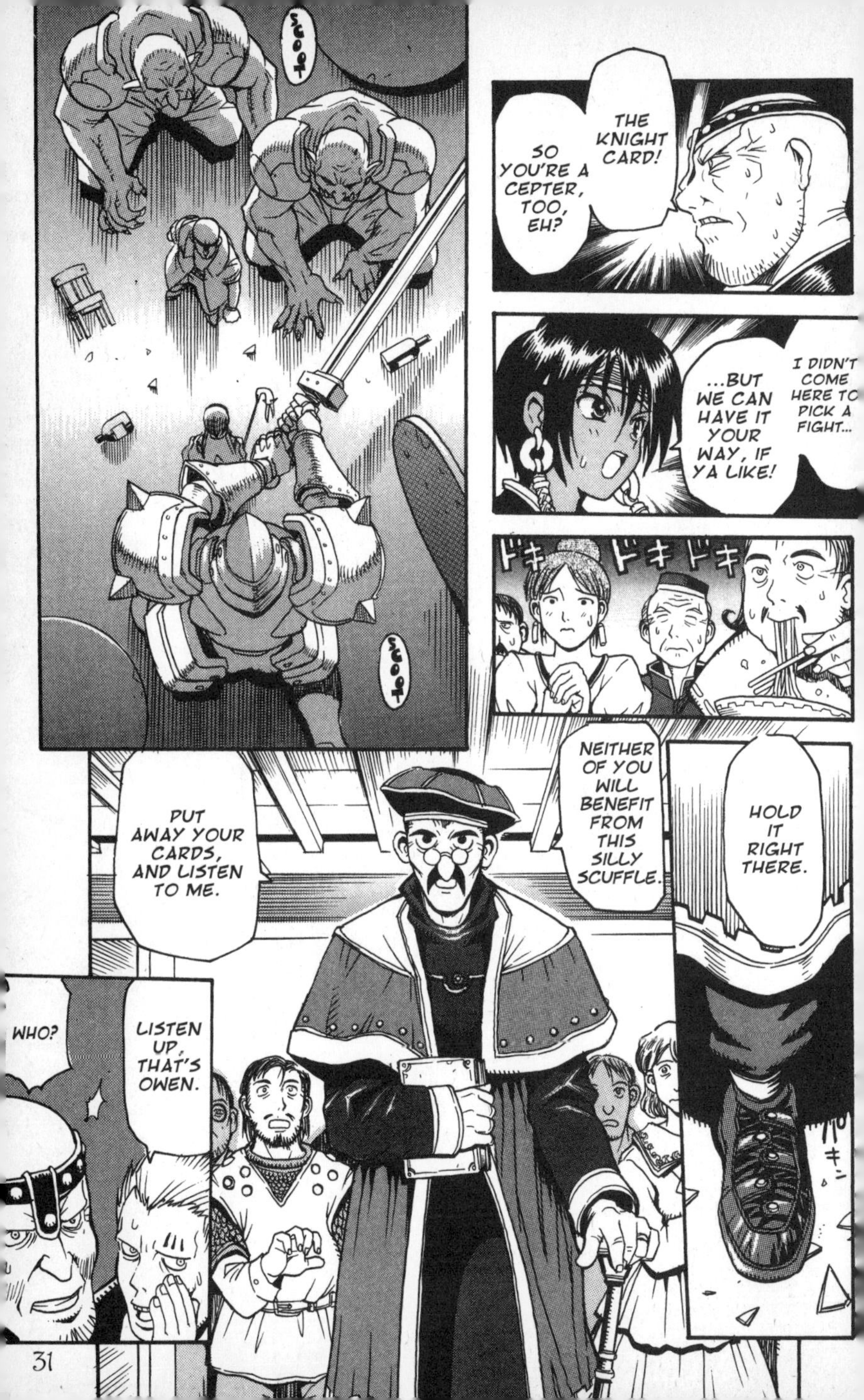
THE KNIGHT CARD!
SO YOU'RE A CEPTER, TOO, EH?
I DIDN'T COME HERE TO PICK A FIGHT...
...BUT WE CAN HAVE IT YOUR WAY, IF YA LIKE!
ドキ
ドキドキ
SCOOT
SCOOT
HOLD IT RIGHT THERE.
パキン
NEITHER OF YOU WILL BENEFIT FROM THIS SILLY SCUFFLE.
PUT AWAY YOUR CARDS, AND LISTEN TO ME.
LISTEN UP. THAT'S OWEN.
WHO?

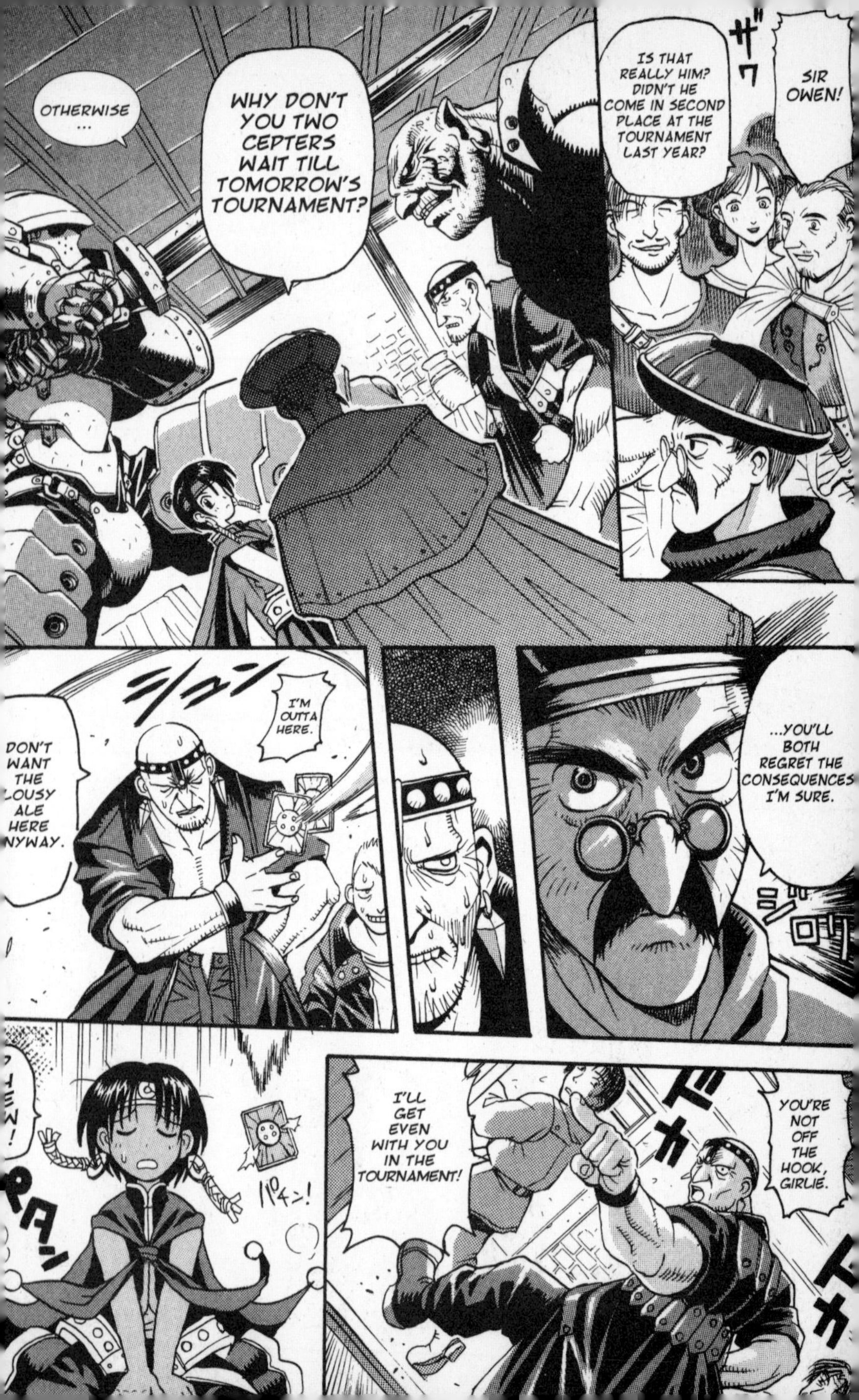
ザワ
SIR OWEN!
IS THAT REALLY HIM? DIDN'T HE COME IN SECOND PLACE AT THE TOURNAMENT LAST YEAR?
WHY DON'T YOU TWO CEPTERS WAIT TILL TOMORROW'S TOURNAMENT?
OTHERWISE...
...YOU'LL BOTH REGRET THE CONSEQUENCES I'M SURE.
I'M OUTTA HERE.
DON'T WANT THE LOUSY ALE HERE NYWAY.
YOU'RE NOT OFF THE HOOK, GIRLIE.
I'LL GET EVEN WITH YOU IN THE TOURNAMENT!

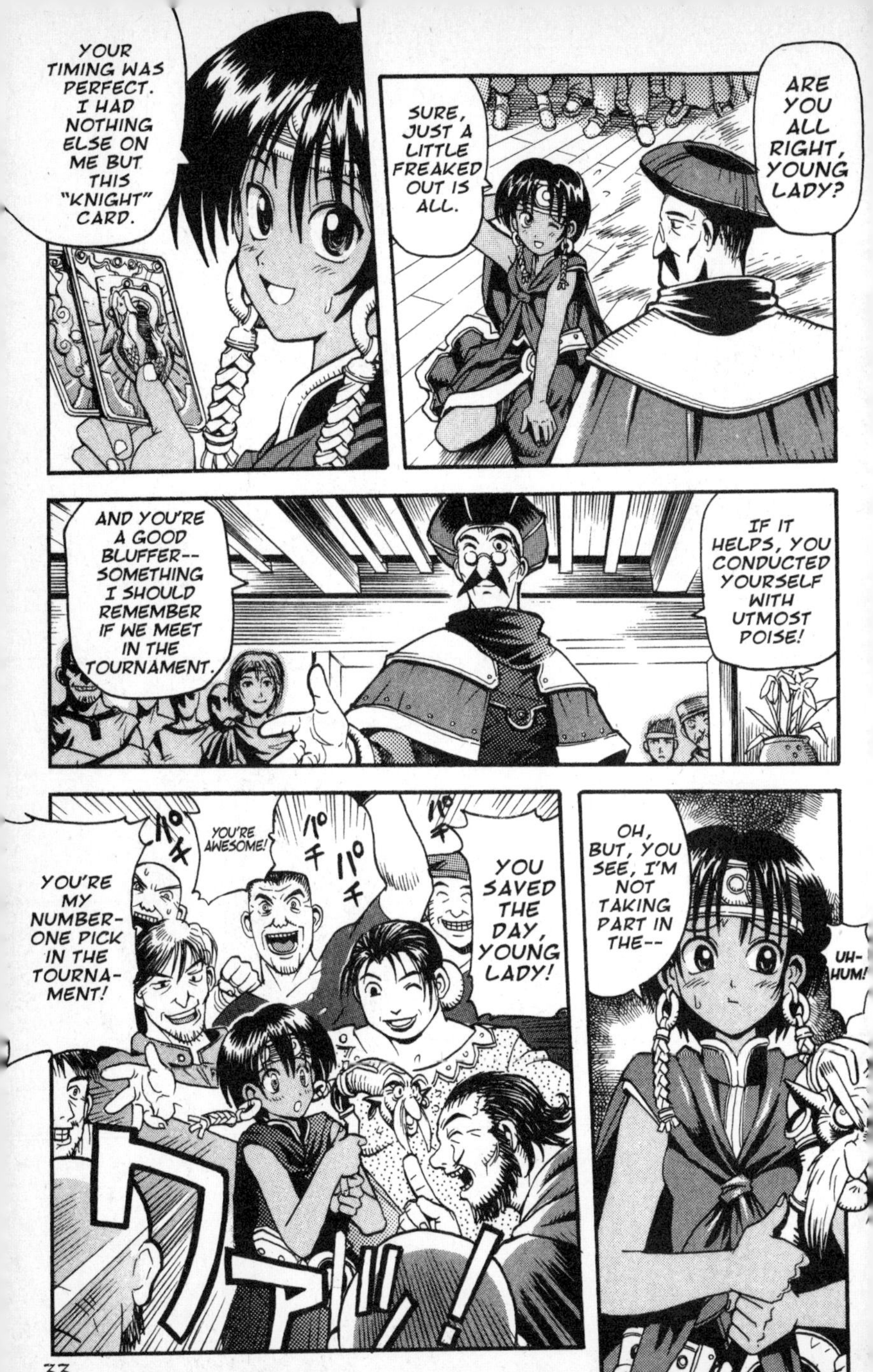
ARE YOU ALL RIGHT, YOUNG LADY?
SURE, JUST A LITTLE FREAKED OUT IS ALL.
YOUR TIMING WAS PERFECT. I HAD NOTHING ELSE ON ME BUT THIS "KNIGHT" CARD.
IF IT HELPS, YOU CONDUCTED YOURSELF WITH UTMOST POISE!
AND YOU'RE A GOOD BLUFFER-- SOMETHING I SHOULD REMEMBER IF WE MEET IN THE TOURNAMENT.
OH, BUT, YOU SEE, I'M NOT TAKING PART IN THE--
UH-HUM!
YOU SAVED THE DAY, YOUNG LADY!
パチ
パチ
YOU'RE AWESOME!
YOU'RE MY NUMBER-ONE PICK IN THE TOURNA-MENT!

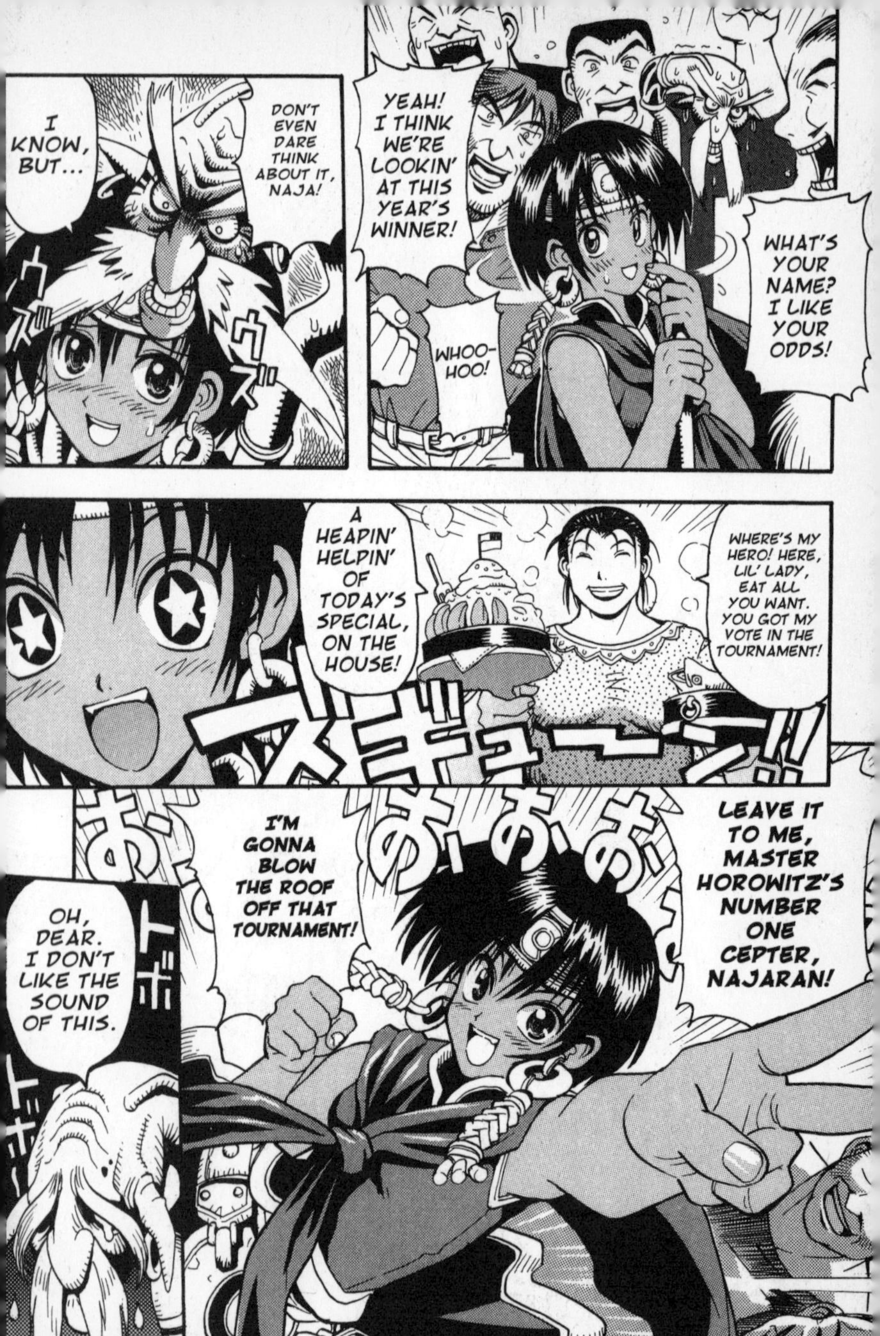
WHAT'S YOUR NAME? I LIKE YOUR ODDS!
YEAH! I THINK WE'RE LOOKIN' AT THIS YEAR'S WINNER!
WHOO-HOO!
DON'T EVEN DARE THINK ABOUT IT, NAJA!
I KNOW, BUT...
WHERE'S MY HERO! HERE, LIL' LADY, EAT ALL YOU WANT. YOU GOT MY VOTE IN THE TOURNAMENT!
A HEAPIN' HELPIN' OF TODAY'S SPECIAL, ON THE HOUSE!
LEAVE IT TO ME, MASTER HOROWITZ'S NUMBER ONE CEPTER, NAJARAN!
I'M GONNA BLOW THE ROOF OFF THAT TOURNAMENT!
OH, DEAR. I DON'T LIKE THE SOUND OF THIS.

Round 1 Najaran, a Novice Cepter – The Beginning of Her Adventure – End

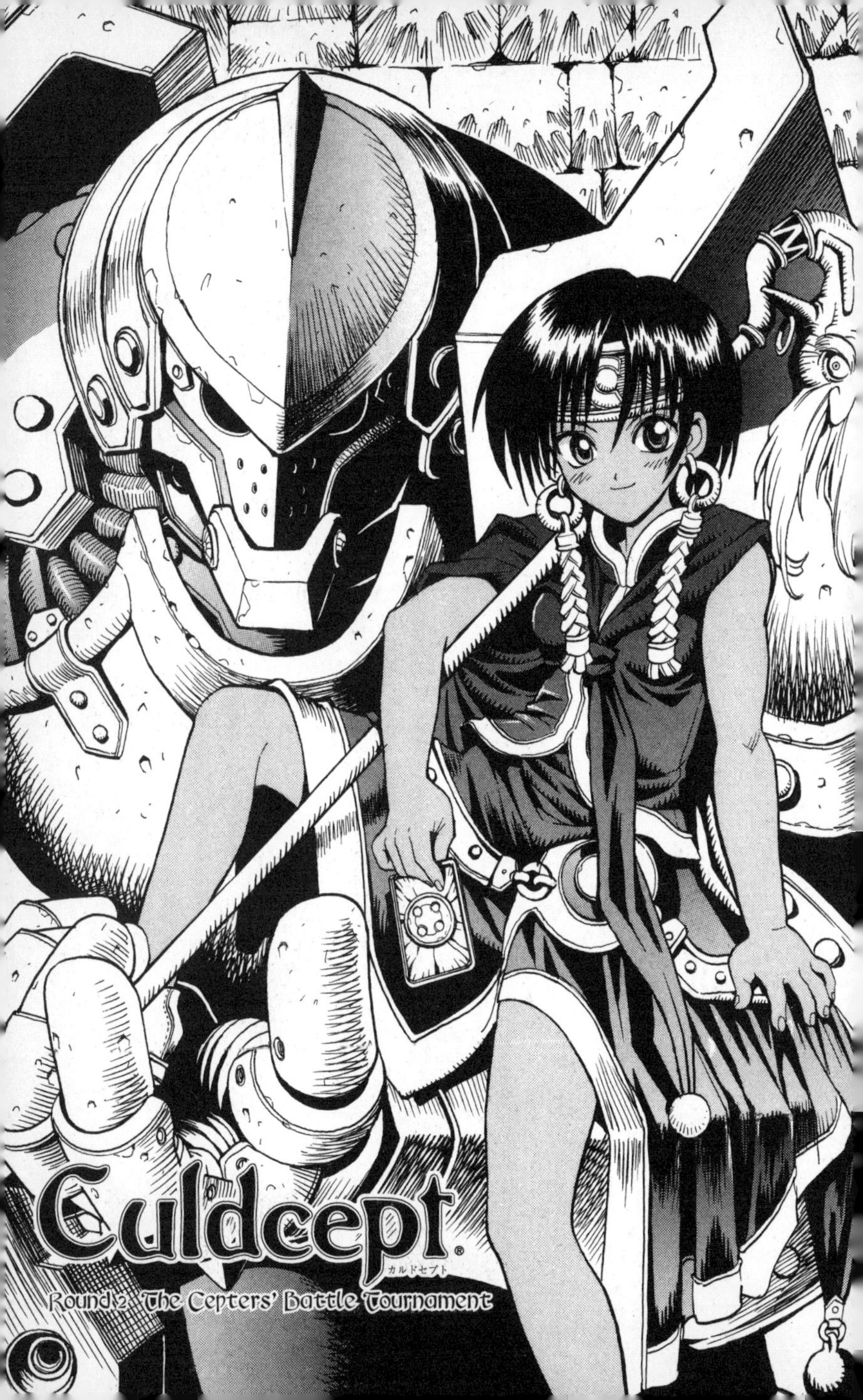
Culdcept
カルドセプト
Round 2 The Cepters' Battle Tournament

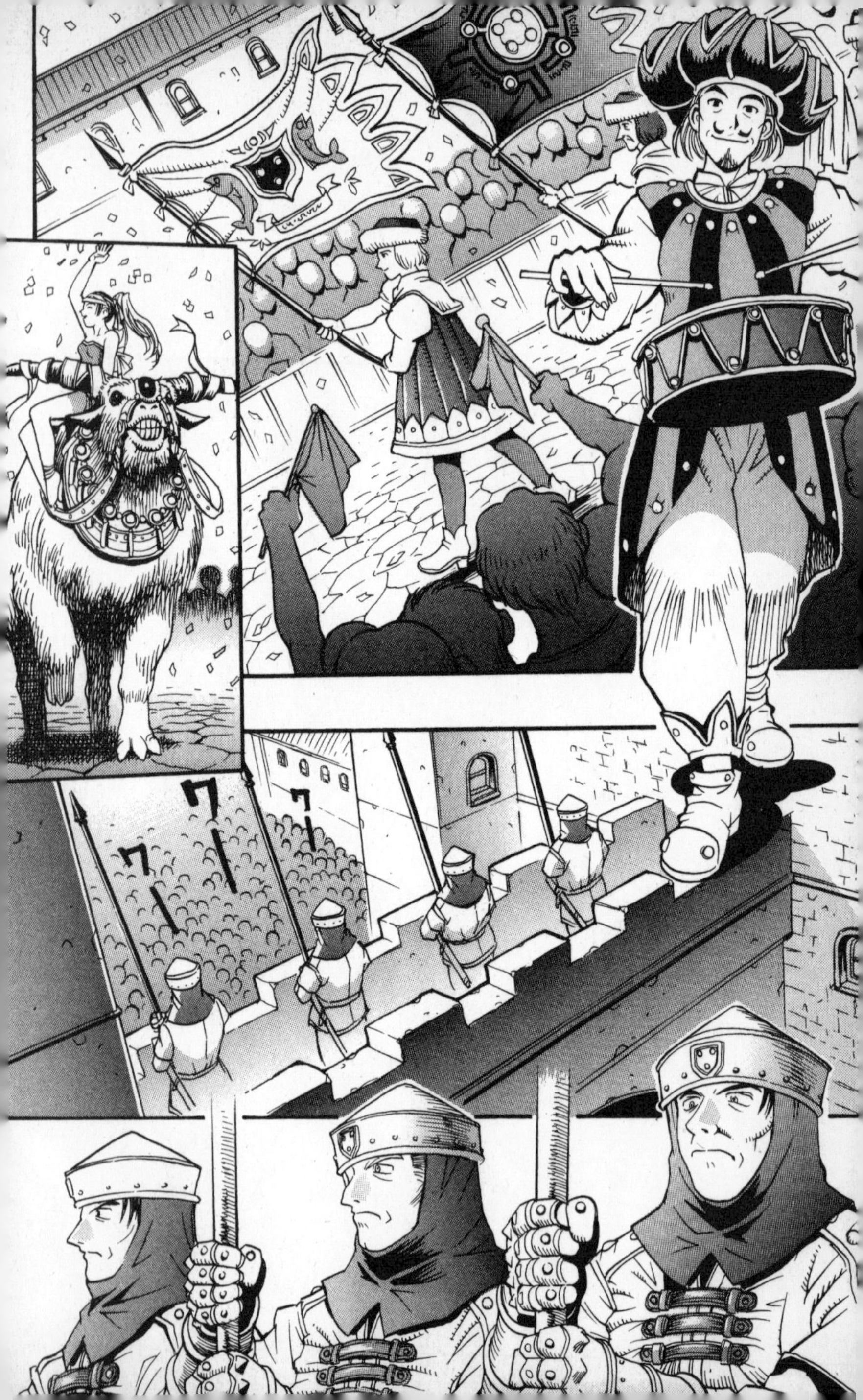
ワー
ワー
ワー

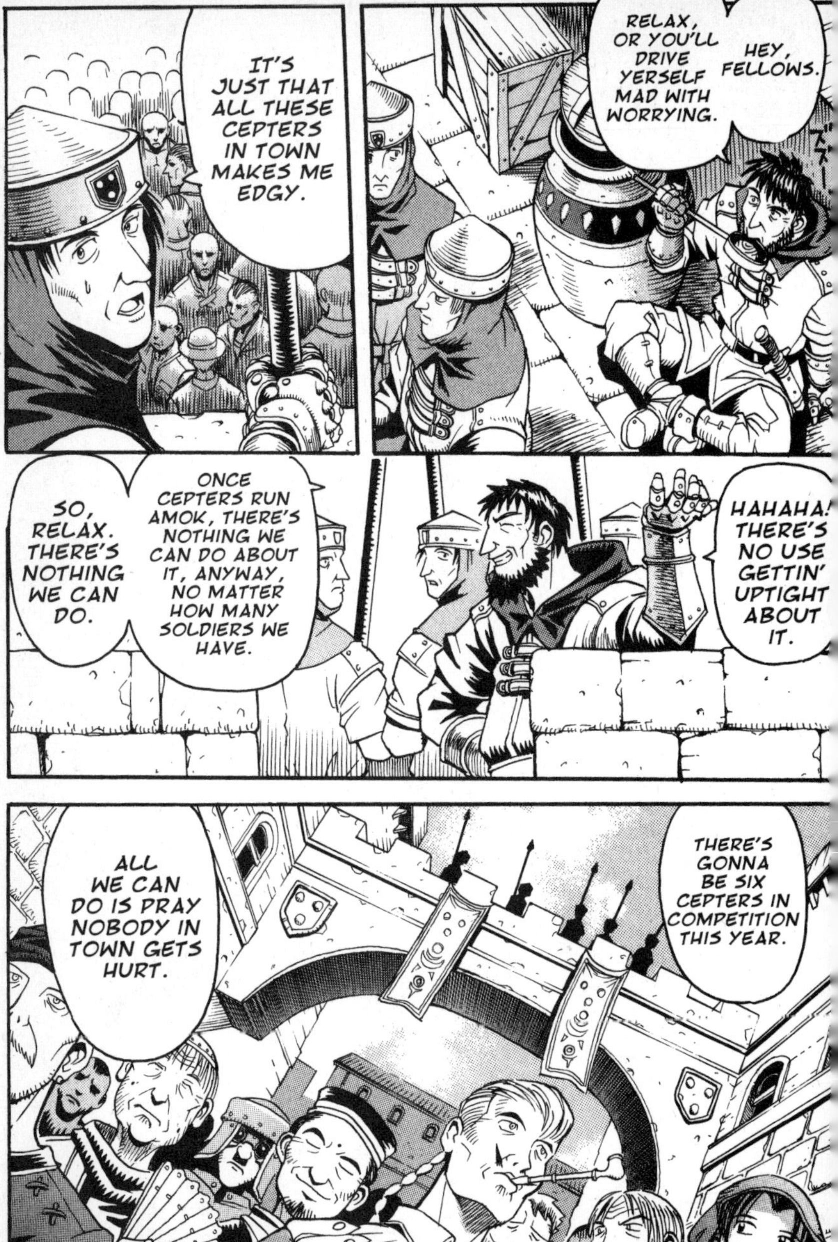
HEY, FELLOWS.
RELAX, OR YOU'LL DRIVE YERSELF MAD WITH WORRYING.
IT'S JUST THAT ALL THESE CEPTERS IN TOWN MAKES ME EDGY.
HAHAHA! THERE'S NO USE GETTIN' UPTIGHT ABOUT IT.
ONCE CEPTERS RUN AMOK, THERE'S NOTHING WE CAN DO ABOUT IT, ANYWAY, NO MATTER HOW MANY SOLDIERS WE HAVE.
SO, RELAX. THERE'S NOTHING WE CAN DO.
THERE'S GONNA BE SIX CEPTERS IN COMPETITION THIS YEAR.
ALL WE CAN DO IS PRAY NOBODY IN TOWN GETS HURT.

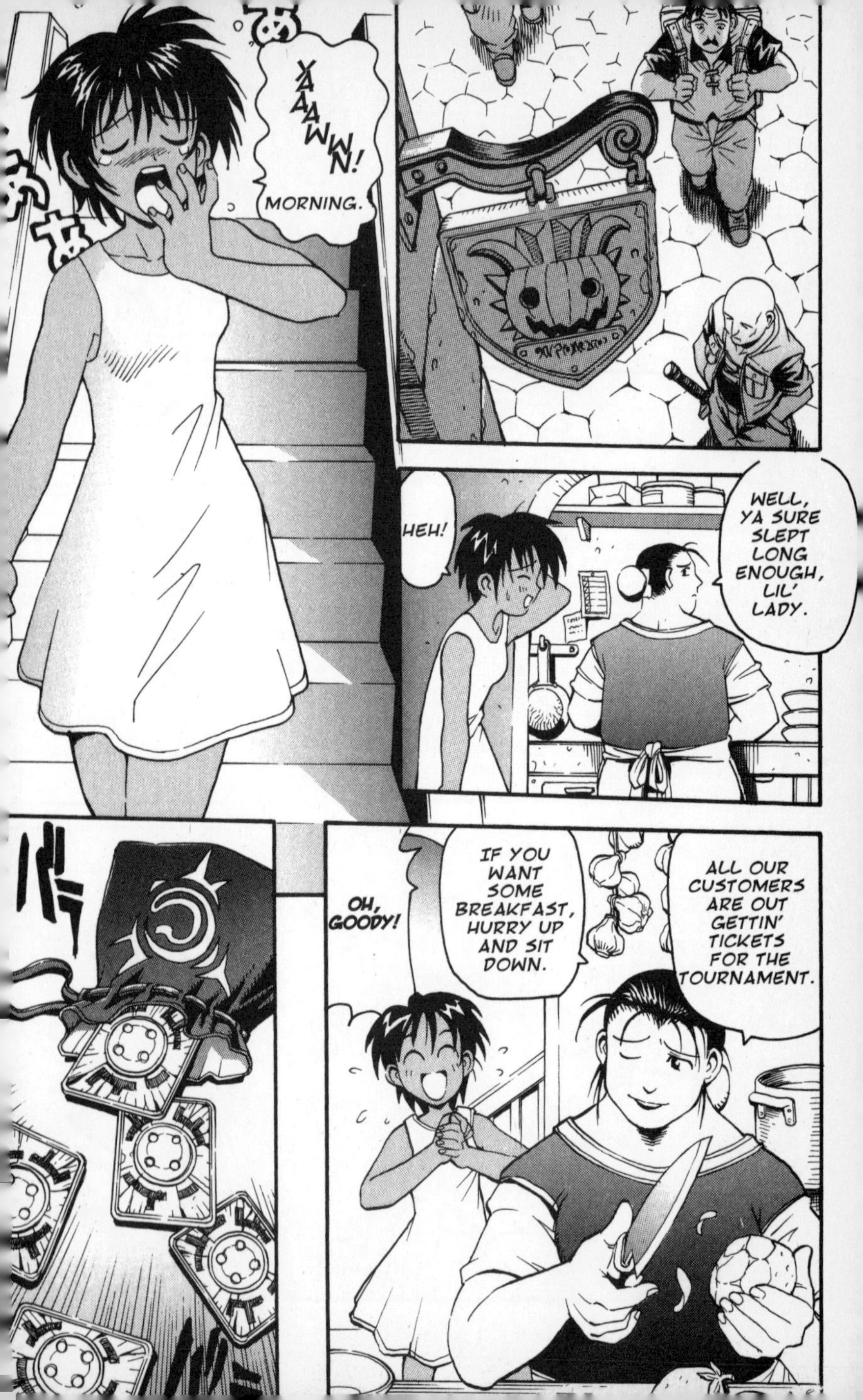
WELL, YA SURE SLEPT LONG ENOUGH, LIL' LADY.
HEH!
YAAAWWN!
MORNING.
ALL OUR CUSTOMERS ARE OUT GETTIN' TICKETS FOR THE TOURNAMENT.
IF YOU WANT SOME BREAKFAST, HURRY UP AND SIT DOWN.
OH, GOODY!

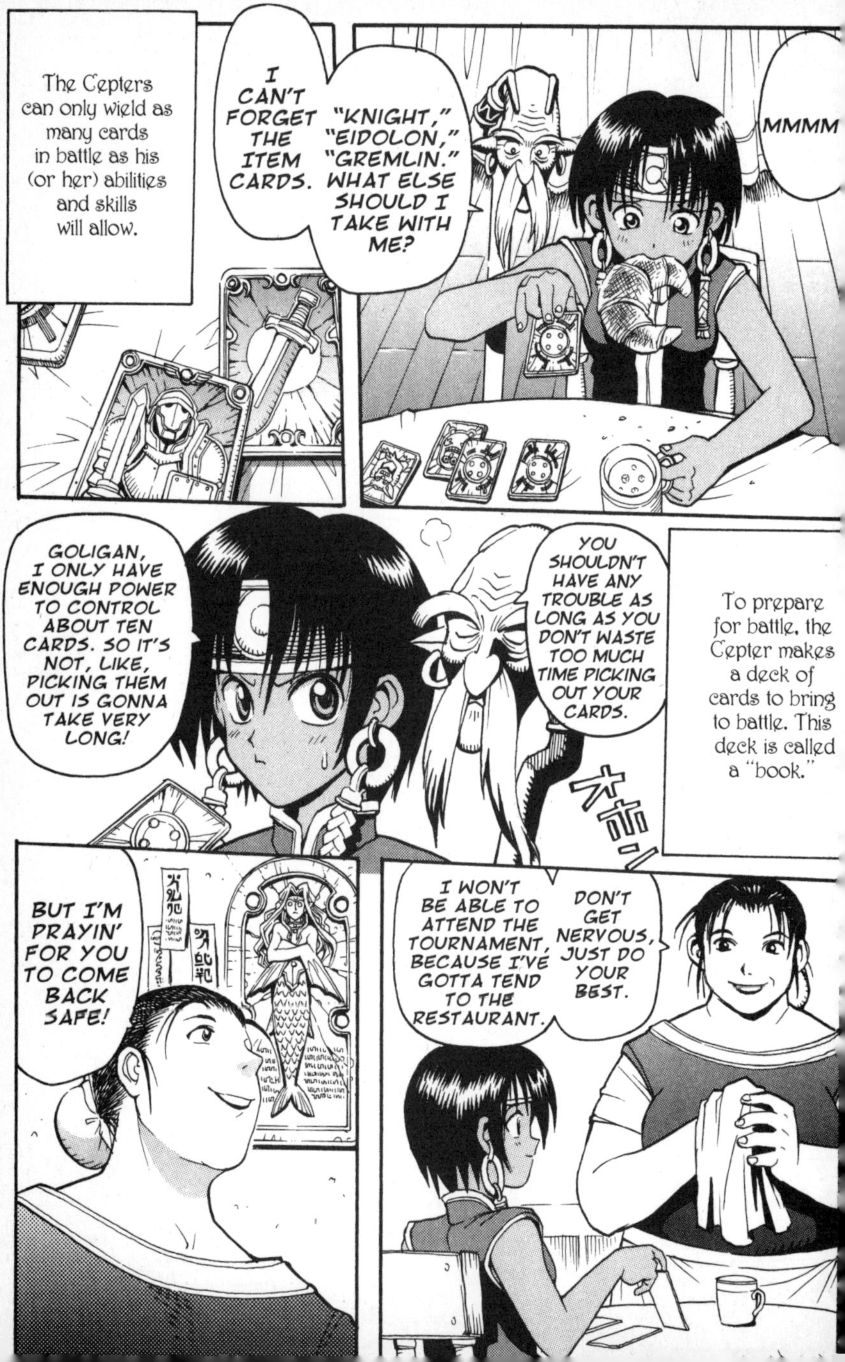
MMMM
"KNIGHT," "EIDOLON," "GREMLIN." WHAT ELSE SHOULD I TAKE WITH ME?
I CAN'T FORGET THE ITEM CARDS.
The Cepters can only wield as many cards in battle as his (or her) abilities and skills will allow.
To prepare for battle, the Cepter makes a deck of cards to bring to battle. This deck is called a "book."
YOU SHOULDN'T HAVE ANY TROUBLE AS LONG AS YOU DON'T WASTE TOO MUCH TIME PICKING OUT YOUR CARDS.
GOLIGAN, I ONLY HAVE ENOUGH POWER TO CONTROL ABOUT TEN CARDS. SO IT'S NOT, LIKE, PICKING THEM OUT IS GONNA TAKE VERY LONG!
DON'T GET NERVOUS, JUST DO YOUR BEST.
I WON'T BE ABLE TO ATTEND THE TOURNAMENT, BECAUSE I'VE GOTTA TEND TO THE RESTAURANT.
BUT I'M PRAYIN' FOR YOU TO COME BACK SAFE!

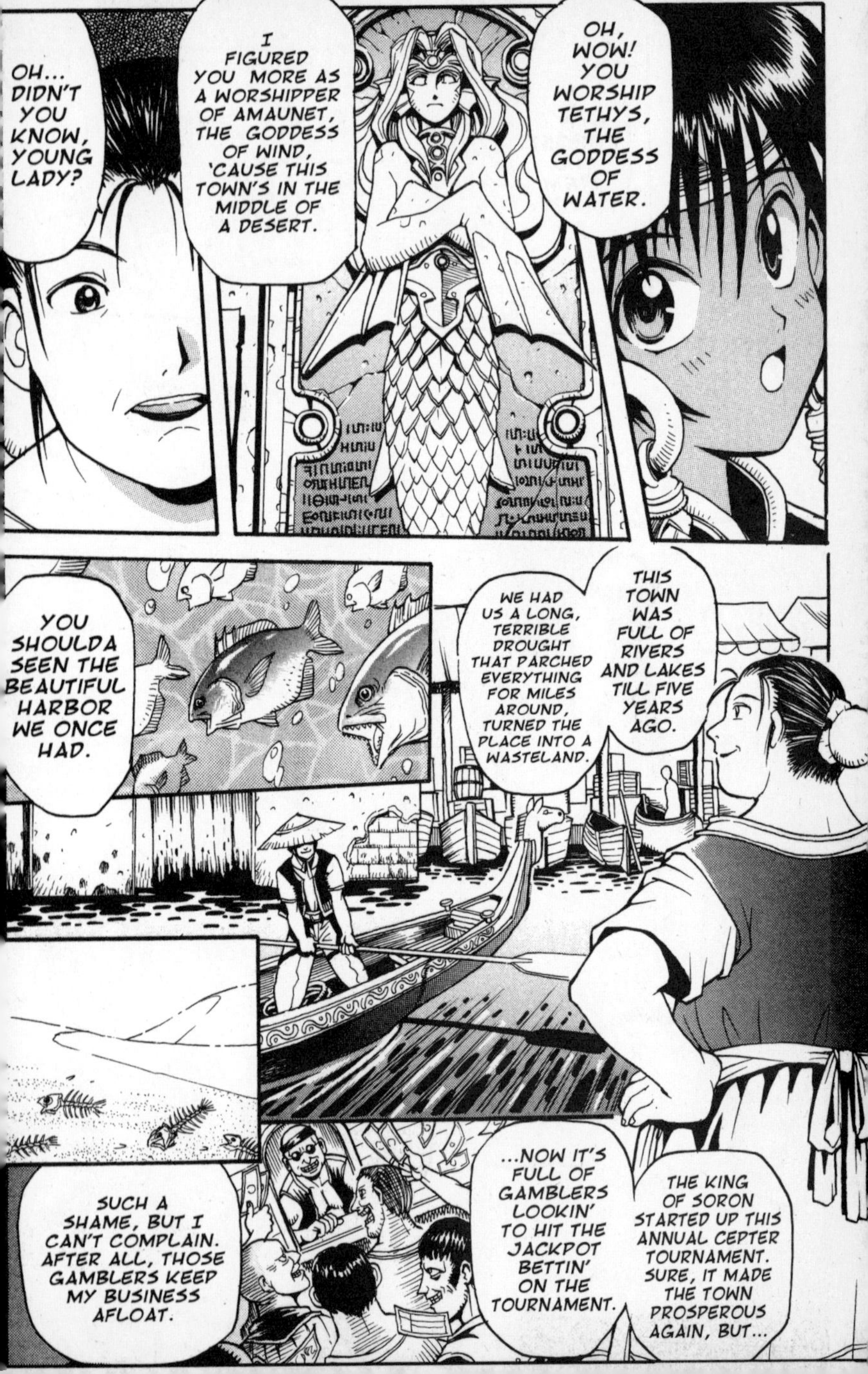
OH, WOW! YOU WORSHIP TETHYS, THE GODDESS OF WATER.
I FIGURED YOU MORE AS A WORSHIPPER OF AMAUNET, THE GODDESS OF WIND, 'CAUSE THIS TOWN'S IN THE MIDDLE OF A DESERT.
OH... DIDN'T YOU KNOW, YOUNG LADY?
THIS TOWN WAS FULL OF RIVERS AND LAKES TILL FIVE YEARS AGO.
WE HAD US A LONG, TERRIBLE DROUGHT THAT PARCHED EVERYTHING FOR MILES AROUND, TURNED THE PLACE INTO A WASTELAND.
YOU SHOULDA SEEN THE BEAUTIFUL HARBOR WE ONCE HAD.
THE KING OF SORON STARTED UP THIS ANNUAL CEPTER TOURNAMENT. SURE, IT MADE THE TOWN PROSPEROUS AGAIN, BUT...
...NOW IT'S FULL OF GAMBLERS LOOKIN' TO HIT THE JACKPOT BETTIN' ON THE TOURNAMENT.
SUCH A SHAME, BUT I CAN'T COMPLAIN. AFTER ALL, THOSE GAMBLERS KEEP MY BUSINESS AFLOAT.

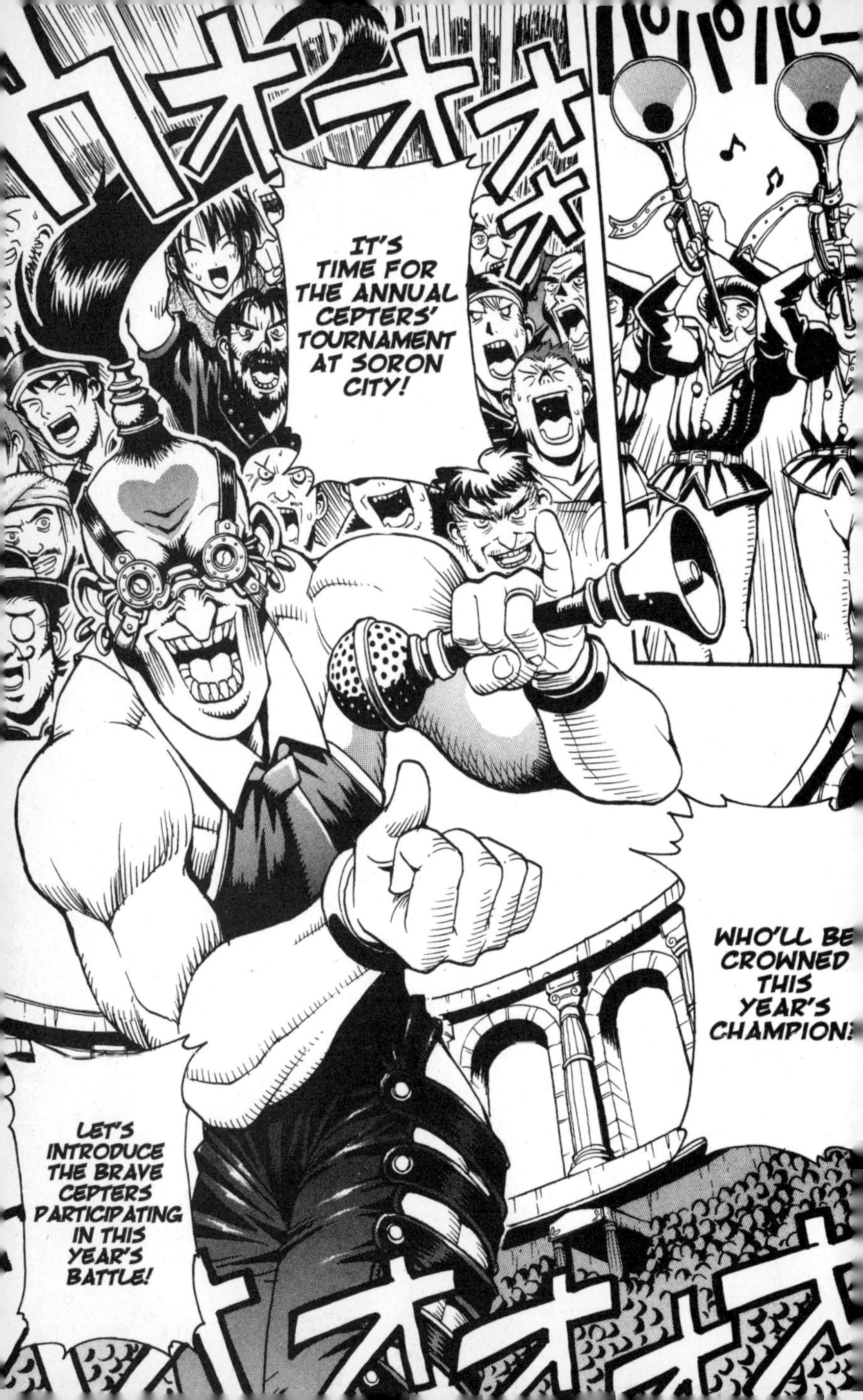
パパパー
IT'S TIME FOR THE ANNUAL CEPTERS' TOURNAMENT AT SORON CITY!
WHO'LL BE CROWNED THIS YEAR'S CHAMPION!
LET'S INTRODUCE THE BRAVE CEPTERS PARTICIPATING IN THIS YEAR'S BATTLE!

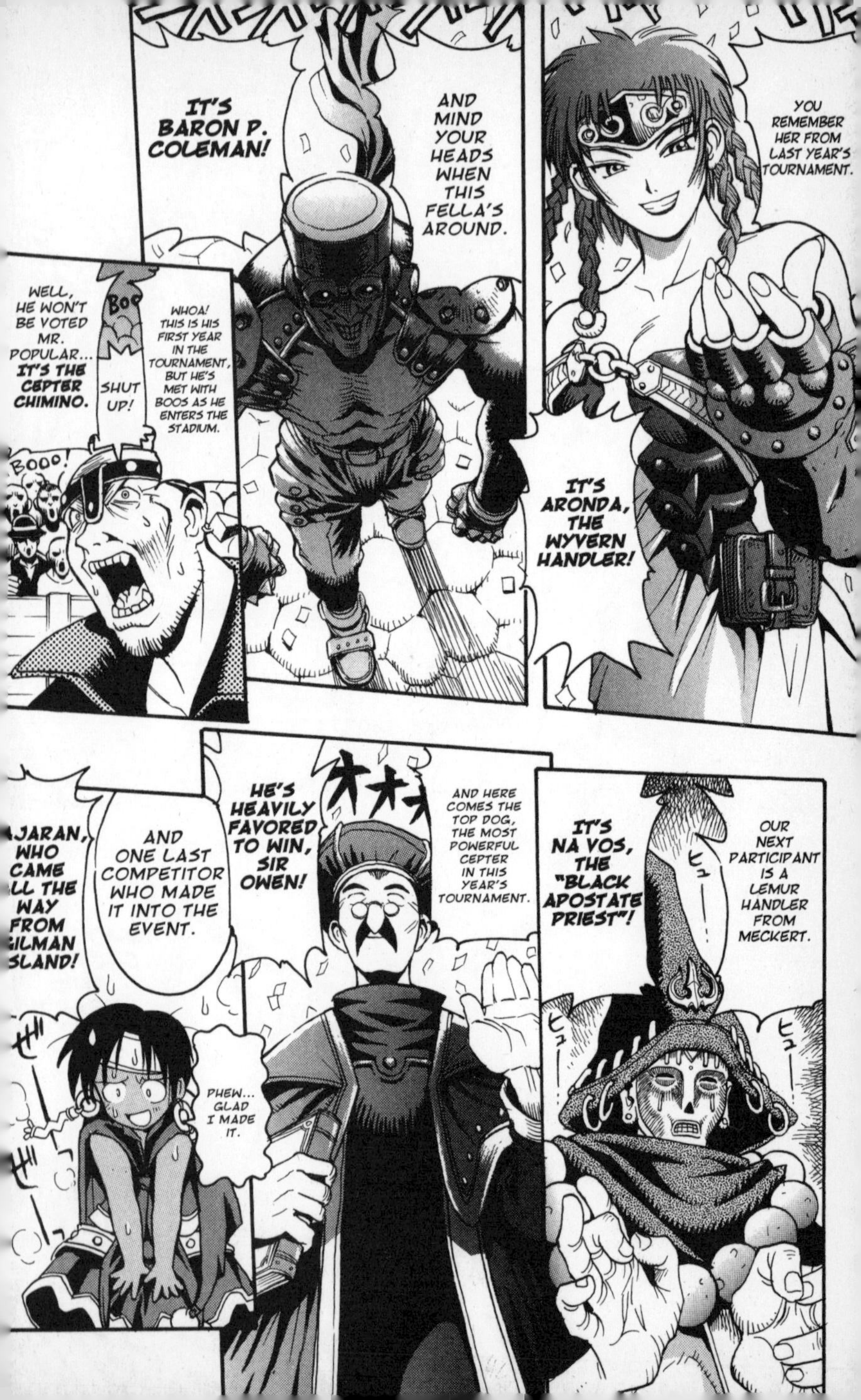
YOU REMEMBER HER FROM LAST YEAR'S TOURNAMENT.
IT'S ARONDA, THE WYVERN HANDLER!
AND MIND YOUR HEADS WHEN THIS FELLA'S AROUND.
IT'S BARON P. COLEMAN!
WHOA! THIS IS HIS FIRST YEAR IN THE TOURNAMENT, BUT HE'S MET WITH BOOS AS HE ENTERS THE STADIUM.
WELL, HE WON'T BE VOTED MR. POPULAR... IT'S THE CEPTER CHIMINO.
BOO
SHUT UP!
BOOO!
OUR NEXT PARTICIPANT IS A LEMUR HANDLER FROM MECKERT.
IT'S NA VOS, THE "BLACK APOSTATE PRIEST"!
ヒュー
ヒュー
ヒュー
AND HERE COMES THE TOP DOG, THE MOST POWERFUL CEPTER IN THIS YEAR'S TOURNAMENT.
HE'S HEAVILY FAVORED TO WIN, SIR OWEN!
オオォ
AND ONE LAST COMPETITOR WHO MADE IT INTO THE EVENT.
AJARAN, WHO CAME LL THE WAY FROM ILMAN SLAND!
PHEW... GLAD I MADE IT.

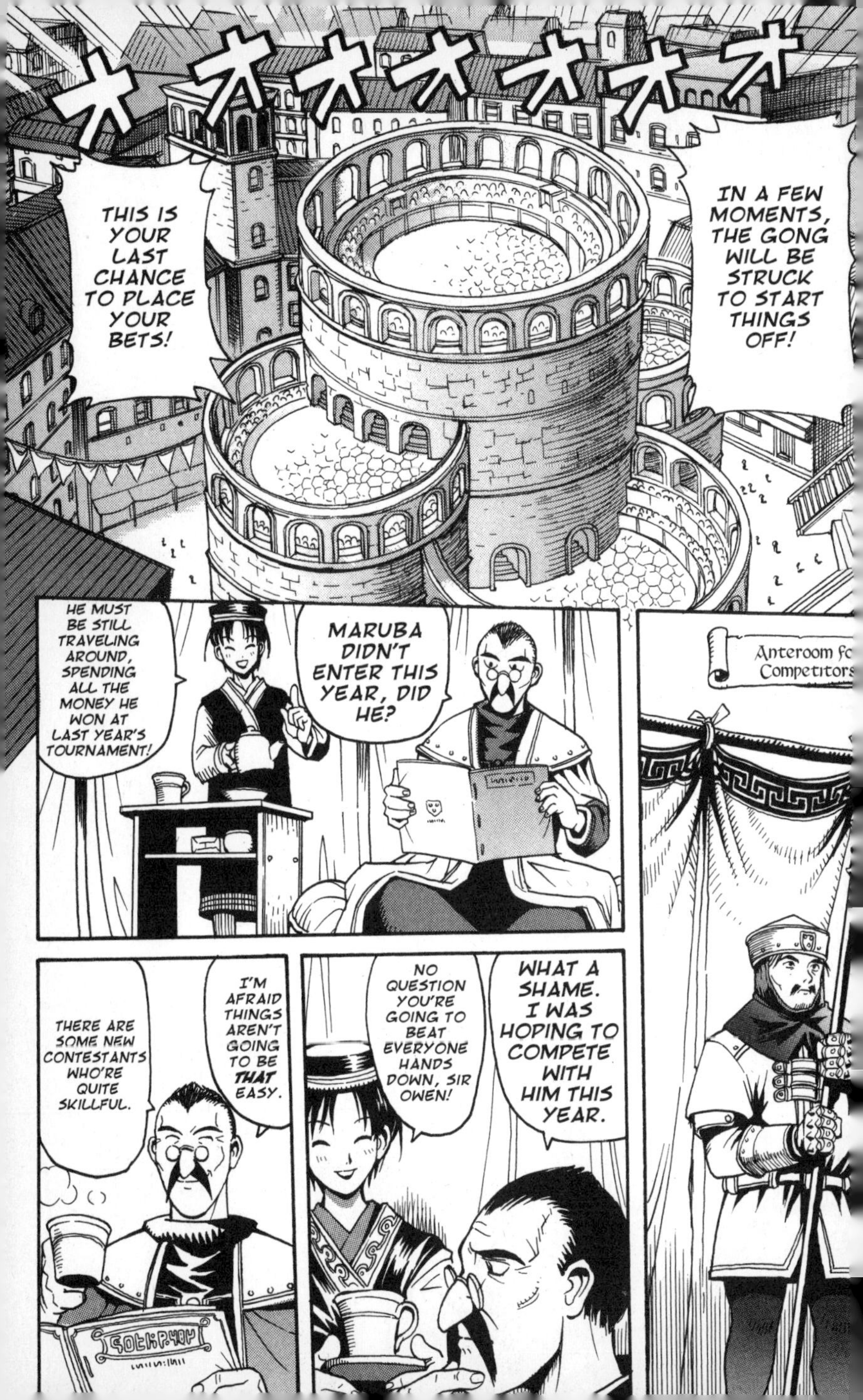

オオオオオオオ
IN A FEW MOMENTS, THE GONG WILL BE STRUCK TO START THINGS OFF!
THIS IS YOUR LAST CHANCE TO PLACE YOUR BETS!
Anteroom fo
Competitors
MARUBA DIDN'T ENTER THIS YEAR, DID HE?
HE MUST BE STILL TRAVELING AROUND, SPENDING ALL THE MONEY HE WON AT LAST YEAR'S TOURNAMENT!
WHAT A SHAME. I WAS HOPING TO COMPETE WITH HIM THIS YEAR.
NO QUESTION YOU'RE GOING TO BEAT EVERYONE HANDS DOWN, SIR OWEN!
I'M AFRAID THINGS AREN'T GOING TO BE ***THAT*** EASY.
THERE ARE SOME NEW CONTESTANTS WHO'RE QUITE SKILLFUL.

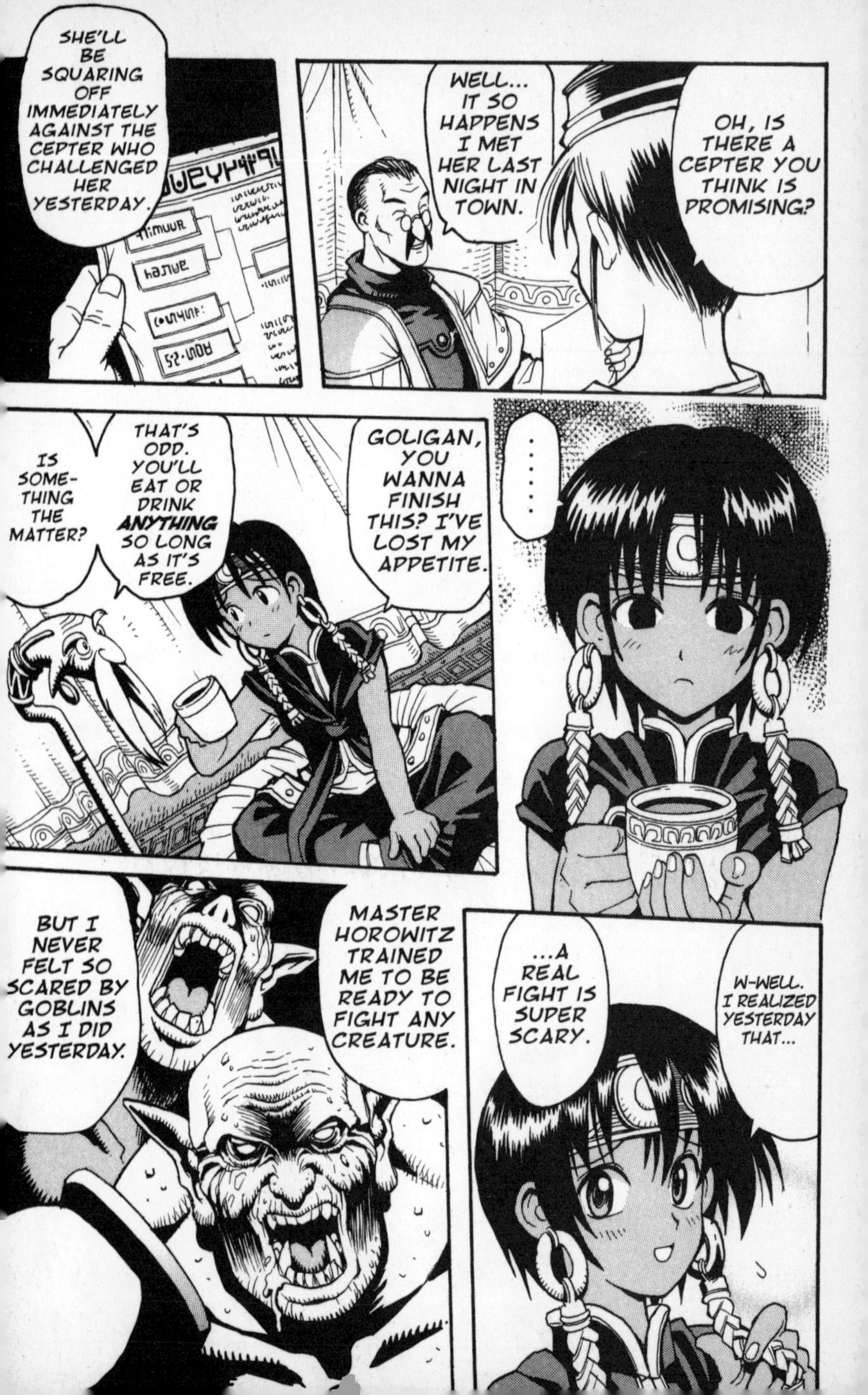
OH, IS THERE A CEPTER YOU THINK IS PROMISING?
WELL... IT SO HAPPENS I MET HER LAST NIGHT IN TOWN.
SHE'LL BE SQUARING OFF IMMEDIATELY AGAINST THE CEPTER WHO CHALLENGED HER YESTERDAY.
......
GOLIGAN, YOU WANNA FINISH THIS? I'VE LOST MY APPETITE.
THAT'S ODD. YOU'LL EAT OR DRINK **ANYTHING** SO LONG AS IT'S FREE.
IS SOMETHING THE MATTER?
W-WELL. I REALIZED YESTERDAY THAT...
...A REAL FIGHT IS SUPER SCARY.
MASTER HOROWITZ TRAINED ME TO BE READY TO FIGHT ANY CREATURE.
BUT I NEVER FELT SO SCARED BY GOBLINS AS I DID YESTERDAY.

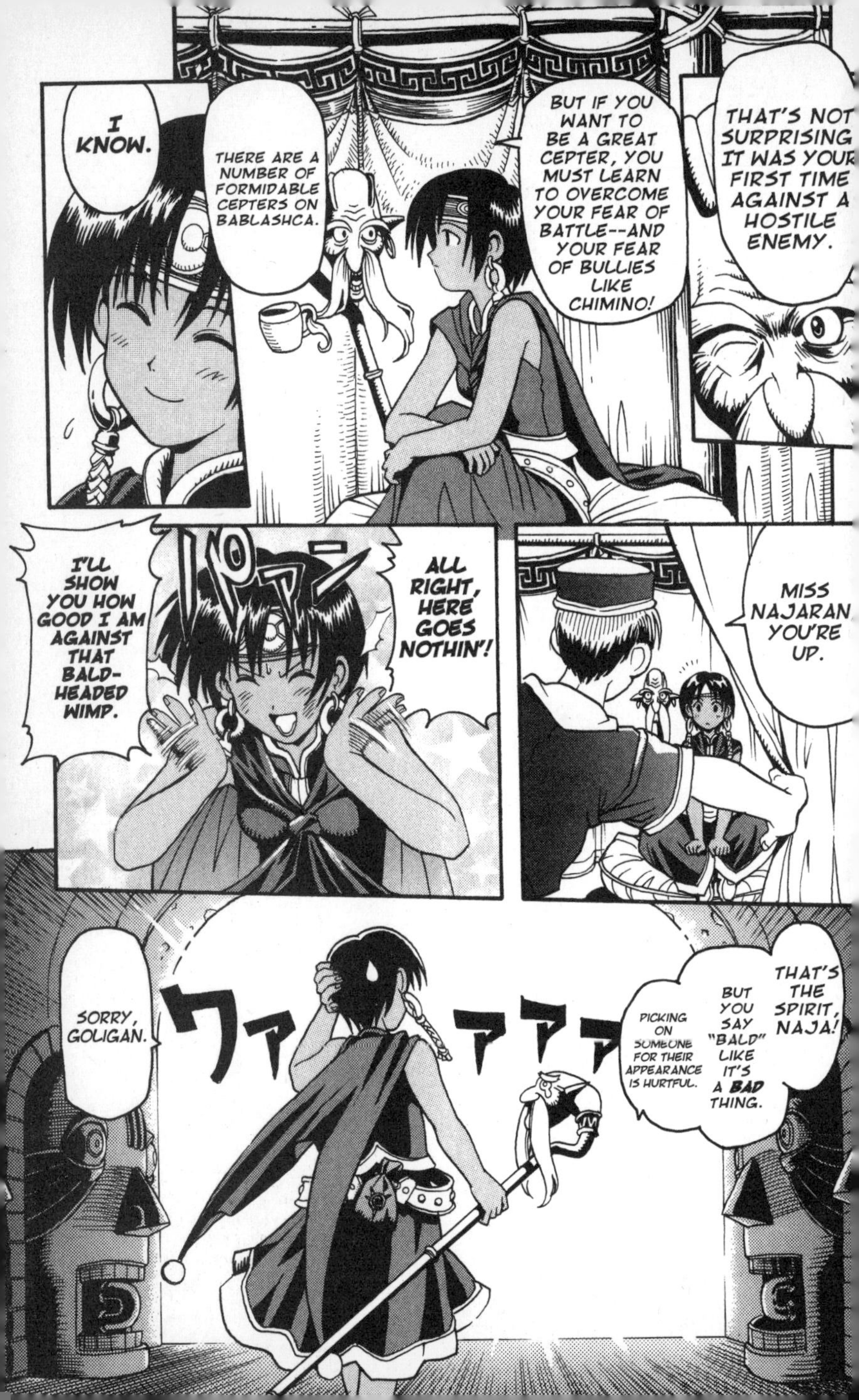
THAT'S NOT SURPRISING IT WAS YOUR FIRST TIME AGAINST A HOSTILE ENEMY.
BUT IF YOU WANT TO BE A GREAT CEPTER, YOU MUST LEARN TO OVERCOME YOUR FEAR OF BATTLE--AND YOUR FEAR OF BULLIES LIKE CHIMINO!
THERE ARE A NUMBER OF FORMIDABLE CEPTERS ON BABLASHCA.
I KNOW.
MISS NAJARAN, YOU'RE UP.
ALL RIGHT, HERE GOES NOTHIN'!
I'LL SHOW YOU HOW GOOD I AM AGAINST THAT BALD-HEADED WIMP.
THAT'S THE SPIRIT, NAJA!
BUT YOU SAY "BALD" LIKE IT'S A **BAD** THING.
PICKING ON SOMEONE FOR THEIR APPEARANCE IS HURTFUL.
SORRY, GOLIGAN.

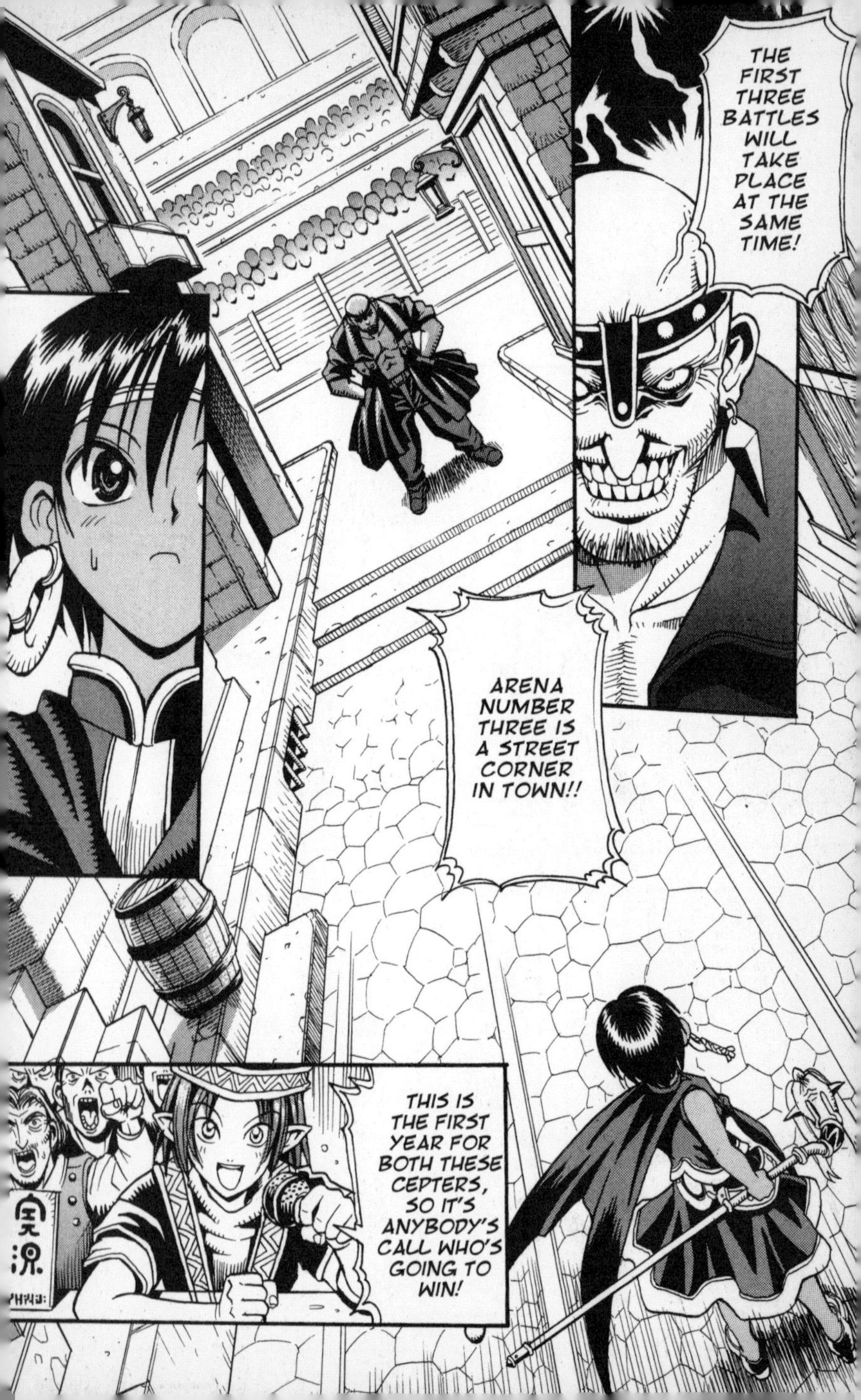
THE FIRST THREE BATTLES WILL TAKE PLACE AT THE SAME TIME!
ARENA NUMBER THREE IS A STREET CORNER IN TOWN!!
THIS IS THE FIRST YEAR FOR BOTH THESE CEPTERS, SO IT'S ANYBODY'S CALL WHO'S GOING TO WIN!

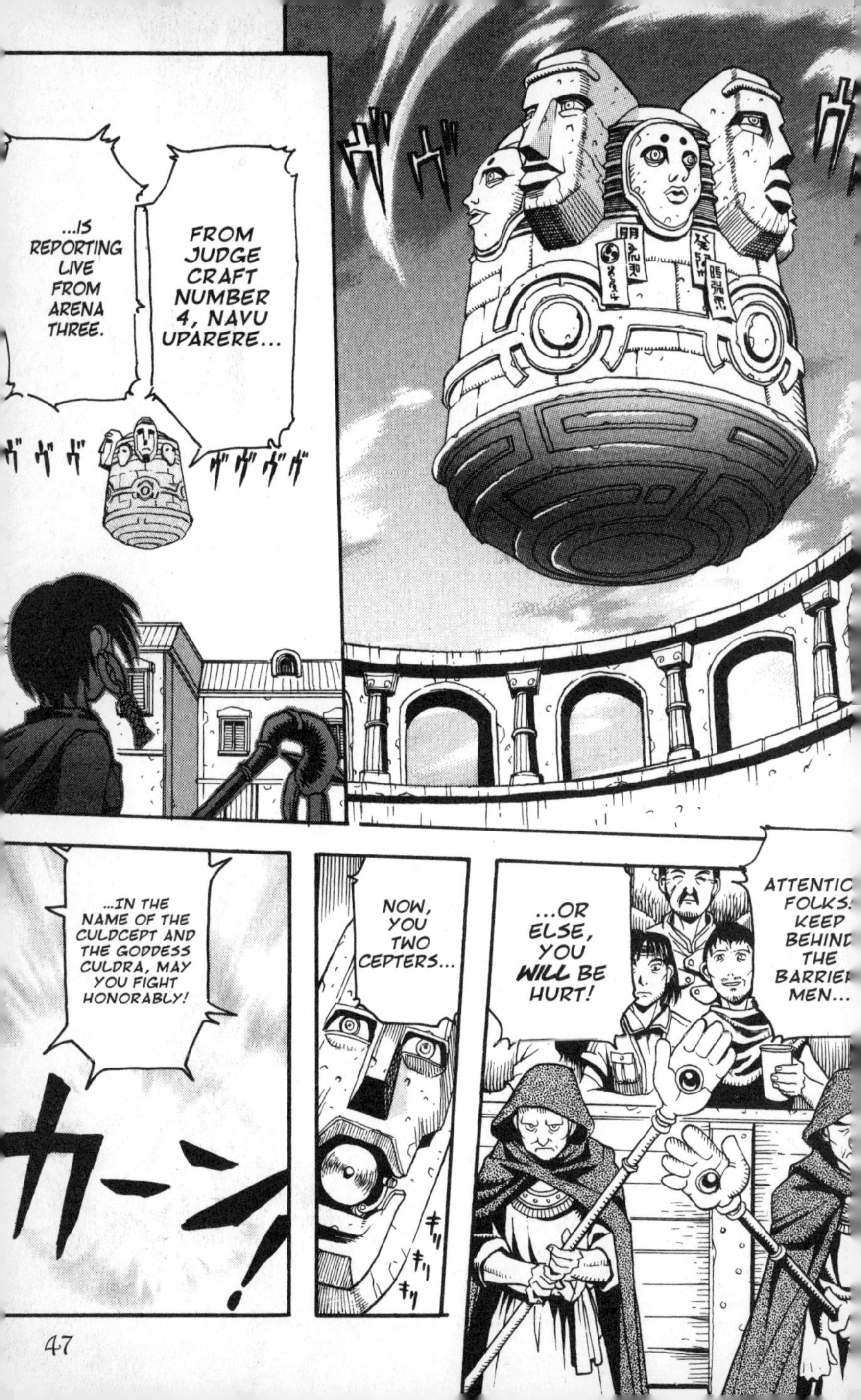
FROM JUDGE CRAFT NUMBER 4, NAVU UPARERE...
...IS REPORTING LIVE FROM ARENA THREE.
ATTENTIO FOLKS! KEEP BEHIND THE BARRIER MEN...
...OR ELSE, YOU **WILL** BE HURT!
NOW, YOU TWO CEPTERS...
...IN THE NAME OF THE CULDCEPT AND THE GODDESS CULDRA, MAY YOU FIGHT HONORABLY!

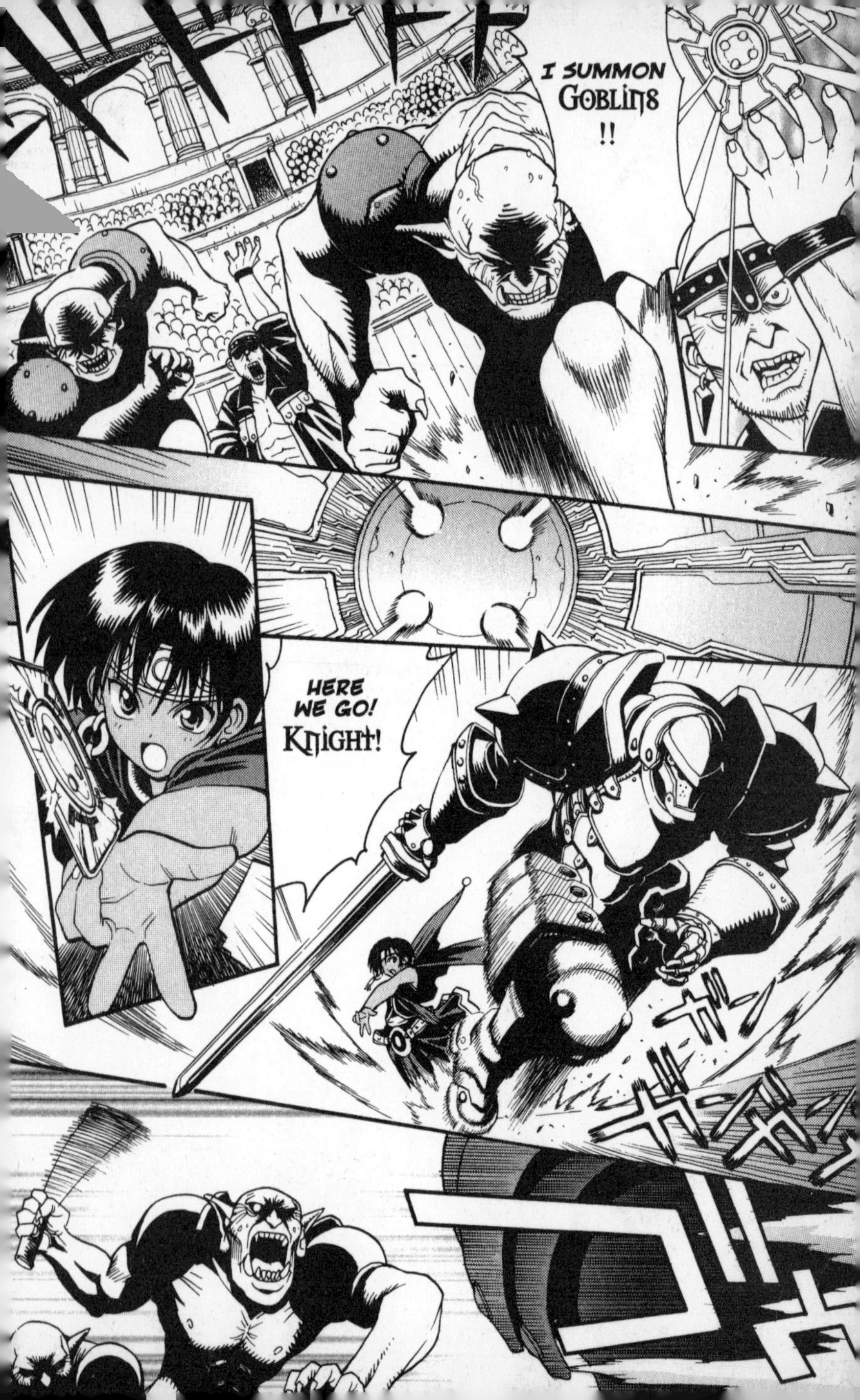
I SUMMON GOBLINS !!
HERE WE GO! KNIGHT!

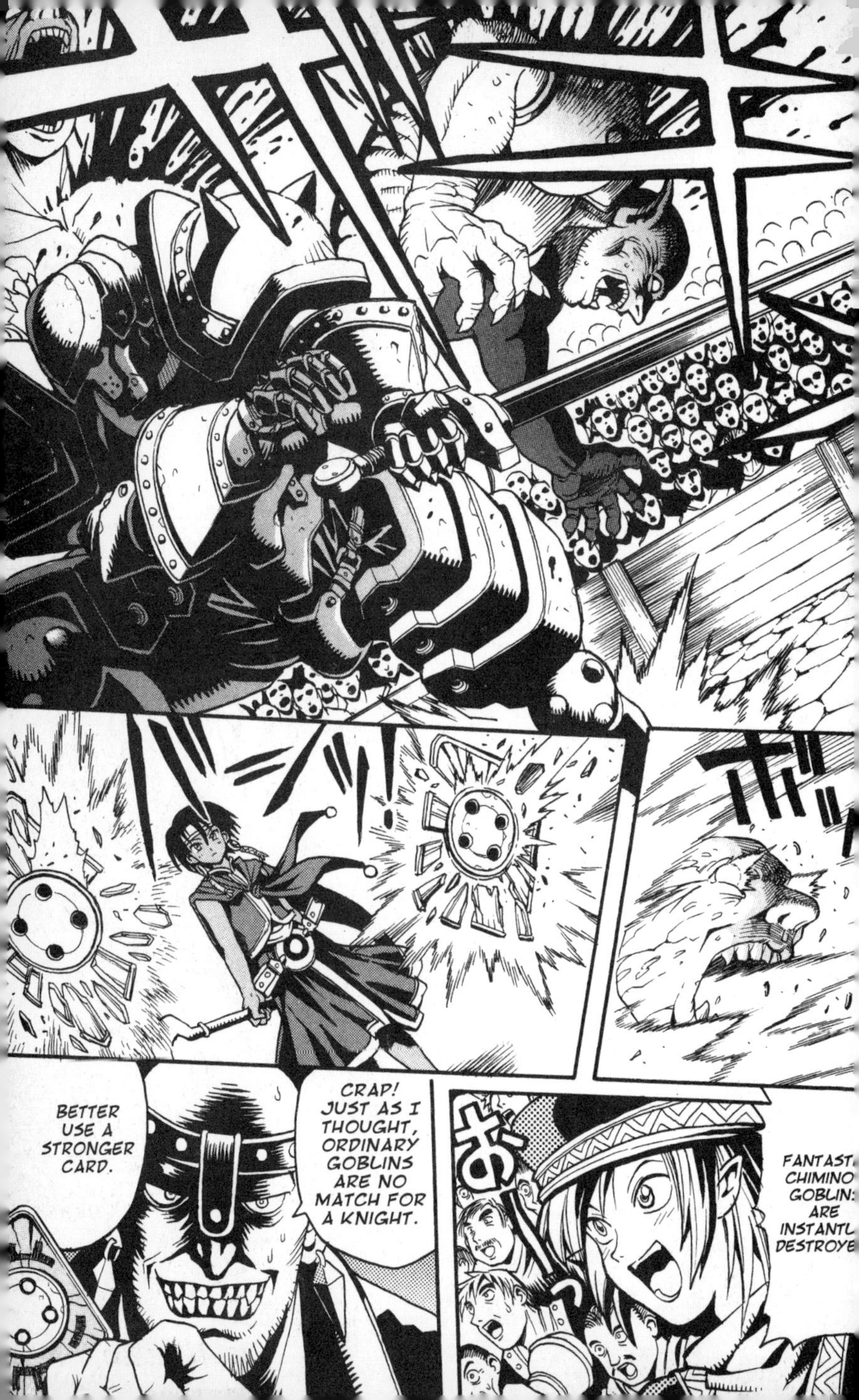
FANTAST CHIMINO GOBLIN: ARE INSTANTL DESTROYE
CRAP! JUST AS I THOUGHT, ORDINARY GOBLINS ARE NO MATCH FOR A KNIGHT.
BETTER USE A STRONGER CARD.

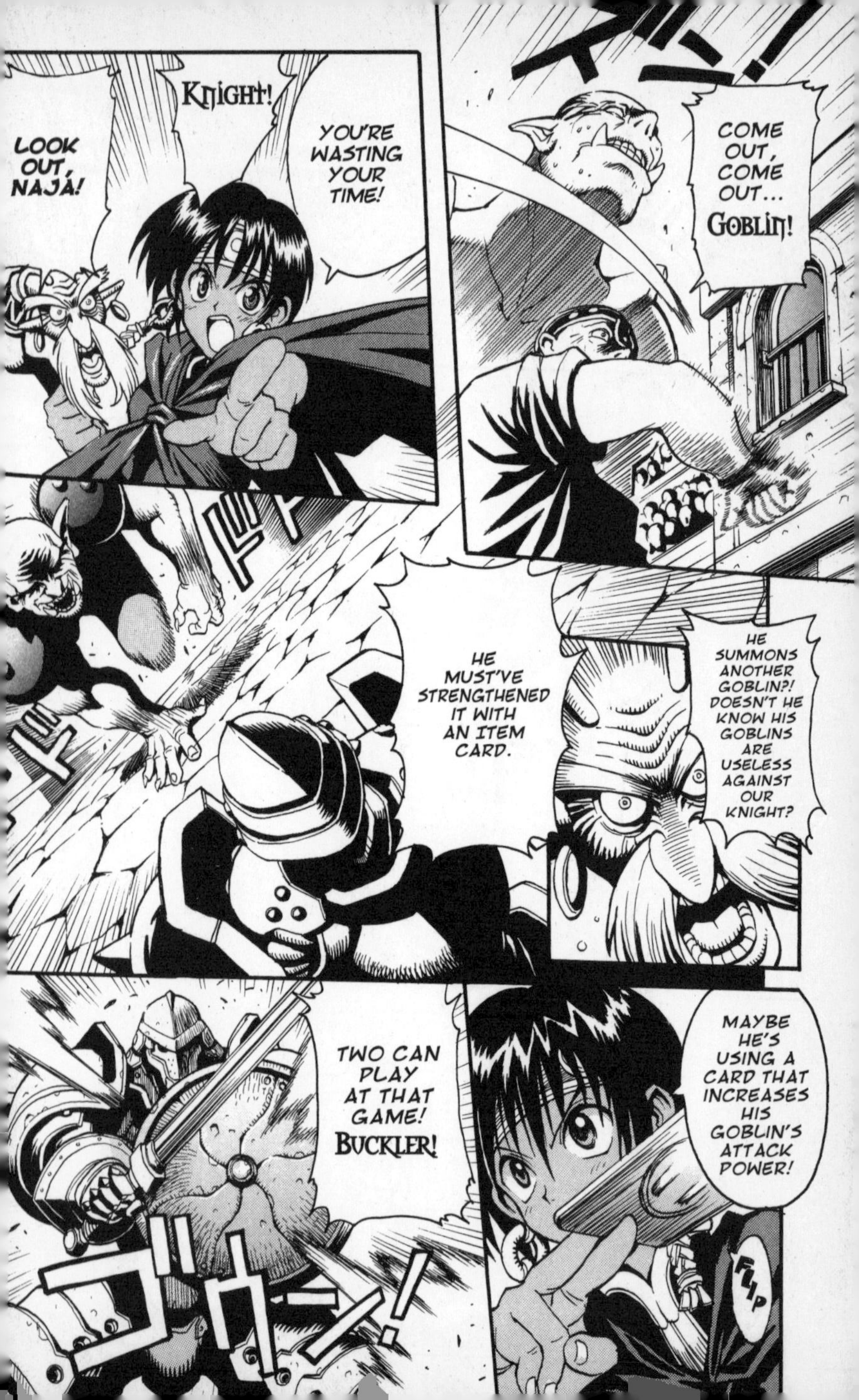
COME OUT, COME OUT... GOBLIN!
KNIGHT!
YOU'RE WASTING YOUR TIME!
LOOK OUT, NAJÁ!
HE SUMMONS ANOTHER GOBLIN?! DOESN'T HE KNOW HIS GOBLINS ARE USELESS AGAINST OUR KNIGHT?
HE MUST'VE STRENGTHENED IT WITH AN ITEM CARD.
MAYBE HE'S USING A CARD THAT INCREASES HIS GOBLIN'S ATTACK POWER!
FLIP
TWO CAN PLAY AT THAT GAME! BUCKLER!

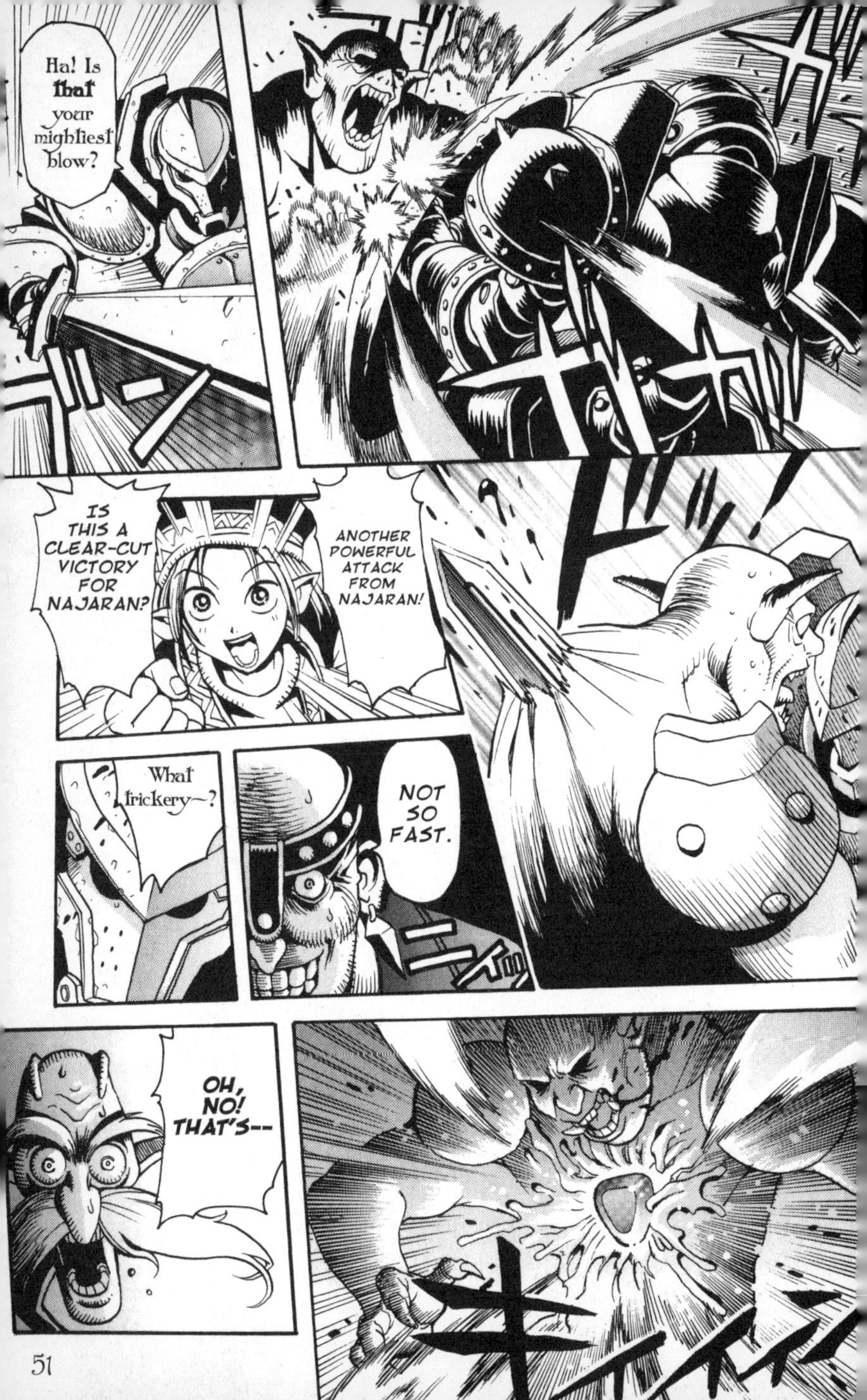
Ha! Is **that** your mightiest blow?
ANOTHER POWERFUL ATTACK FROM NAJARAN!
IS THIS A CLEAR-CUT VICTORY FOR NAJARAN?
NOT SO FAST.
What trickery~?
OH, NO! THAT'S--

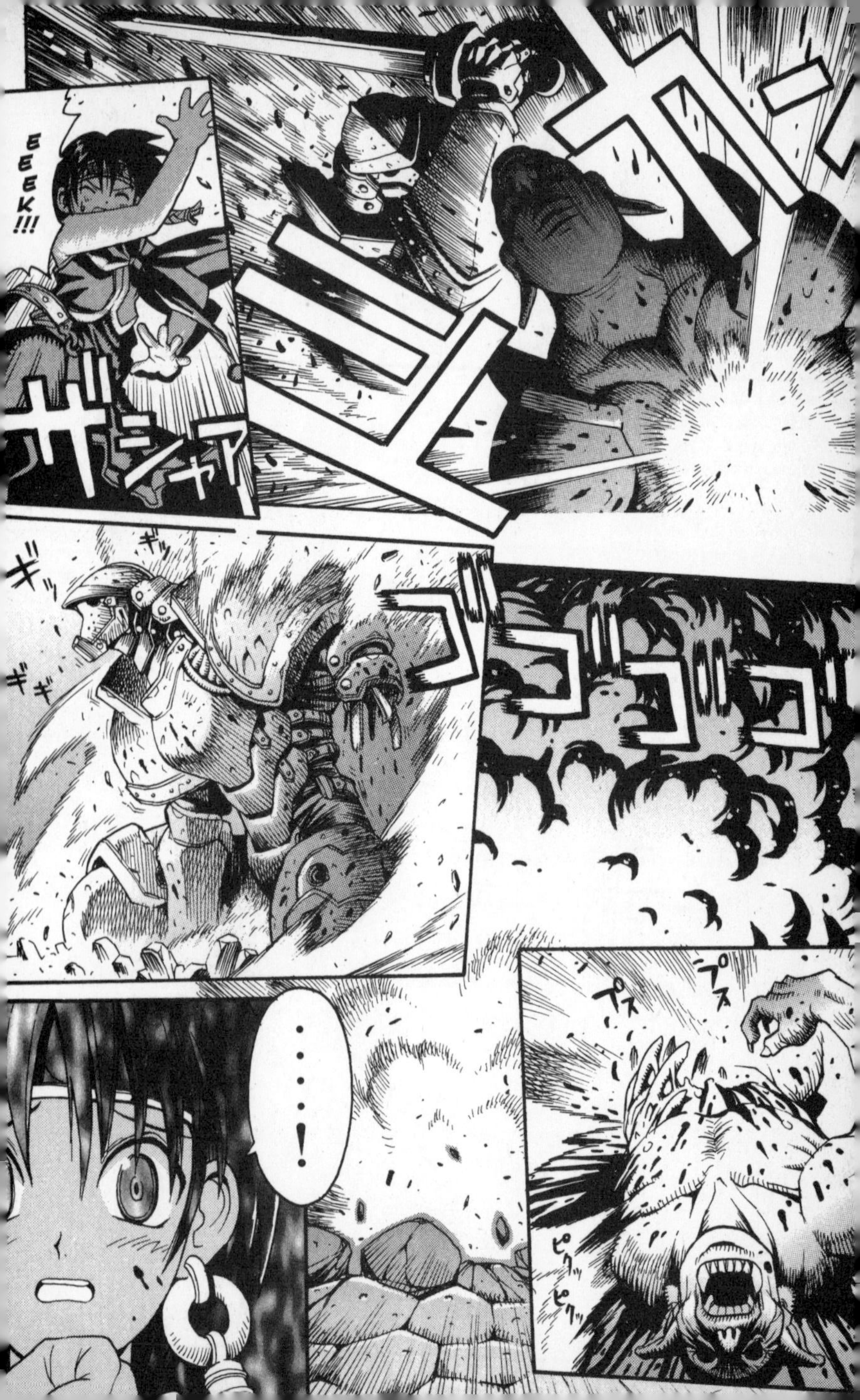
EEEK!!!
ザシャア
ゴゴゴゴ
ギッ
ギッ
ギギ
プス
プス
ピクッ
ピクッ
...!

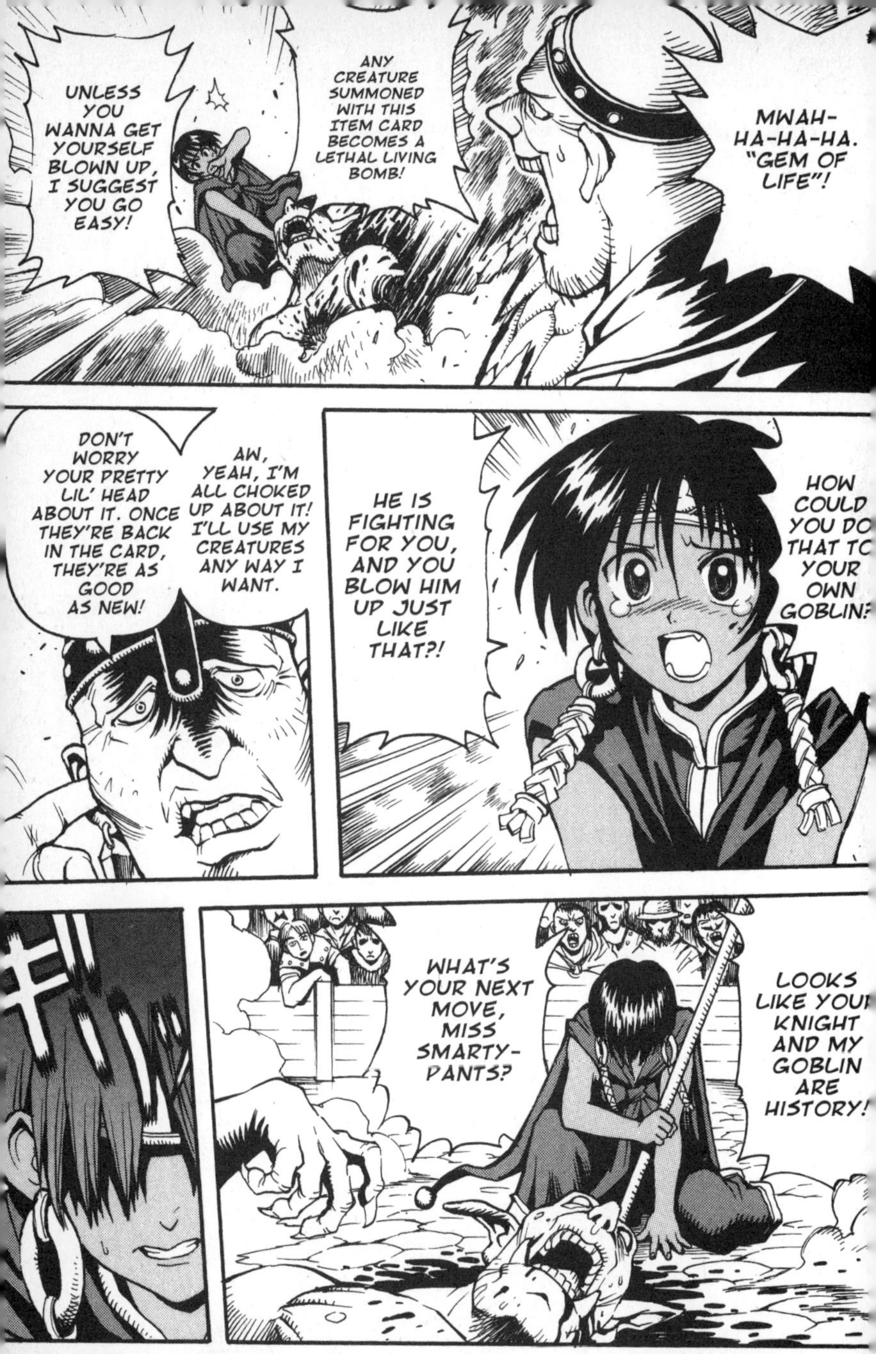
MWAH-HA-HA-HA. "GEM OF LIFE"!
ANY CREATURE SUMMONED WITH THIS ITEM CARD BECOMES A LETHAL LIVING BOMB!
UNLESS YOU WANNA GET YOURSELF BLOWN UP, I SUGGEST YOU GO EASY!
HOW COULD YOU DO THAT TO YOUR OWN GOBLIN?
HE IS FIGHTING FOR YOU, AND YOU BLOW HIM UP JUST LIKE THAT?!
AW, YEAH, I'M ALL CHOKED UP ABOUT IT! I'LL USE MY CREATURES ANY WAY I WANT.
DON'T WORRY YOUR PRETTY LIL' HEAD ABOUT IT. ONCE THEY'RE BACK IN THE CARD, THEY'RE AS GOOD AS NEW!
LOOKS LIKE YOUR KNIGHT AND MY GOBLIN ARE HISTORY!
WHAT'S YOUR NEXT MOVE, MISS SMARTY-PANTS?

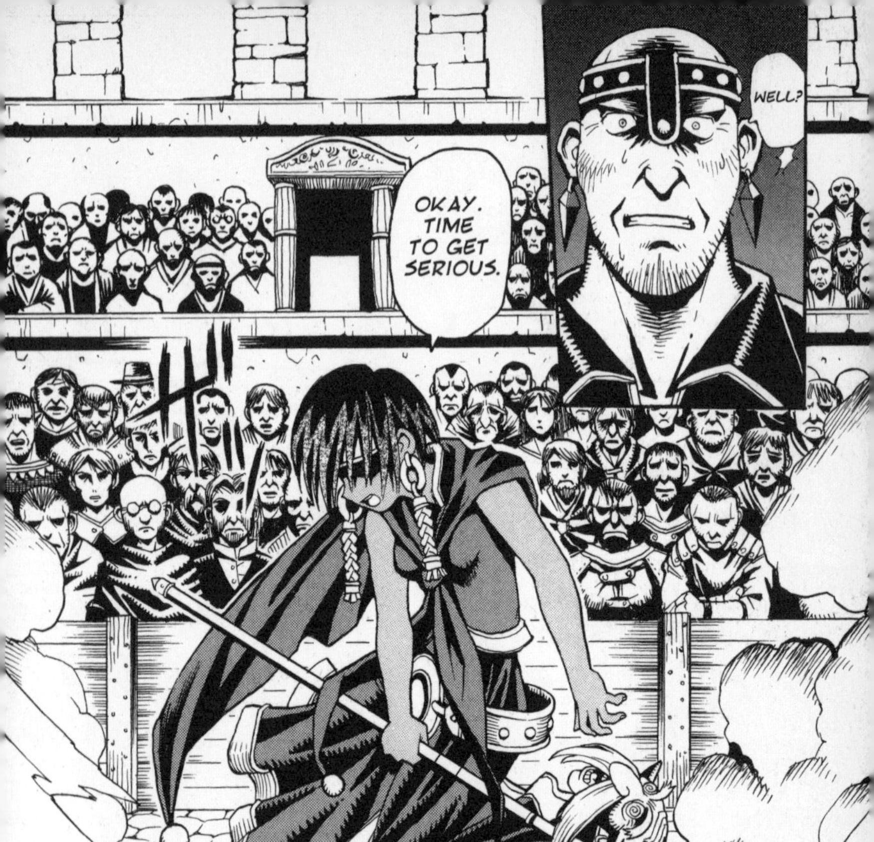
WELL?
OKAY. TIME TO GET SERIOUS.
Round 2: The Cepters' Battle Tournament — End

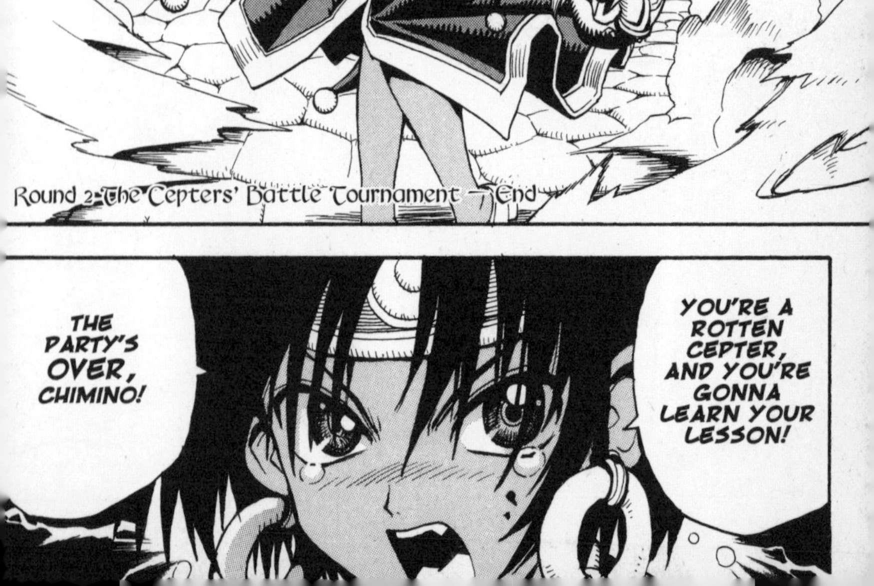
YOU'RE A ROTTEN CEPTER, AND YOU'RE GONNA LEARN YOUR LESSON!
THE PARTY'S OVER, CHIMINO!

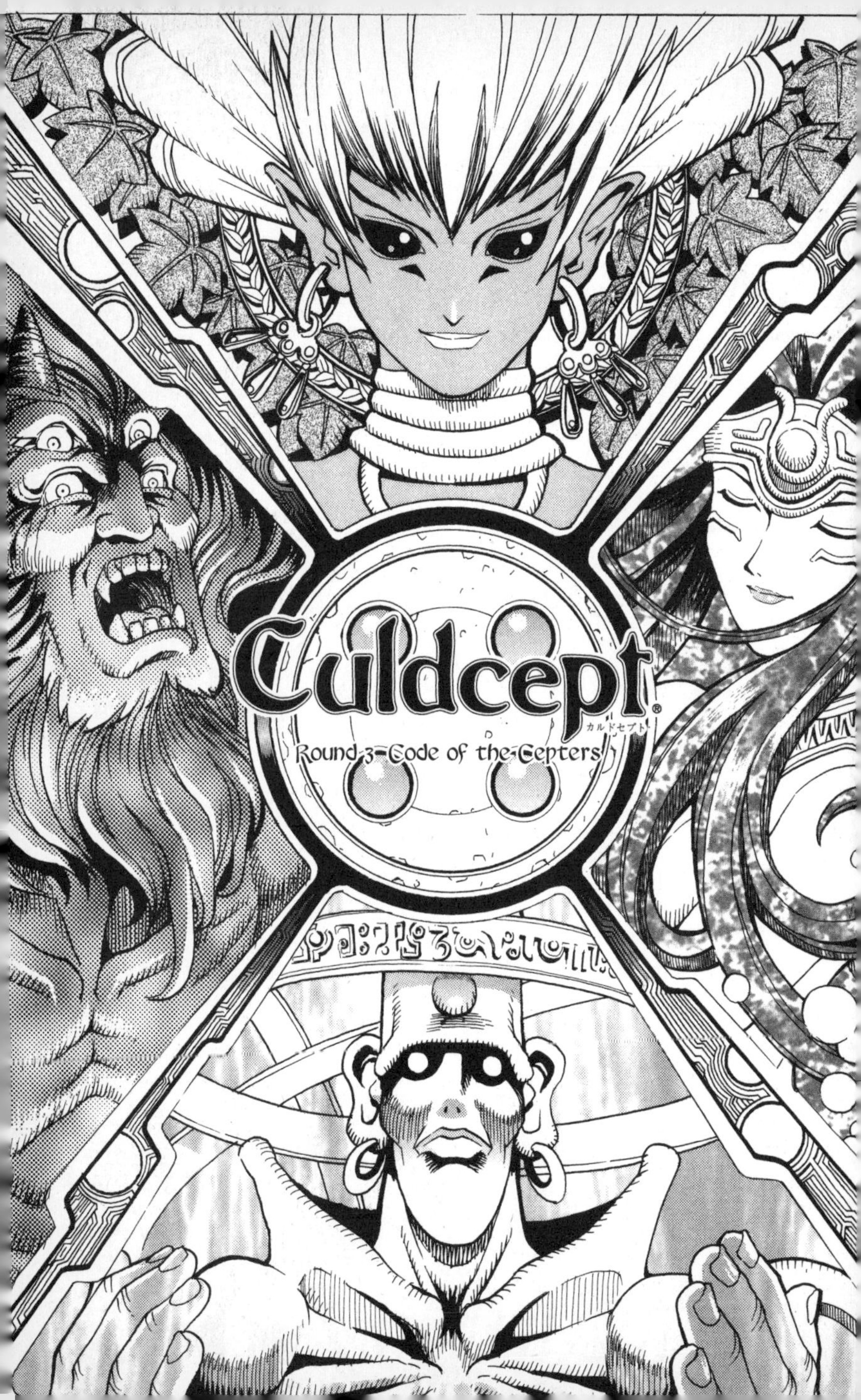
Culdcept®
カルドセプト
Round 3 - Code of the Cepters

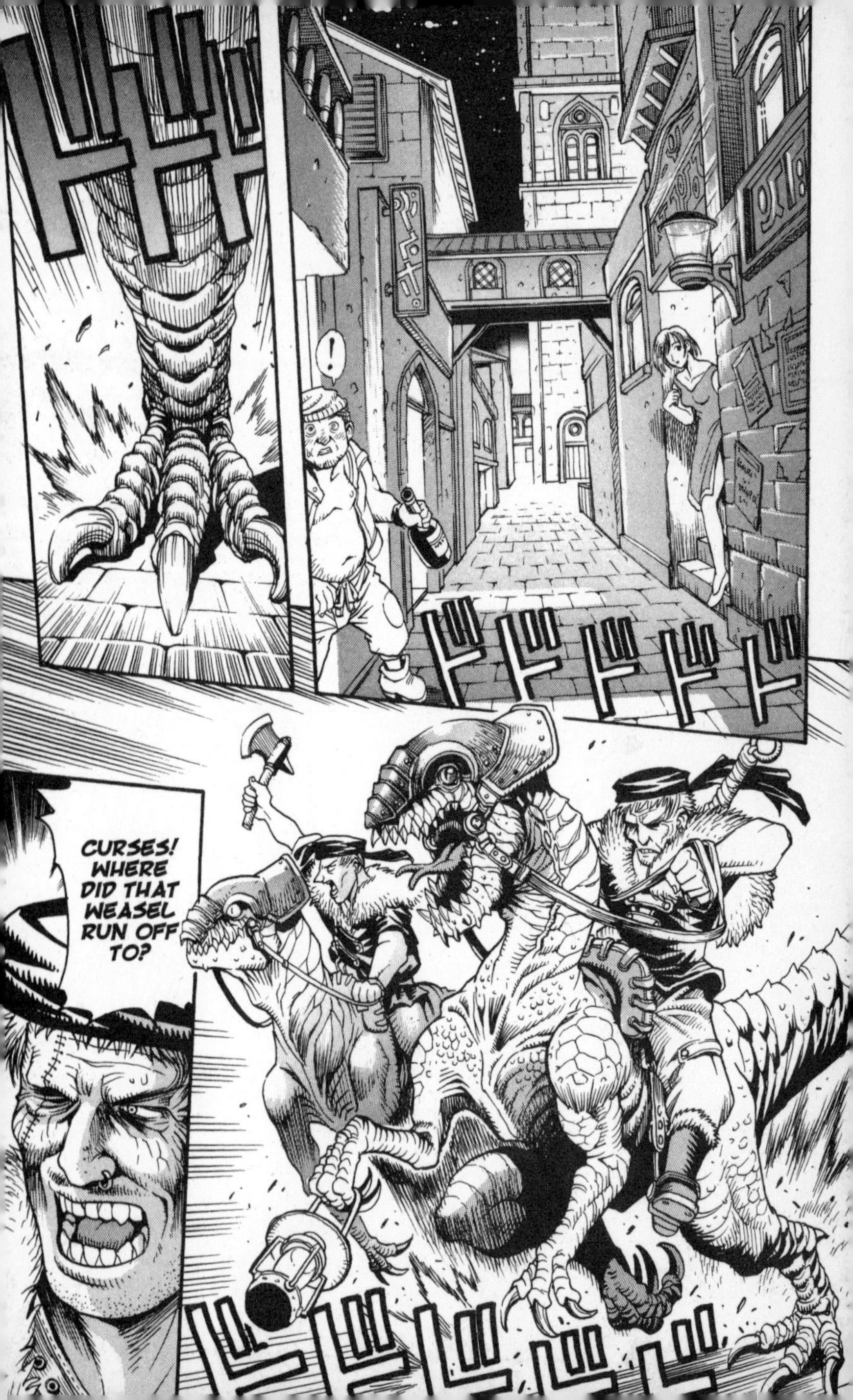
!
CURSES! WHERE DID THAT WEASEL RUN OFF TO?

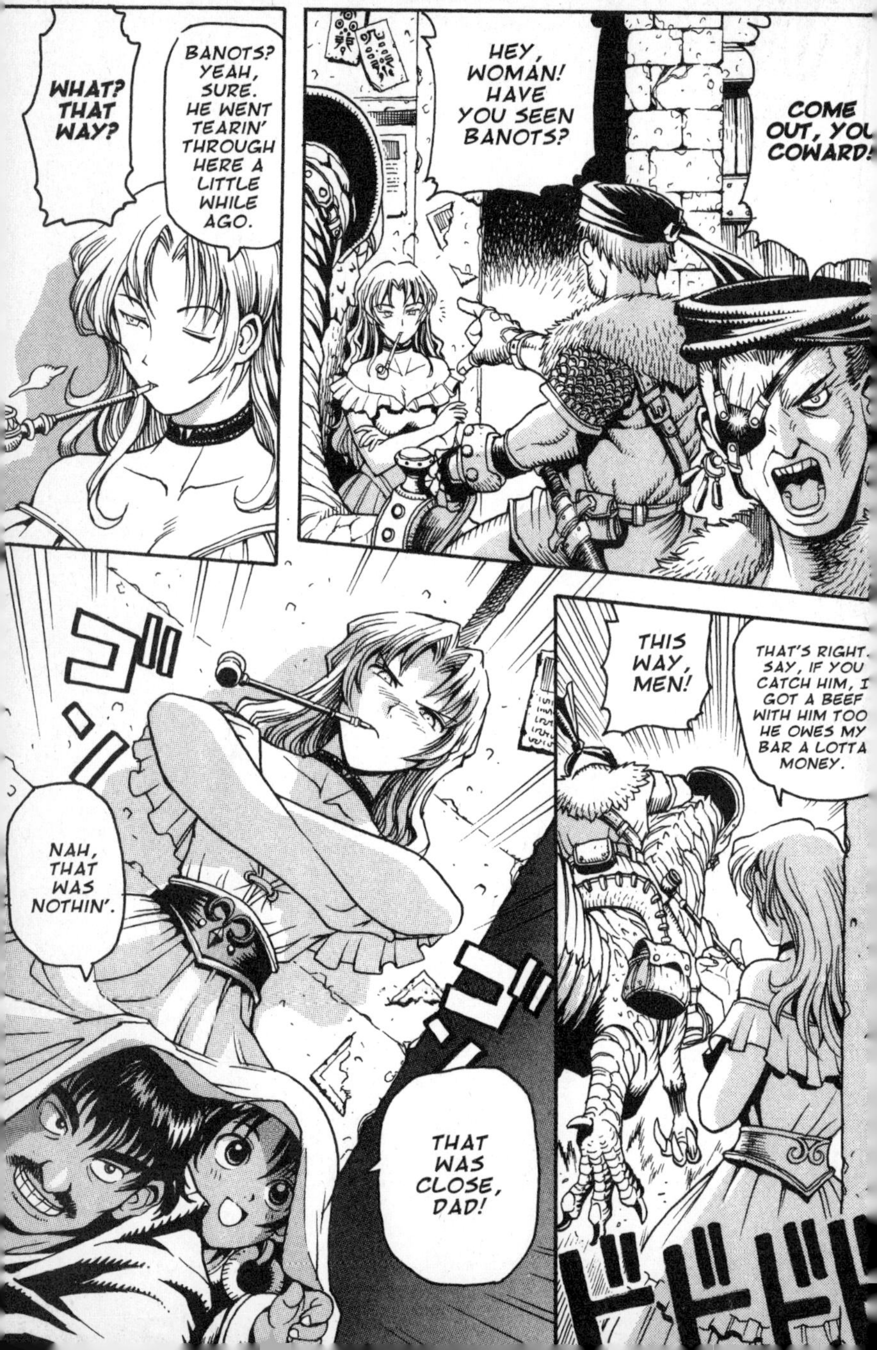
COME OUT, YOU COWARD!
HEY, WOMAN! HAVE YOU SEEN BANOTS?
BANOTS? YEAH, SURE. HE WENT TEARIN' THROUGH HERE A LITTLE WHILE AGO.
WHAT? THAT WAY?
THAT'S RIGHT. SAY, IF YOU CATCH HIM, I GOT A BEEF WITH HIM TOO HE OWES MY BAR A LOTTA MONEY.
THIS WAY, MEN!
THAT WAS CLOSE, DAD!
NAH, THAT WAS NOTHIN'.

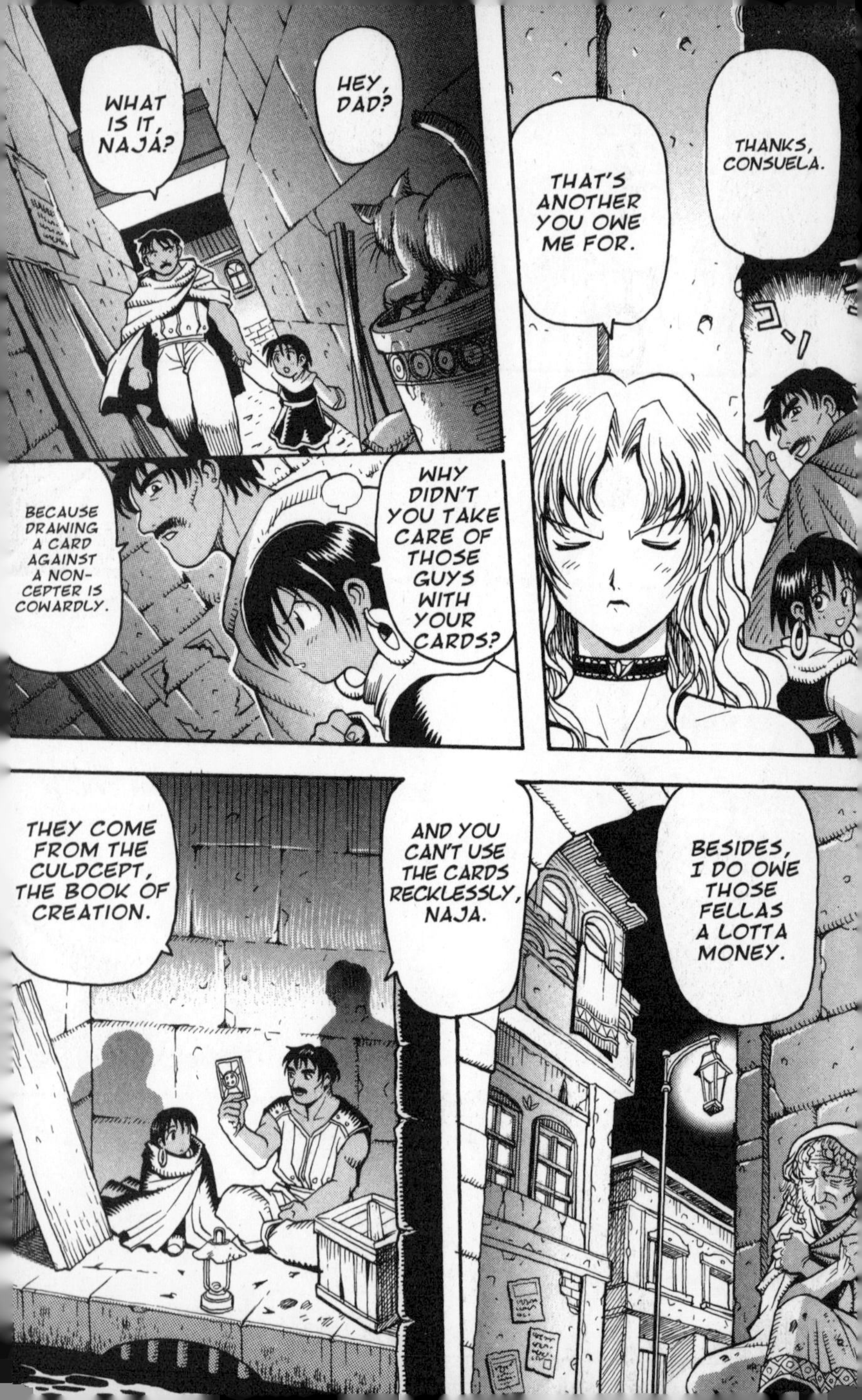
THANKS, CONSUELA.
THAT'S ANOTHER YOU OWE ME FOR.
HEY, DAD?
WHAT IS IT, NAJA?
WHY DIDN'T YOU TAKE CARE OF THOSE GUYS WITH YOUR CARDS?
BECAUSE DRAWING A CARD AGAINST A NON-CEPTER IS COWARDLY.
BESIDES, I DO OWE THOSE FELLAS A LOTTA MONEY.
AND YOU CAN'T USE THE CARDS RECKLESSLY, NAJA.
THEY COME FROM THE CULDCEPT, THE BOOK OF CREATION.

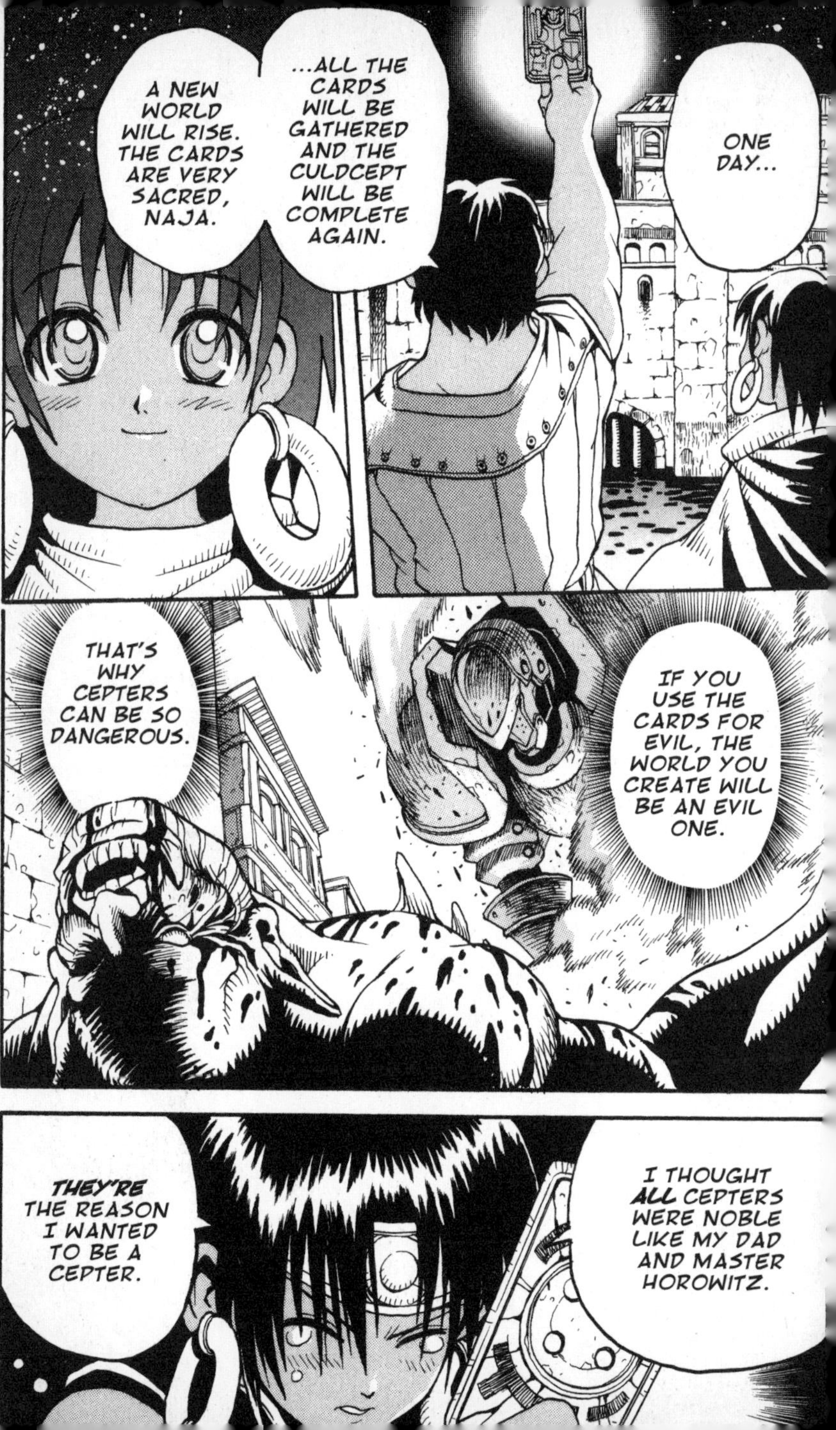
ONE DAY...
...ALL THE CARDS WILL BE GATHERED AND THE CULDCEPT WILL BE COMPLETE AGAIN.
A NEW WORLD WILL RISE. THE CARDS ARE VERY SACRED, NAJA.
IF YOU USE THE CARDS FOR EVIL, THE WORLD YOU CREATE WILL BE AN EVIL ONE.
THAT'S WHY CEPTERS CAN BE SO DANGEROUS.
I THOUGHT **ALL** CEPTERS WERE NOBLE LIKE MY DAD AND MASTER HOROWITZ.
THEY'RE THE REASON I WANTED TO BE A CEPTER.

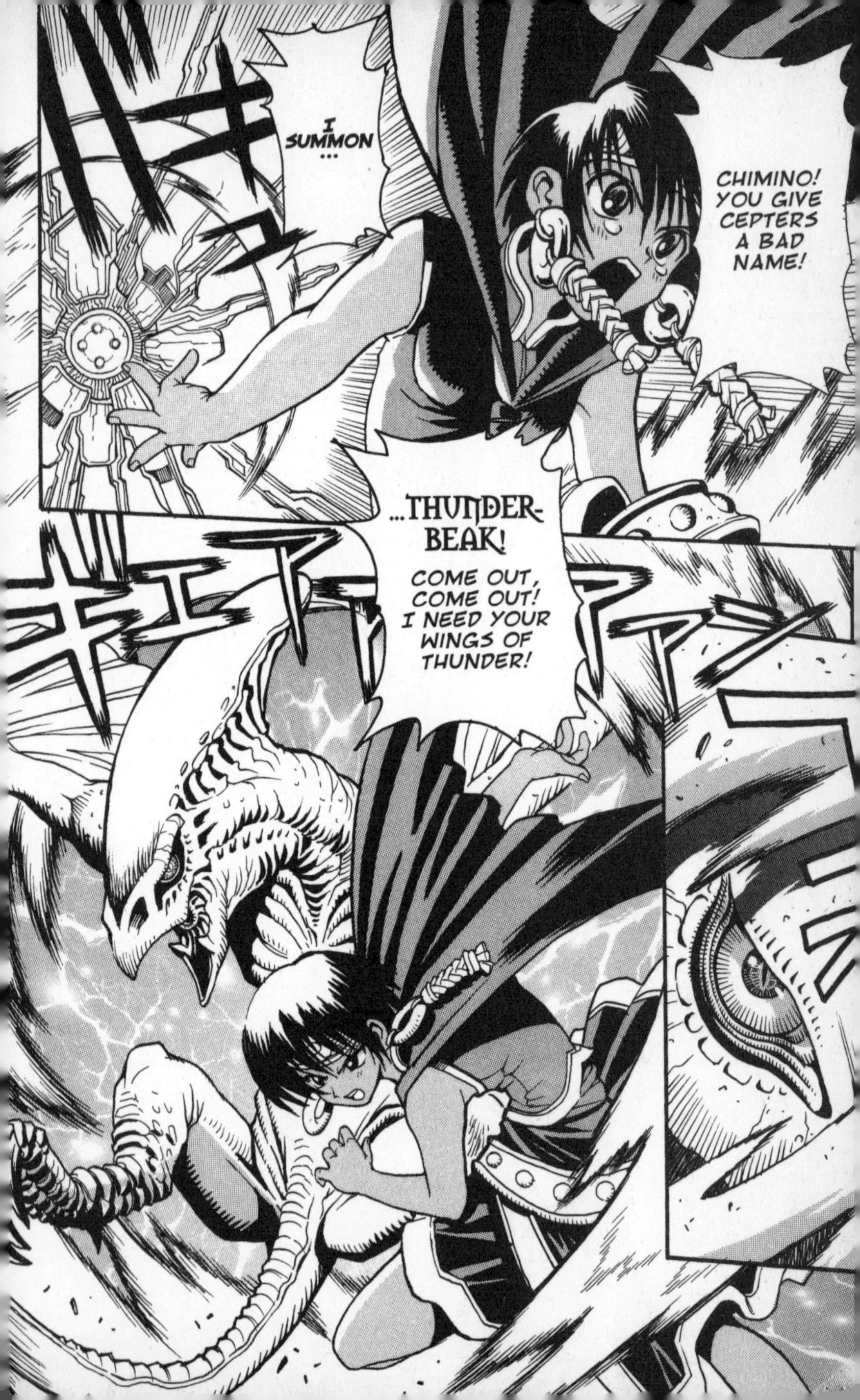
CHIMINO! YOU GIVE CEPTERS A BAD NAME!
I SUMMON...
...THUNDER-BEAK!
COME OUT, COME OUT! I NEED YOUR WINGS OF THUNDER!

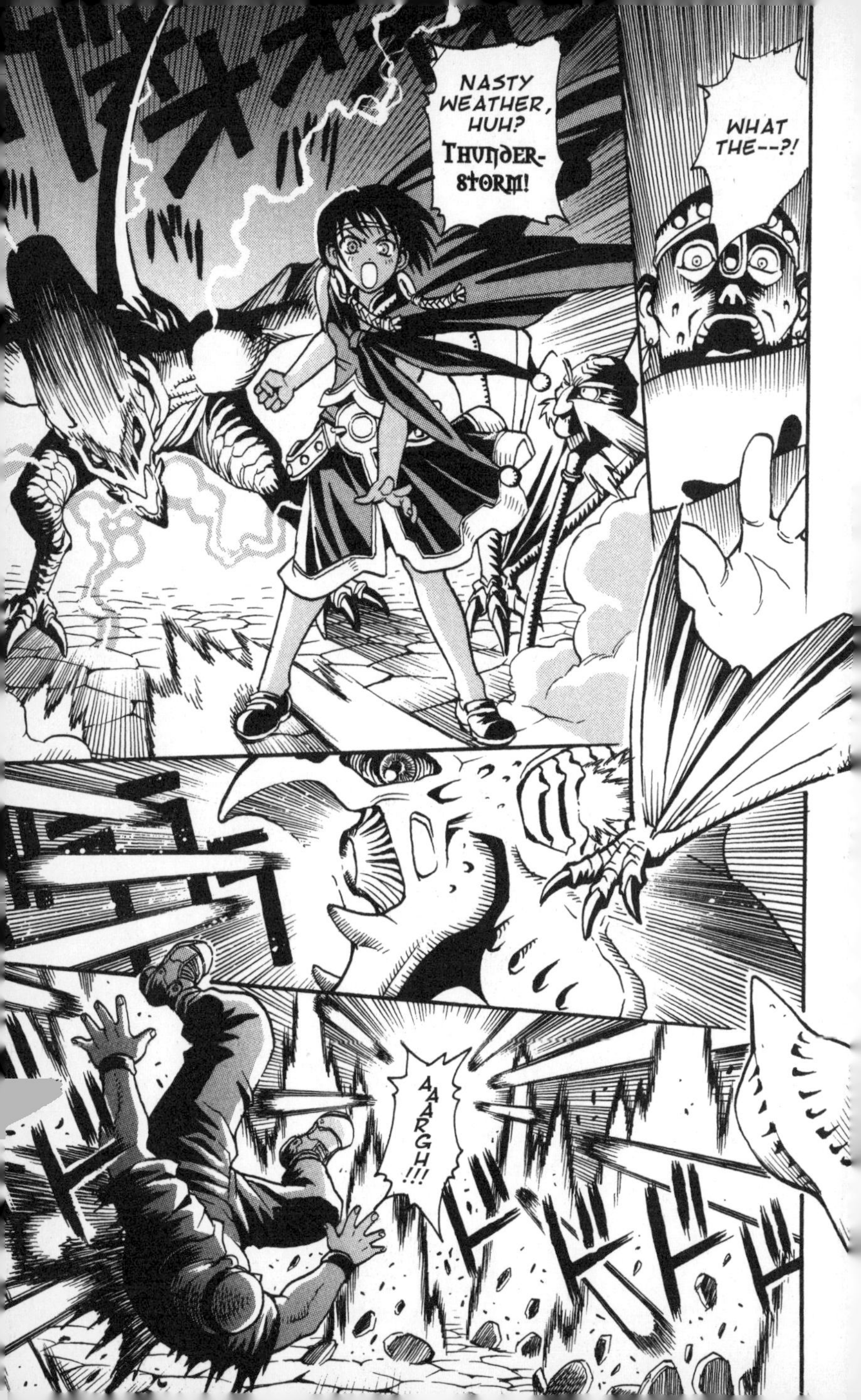
WHAT THE--?!
NASTY WEATHER, HUH? THUNDER-STORM!
AAARGH!!!

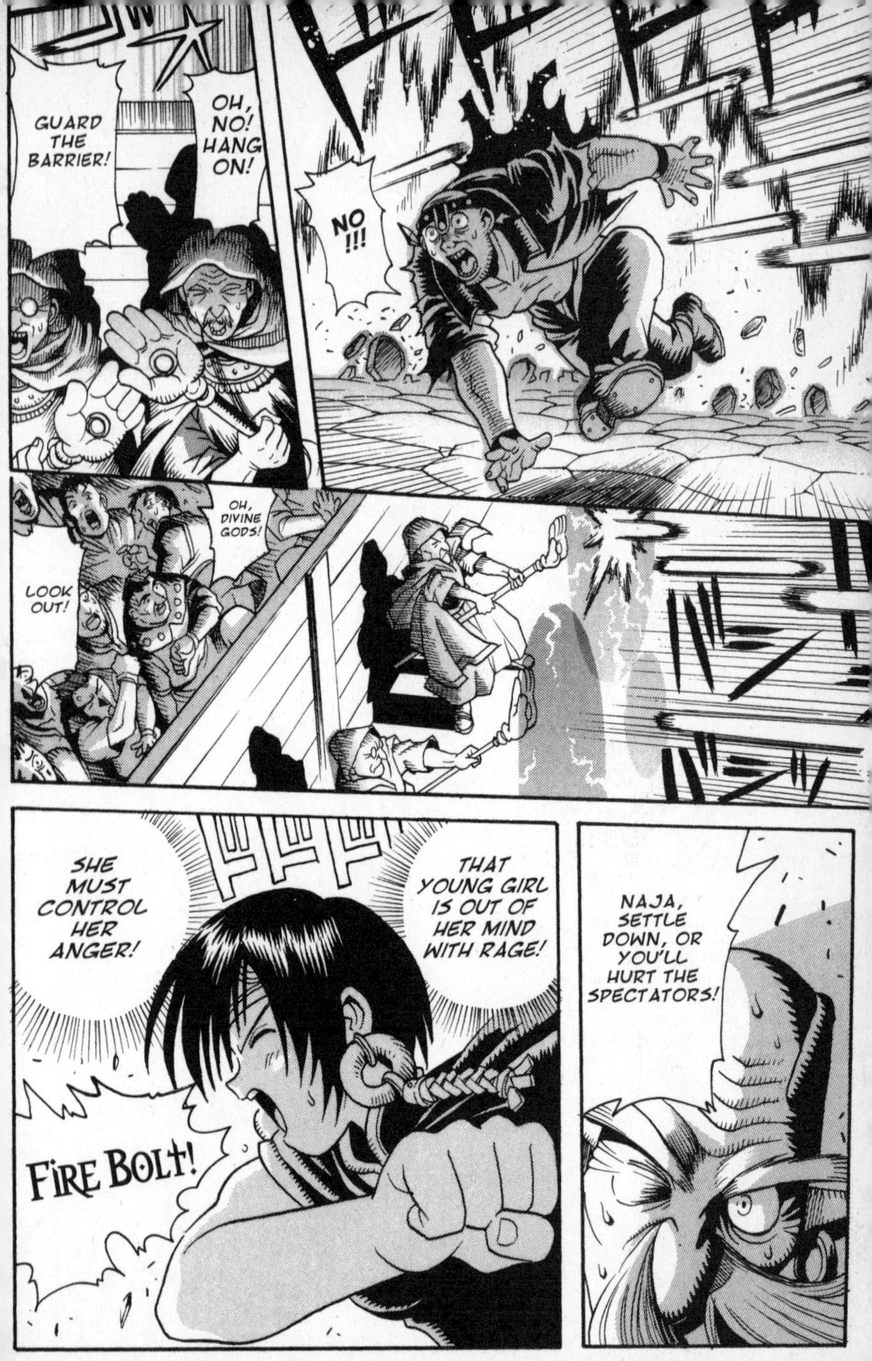
NO !!!
OH, NO! HANG ON!
GUARD THE BARRIER!
OH, DIVINE GODS!
LOOK OUT!
NAJA, SETTLE DOWN, OR YOU'LL HURT THE SPECTATORS!
THAT YOUNG GIRL IS OUT OF HER MIND WITH RAGE!
SHE MUST CONTROL HER ANGER!
FIRE BOLT!

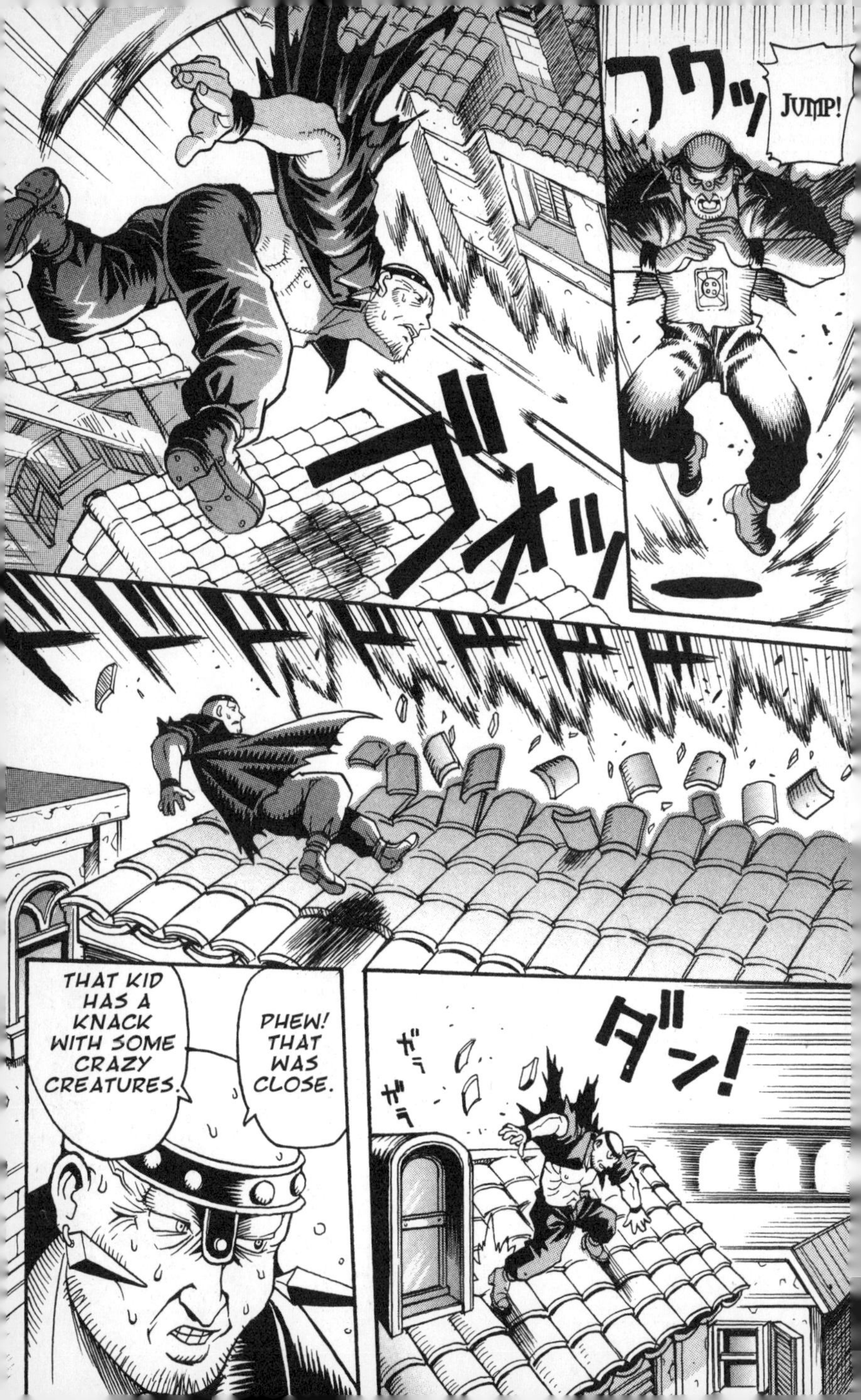

フワッ
JUMP!
ゴオッ
ドドドドドドドドド
ダン!
ガラ
ガラ
PHEW! THAT WAS CLOSE.
THAT KID HAS A KNACK WITH SOME CRAZY CREATURES.

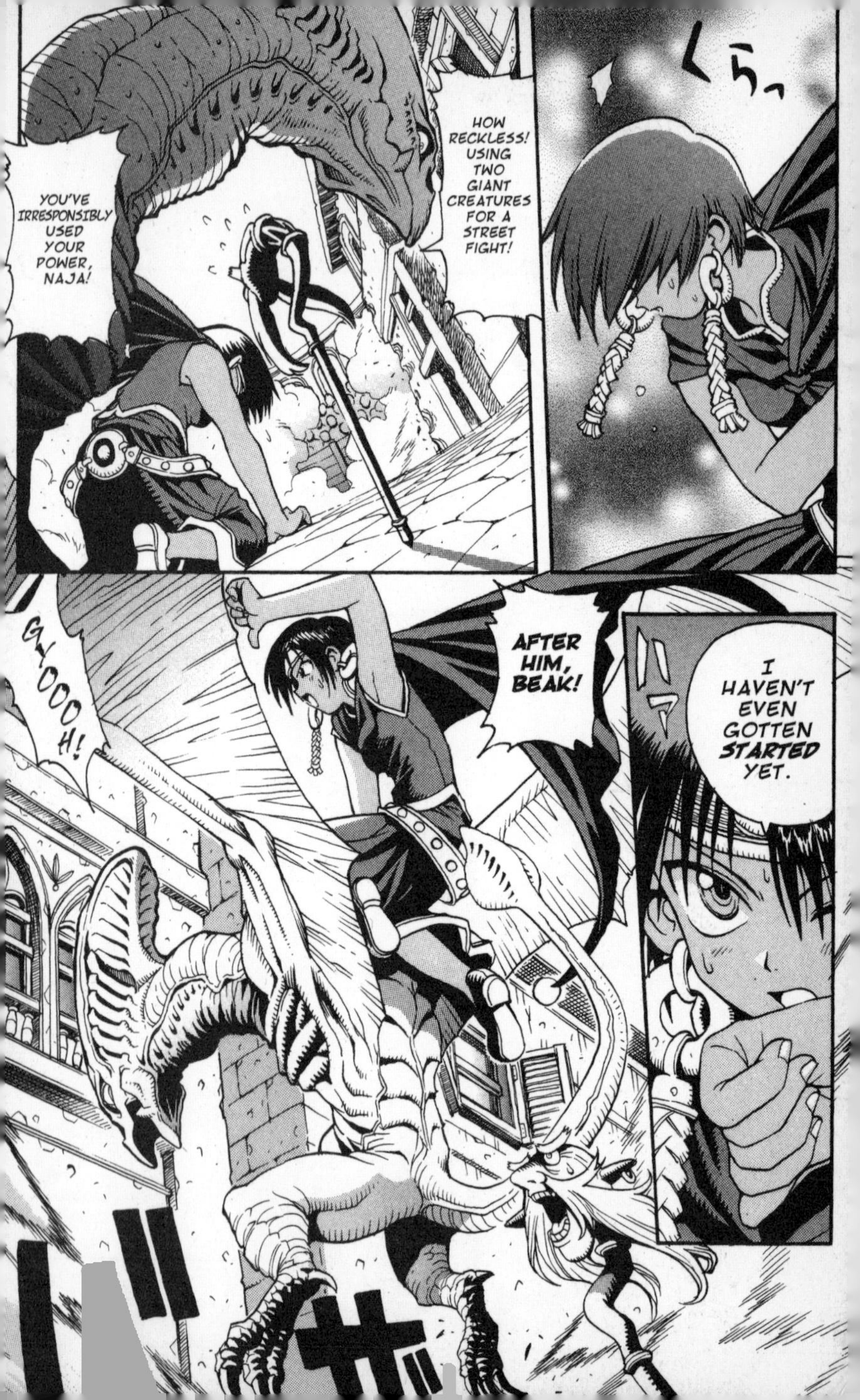
HOW RECKLESS! USING TWO GIANT CREATURES FOR A STREET FIGHT!
YOU'VE IRRESPONSIBLY USED YOUR POWER, NAJA!
I HAVEN'T EVEN GOTTEN **STARTED** YET.
AFTER HIM, BEAK!
GWOOOOH!

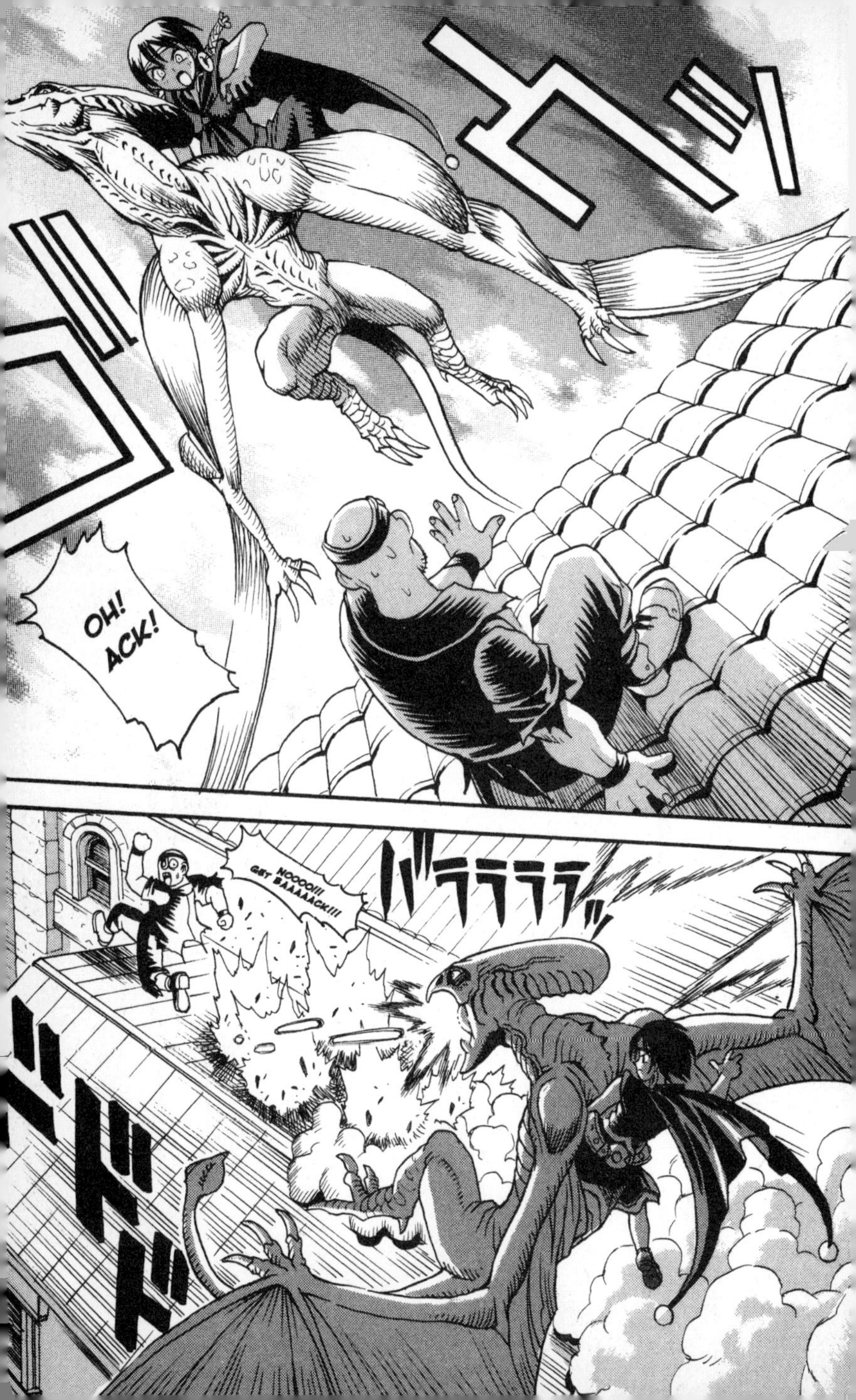
OH! ACK!
NOOOO!!! GET BAAAAACK!!!
バラララララッ

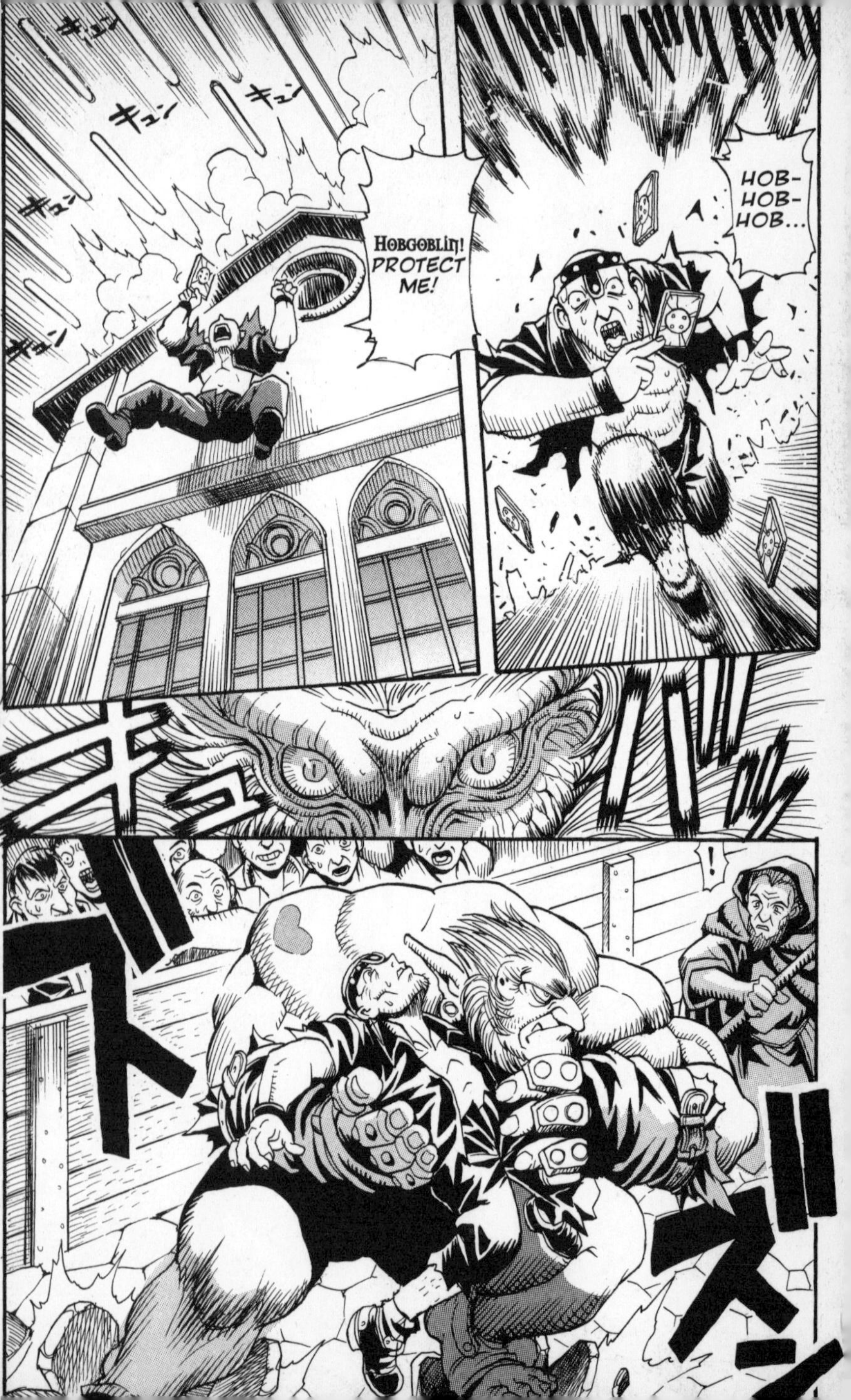
HOB-
HOB-
HOB...
HOBGOBLIN! PROTECT ME!
!

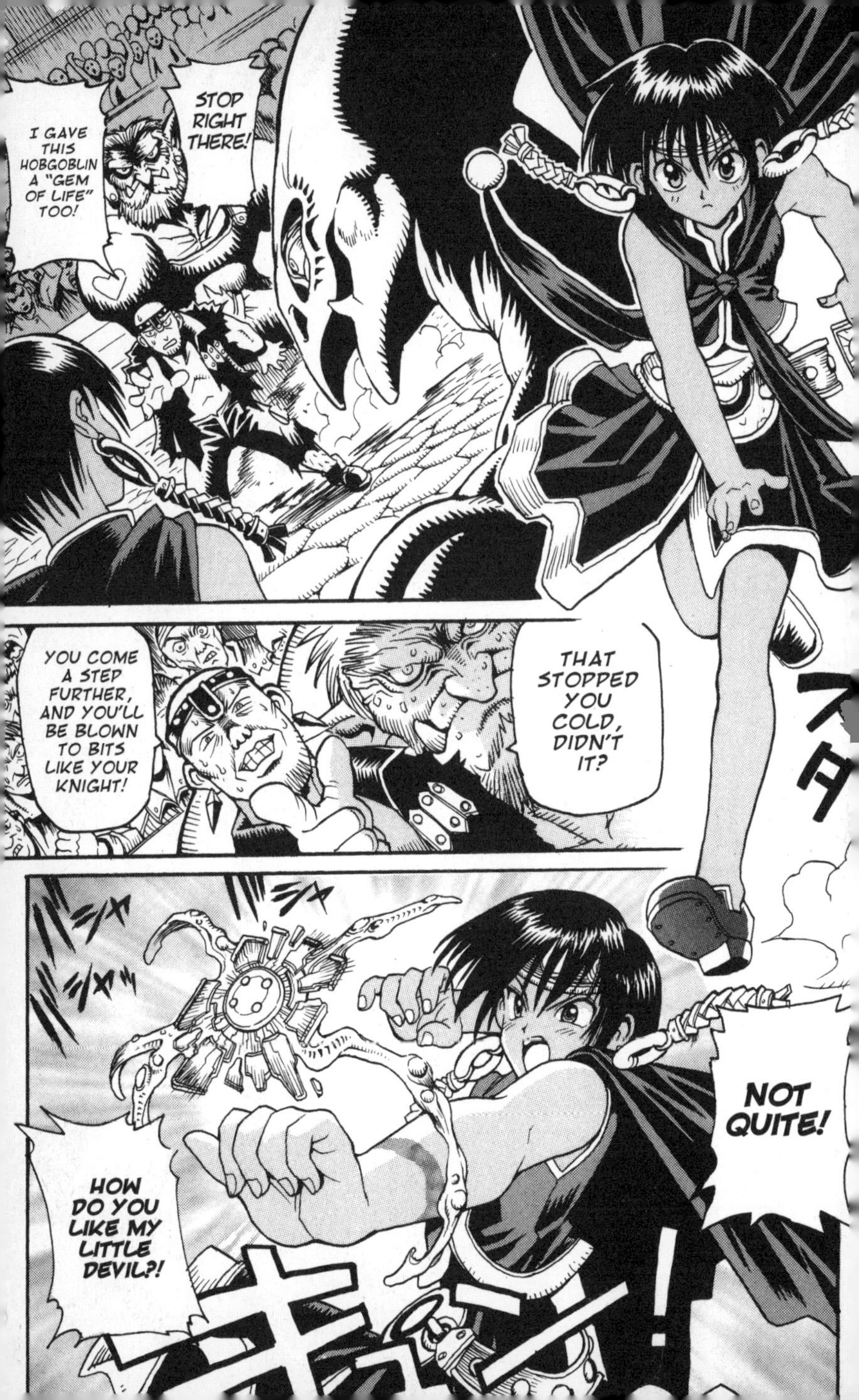
STOP RIGHT THERE!
I GAVE THIS HOBGOBLIN A "GEM OF LIFE" TOO!
THAT STOPPED YOU COLD, DIDN'T IT?
YOU COME A STEP FURTHER, AND YOU'LL BE BLOWN TO BITS LIKE YOUR KNIGHT!
NOT QUITE!
HOW DO YOU LIKE MY LITTLE DEVIL?!

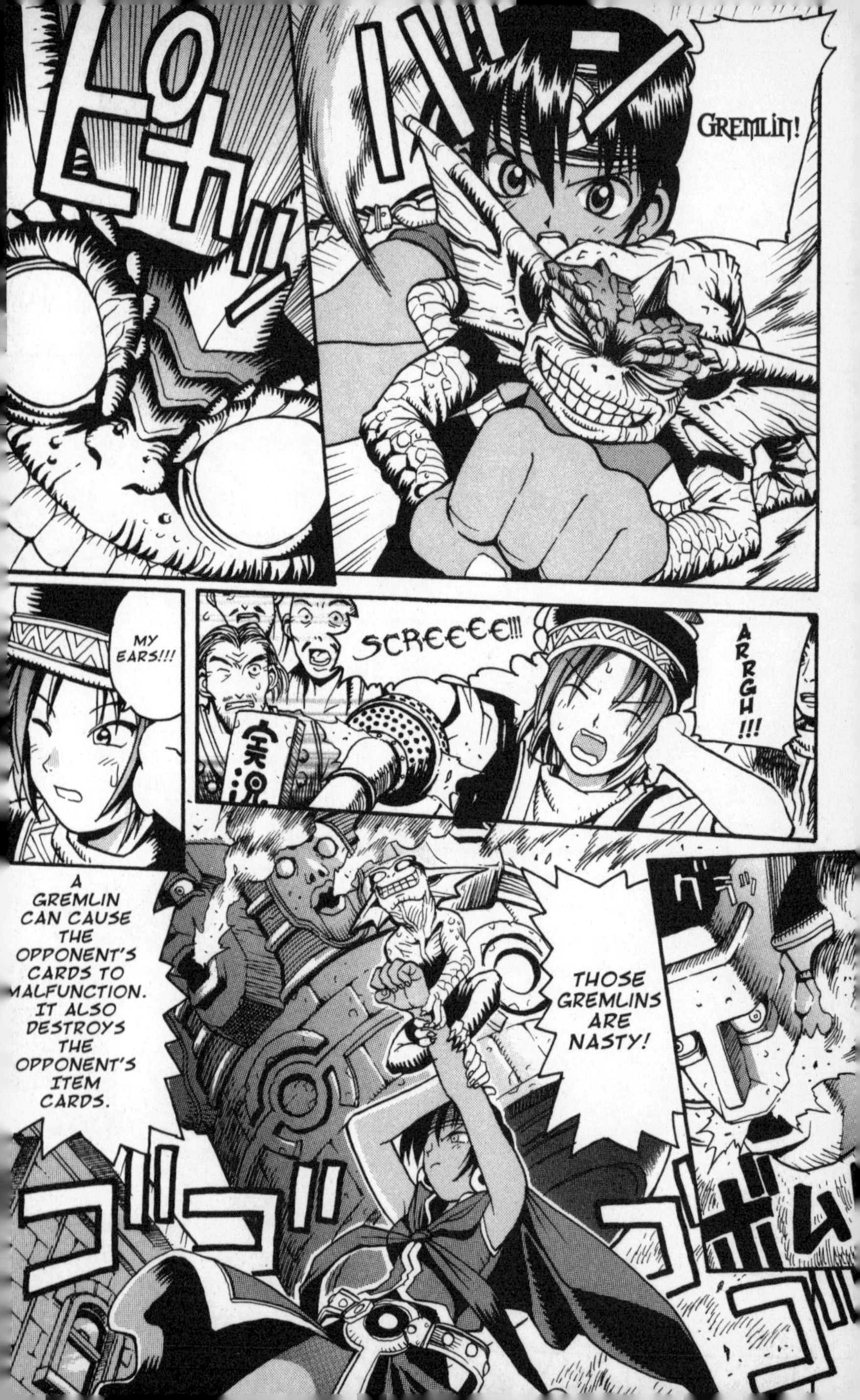
GREMLIN!
ARRGH!!!
SCREEEEE!!!
MY EARS!!!
THOSE GREMLINS ARE NASTY!
A GREMLIN CAN CAUSE THE OPPONENT'S CARDS TO MALFUNCTION. IT ALSO DESTROYS THE OPPONENT'S ITEM CARDS.

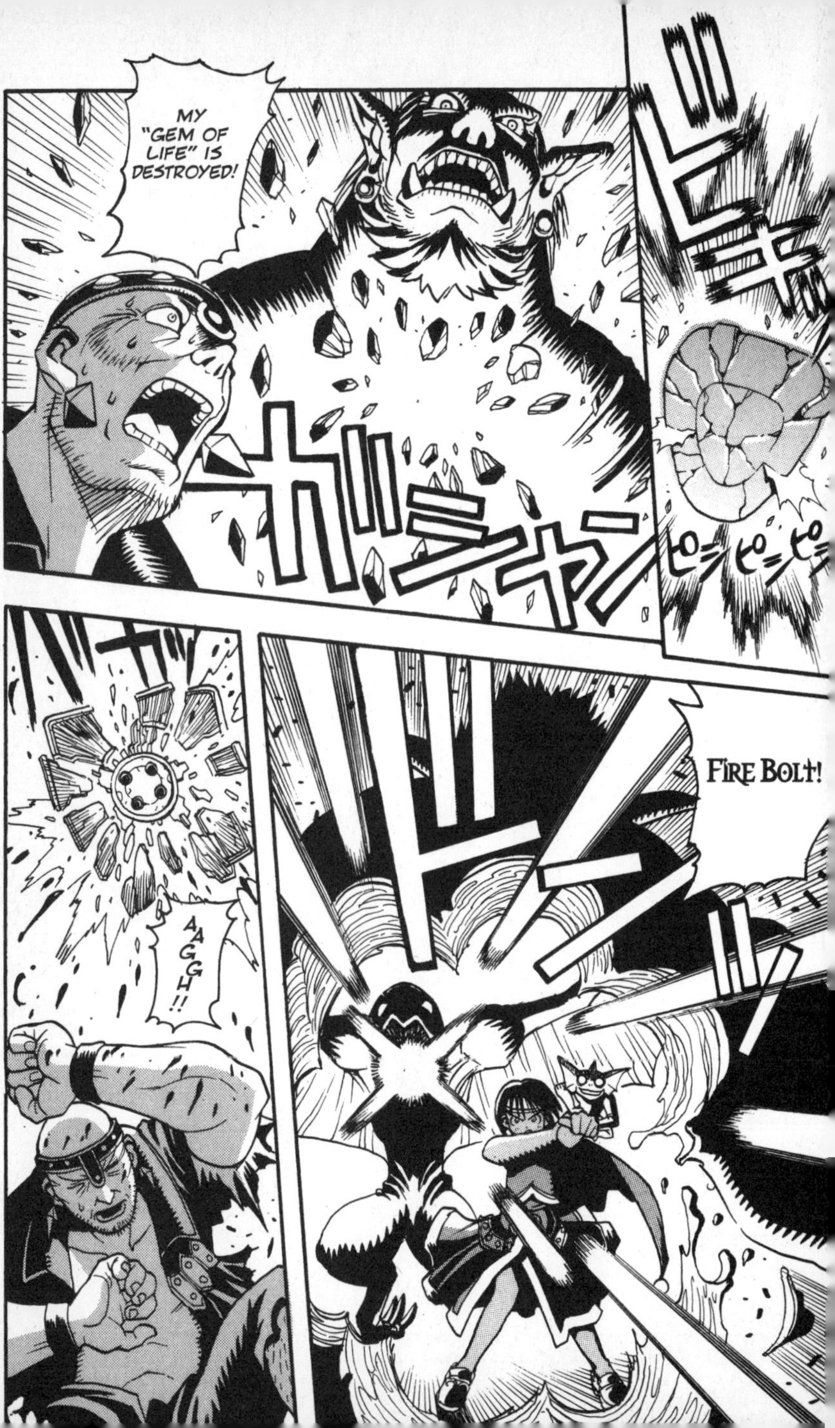

MY "GEM OF LIFE" IS DESTROYED!
ガシャン
FIRE BOLT!
AAGGH!!

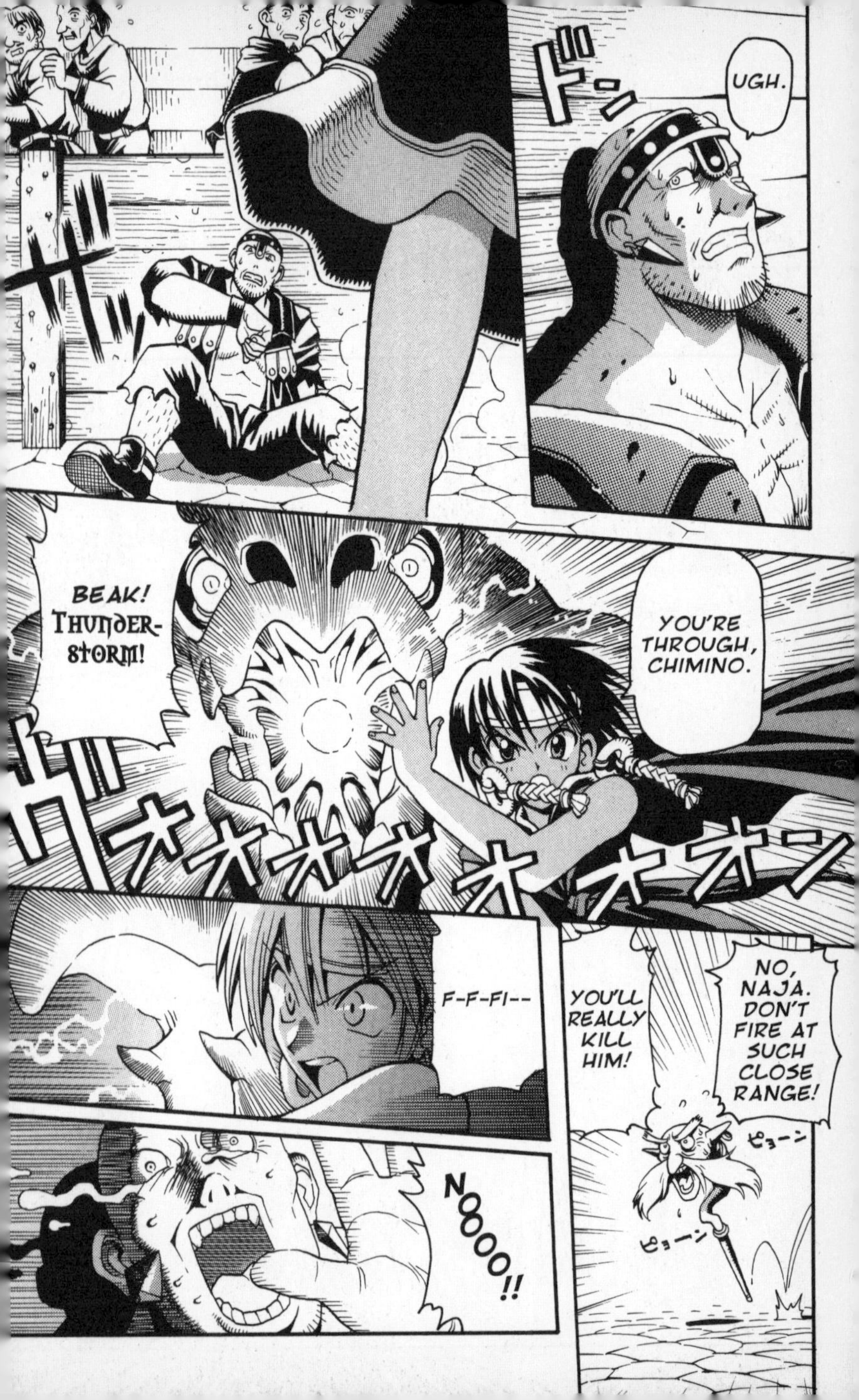
UGH.
YOU'RE THROUGH, CHIMINO.
BEAK! THUNDER-STORM!
NO, NAJA. DON'T FIRE AT SUCH CLOSE RANGE!
YOU'LL REALLY KILL HIM!
ピョーン
ピョーン
F-F-FI--
NOOOO!!

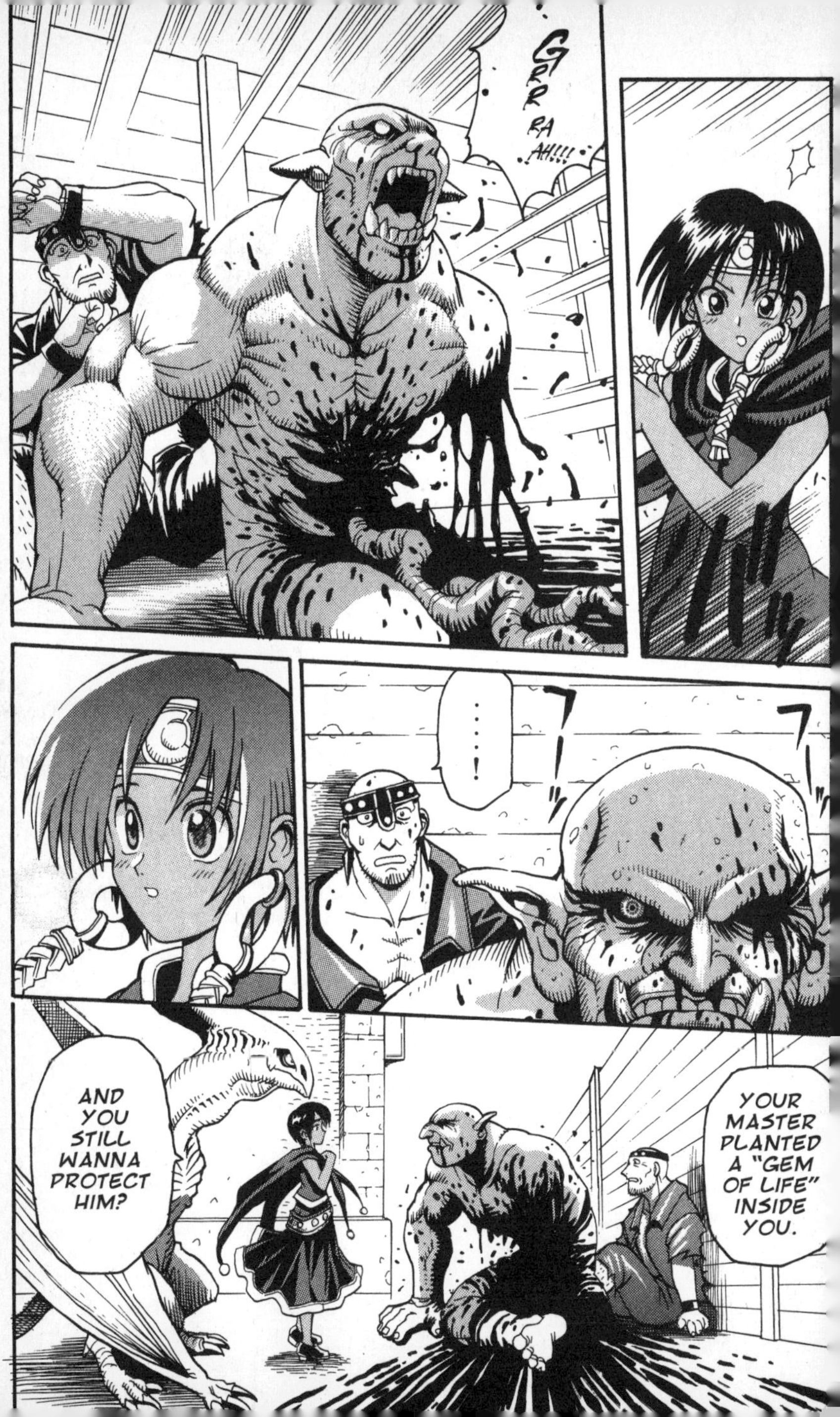
GRRR RAAH!!!
....!
YOUR MASTER PLANTED A "GEM OF LIFE" INSIDE YOU.
AND YOU STILL WANNA PROTECT HIM?

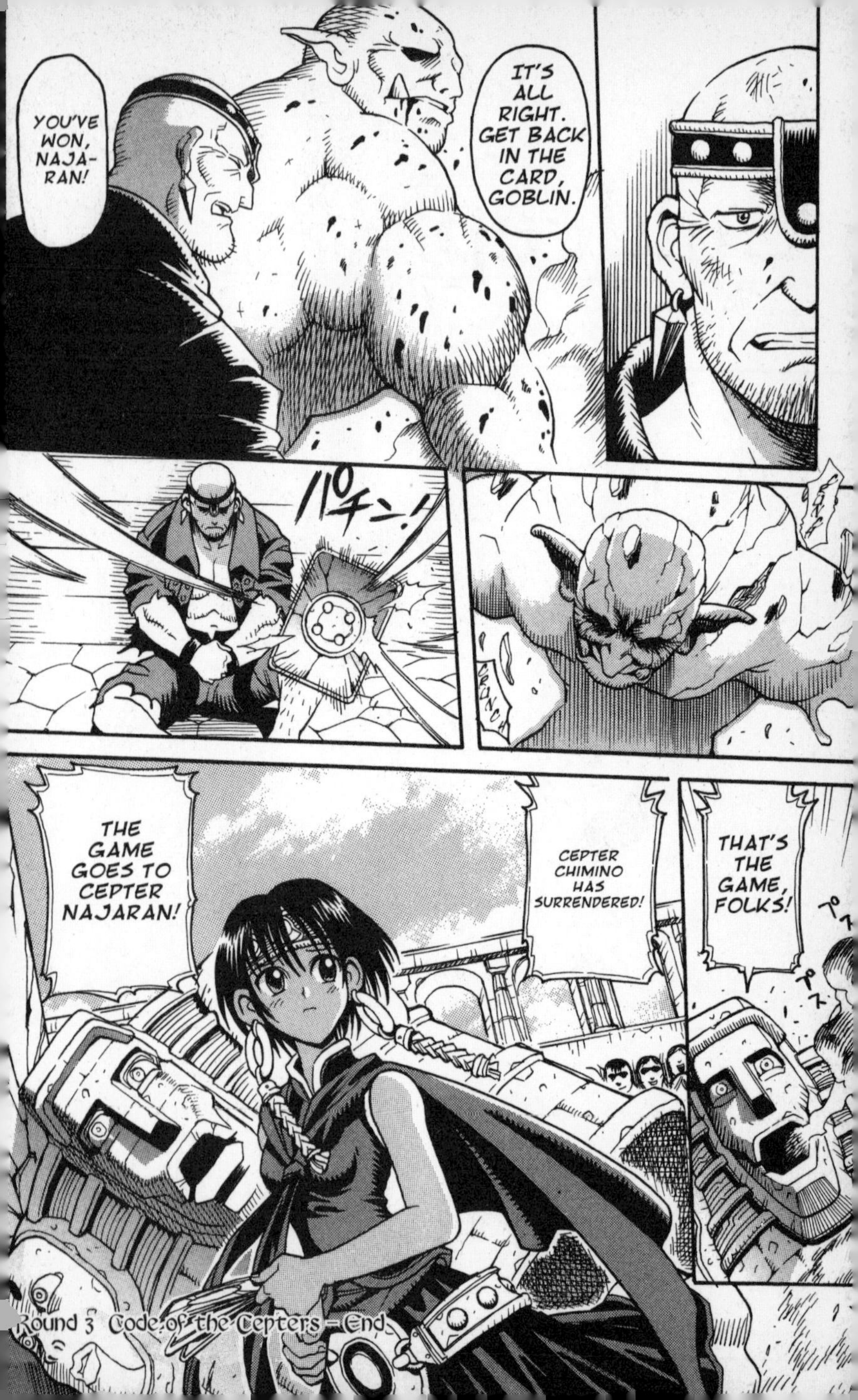
IT'S ALL RIGHT. GET BACK IN THE CARD, GOBLIN.
YOU'VE WON, NAJARAN!
CRUNCH
パチン!
THAT'S THE GAME, FOLKS!
CEPTER CHIMINO HAS SURRENDERED!
THE GAME GOES TO CEPTER NAJARAN!
Round 3 Code of the Cepters - End

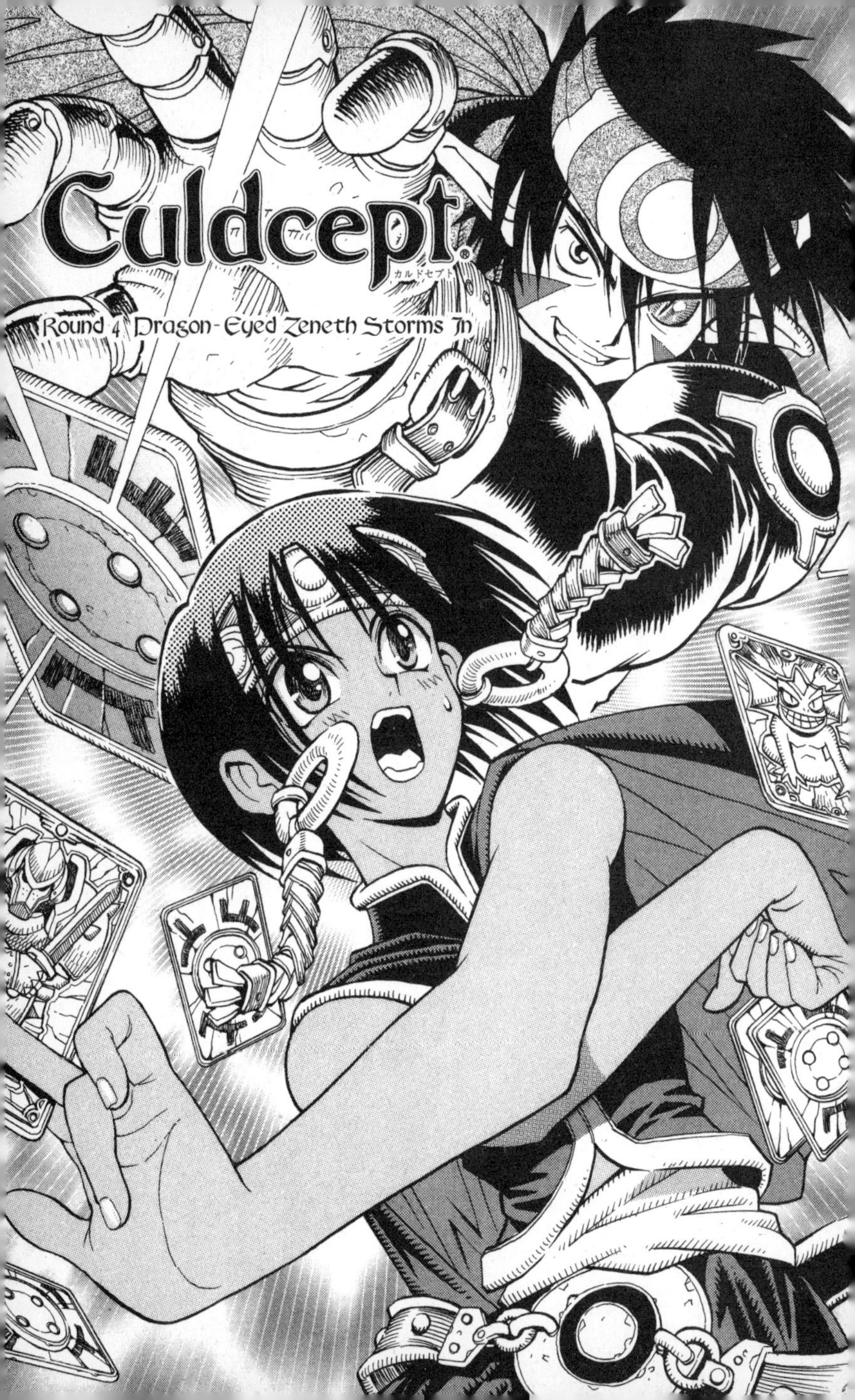
Culdcept®
カルドセプト
Round 4 Dragon-Eyed Zeneth Storms In

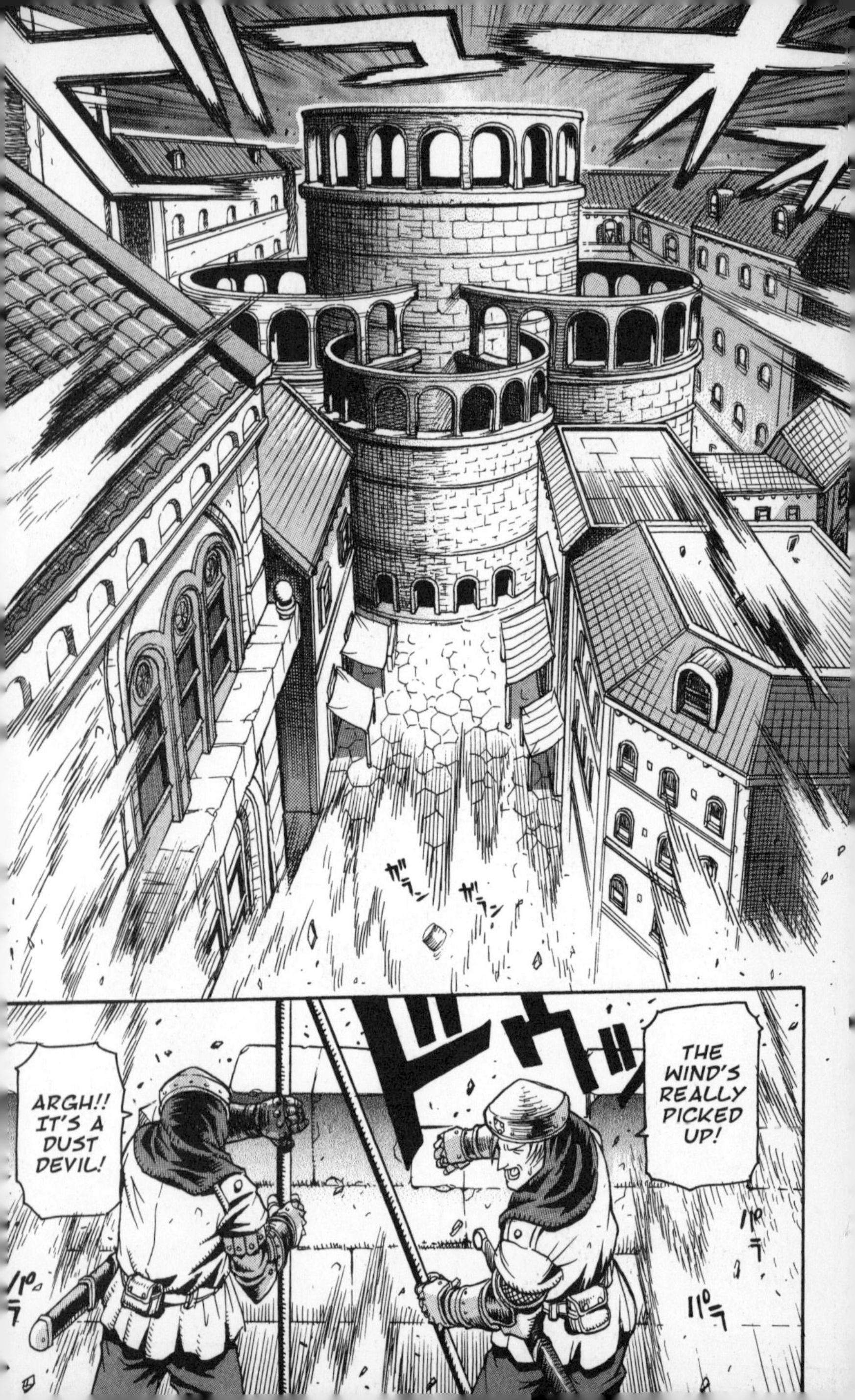
ガラン ガラン
THE WIND'S REALLY PICKED UP!
ARGH!! IT'S A DUST DEVIL!
パラ パラ

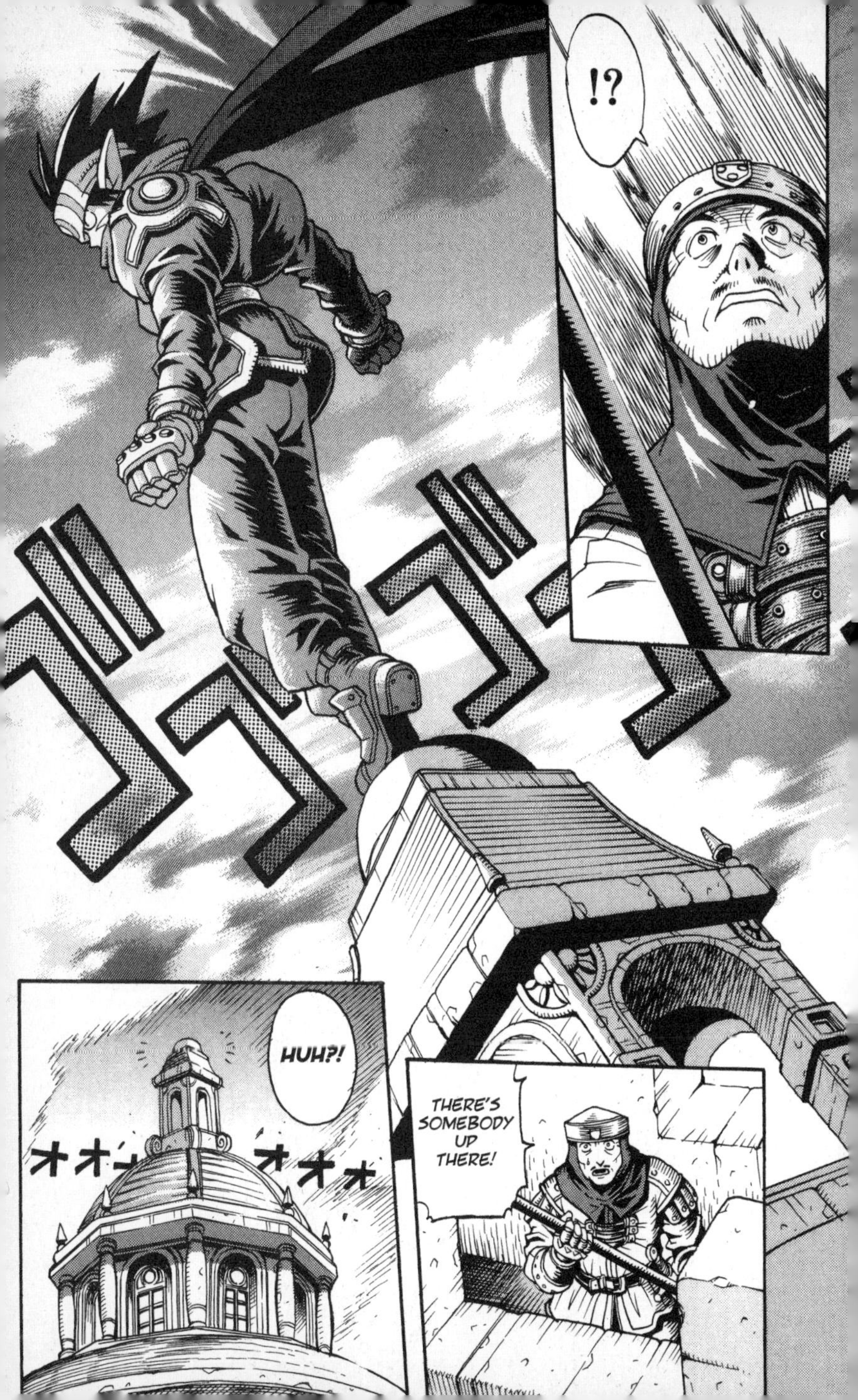
!?
ゴゴゴゴ
THERE'S SOMEBODY UP THERE!
HUH?!
オオー
オオオ

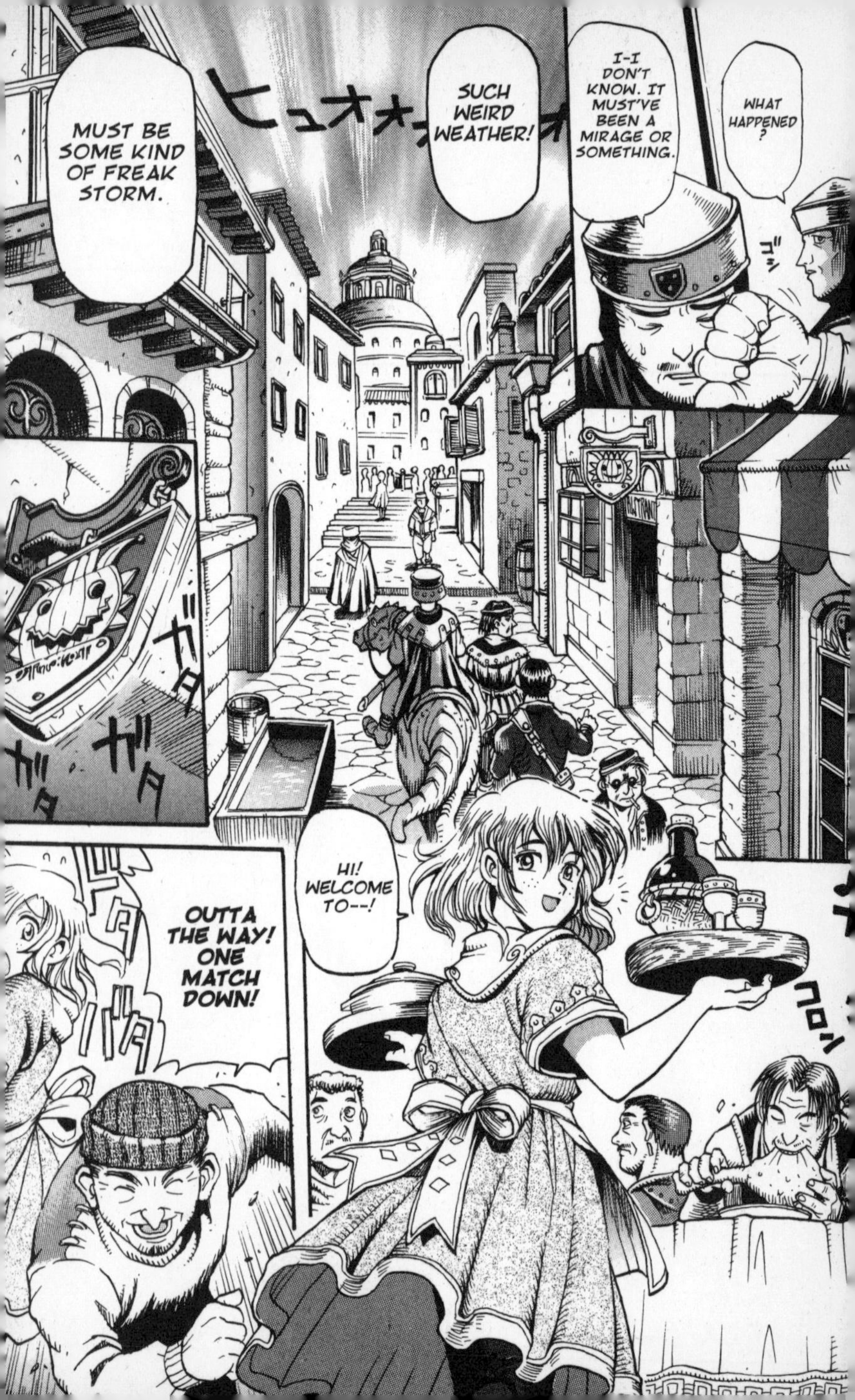
WHAT HAPPENED?
I-I DON'T KNOW. IT MUST'VE BEEN A MIRAGE OR SOMETHING.
SUCH WEIRD WEATHER!
MUST BE SOME KIND OF FREAK STORM.
HI! WELCOME TO--!
OUTTA THE WAY! ONE MATCH DOWN!

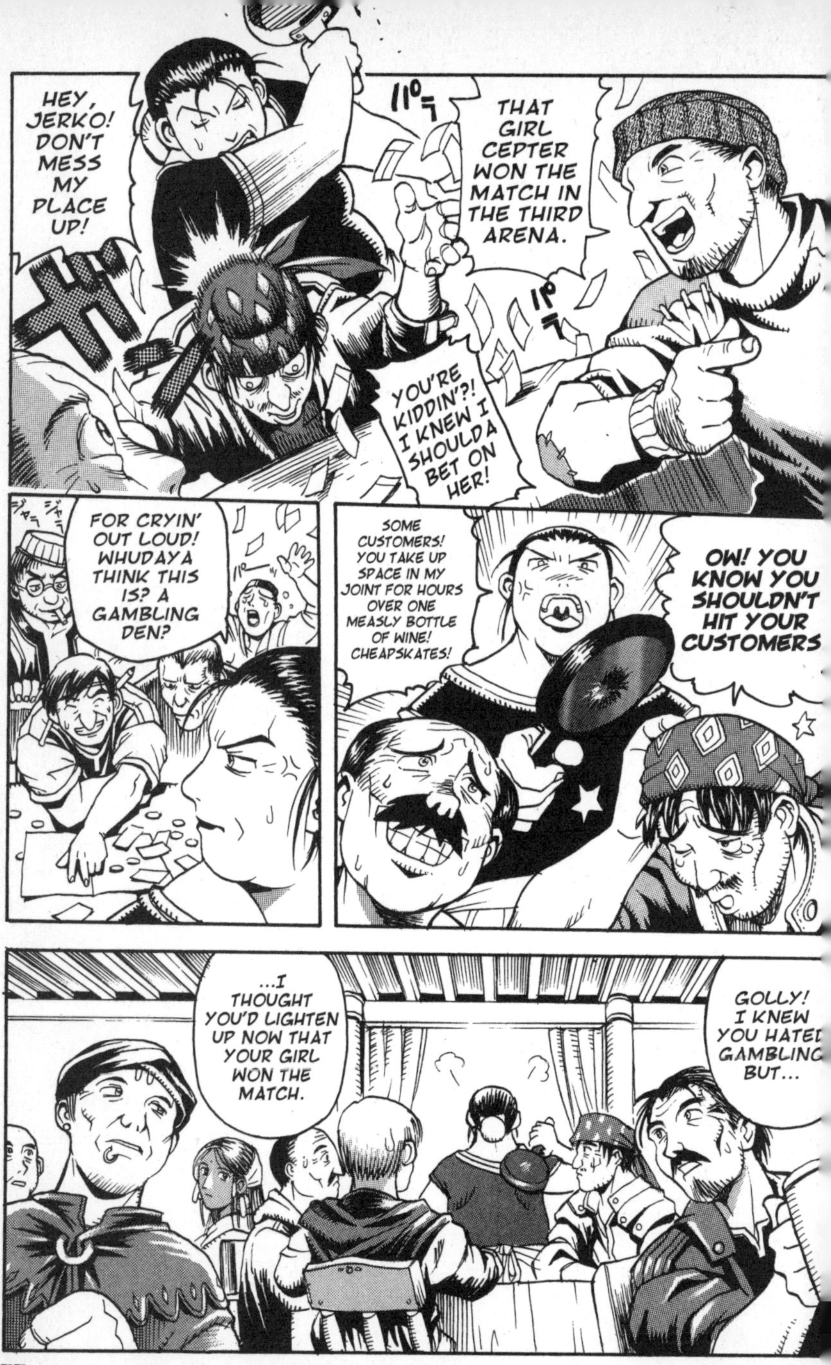

THAT GIRL CEPTER WON THE MATCH IN THE THIRD ARENA.
HEY, JERKO! DON'T MESS MY PLACE UP!
YOU'RE KIDDIN'?! I KNEW I SHOULDA BET ON HER!
OW! YOU KNOW YOU SHOULDN'T HIT YOUR CUSTOMERS
SOME CUSTOMERS! YOU TAKE UP SPACE IN MY JOINT FOR HOURS OVER ONE MEASLY BOTTLE OF WINE! CHEAPSKATES!
FOR CRYIN' OUT LOUD! WHUDAYA THINK THIS IS? A GAMBLING DEN?
GOLLY! I KNEW YOU HATED GAMBLING BUT...
...I THOUGHT YOU'D LIGHTEN UP NOW THAT YOUR GIRL WON THE MATCH.

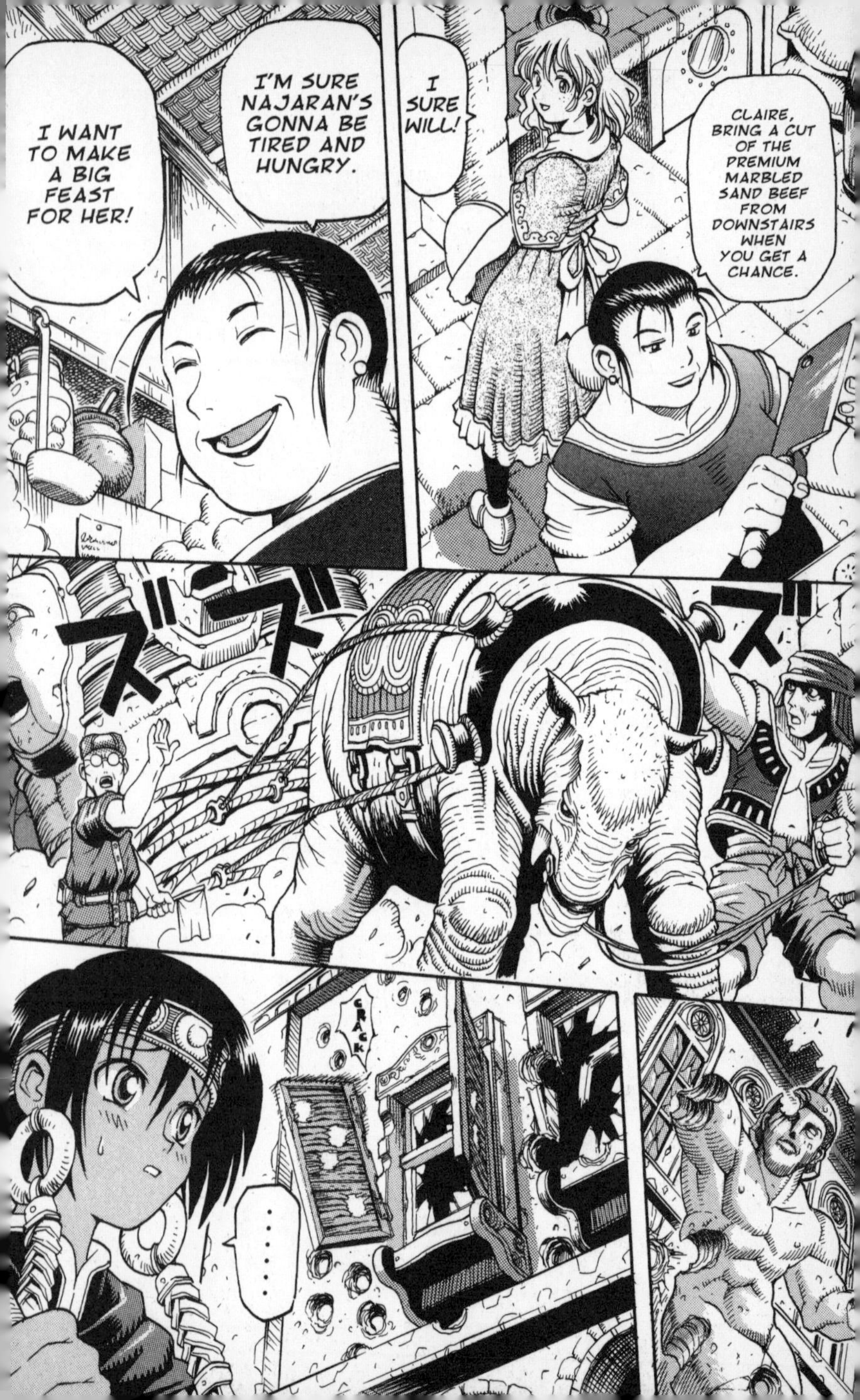
CLAIRE, BRING A CUT OF THE PREMIUM MARBLED SAND BEEF FROM DOWNSTAIRS WHEN YOU GET A CHANCE.
I SURE WILL!
I'M SURE NAJARAN'S GONNA BE TIRED AND HUNGRY.
I WANT TO MAKE A BIG FEAST FOR HER!
ズ
ズ
ズ
CRACK
......

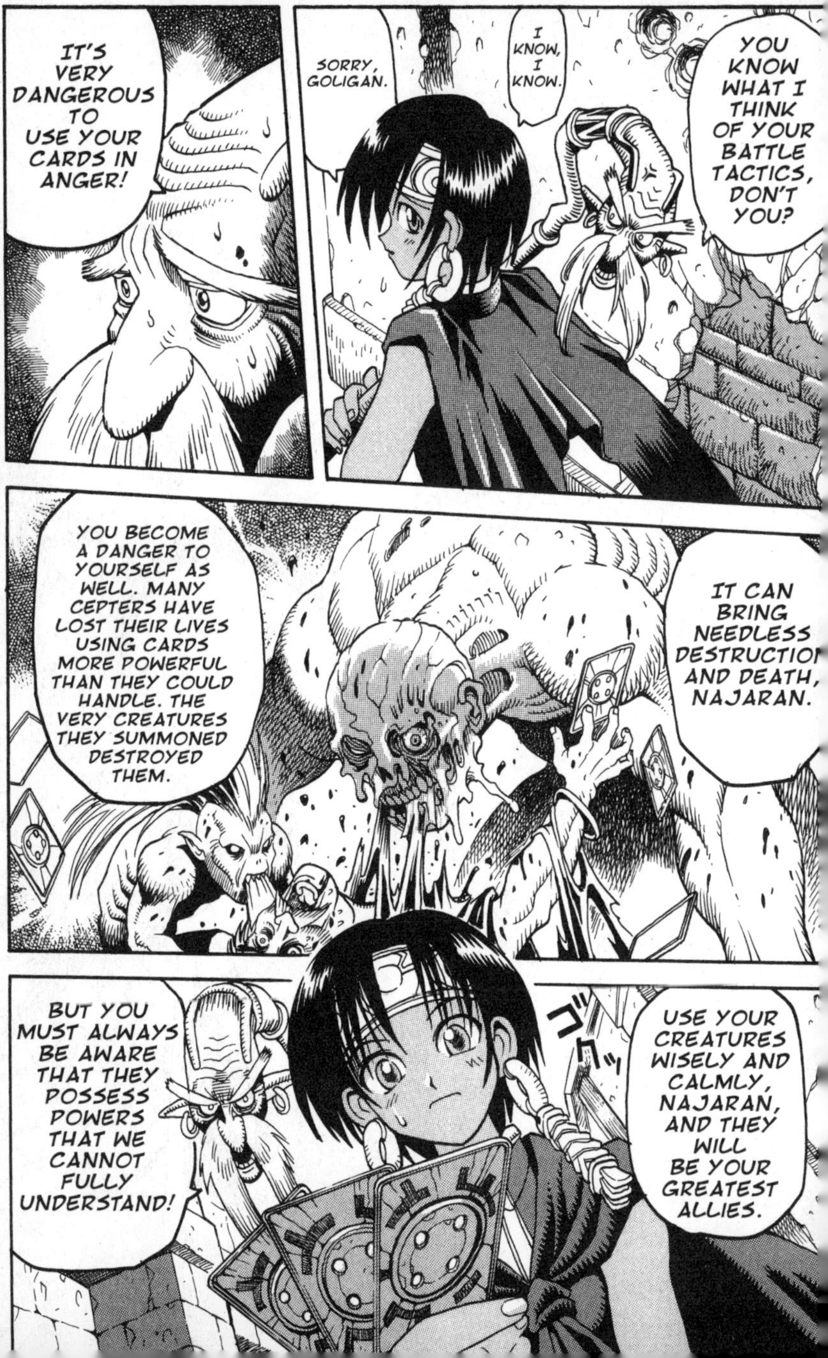
YOU KNOW WHAT I THINK OF YOUR BATTLE TACTICS, DON'T YOU?
I KNOW, I KNOW.
SORRY, GOLIGAN.
IT'S VERY DANGEROUS TO USE YOUR CARDS IN ANGER!
IT CAN BRING NEEDLESS DESTRUCTIO AND DEATH, NAJARAN.
YOU BECOME A DANGER TO YOURSELF AS WELL. MANY CEPTERS HAVE LOST THEIR LIVES USING CARDS MORE POWERFUL THAN THEY COULD HANDLE. THE VERY CREATURES THEY SUMMONED DESTROYED THEM.
USE YOUR CREATURES WISELY AND CALMLY, NAJARAN, AND THEY WILL BE YOUR GREATEST ALLIES.
ゴクッ
BUT YOU MUST ALWAYS BE AWARE THAT THEY POSSESS POWERS THAT WE CANNOT FULLY UNDERSTAND!

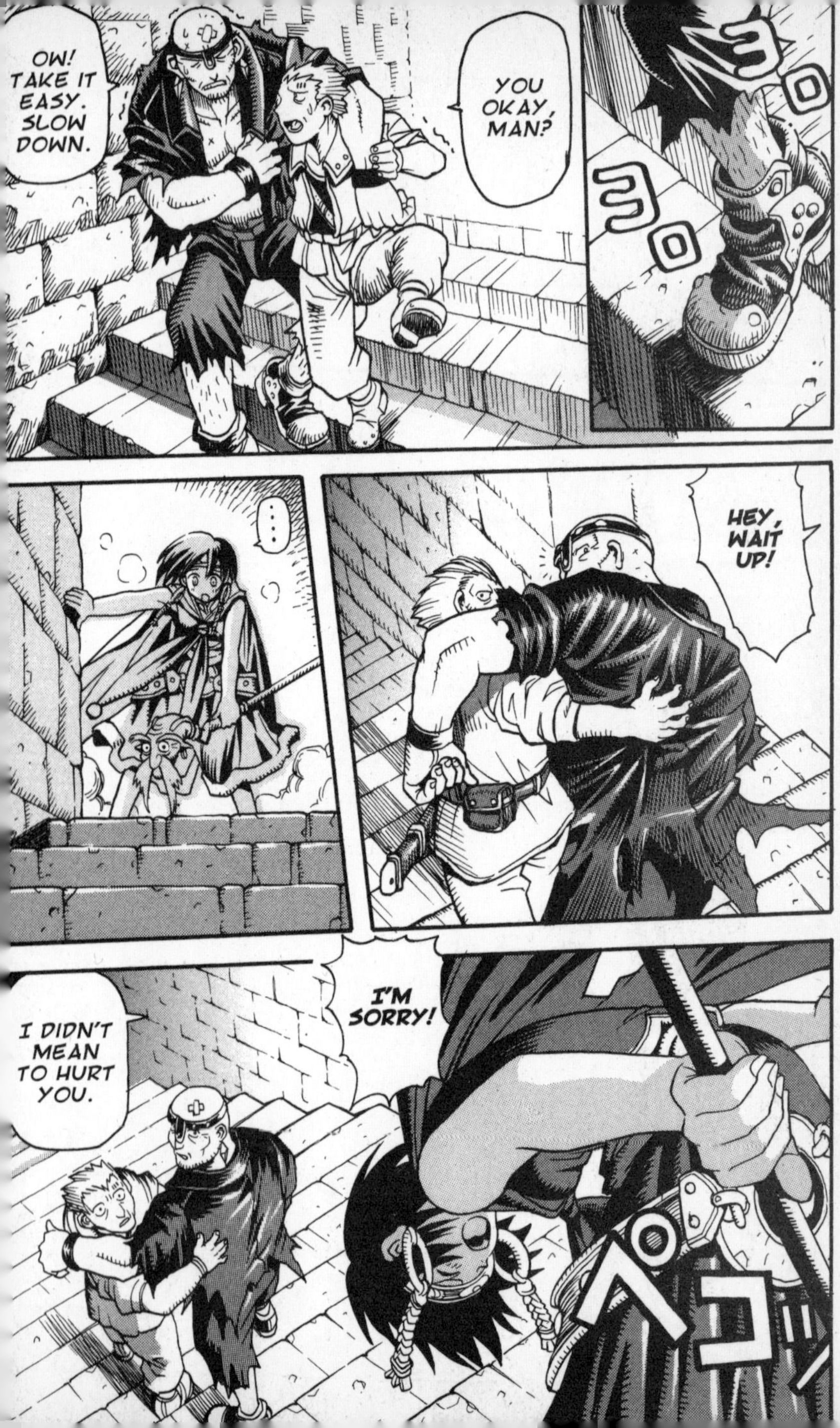
コロ
コロ
YOU OKAY, MAN?
OW! TAKE IT EASY. SLOW DOWN.
HEY, WAIT UP!
...
I'M SORRY!
ペコ
I DIDN'T MEAN TO HURT YOU.

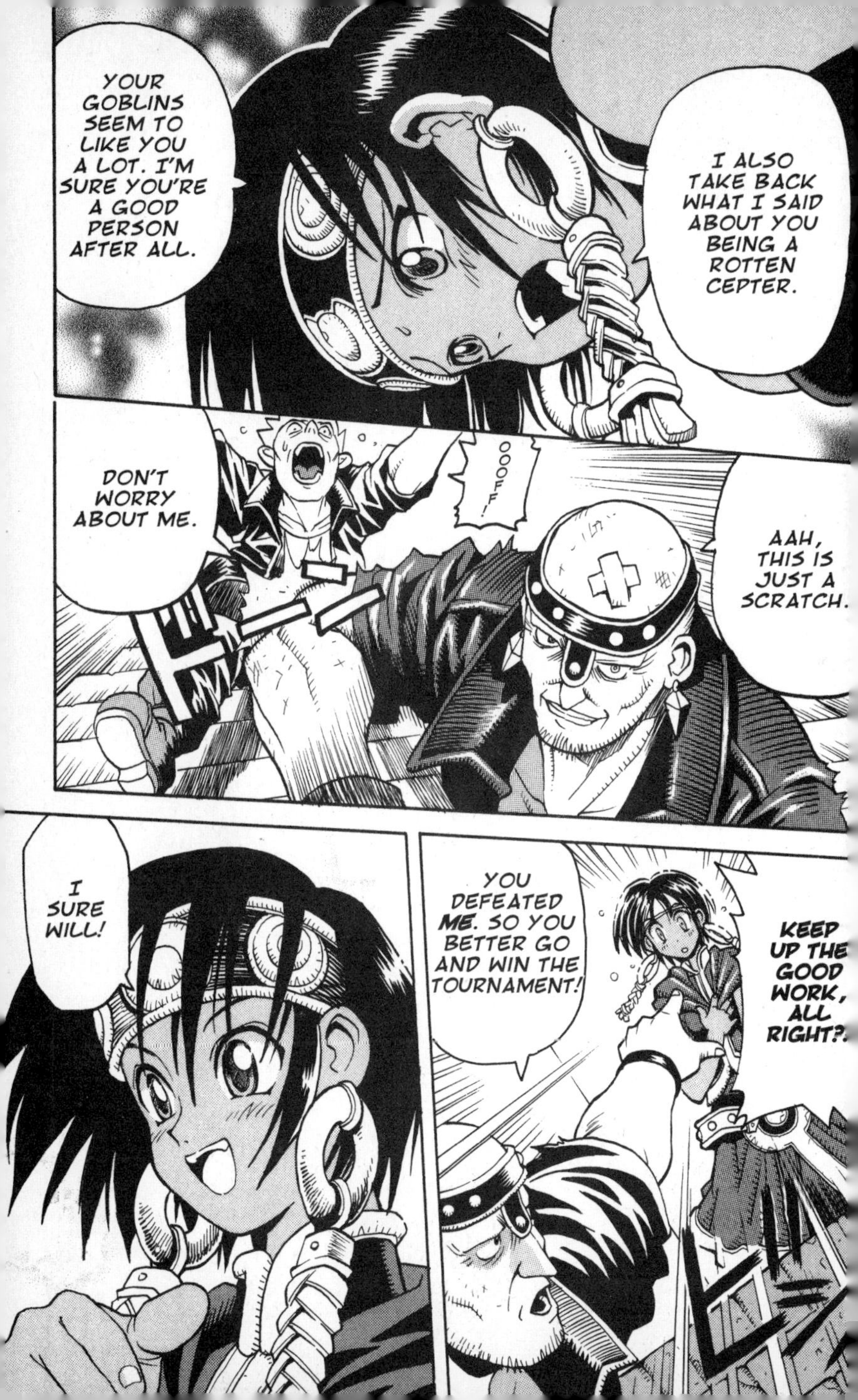
I ALSO TAKE BACK WHAT I SAID ABOUT YOU BEING A ROTTEN CEPTER.
YOUR GOBLINS SEEM TO LIKE YOU A LOT. I'M SURE YOU'RE A GOOD PERSON AFTER ALL.
AAH, THIS IS JUST A SCRATCH.
OOOFF!
DON'T WORRY ABOUT ME.
KEEP UP THE GOOD WORK, ALL RIGHT?
YOU DEFEATED **ME**. SO YOU BETTER GO AND WIN THE TOURNAMENT!
I SURE WILL!

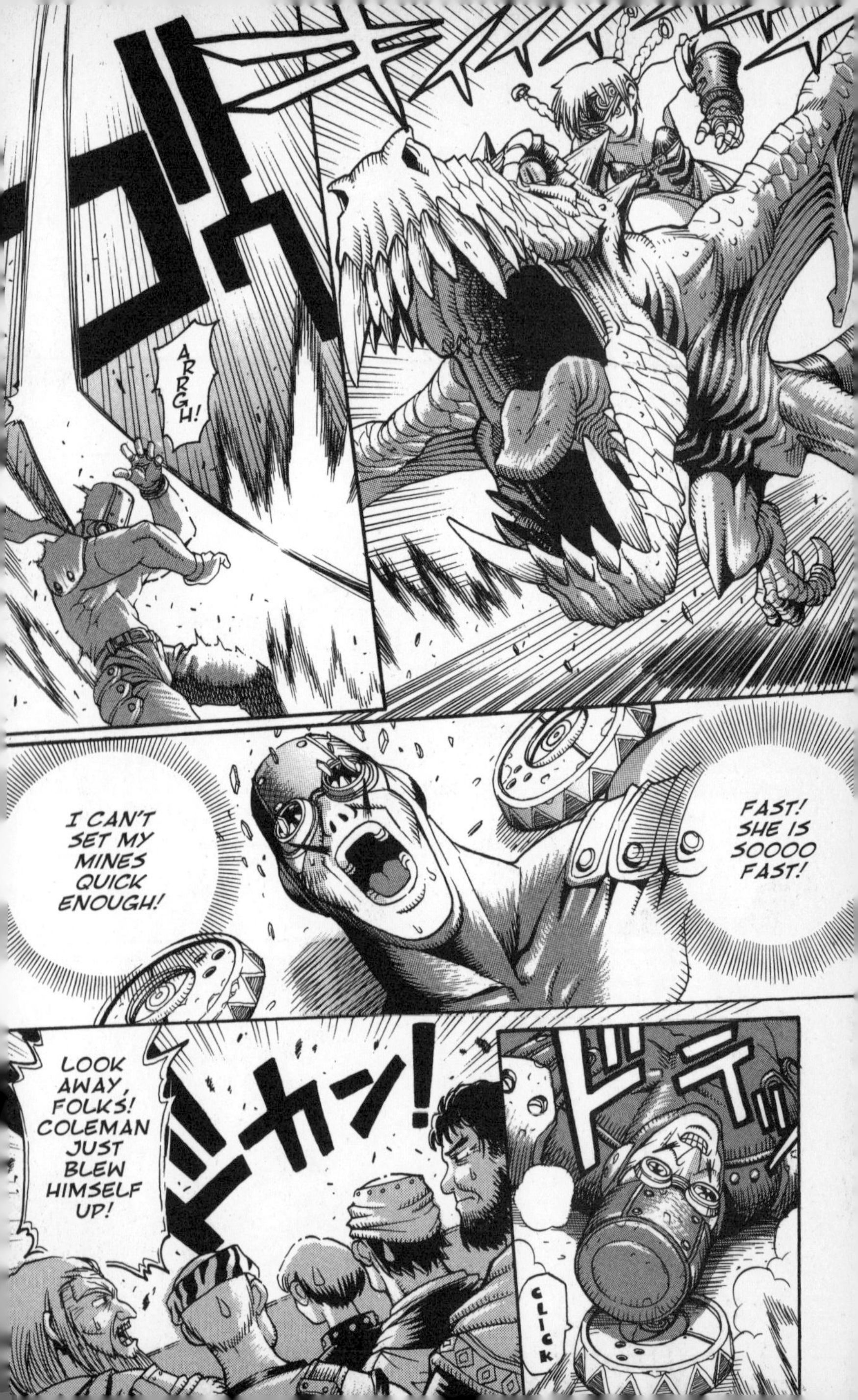
ARRGH!
FAST! SHE IS SOOOO FAST!
I CAN'T SET MY MINES QUICK ENOUGH!
CLICK
LOOK AWAY, FOLKS! COLEMAN JUST BLEW HIMSELF UP!

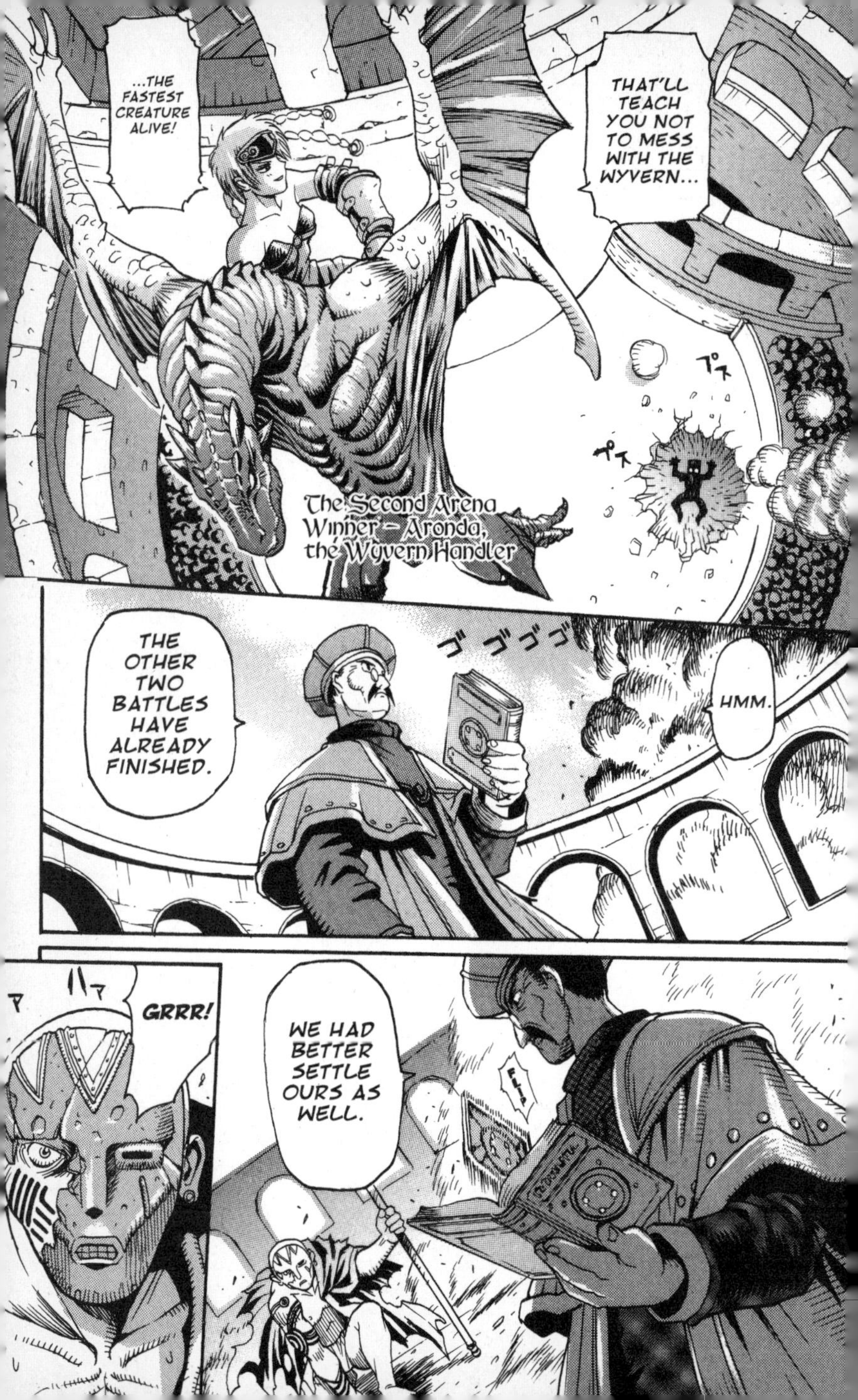

THAT'LL TEACH YOU NOT TO MESS WITH THE WYVERN...
...THE FASTEST CREATURE ALIVE!
The Second Arena Winner – Aronda, the Wyvern Handler
HMM.
THE OTHER TWO BATTLES HAVE ALREADY FINISHED.
FLIP
WE HAD BETTER SETTLE OURS AS WELL.
GRRR!

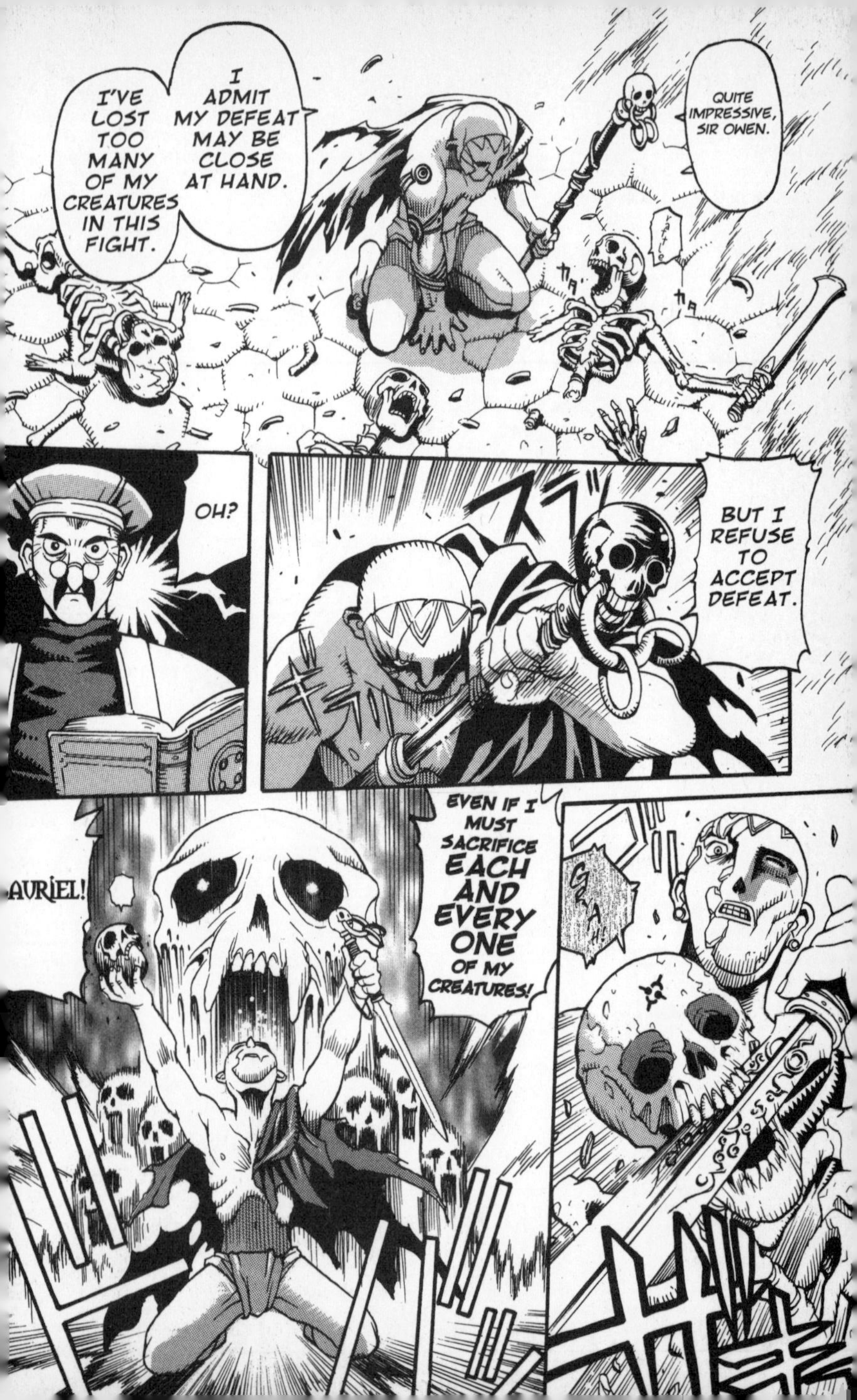
QUITE IMPRESSIVE, SIR OWEN.
I ADMIT MY DEFEAT MAY BE CLOSE AT HAND.
I'VE LOST TOO MANY OF MY CREATURES IN THIS FIGHT.
BUT I REFUSE TO ACCEPT DEFEAT.
OH?
EVEN IF I MUST SACRIFICE EACH AND EVERY ONE OF MY CREATURES!
AURIEL!

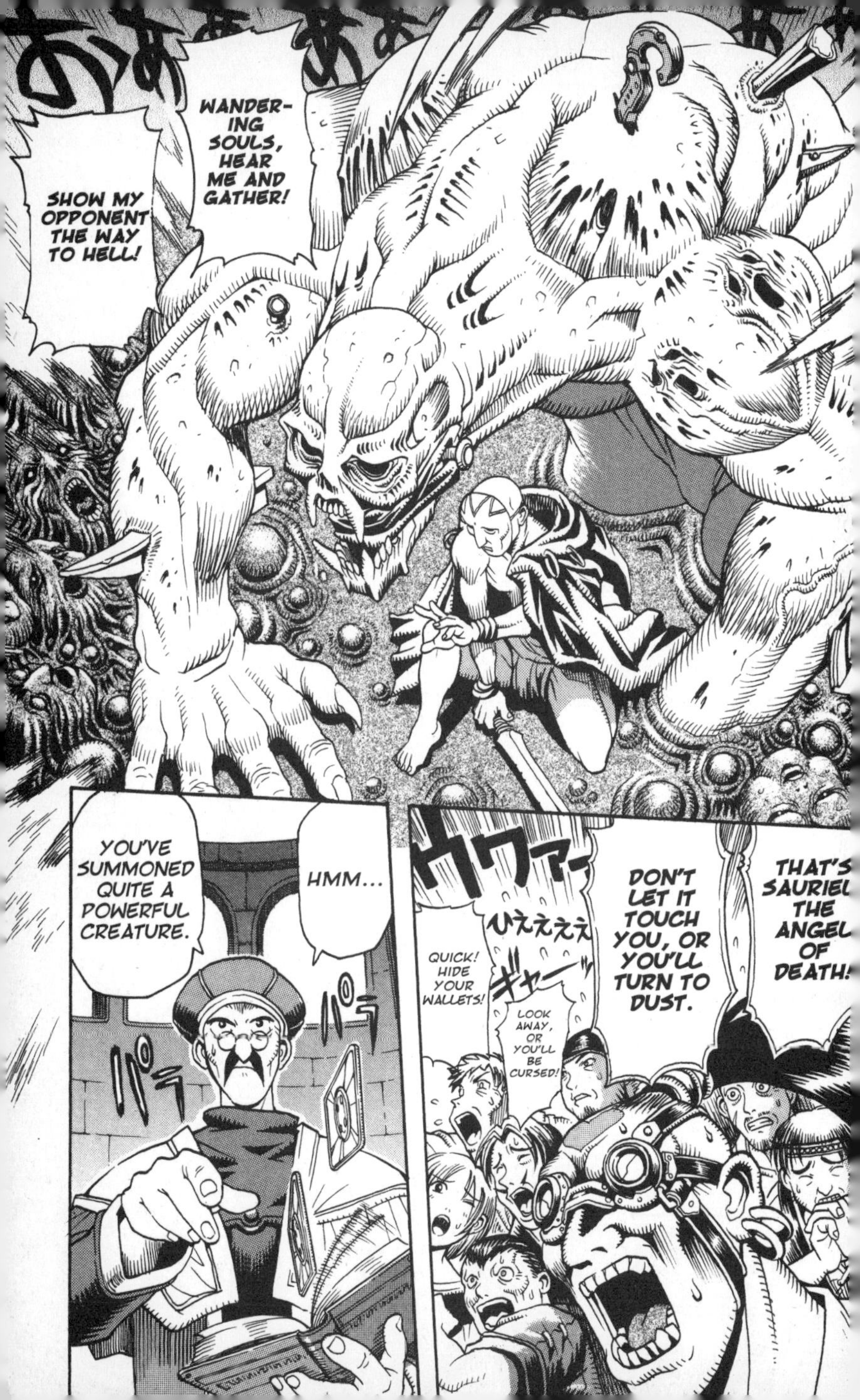
WANDERING SOULS, HEAR ME AND GATHER!
SHOW MY OPPONENT THE WAY TO HELL!
THAT'S SAURIEL THE ANGEL OF DEATH!
DON'T LET IT TOUCH YOU, OR YOU'LL TURN TO DUST.
ウワァー
ひえええ
QUICK! HIDE YOUR WALLETS!
ギャー
LOOK AWAY, OR YOU'LL BE CURSED!
HMM...
YOU'VE SUMMONED QUITE A POWERFUL CREATURE.
パラ
パラ

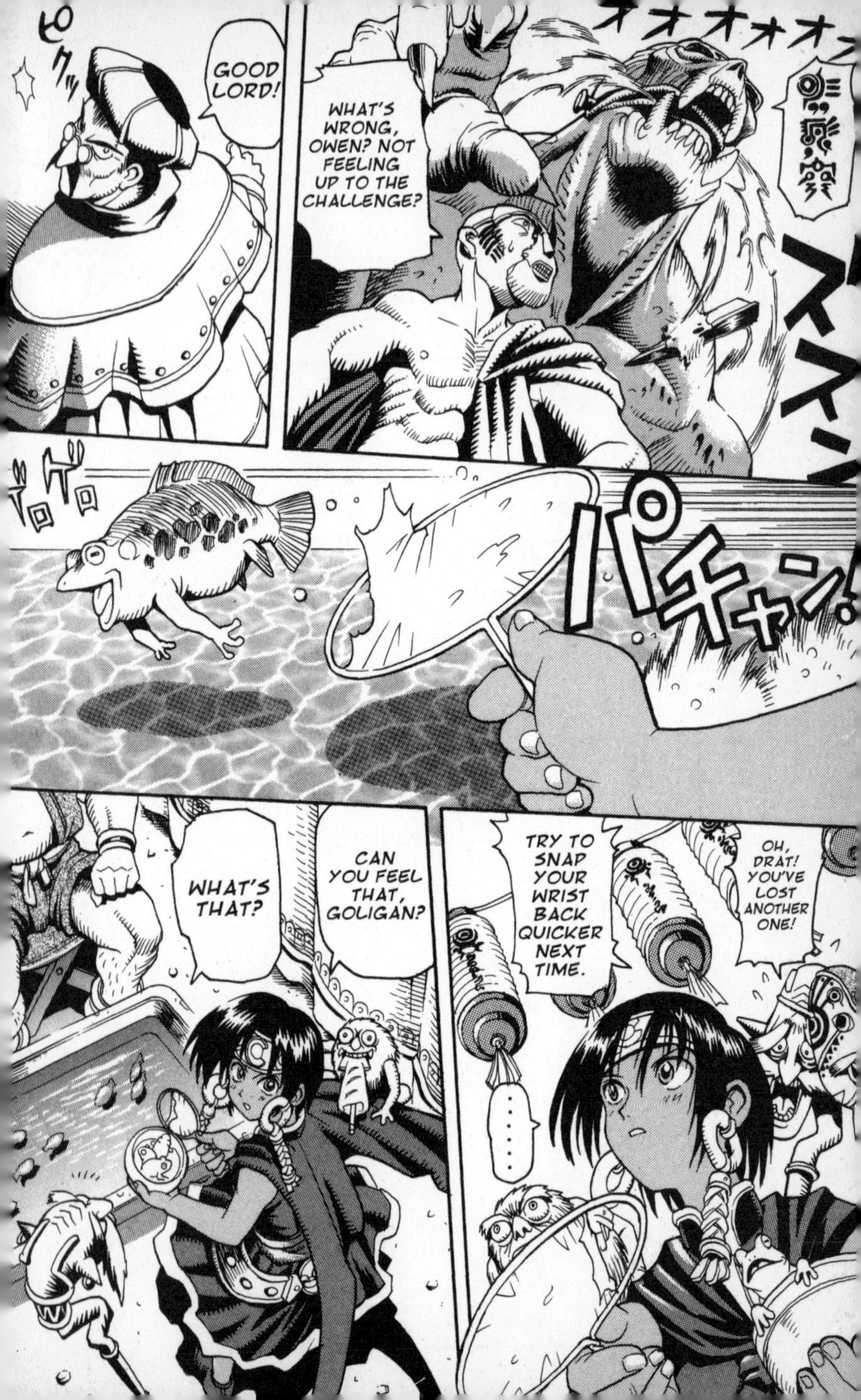
オオオオオ
WHAT'S WRONG, OWEN? NOT FEELING UP TO THE CHALLENGE?
GOOD LORD!
ピクッ
パチャン!
ゲロゲロ
OH, DRAT! YOU'VE LOST ANOTHER ONE!
TRY TO SNAP YOUR WRIST BACK QUICKER NEXT TIME.
......
CAN YOU FEEL THAT, GOLIGAN?
WHAT'S THAT?

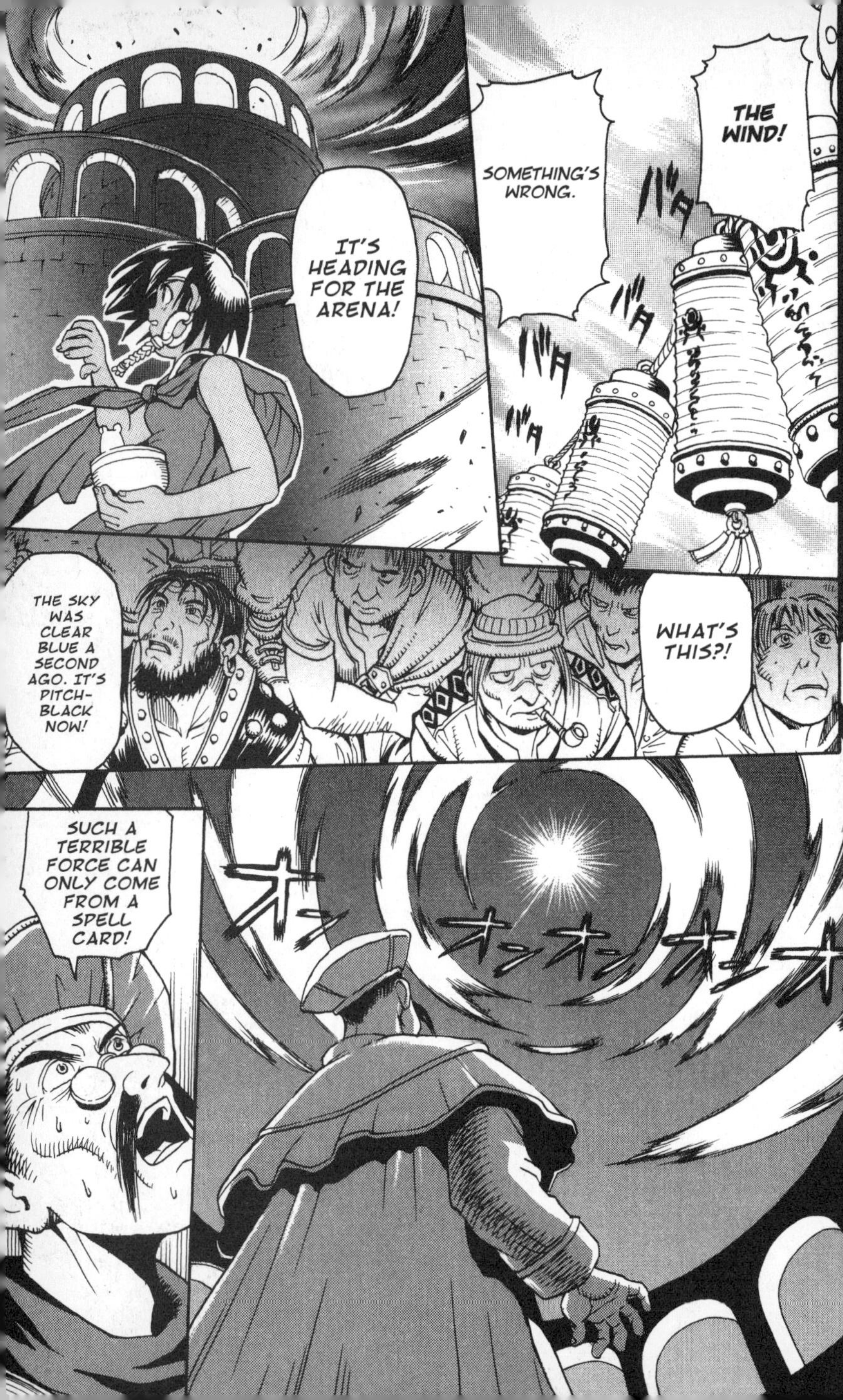
THE WIND!
SOMETHING'S WRONG.
IT'S HEADING FOR THE ARENA!
WHAT'S THIS?!
THE SKY WAS CLEAR BLUE A SECOND AGO. IT'S PITCH-BLACK NOW!
SUCH A TERRIBLE FORCE CAN ONLY COME FROM A SPELL CARD!

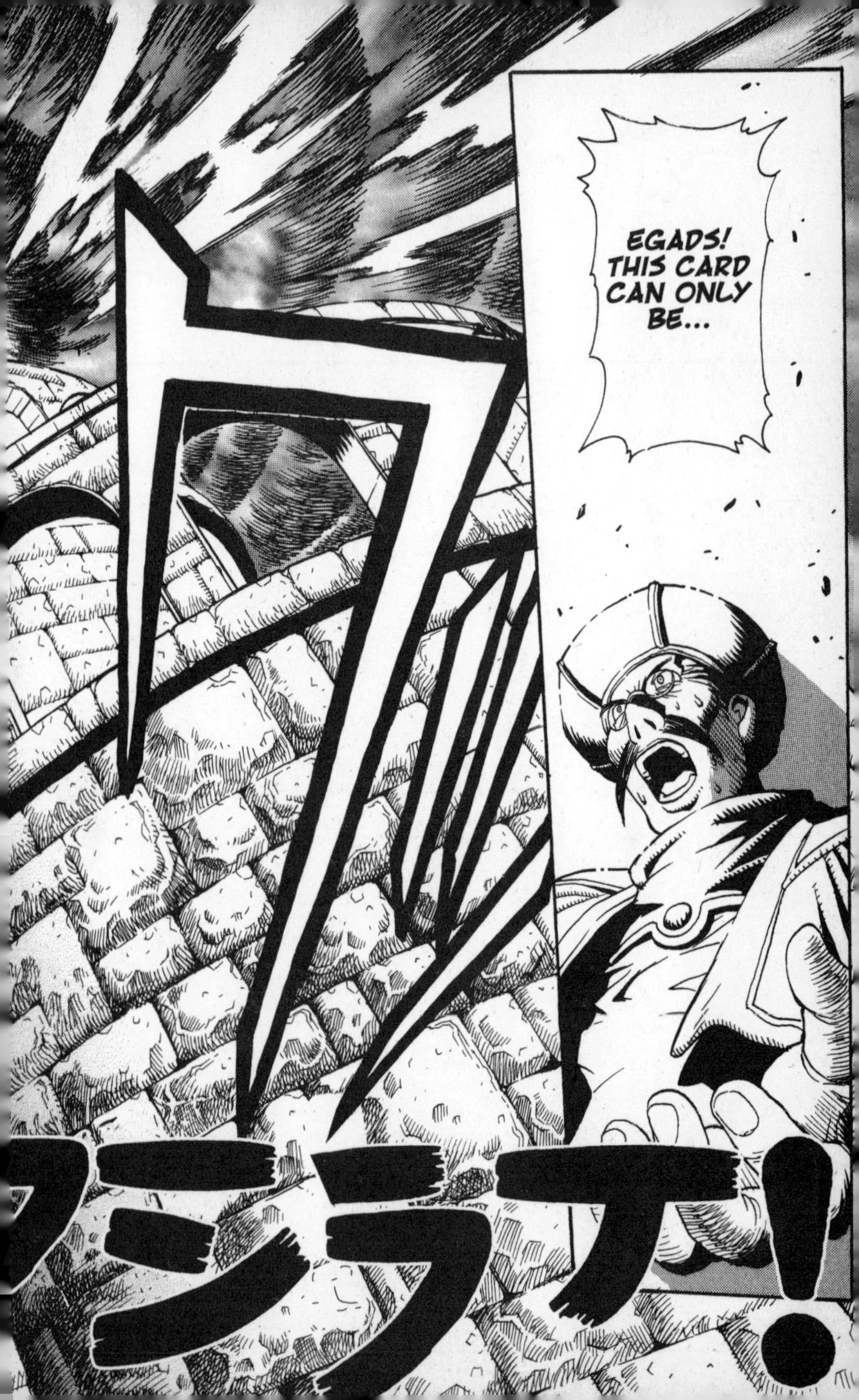
EGADS! THIS CARD CAN ONLY BE...

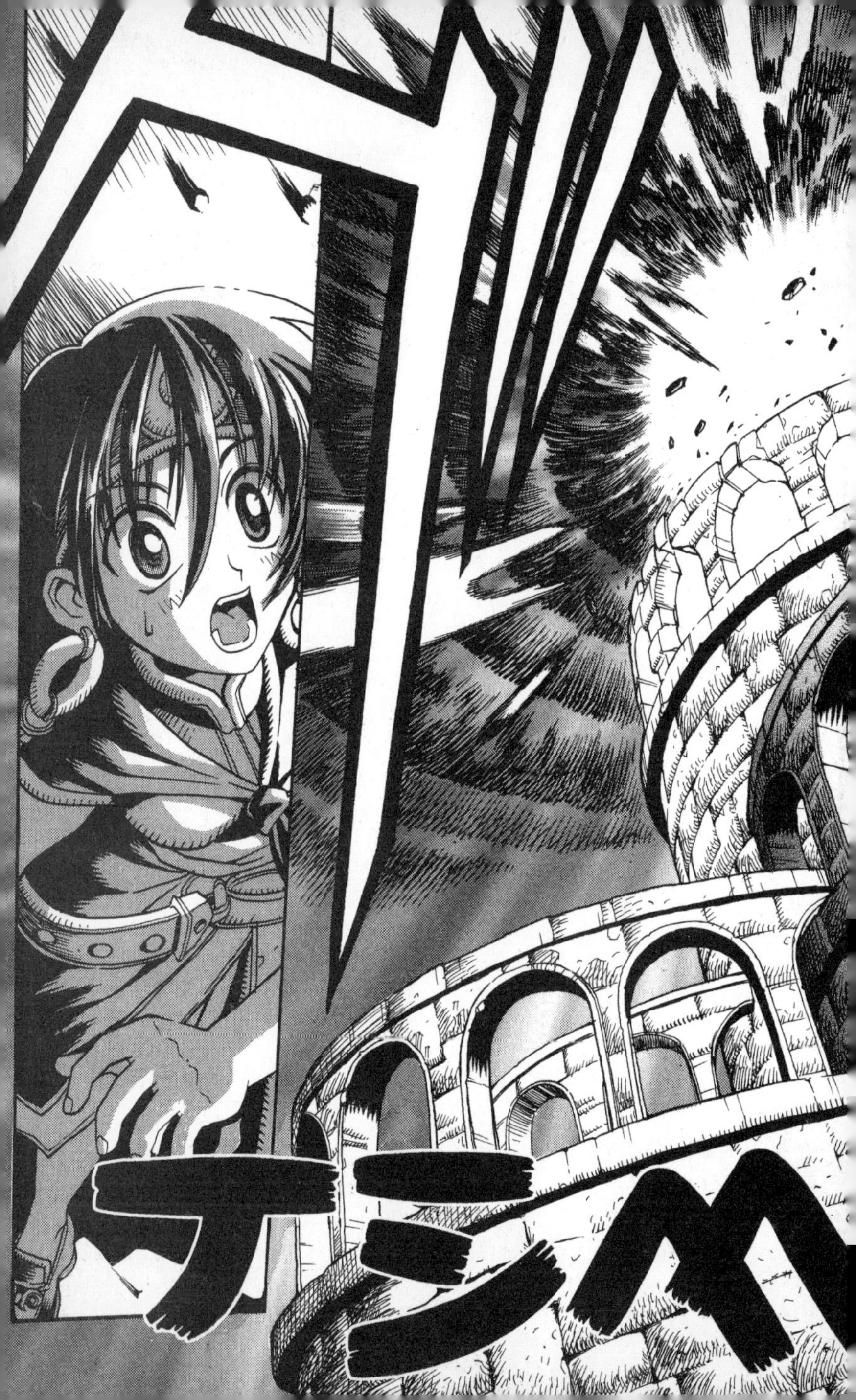

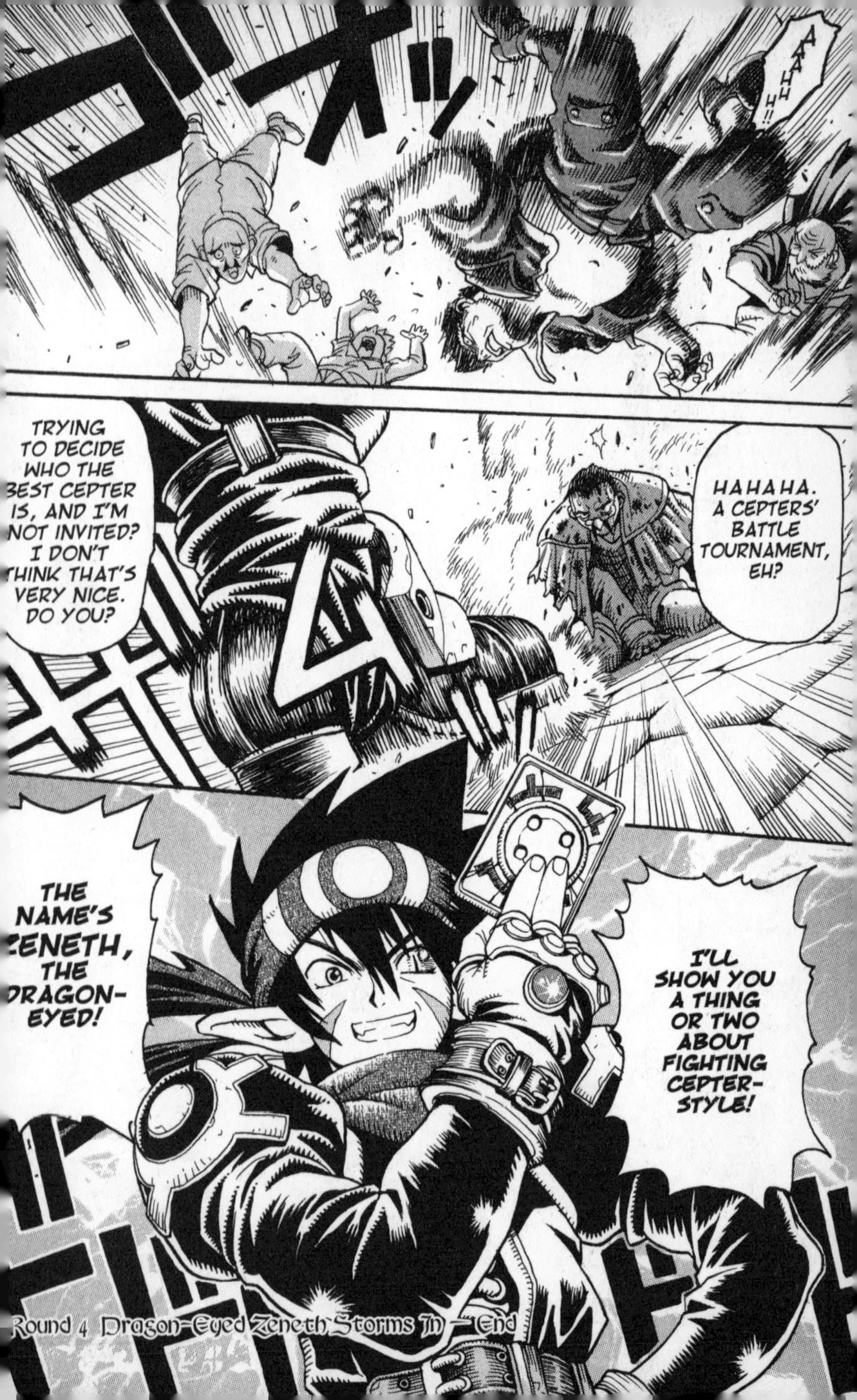
AAAAHH!!
HAHAHA. A CEPTERS' BATTLE TOURNAMENT, EH?
TRYING TO DECIDE WHO THE BEST CEPTER IS, AND I'M NOT INVITED? I DON'T THINK THAT'S VERY NICE. DO YOU?
THE NAME'S ZENETH, THE DRAGON-EYED!
I'LL SHOW YOU A THING OR TWO ABOUT FIGHTING CEPTER-STYLE!
Round 4 Dragon-Eyed Zeneth Storms In — End

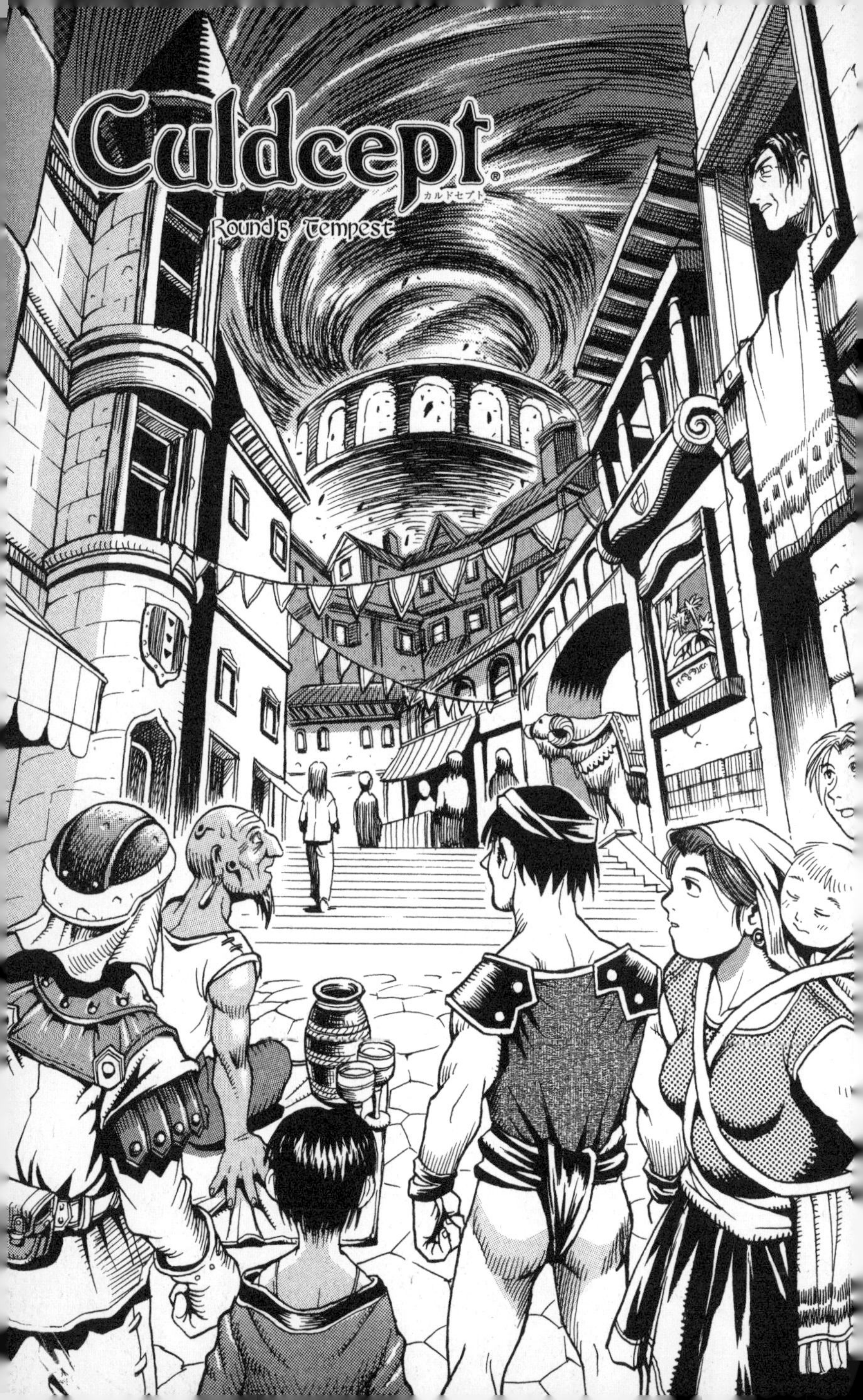
Culdcept®
カルドセプト
Round 5 Tempest

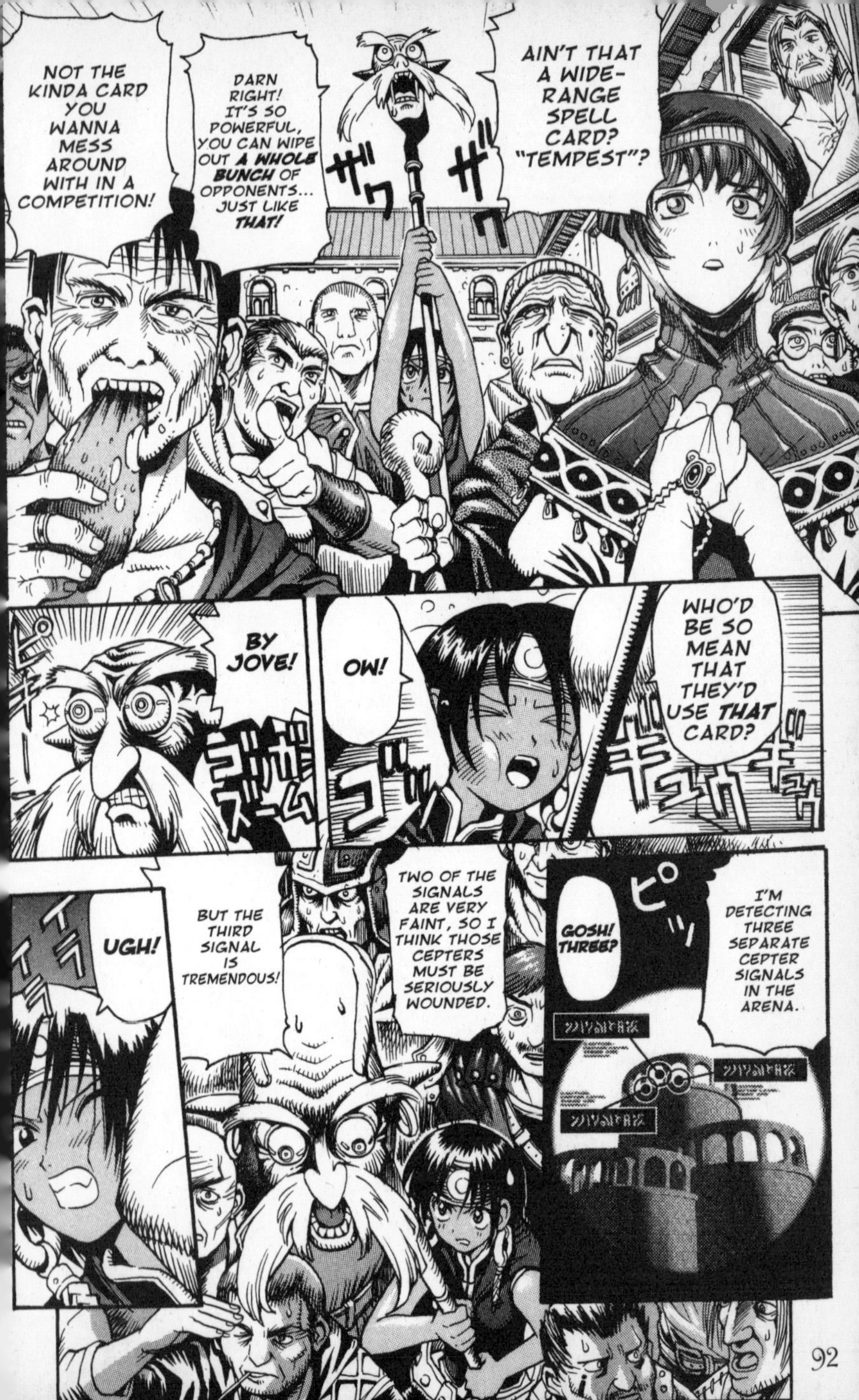
AIN'T THAT A WIDE-RANGE SPELL CARD? "TEMPEST"?
DARN RIGHT! IT'S SO POWERFUL, YOU CAN WIPE OUT A WHOLE BUNCH OF OPPONENTS... JUST LIKE THAT!
NOT THE KINDA CARD YOU WANNA MESS AROUND WITH IN A COMPETITION!
WHO'D BE SO MEAN THAT THEY'D USE THAT CARD?
OW!
BY JOVE!
I'M DETECTING THREE SEPARATE CEPTER SIGNALS IN THE ARENA.
GOSH! THREE?
TWO OF THE SIGNALS ARE VERY FAINT, SO I THINK THOSE CEPTERS MUST BE SERIOUSLY WOUNDED.
BUT THE THIRD SIGNAL IS TREMENDOUS!
UGH!

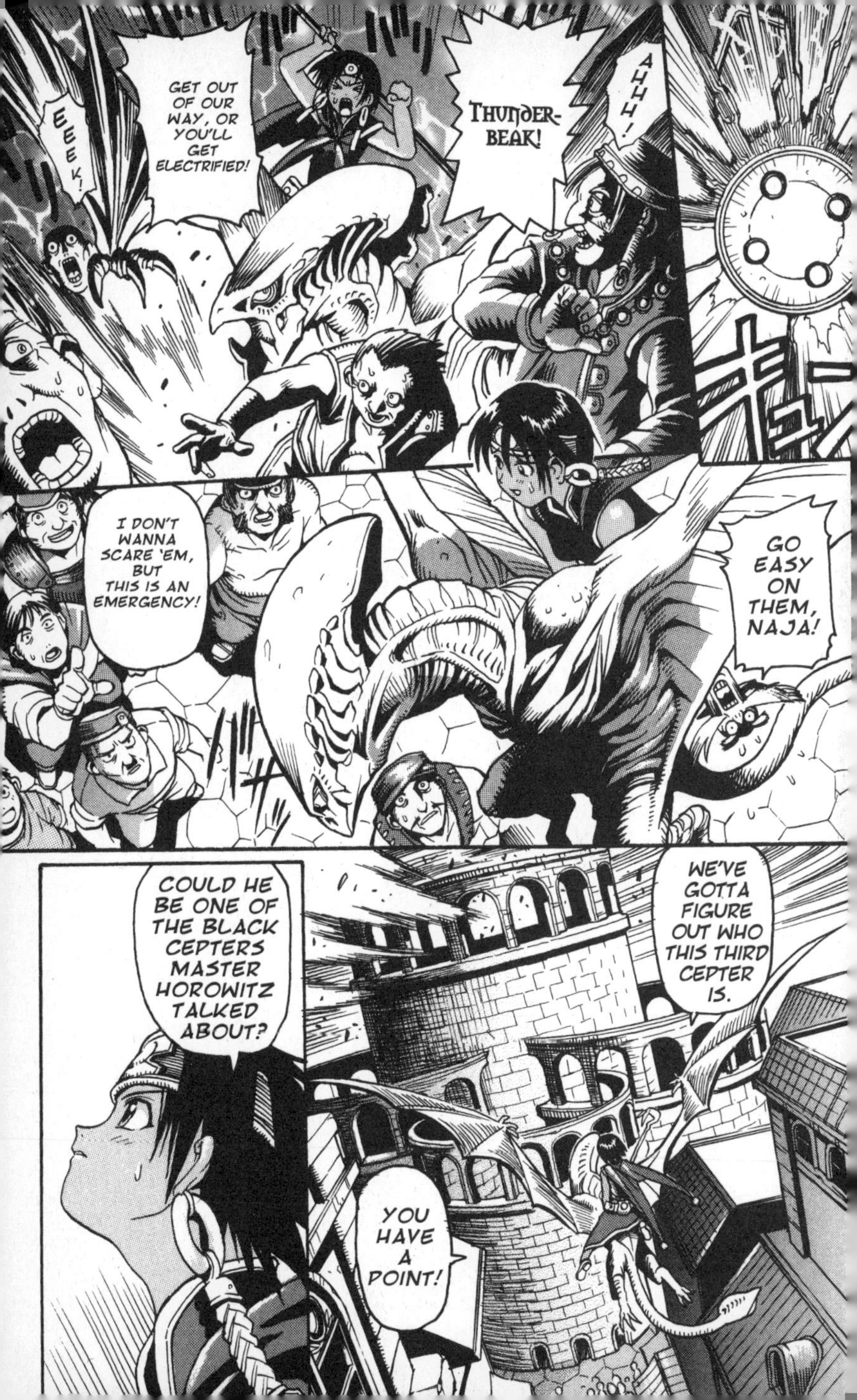

AHHH!
THUNDER-BEAK!
GET OUT OF OUR WAY, OR YOU'LL GET ELECTRIFIED!
EEEK!
GO EASY ON THEM, NAJA!
I DON'T WANNA SCARE 'EM, BUT THIS IS AN EMERGENCY!
WE'VE GOTTA FIGURE OUT WHO THIS THIRD CEPTER IS.
COULD HE BE ONE OF THE BLACK CEPTERS MASTER HOROWITZ TALKED ABOUT?
YOU HAVE A POINT!

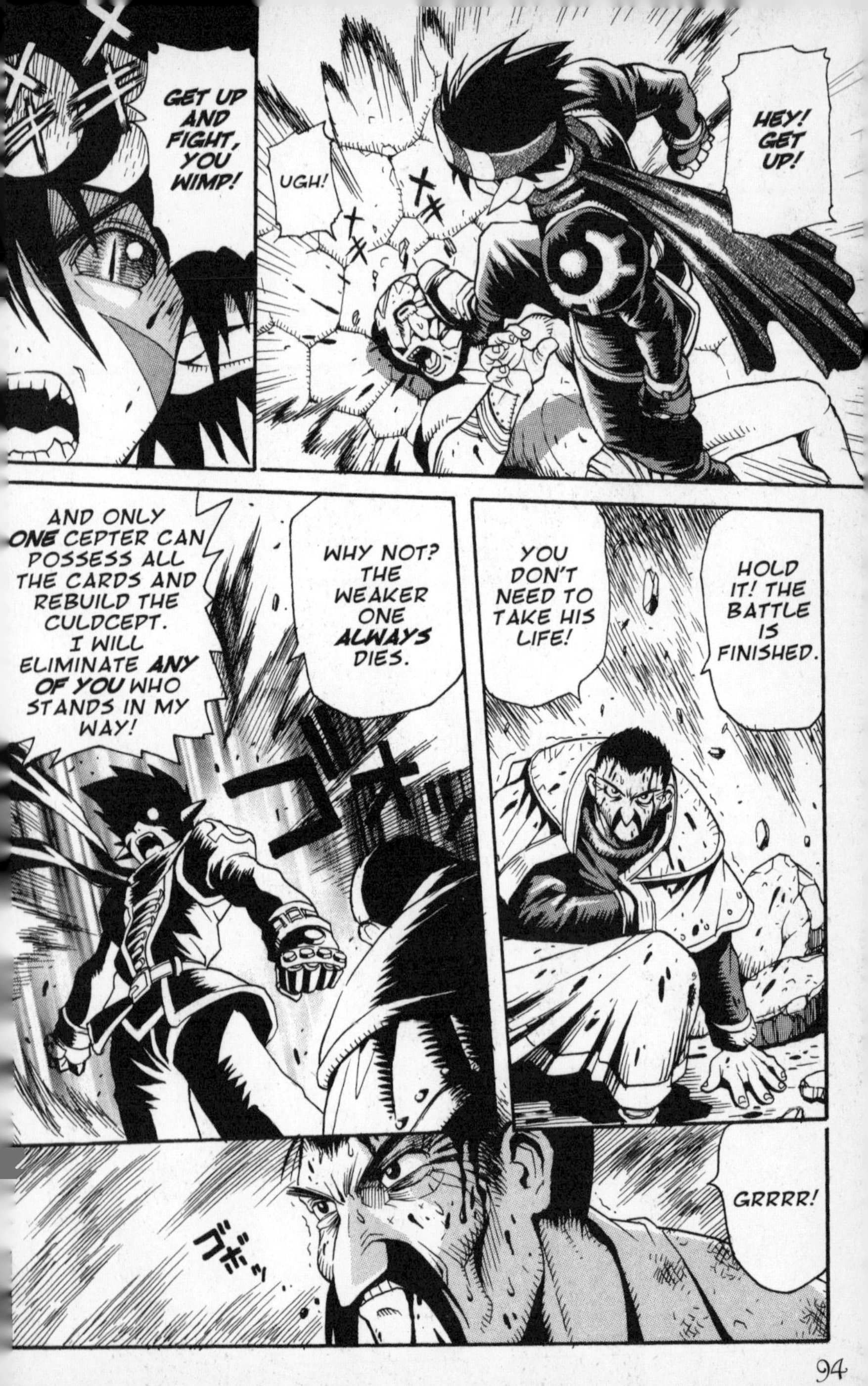
HEY! GET UP!
UGH!
GET UP AND FIGHT, YOU WIMP!
HOLD IT! THE BATTLE IS FINISHED.
YOU DON'T NEED TO TAKE HIS LIFE!
WHY NOT? THE WEAKER ONE ALWAYS DIES.
AND ONLY ONE CEPTER CAN POSSESS ALL THE CARDS AND REBUILD THE CULDCEPT. I WILL ELIMINATE ANY OF YOU WHO STANDS IN MY WAY!
ゴオッ
GRRRR!
ゴボッ

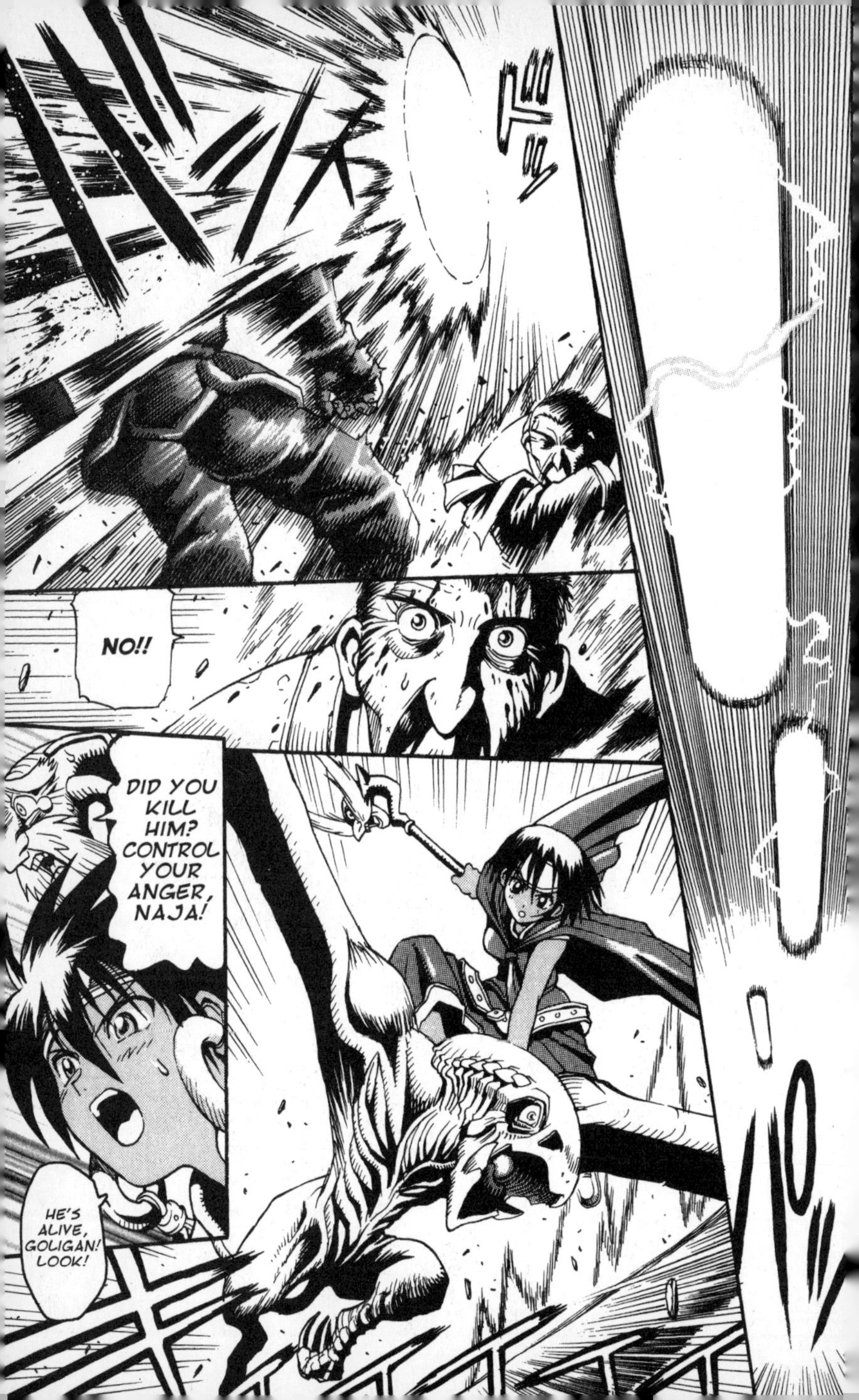
NO!!
DID YOU KILL HIM? CONTROL YOUR ANGER, NAJA!
HE'S ALIVE, GOLIGAN! LOOK!

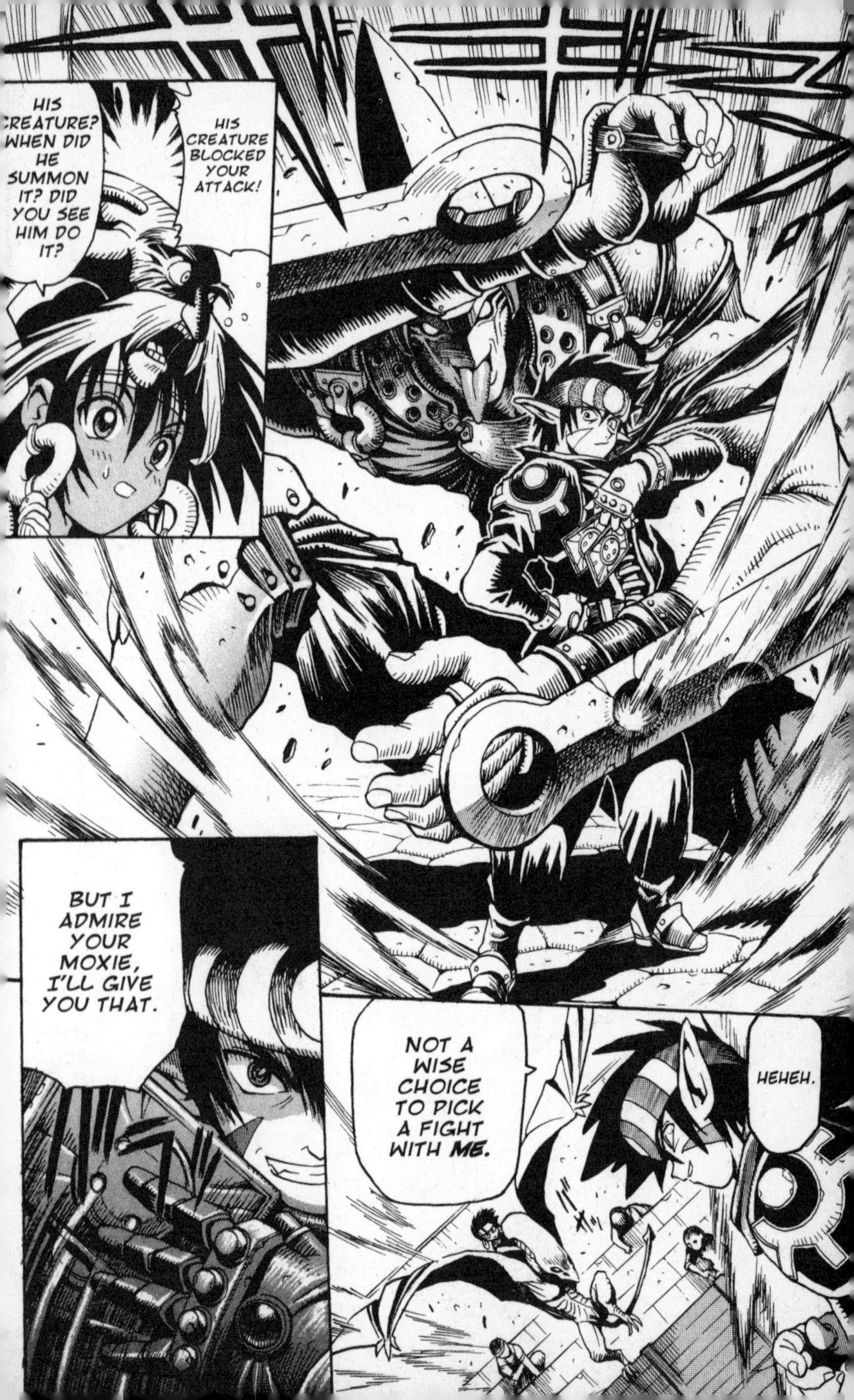
HIS CREATURE BLOCKED YOUR ATTACK!
HIS CREATURE? WHEN DID HE SUMMON IT? DID YOU SEE HIM DO IT?
HEHEH.
NOT A WISE CHOICE TO PICK A FIGHT WITH ME.
BUT I ADMIRE YOUR MOXIE, I'LL GIVE YOU THAT.

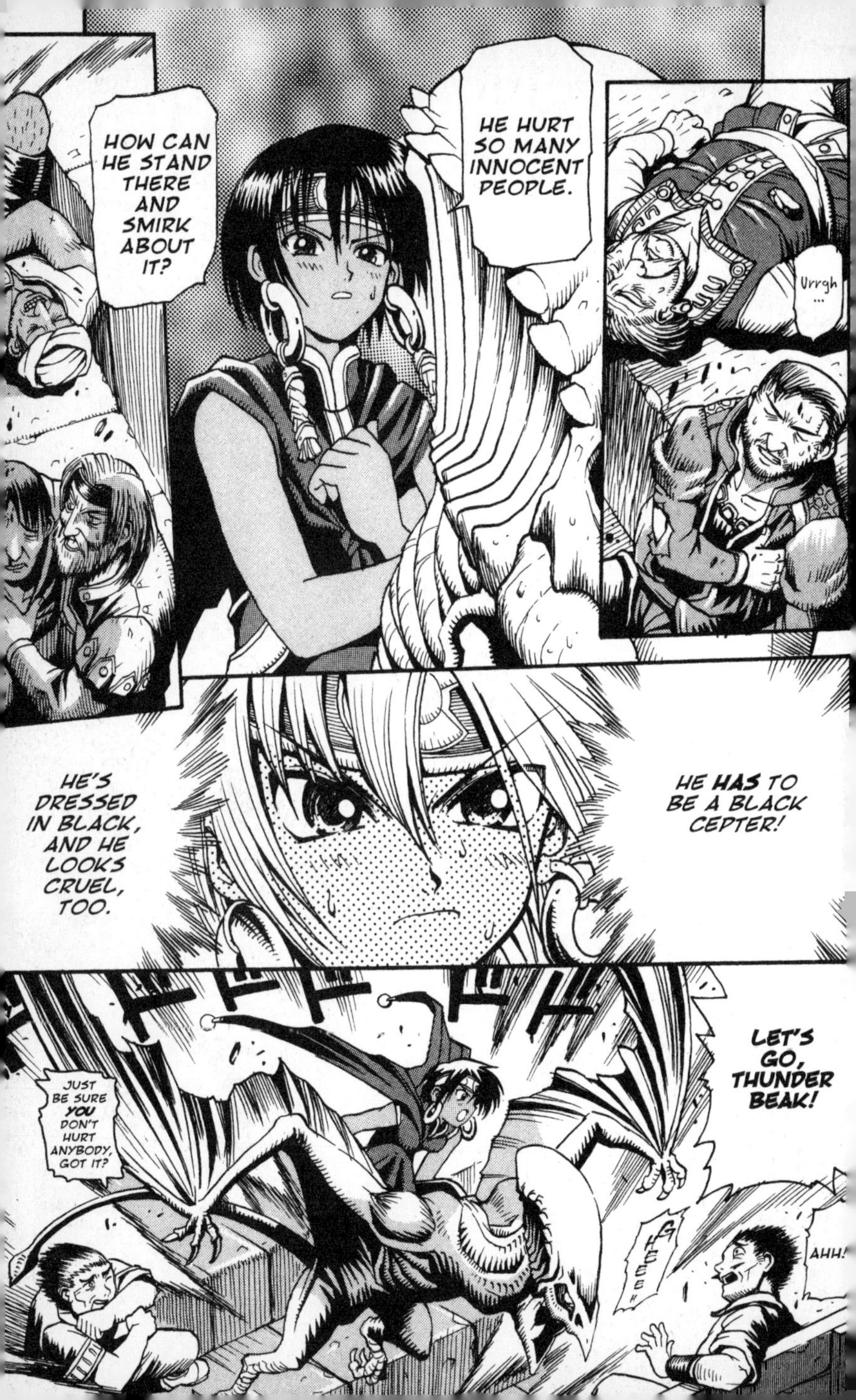
Urrgh...
HE HURT SO MANY INNOCENT PEOPLE.
HOW CAN HE STAND THERE AND SMIRK ABOUT IT?
HE HAS TO BE A BLACK CEPTER!
HE'S DRESSED IN BLACK, AND HE LOOKS CRUEL, TOO.
LET'S GO, THUNDER BEAK!
AHH!
GHEEE!!
JUST BE SURE YOU DON'T HURT ANYBODY, GOT IT?

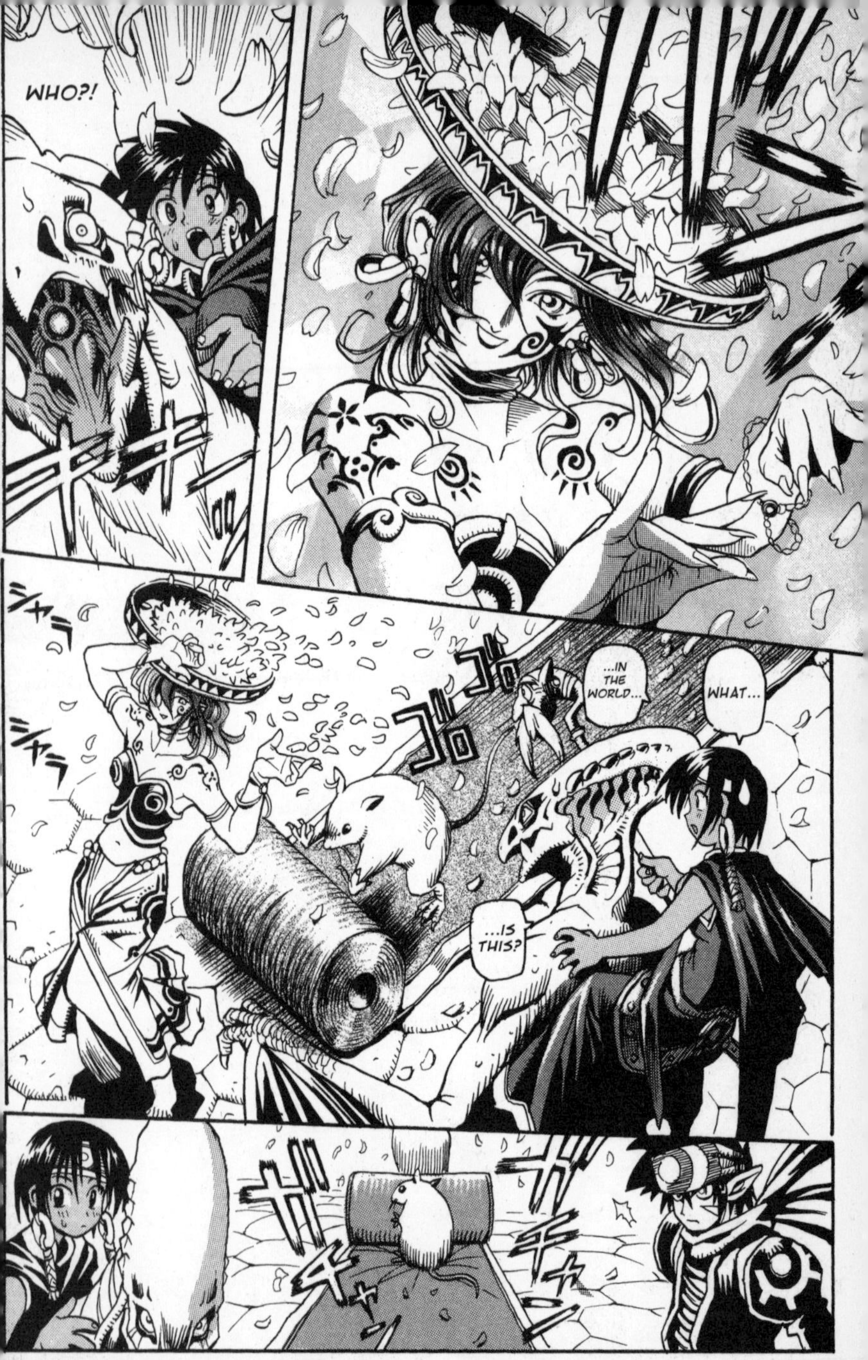
WHO?!
WHAT...
...IN THE WORLD...
...IS THIS?

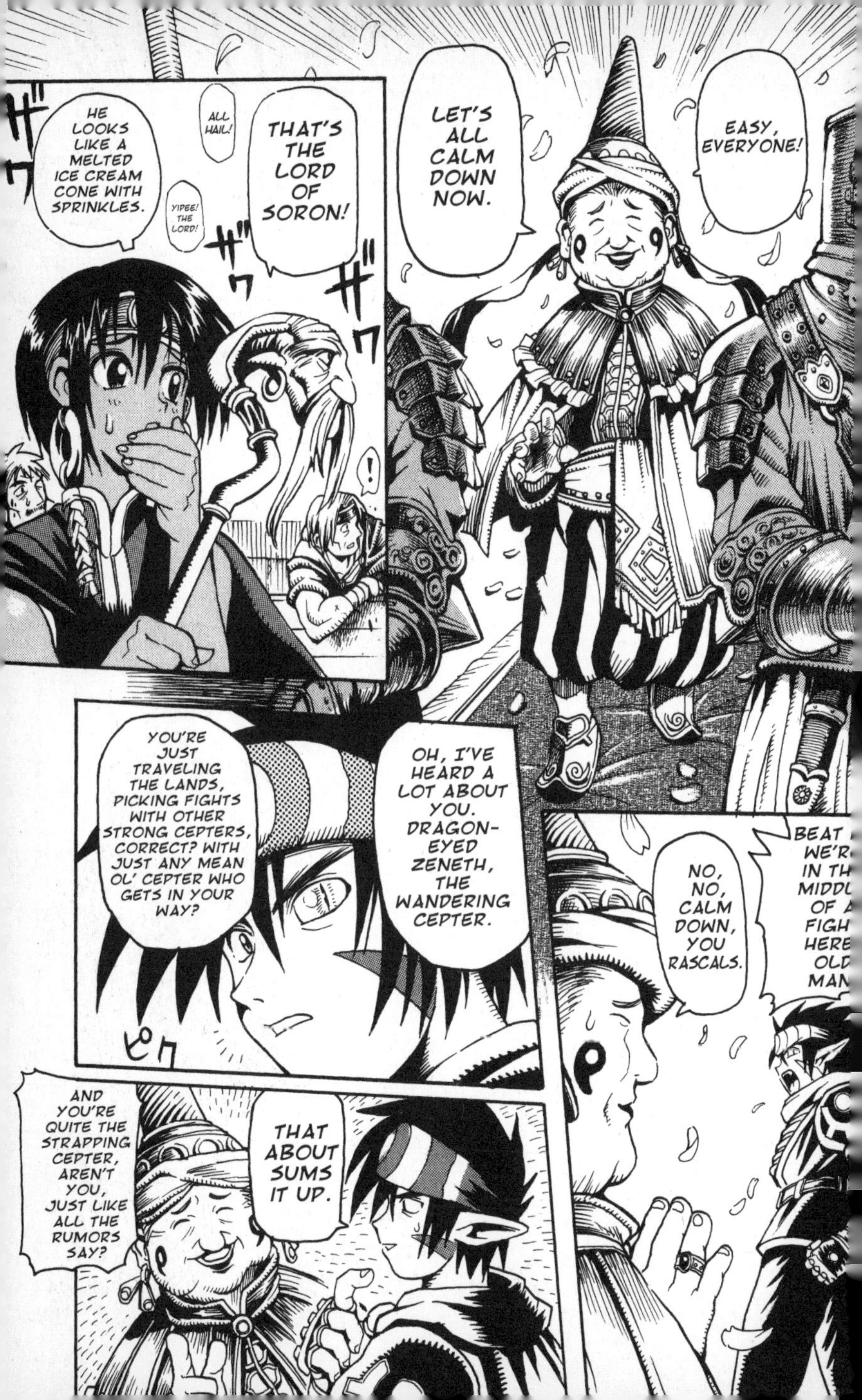
EASY, EVERYONE!
LET'S ALL CALM DOWN NOW.
THAT'S THE LORD OF SORON!
ALL HAIL!
YIPEE! THE LORD!
HE LOOKS LIKE A MELTED ICE CREAM CONE WITH SPRINKLES.
ザワ
ザワ
ザワ
BEAT I WE'R IN TH MIDDL OF A FIGH HERE OLD MAN
NO, NO, CALM DOWN, YOU RASCALS.
OH, I'VE HEARD A LOT ABOUT YOU. DRAGON-EYED ZENETH, THE WANDERING CEPTER.
YOU'RE JUST TRAVELING THE LANDS, PICKING FIGHTS WITH OTHER STRONG CEPTERS, CORRECT? WITH JUST ANY MEAN OL' CEPTER WHO GETS IN YOUR WAY?
ピク
THAT ABOUT SUMS IT UP.
AND YOU'RE QUITE THE STRAPPING CEPTER, AREN'T YOU, JUST LIKE ALL THE RUMORS SAY?

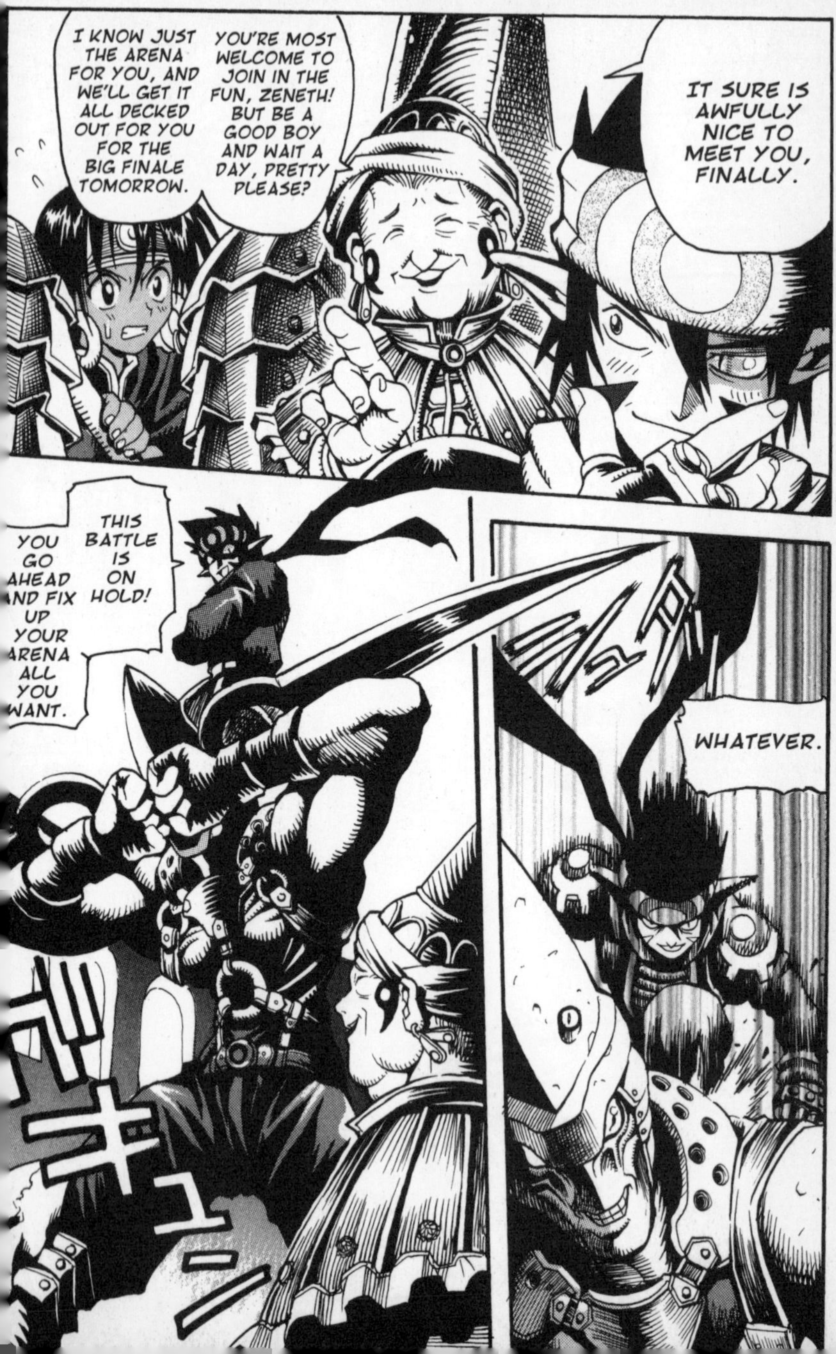
IT SURE IS AWFULLY NICE TO MEET YOU, FINALLY.
YOU'RE MOST WELCOME TO JOIN IN THE FUN, ZENETH! BUT BE A GOOD BOY AND WAIT A DAY, PRETTY PLEASE?
I KNOW JUST THE ARENA FOR YOU, AND WE'LL GET IT ALL DECKED OUT FOR YOU FOR THE BIG FINALE TOMORROW.
WHATEVER.
THIS BATTLE IS ON HOLD!
YOU GO AHEAD AND FIX UP YOUR ARENA ALL YOU WANT.

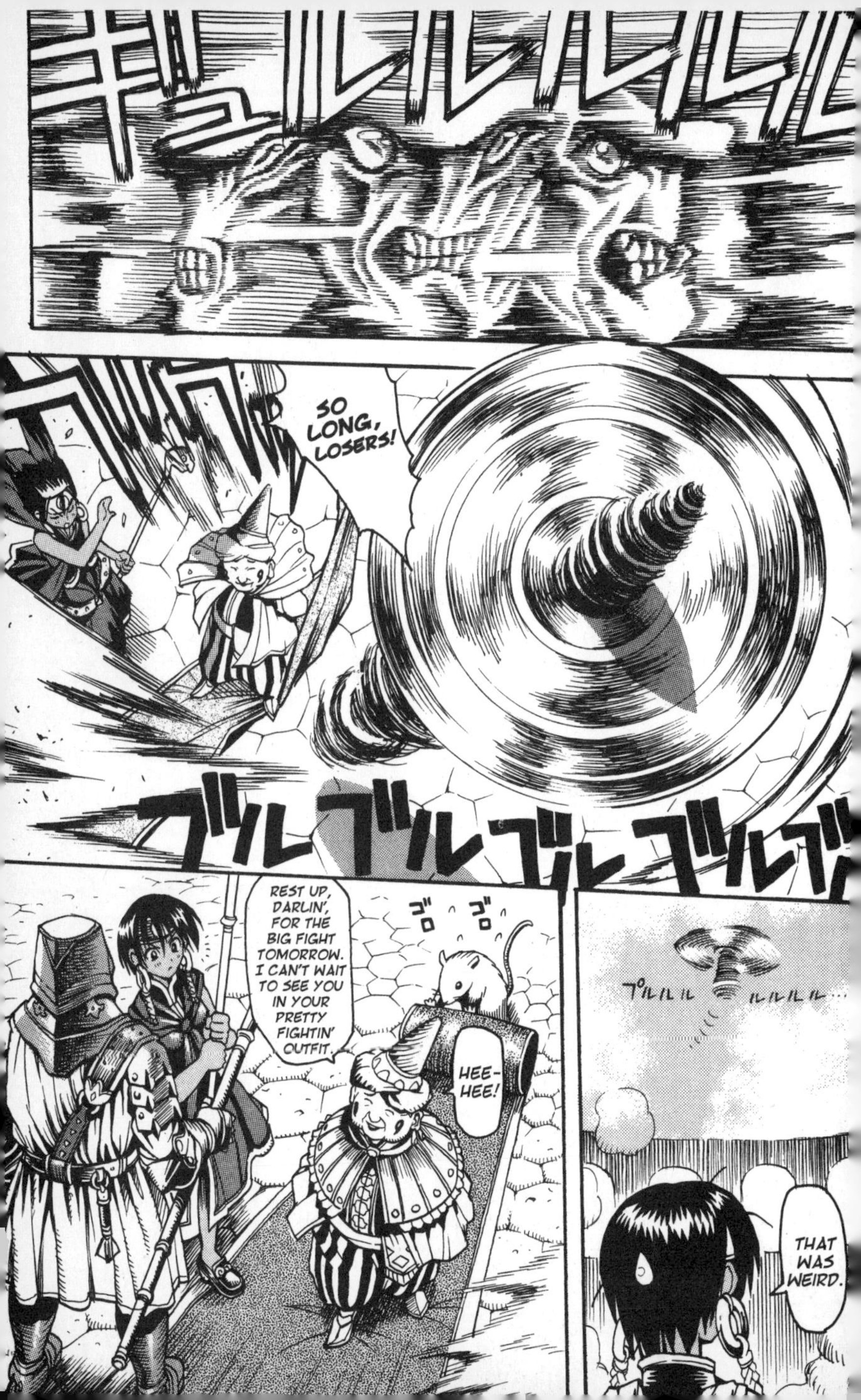
キュルルルルル
SO LONG, LOSERS!
ブルブルブルブ
プルルル ルルルル…
THAT WAS WEIRD.
REST UP, DARLIN', FOR THE BIG FIGHT TOMORROW. I CAN'T WAIT TO SEE YOU IN YOUR PRETTY FIGHTIN' OUTFIT.
ゴロ ゴロ
HEE-HEE!

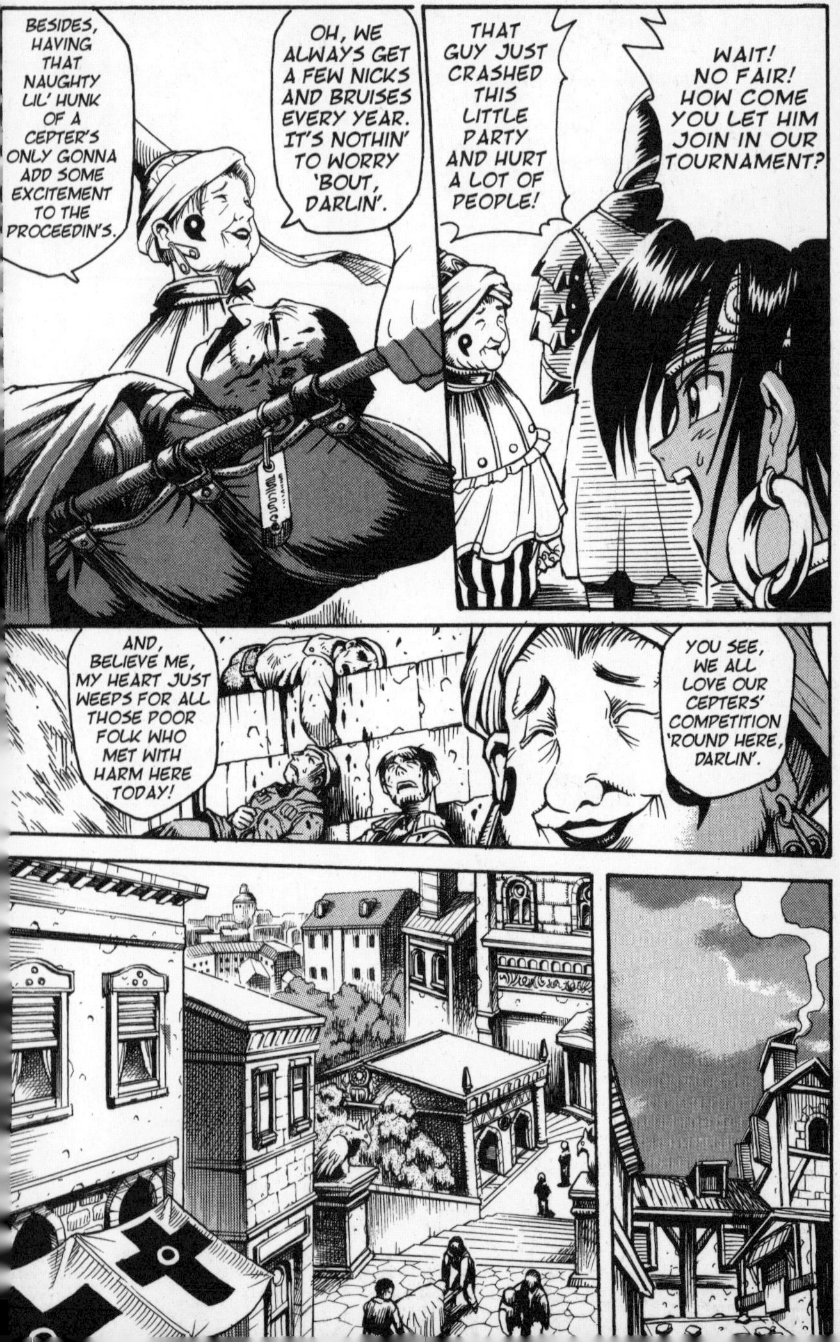
WAIT! NO FAIR! HOW COME YOU LET HIM JOIN IN OUR TOURNAMENT?
THAT GUY JUST CRASHED THIS LITTLE PARTY AND HURT A LOT OF PEOPLE!
OH, WE ALWAYS GET A FEW NICKS AND BRUISES EVERY YEAR. IT'S NOTHIN' TO WORRY 'BOUT, DARLIN'.
BESIDES, HAVING THAT NAUGHTY LIL' HUNK OF A CEPTER'S ONLY GONNA ADD SOME EXCITEMENT TO THE PROCEEDIN'S.
YOU SEE, WE ALL LOVE OUR CEPTERS' COMPETITION 'ROUND HERE, DARLIN'.
AND, BELIEVE ME, MY HEART JUST WEEPS FOR ALL THOSE POOR FOLK WHO MET WITH HARM HERE TODAY!

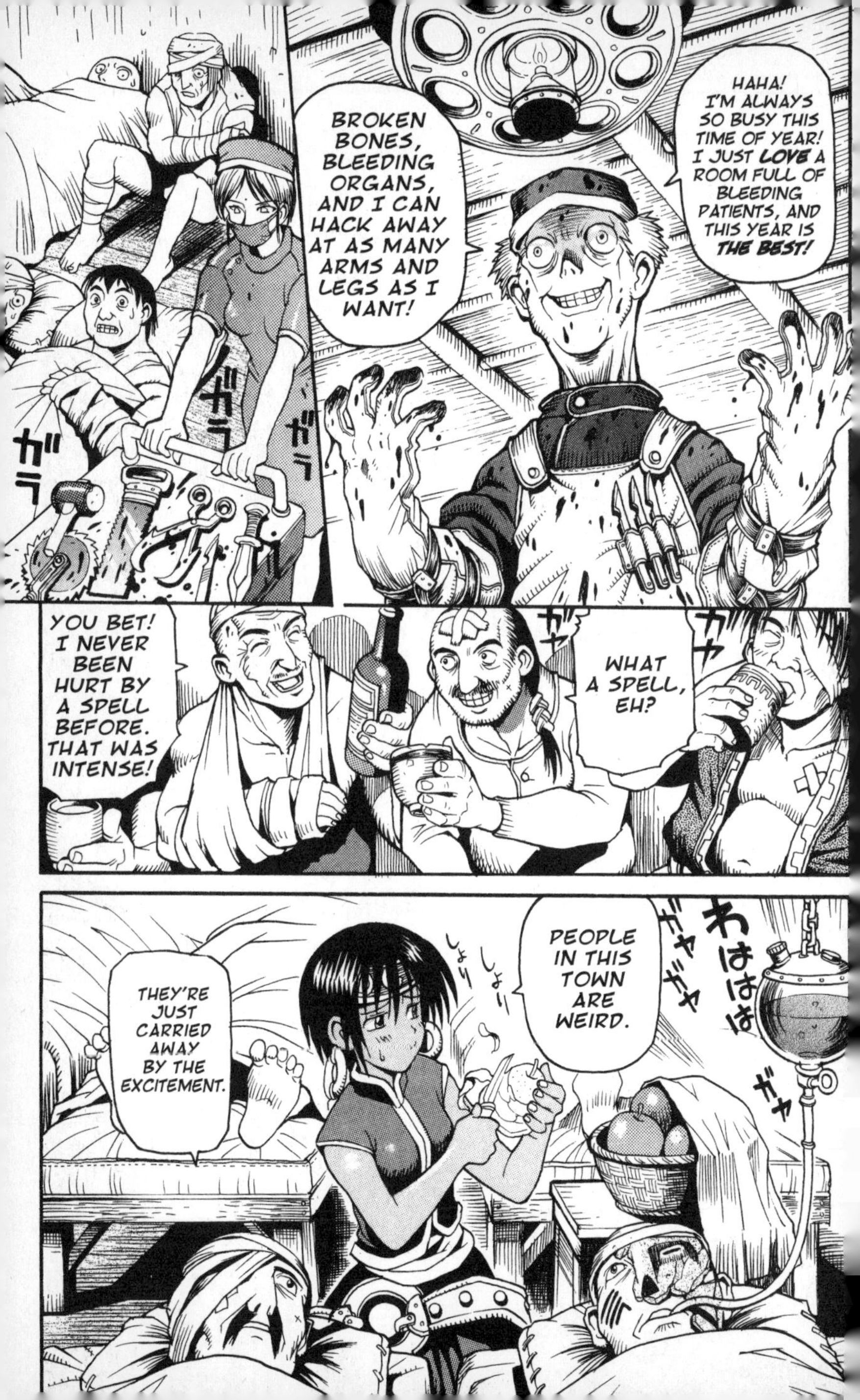
HAHA! I'M ALWAYS SO BUSY THIS TIME OF YEAR! I JUST LOVE A ROOM FULL OF BLEEDING PATIENTS, AND THIS YEAR IS THE BEST!
BROKEN BONES, BLEEDING ORGANS, AND I CAN HACK AWAY AT AS MANY ARMS AND LEGS AS I WANT!
ガラ
ガラ
ガラ
ガヤ
ガヤ
WHAT A SPELL, EH?
YOU BET! I NEVER BEEN HURT BY A SPELL BEFORE. THAT WAS INTENSE!
わははは
ガヤガヤ
ガヤ
PEOPLE IN THIS TOWN ARE WEIRD.
しょり
しょり
THEY'RE JUST CARRIED AWAY BY THE EXCITEMENT.

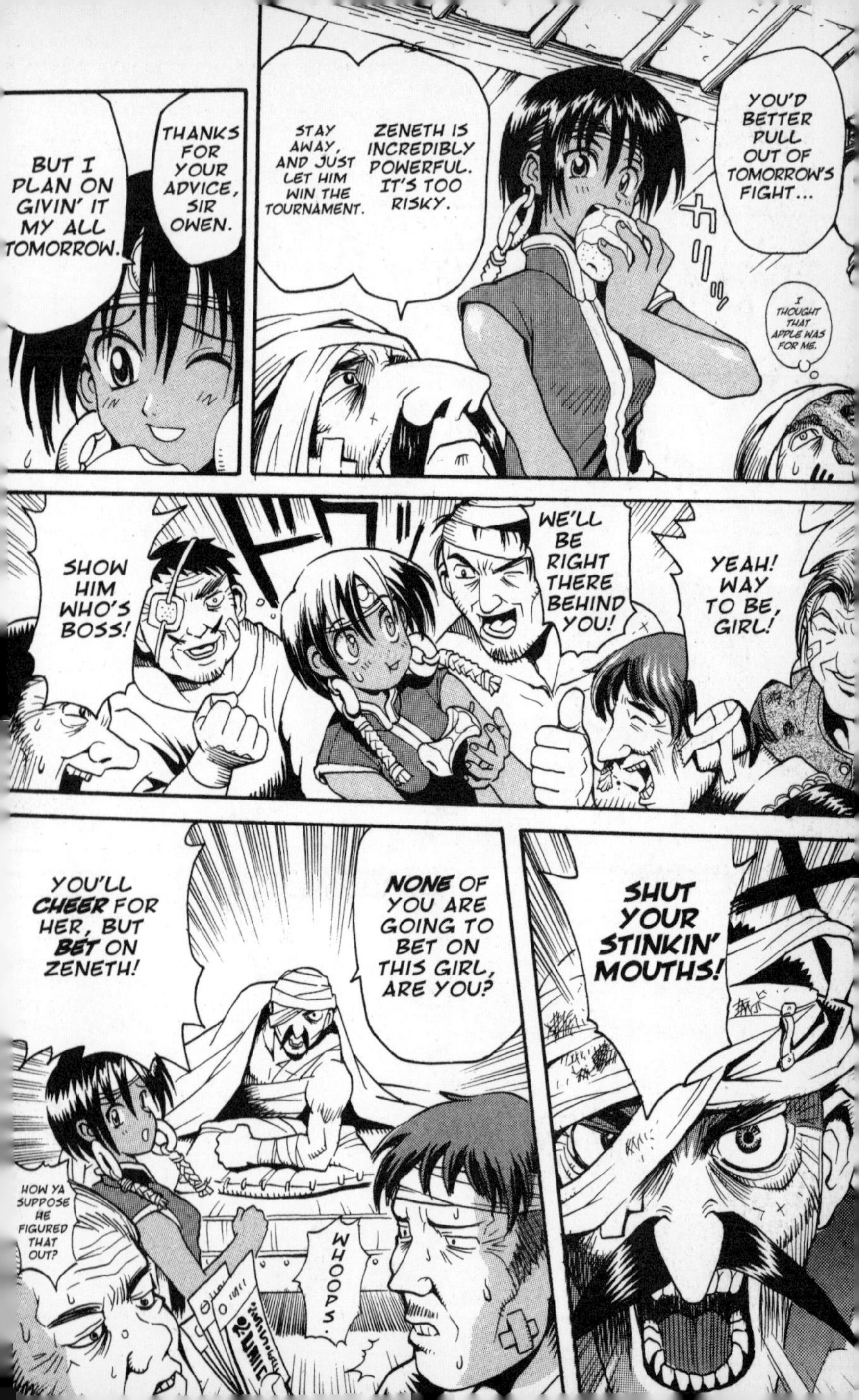
YOU'D BETTER PULL OUT OF TOMORROW'S FIGHT...
ZENETH IS INCREDIBLY POWERFUL. IT'S TOO RISKY.
STAY AWAY, AND JUST LET HIM WIN THE TOURNAMENT.
I THOUGHT THAT APPLE WAS FOR ME.
THANKS FOR YOUR ADVICE, SIR OWEN.
BUT I PLAN ON GIVIN' IT MY ALL TOMORROW.
YEAH! WAY TO BE, GIRL!
WE'LL BE RIGHT THERE BEHIND YOU!
SHOW HIM WHO'S BOSS!
SHUT YOUR STINKIN' MOUTHS!
NONE OF YOU ARE GOING TO BET ON THIS GIRL, ARE YOU?
YOU'LL CHEER FOR HER, BUT BET ON ZENETH!
WHOOPS.
HOW YA SUPPOSE HE FIGURED THAT OUT?

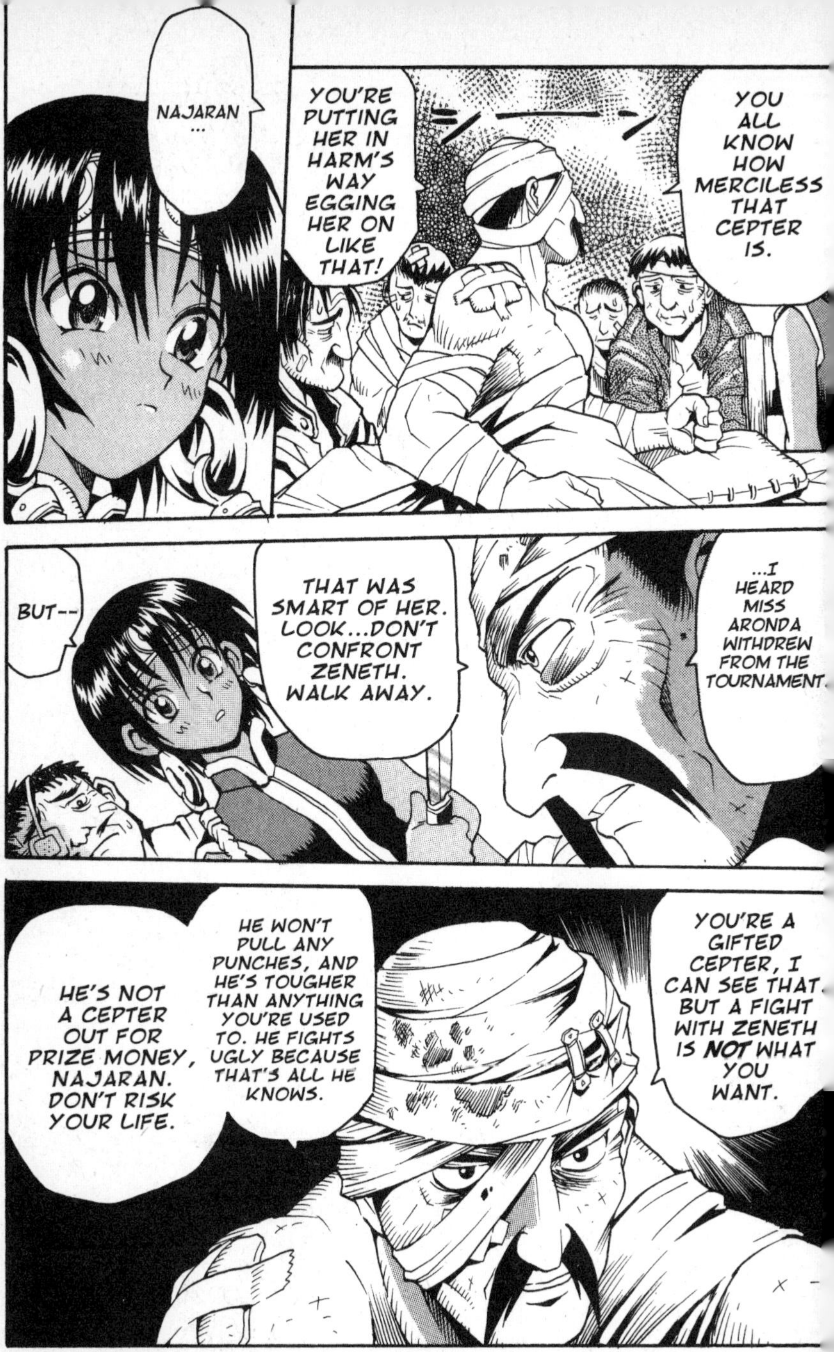
YOU ALL KNOW HOW MERCILESS THAT CEPTER IS.
YOU'RE PUTTING HER IN HARM'S WAY EGGING HER ON LIKE THAT!
NAJARAN ...
...I HEARD MISS ARONDA WITHDREW FROM THE TOURNAMENT.
THAT WAS SMART OF HER. LOOK...DON'T CONFRONT ZENETH. WALK AWAY.
BUT--
YOU'RE A GIFTED CEPTER, I CAN SEE THAT. BUT A FIGHT WITH ZENETH IS **NOT** WHAT YOU WANT.
HE WON'T PULL ANY PUNCHES, AND HE'S TOUGHER THAN ANYTHING YOU'RE USED TO. HE FIGHTS UGLY BECAUSE THAT'S ALL HE KNOWS.
HE'S NOT A CEPTER OUT FOR PRIZE MONEY, NAJARAN. DON'T RISK YOUR LIFE.

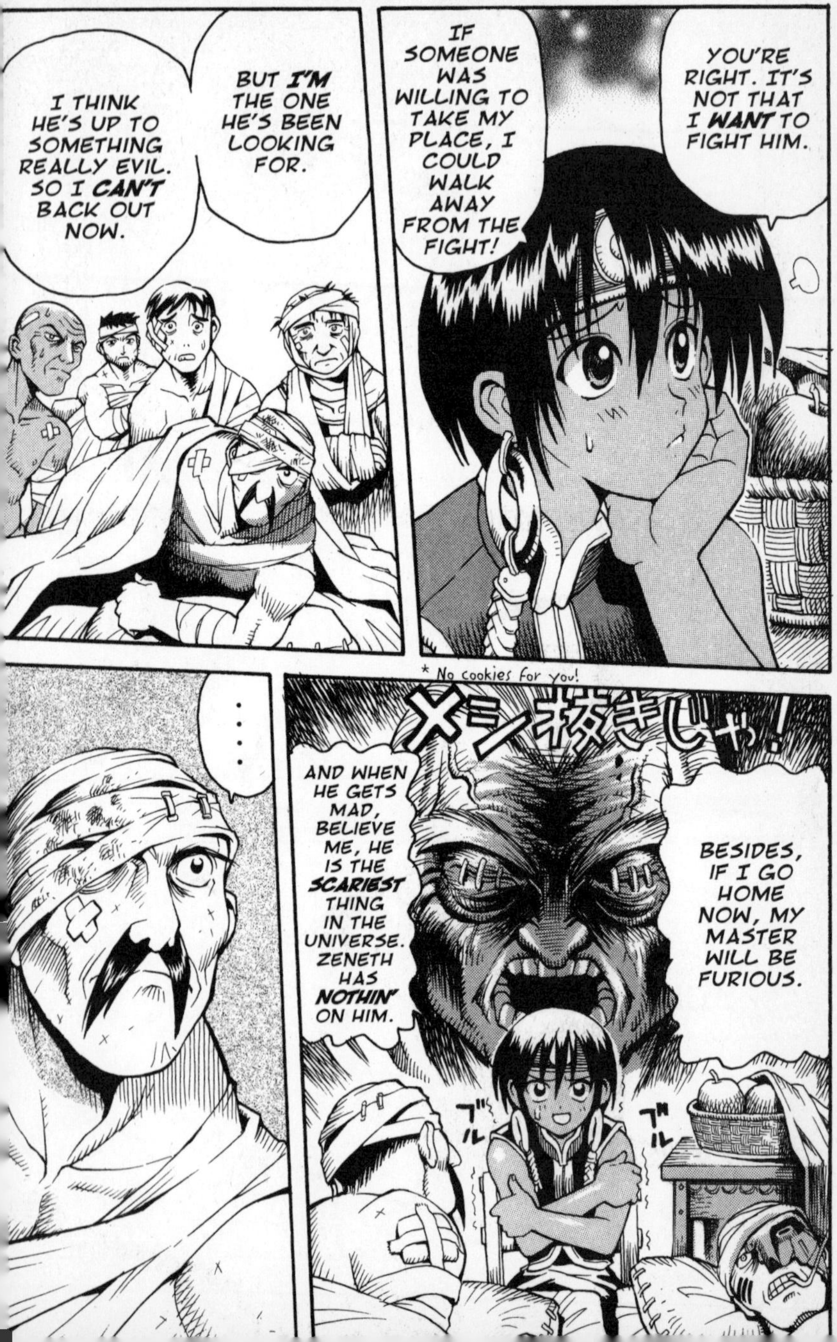
YOU'RE RIGHT. IT'S NOT THAT I WANT TO FIGHT HIM.
IF SOMEONE WAS WILLING TO TAKE MY PLACE, I COULD WALK AWAY FROM THE FIGHT!
BUT I'M THE ONE HE'S BEEN LOOKING FOR.
I THINK HE'S UP TO SOMETHING REALLY EVIL. SO I CAN'T BACK OUT NOW.
* No cookies for you!
メシ抜きじゃ!
BESIDES, IF I GO HOME NOW, MY MASTER WILL BE FURIOUS.
AND WHEN HE GETS MAD, BELIEVE ME, HE IS THE SCARIEST THING IN THE UNIVERSE. ZENETH HAS NOTHIN' ON HIM.
ブル
ブル
.....

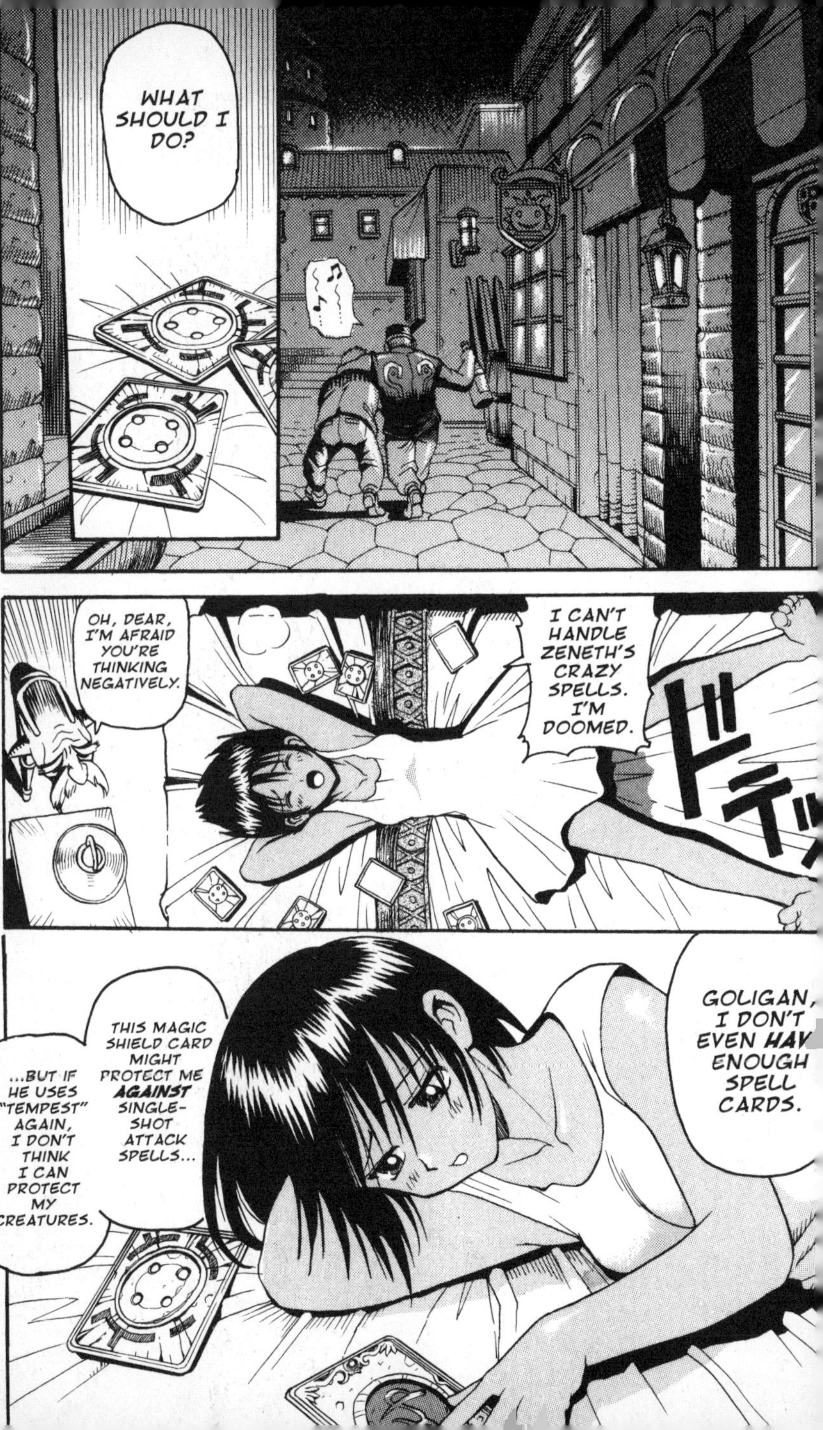
WHAT SHOULD I DO?
I CAN'T HANDLE ZENETH'S CRAZY SPELLS. I'M DOOMED.
ドテッ
OH, DEAR, I'M AFRAID YOU'RE THINKING NEGATIVELY.
GOLIGAN, I DON'T EVEN **HAV** ENOUGH SPELL CARDS.
THIS MAGIC SHIELD CARD MIGHT PROTECT ME ***AGAINST*** SINGLE-SHOT ATTACK SPELLS...
...BUT IF HE USES "TEMPEST" AGAIN, I DON'T THINK I CAN PROTECT MY CREATURES.

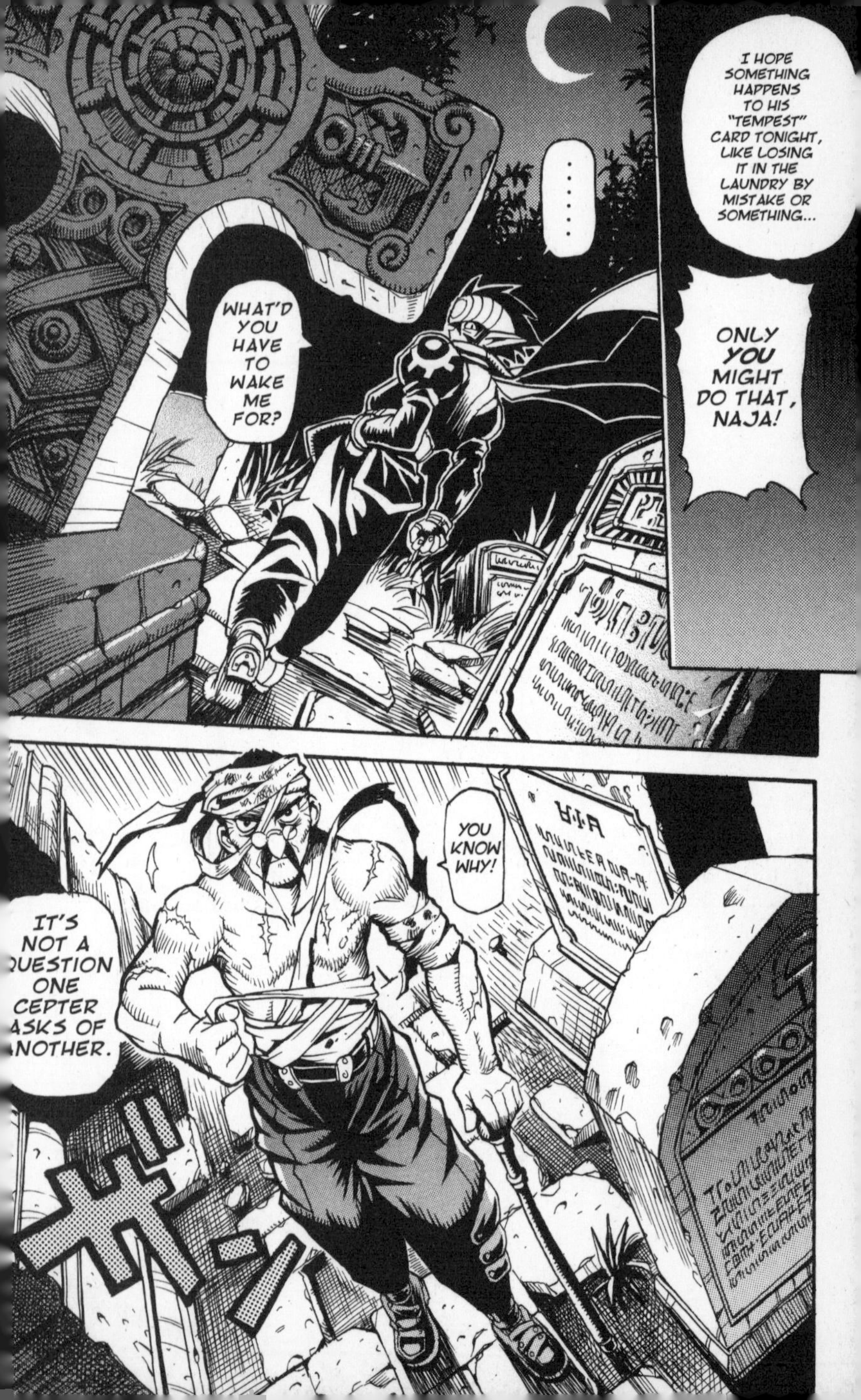
I HOPE SOMETHING HAPPENS TO HIS "TEMPEST" CARD TONIGHT, LIKE LOSING IT IN THE LAUNDRY BY MISTAKE OR SOMETHING...
ONLY *YOU* MIGHT DO THAT, NAJA!
......
WHAT'D YOU HAVE TO WAKE ME FOR?
YOU KNOW WHY!
IT'S NOT A QUESTION ONE CEPTER ASKS OF ANOTHER.

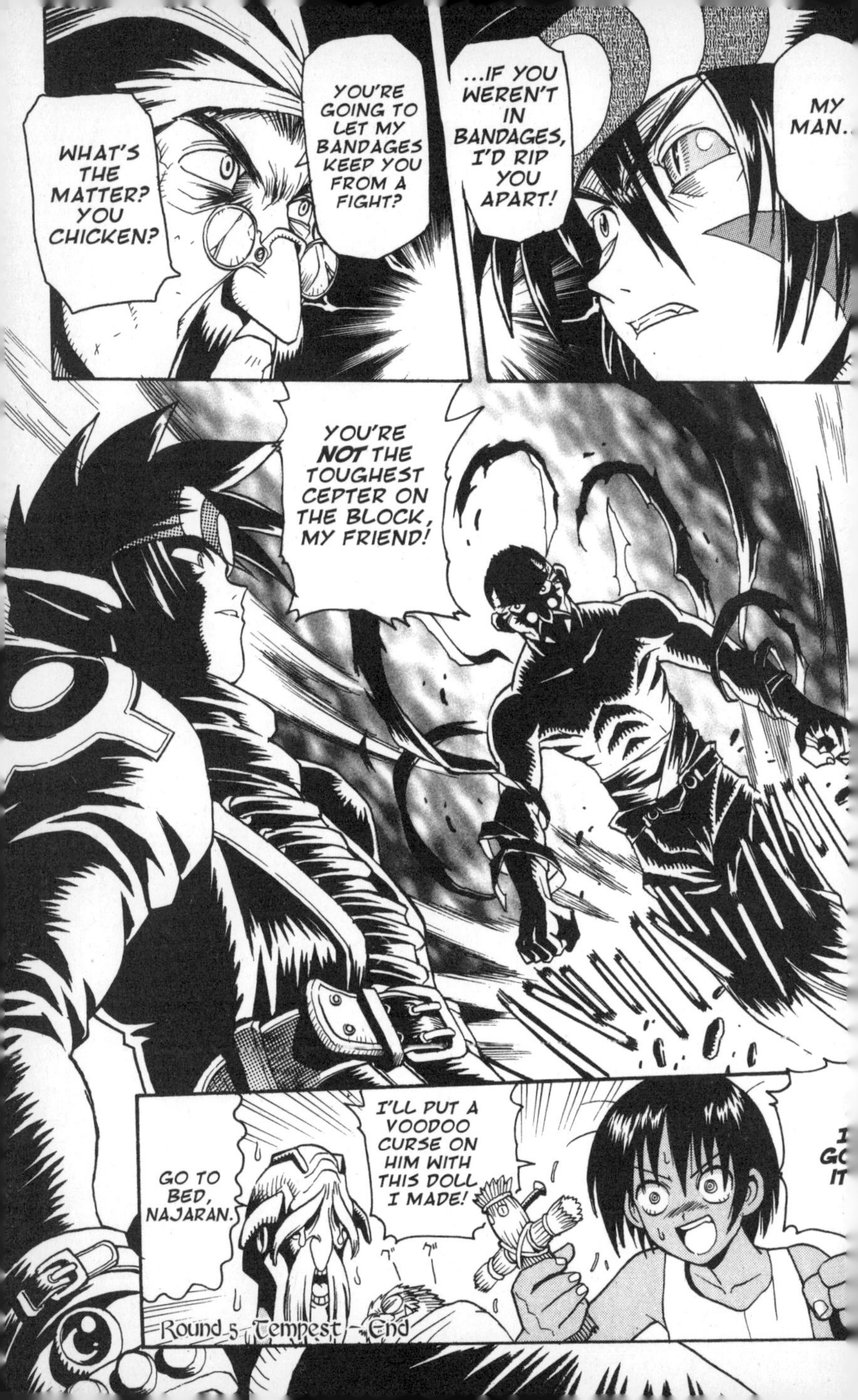
MY MAN...
...IF YOU WEREN'T IN BANDAGES, I'D RIP YOU APART!
YOU'RE GOING TO LET MY BANDAGES KEEP YOU FROM A FIGHT?
WHAT'S THE MATTER? YOU CHICKEN?
YOU'RE **NOT** THE TOUGHEST CEPTER ON THE BLOCK, MY FRIEND!
I'LL PUT A VOODOO CURSE ON HIM WITH THIS DOLL I MADE!
GO TO BED, NAJARAN.
Round 5 Tempest End

Aeolian Creatures

AEOLIAN CREATURES ARE BEASTS OF THE AIR. THEY ARE
SWIFT FIGHTERS WITH NOTABLE ATTACK CAPABILITIES.
STAYING AHEAD OF THE OPPONENT IS CRUCIAL IN A
CEPTER BATTLE!

Najaran

Knight

Attack Points	50
Defense Points	40
Summon Cost	110
Special Abilities	Especially effective against Dragon creatures.

THIS IS ONE OF THE MOST POWERFUL CARDS IN MY BOOK IN TERMS OF BOTH ATTACK AND DEFENSE POINTS. HE IS ALSO GOOD AT PEELING POTATOES AND SPLITTING WOOD. SUCH A USEFUL CREATURE!

Gremlin

Attack Points	20
Defense Points	30
Summon Cost	70
Special Abilities	Destruction of Item Cards.

HE IS A LITTLE DEVIL WHO CAN DESTROY AN OPPONENT'S ITEM CARDS. REGARDLESS OF HIS LOW ATTACK POINTS, HE IS SOMETIMES VERY STRONG AND QUITE USEFUL. UNFORTUNATELY, HE IS NOT MUCH FOR DOMESTIC CHORES BECAUSE HE TENDS TO DESTROY THINGS AROUND THE HOUSE. YIKES!

Thunderbeak

Attack Points	50
Defense Points	20
Summon Cost	70
Special Abilities	Preemptive attacks, can paralyze Water creatures.

HE IS A THUNDER DRAGON WHOSE ATTACK POINTS ARE AS HIGH AS A KNIGHT'S. RIDING HIM IS NOT VERY COMFORTABLE, BECAUSE YOU SOMETIMES FEEL ELECTRIC SHOCKS FROM HIM!

Eidolon

Attack Points	30
Defense Points	40
Summon Cost	50
Special Abilities	None.

ALTHOUGH HE LOOKS LIKE NOTHING MORE THAN A FLUFFY SNOWMAN, HE IS ACTUALLY PRETTY POWERFUL. HE CAN BEAT GOBLINS VERY EASILY. HE ALSO HELPS ME WASH DISHES SINCE HE IS ALSO A WALKING SCRUB BRUSH!

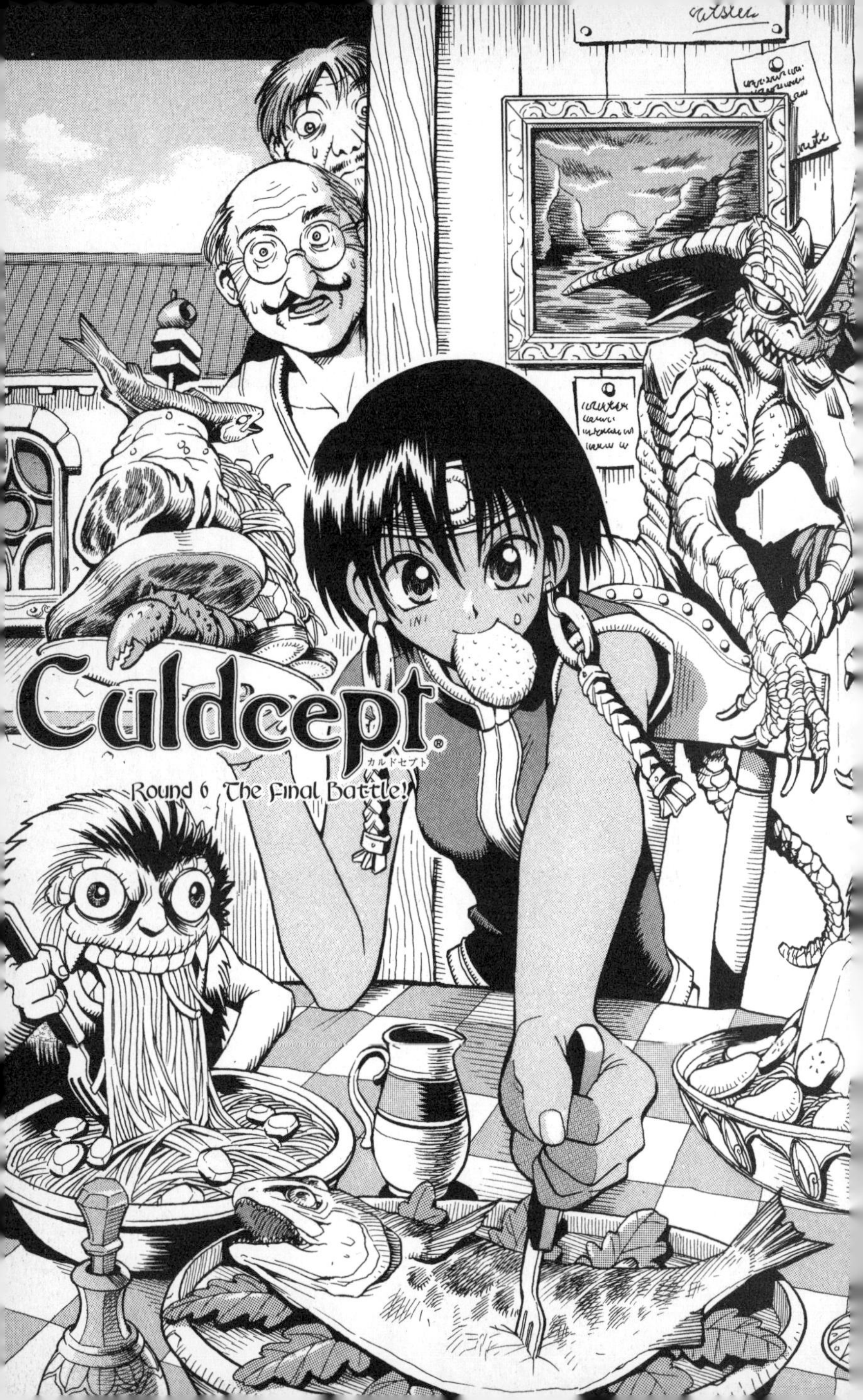
Culdcept®
カルドセプト
Round 6 The Final Battle!

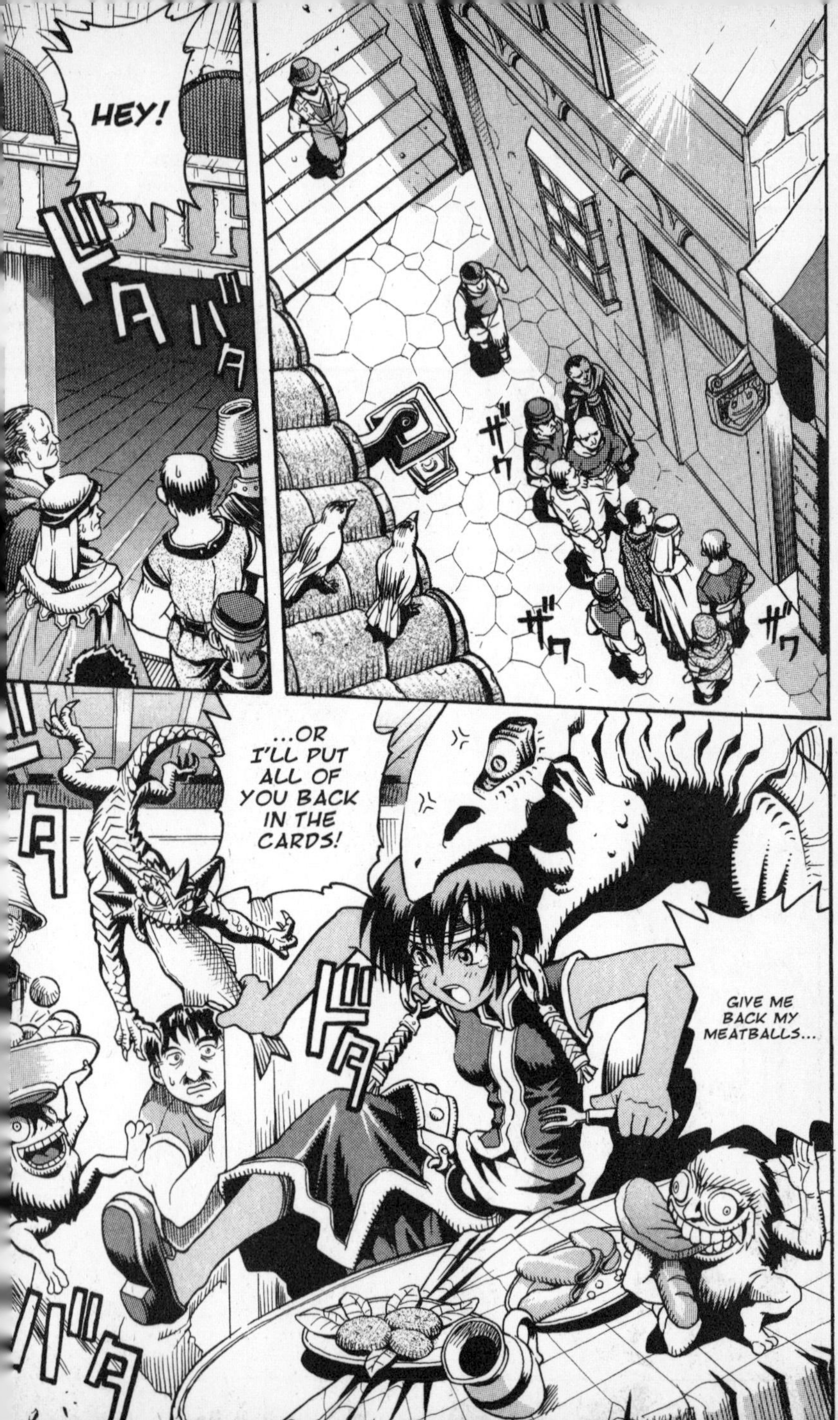
ザワ
ザワ
ザワ
HEY!
ドタバタ
GIVE ME BACK MY MEATBALLS...
...OR I'LL PUT ALL OF YOU BACK IN THE CARDS!
ドタ
ドタ
バタ

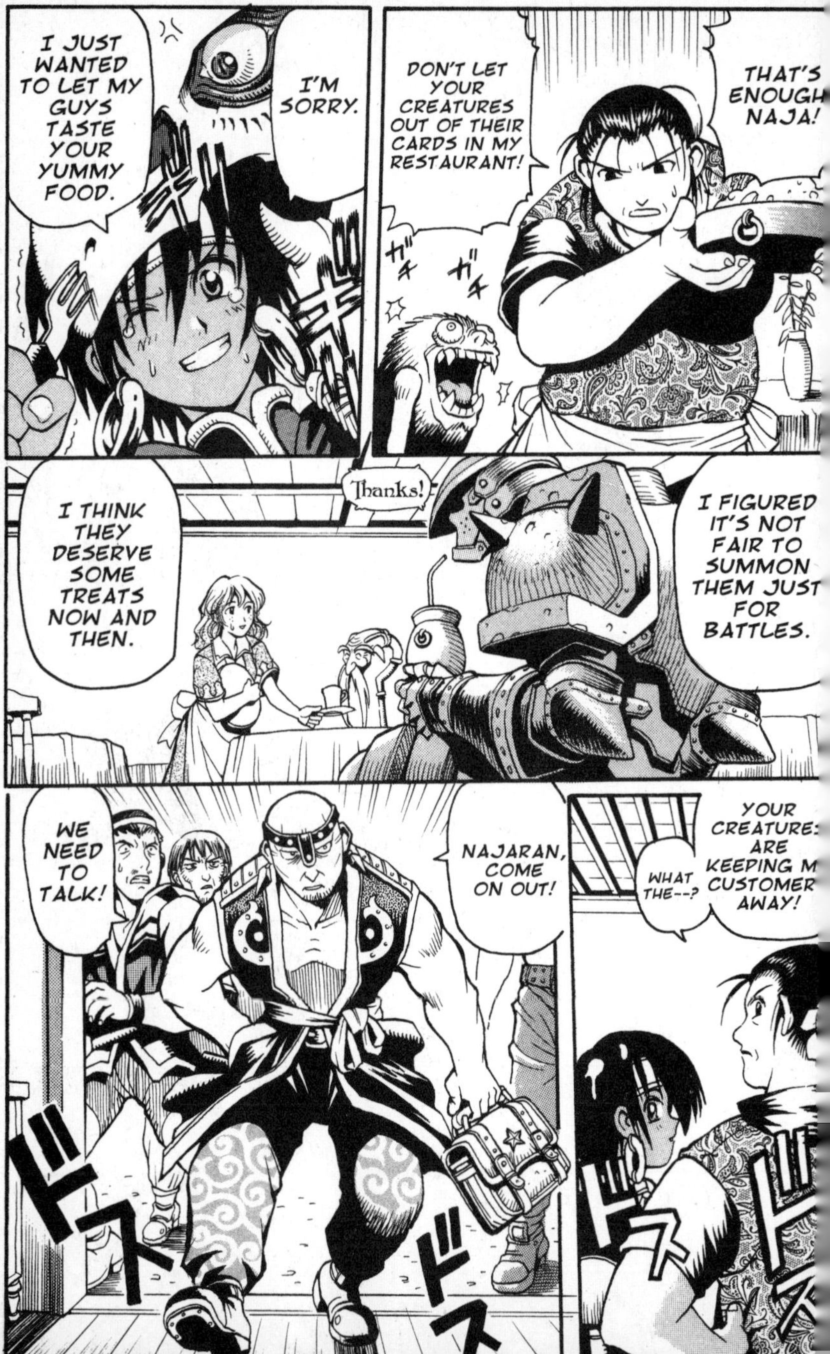
THAT'S ENOUGH NAJA!
DON'T LET YOUR CREATURES OUT OF THEIR CARDS IN MY RESTAURANT!
ガチ
ガチ
I'M SORRY.
I JUST WANTED TO LET MY GUYS TASTE YOUR YUMMY FOOD.
I FIGURED IT'S NOT FAIR TO SUMMON THEM JUST FOR BATTLES.
Thanks!
I THINK THEY DESERVE SOME TREATS NOW AND THEN.
YOUR CREATURE ARE KEEPING M CUSTOMER AWAY!
WHAT THE--?
ドス
ドス
NAJARAN, COME ON OUT!
WE NEED TO TALK!
ドス
ドス

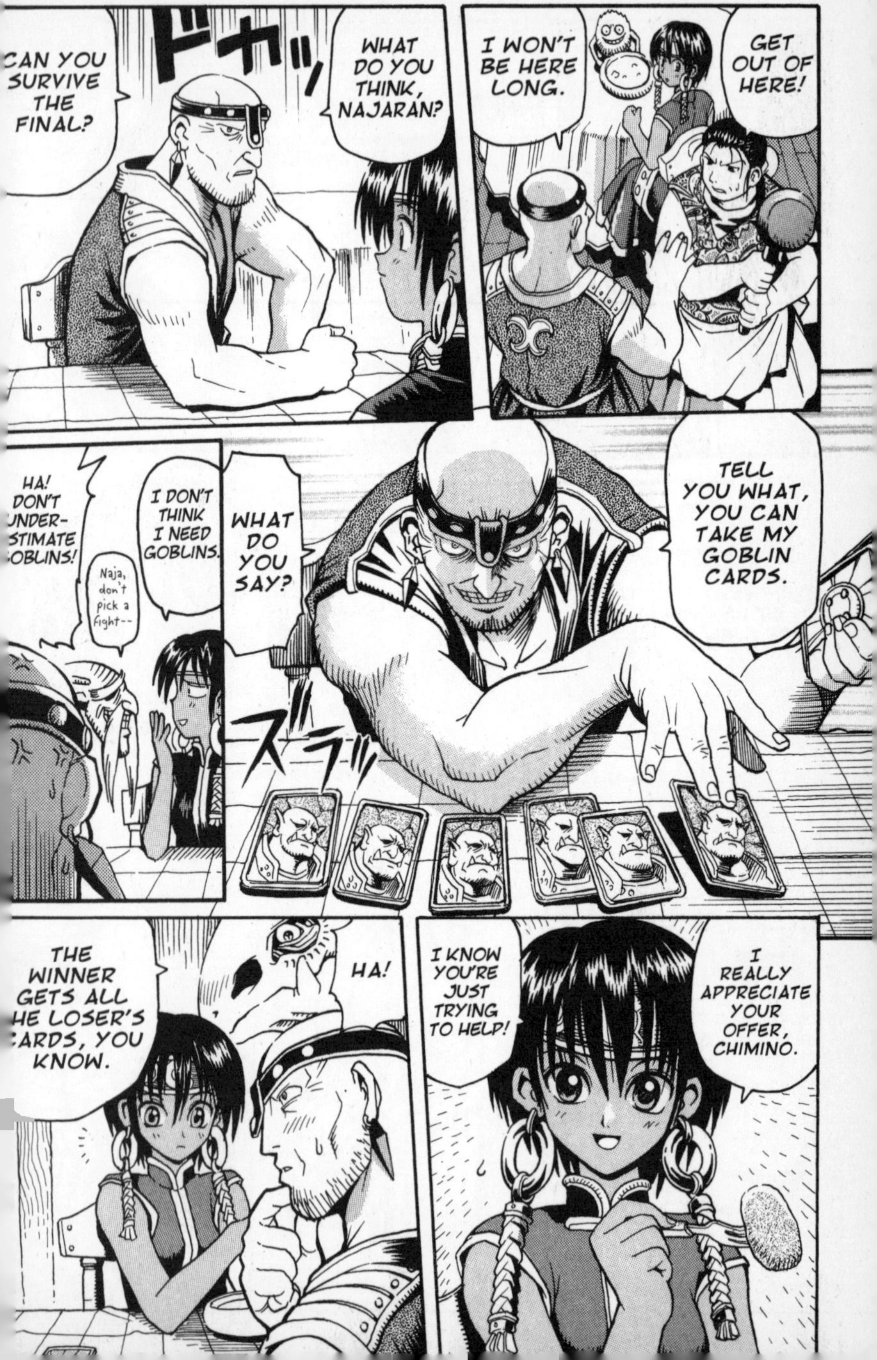
GET OUT OF HERE!
I WON'T BE HERE LONG.
ドカッ
WHAT DO YOU THINK, NAJARAN?
CAN YOU SURVIVE THE FINAL?
TELL YOU WHAT, YOU CAN TAKE MY GOBLIN CARDS.
WHAT DO YOU SAY?
ズラッ
I DON'T THINK I NEED GOBLINS.
HA! DON'T UNDER- STIMATE OBLINS!
Naja, don't pick a fight--
I REALLY APPRECIATE YOUR OFFER, CHIMINO.
I KNOW YOU'RE JUST TRYING TO HELP!
HA!
THE WINNER GETS ALL HE LOSER'S ARDS, YOU KNOW.

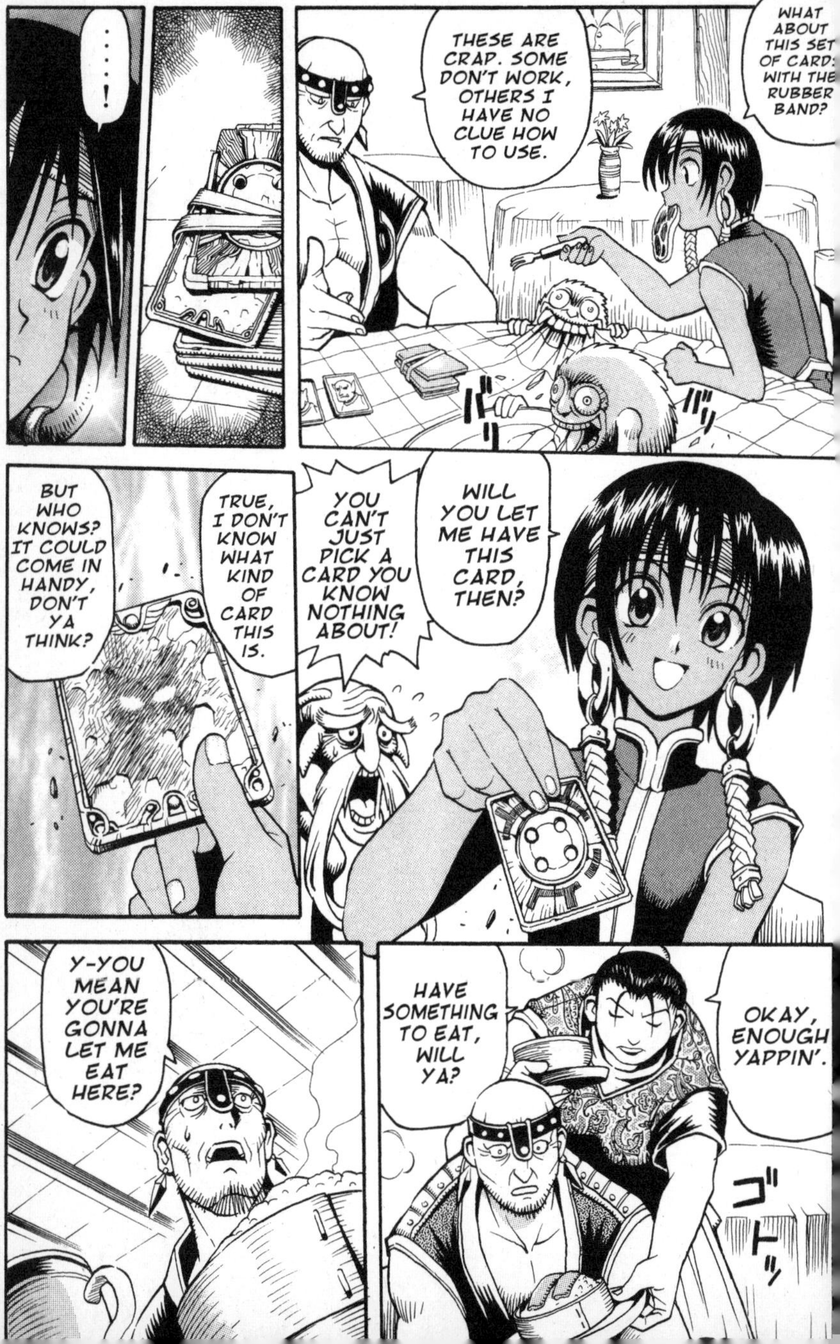
WHAT ABOUT THIS SET OF CARDS WITH THE RUBBER BAND?
THESE ARE CRAP. SOME DON'T WORK, OTHERS I HAVE NO CLUE HOW TO USE.
バリ
バリ
……!
WILL YOU LET ME HAVE THIS CARD, THEN?
YOU CAN'T JUST PICK A CARD YOU KNOW NOTHING ABOUT!
TRUE, I DON'T KNOW WHAT KIND OF CARD THIS IS.
BUT WHO KNOWS? IT COULD COME IN HANDY, DON'T YA THINK?
OKAY, ENOUGH YAPPIN'.
HAVE SOMETHING TO EAT, WILL YA?
ゴトッ
Y-YOU MEAN YOU'RE GONNA LET ME EAT HERE?

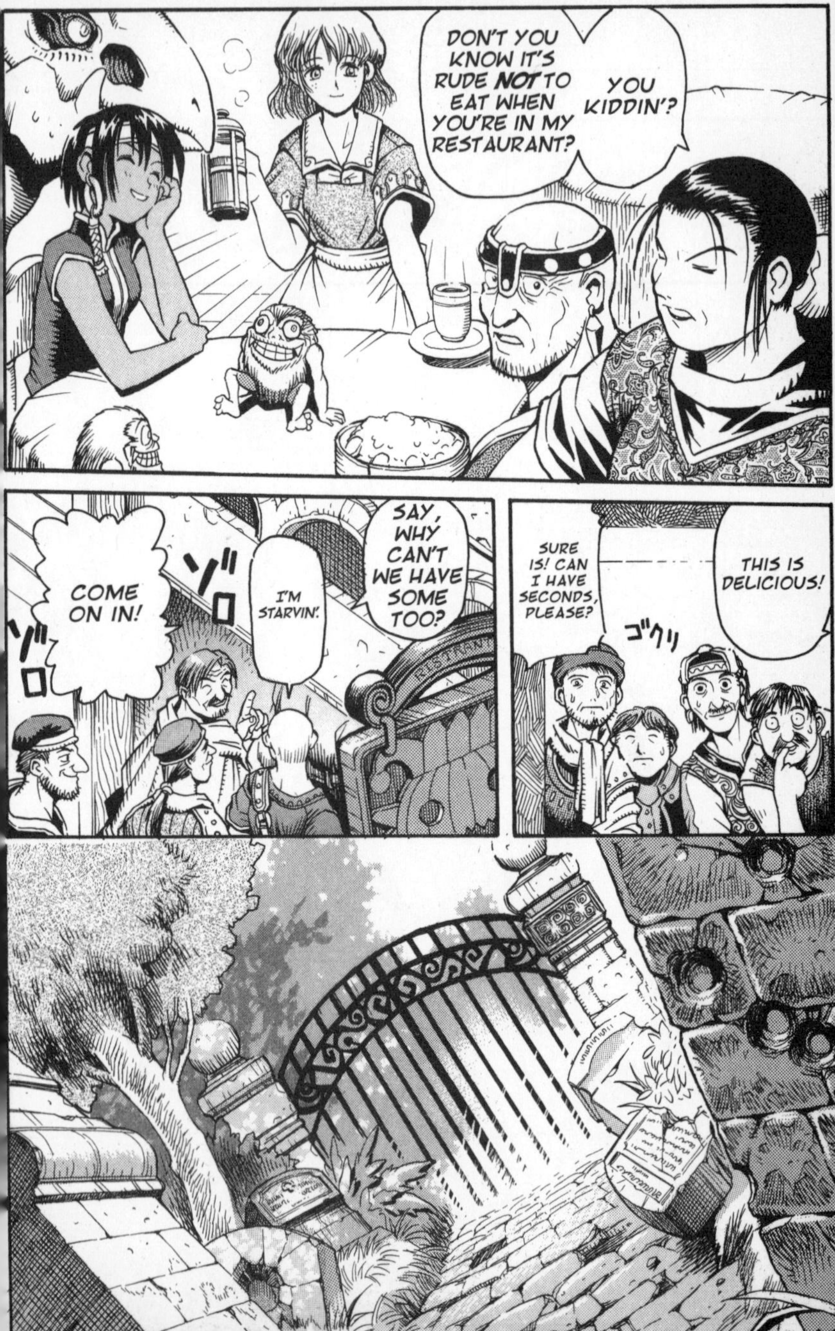
YOU KIDDIN'?
DON'T YOU KNOW IT'S RUDE **NOT** TO EAT WHEN YOU'RE IN MY RESTAURANT?
THIS IS DELICIOUS!
SURE IS! CAN I HAVE SECONDS, PLEASE?
ゴクリ
SAY, WHY CAN'T WE HAVE SOME TOO?
I'M STARVIN'.
ゾロ
COME ON IN!
ゾロ

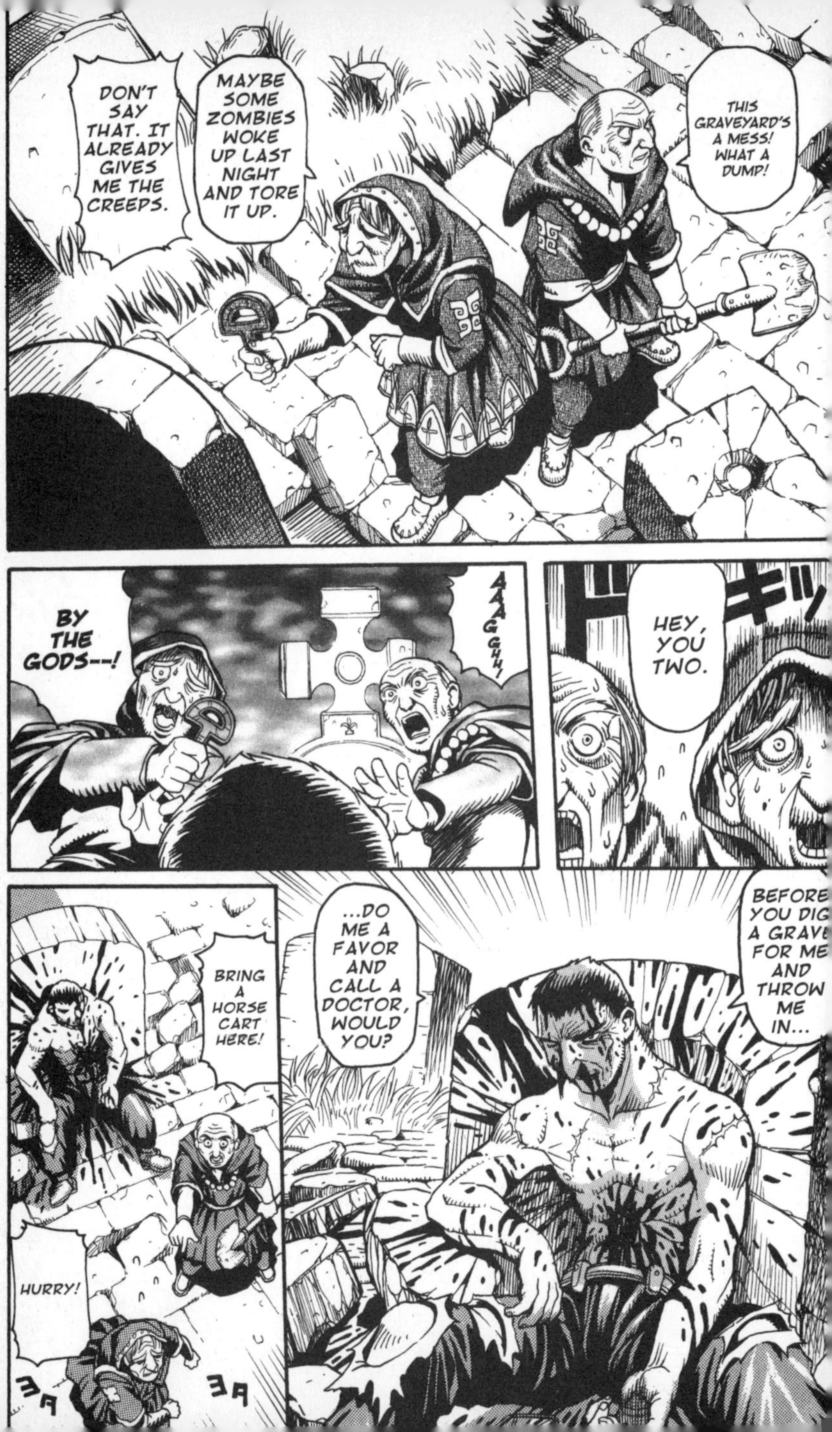
THIS GRAVEYARD'S A MESS! WHAT A DUMP!
MAYBE SOME ZOMBIES WOKE UP LAST NIGHT AND TORE IT UP.
DON'T SAY THAT. IT ALREADY GIVES ME THE CREEPS.
HEY, YOU TWO.
AAAAGGHH!
BY THE GODS--!
BEFORE YOU DIG A GRAVE FOR ME AND THROW ME IN...
...DO ME A FAVOR AND CALL A DOCTOR, WOULD YOU?
BRING A HORSE CART HERE!
HURRY!

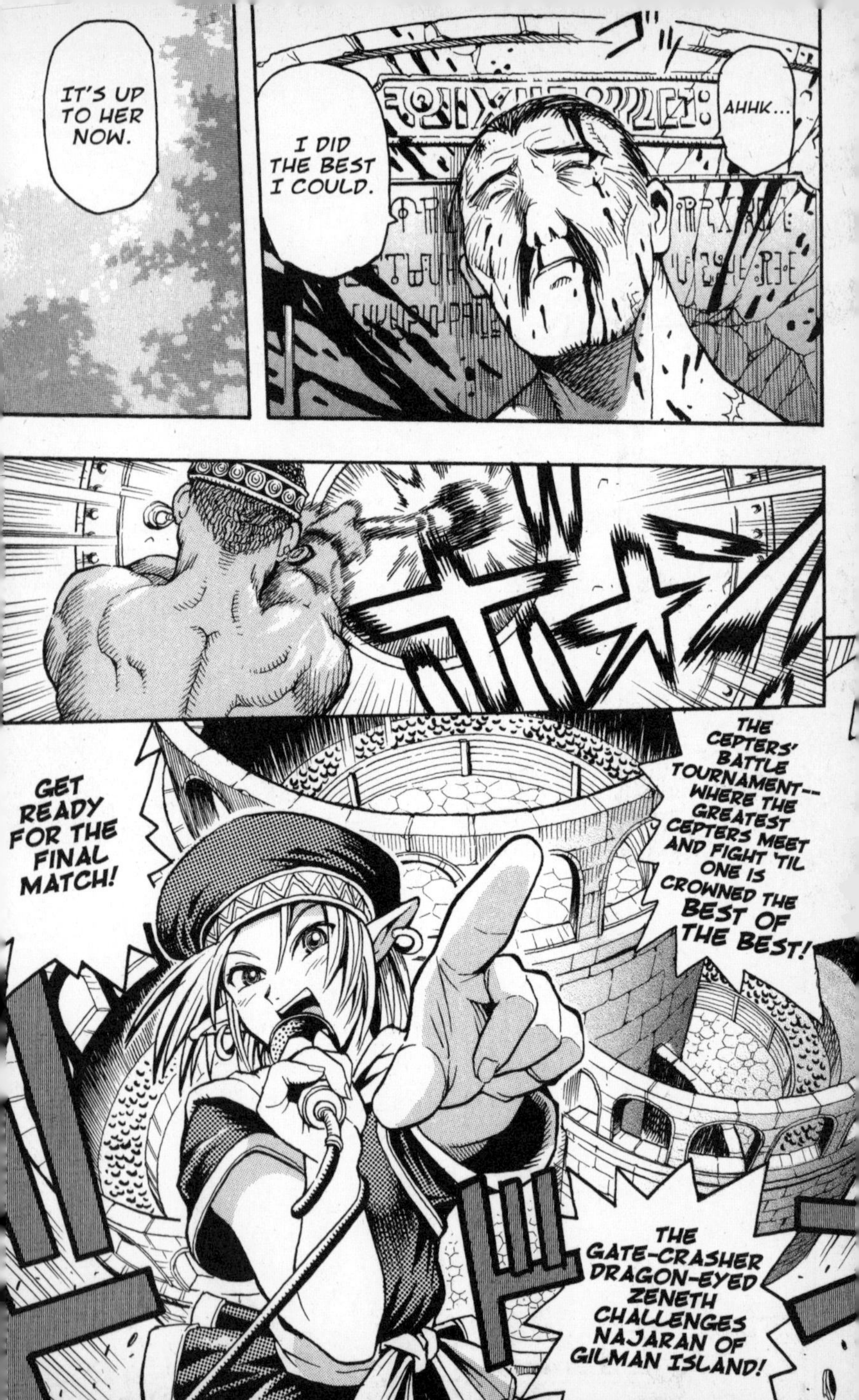
AHHK...
I DID THE BEST I COULD.
IT'S UP TO HER NOW.
THE CEPTERS' BATTLE TOURNAMENT-- WHERE THE GREATEST CEPTERS MEET AND FIGHT 'TIL ONE IS CROWNED THE BEST OF THE BEST!
GET READY FOR THE FINAL MATCH!
THE GATE-CRASHER DRAGON-EYED ZENETH CHALLENGES NAJARAN OF GILMAN ISLAND!

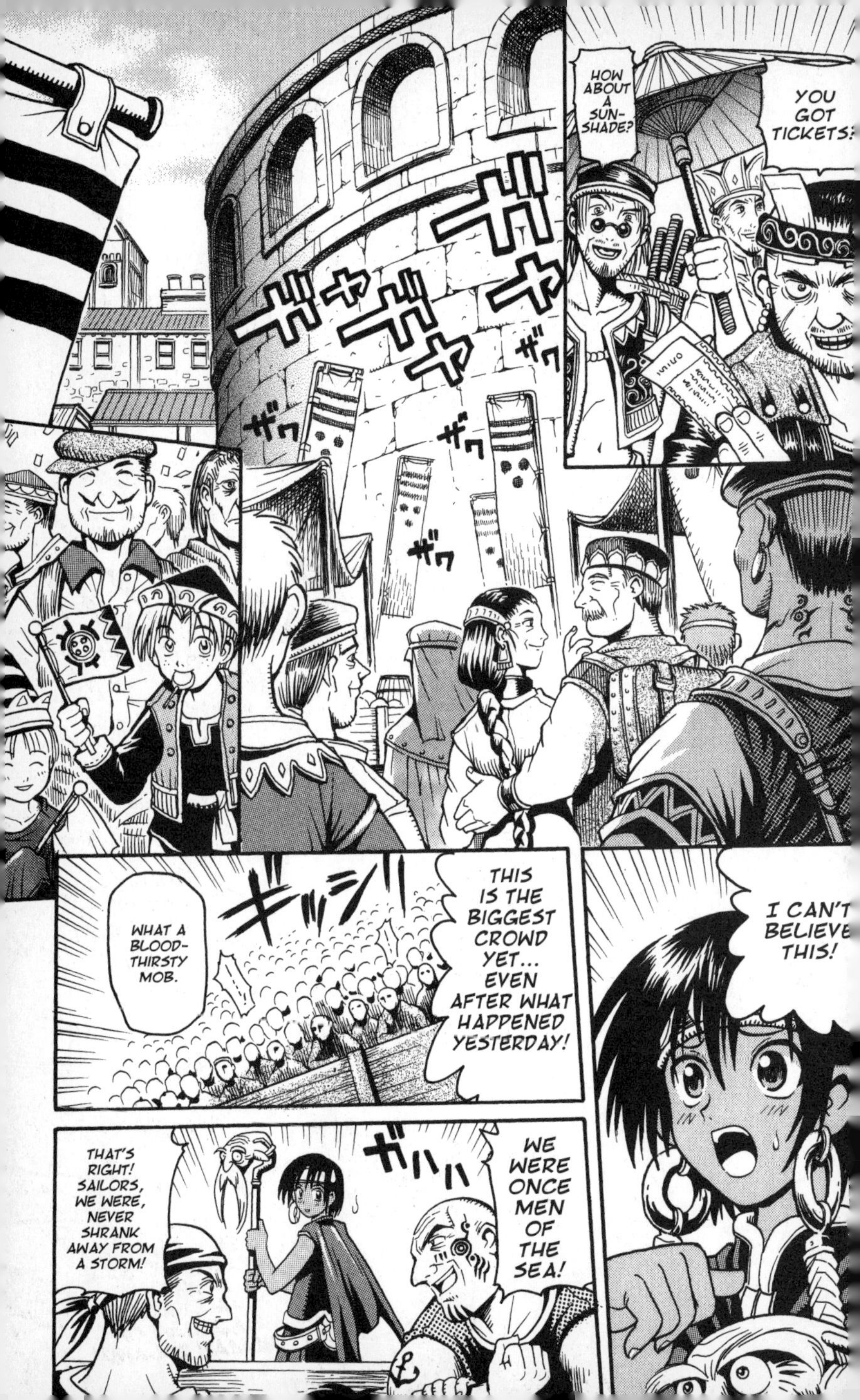
YOU GOT TICKETS!?
HOW ABOUT A SUN-SHADE?
ガヤガヤ
ガヤガヤ
ザワ
ザワ
ザワ
ザワ
I CAN'T BELIEVE THIS!
THIS IS THE BIGGEST CROWD YET... EVEN AFTER WHAT HAPPENED YESTERDAY!
ギッシリ
WHAT A BLOOD-THIRSTY MOB.
WE WERE ONCE MEN OF THE SEA!
ガハハ
THAT'S RIGHT! SAILORS, WE WERE, NEVER SHRANK AWAY FROM A STORM!

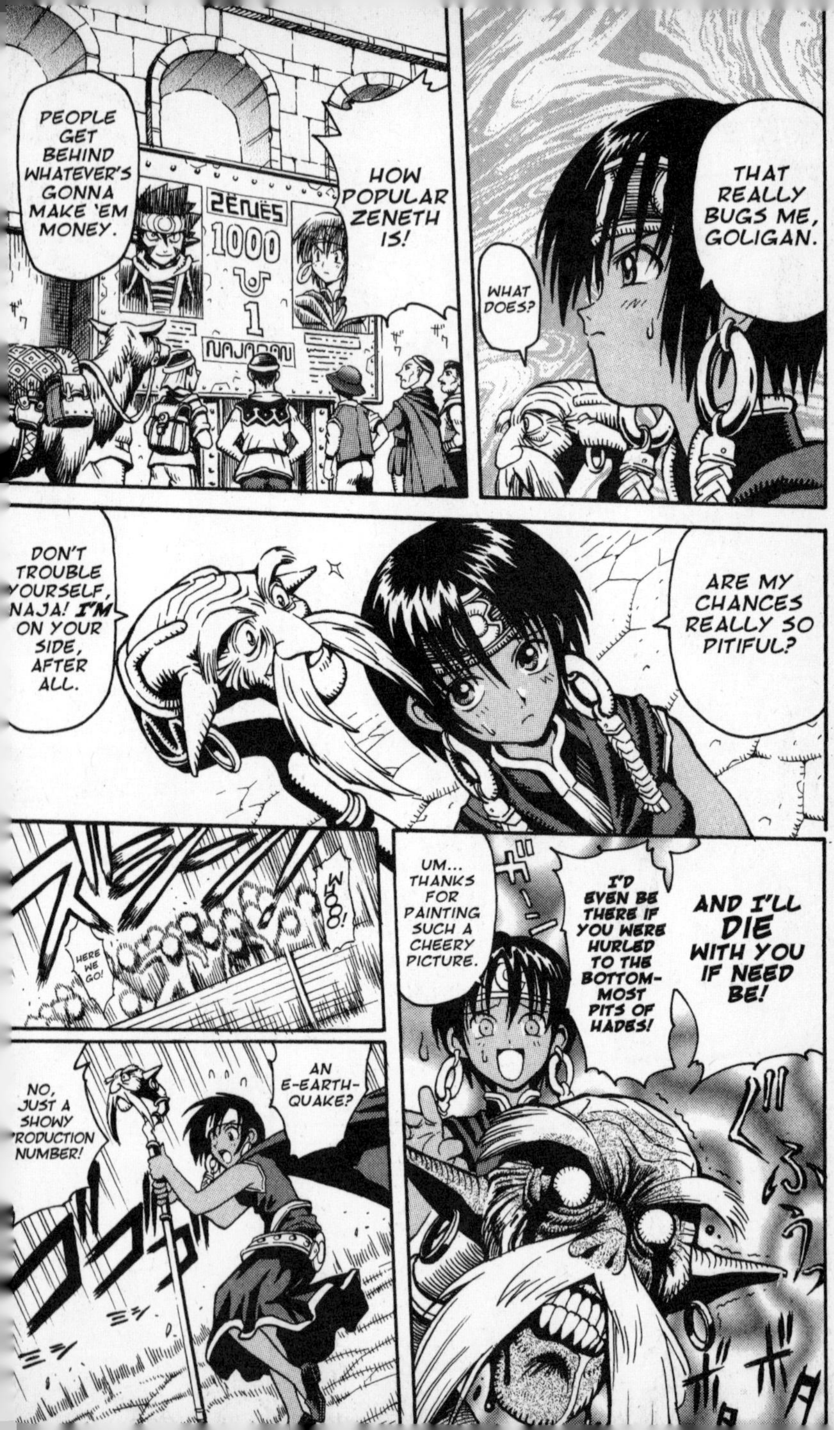
THAT REALLY BUGS ME, GOLIGAN.
WHAT DOES?
HOW POPULAR ZENETH IS!
PEOPLE GET BEHIND WHATEVER'S GONNA MAKE 'EM MONEY.
ARE MY CHANCES REALLY SO PITIFUL?
DON'T TROUBLE YOURSELF, NAJA! **I'M** ON YOUR SIDE, AFTER ALL.
AND I'LL DIE WITH YOU IF NEED BE!
I'D EVEN BE THERE IF YOU WERE HURLED TO THE BOTTOM-MOST PITS OF HADES!
UM... THANKS FOR PAINTING SUCH A CHEERY PICTURE.
WHOO!
HERE WE GO!
AN E-EARTH-QUAKE?
NO, JUST A SHOWY PRODUCTION NUMBER!

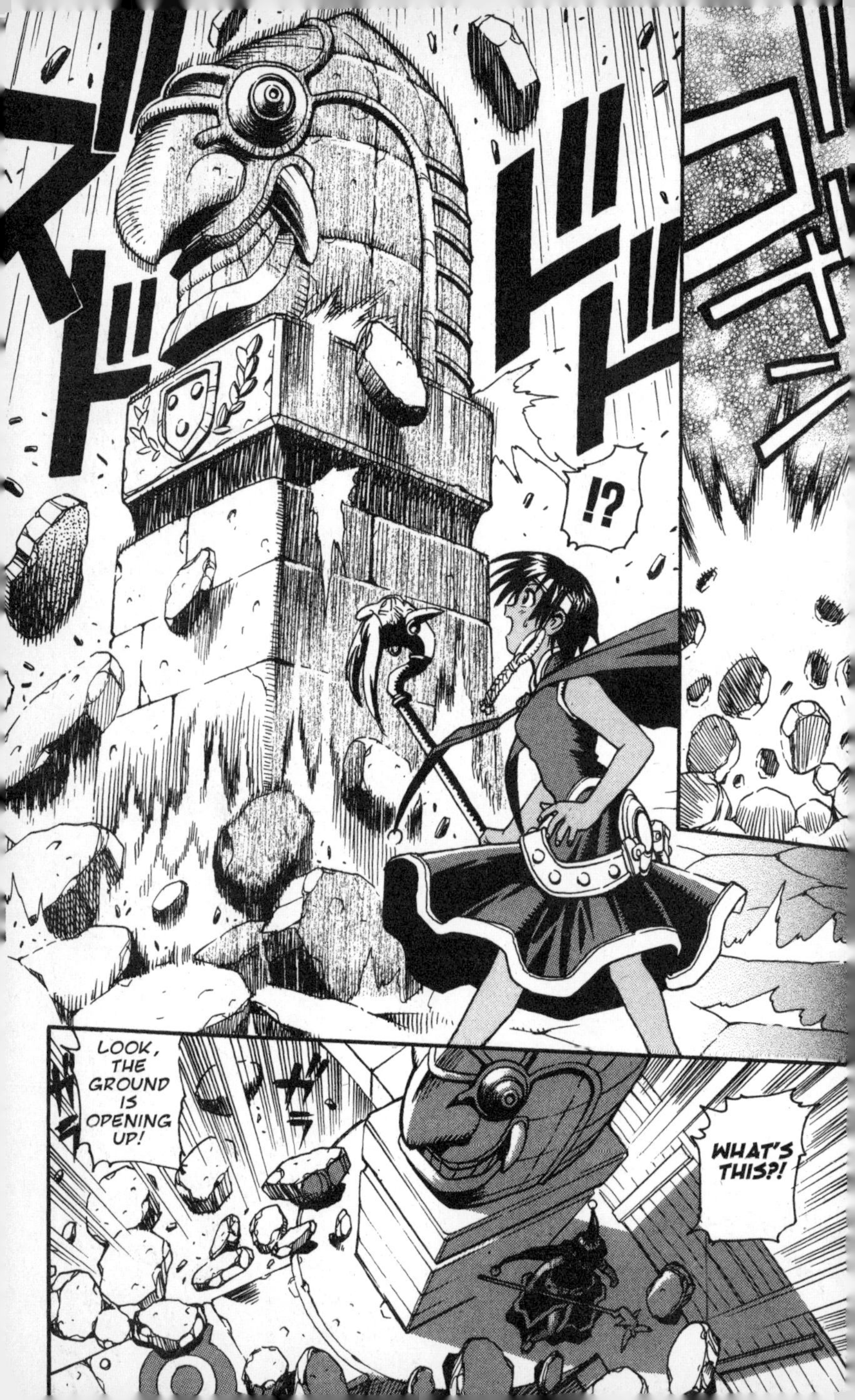
!?
WHAT'S THIS?!
LOOK, THE GROUND IS OPENING UP!

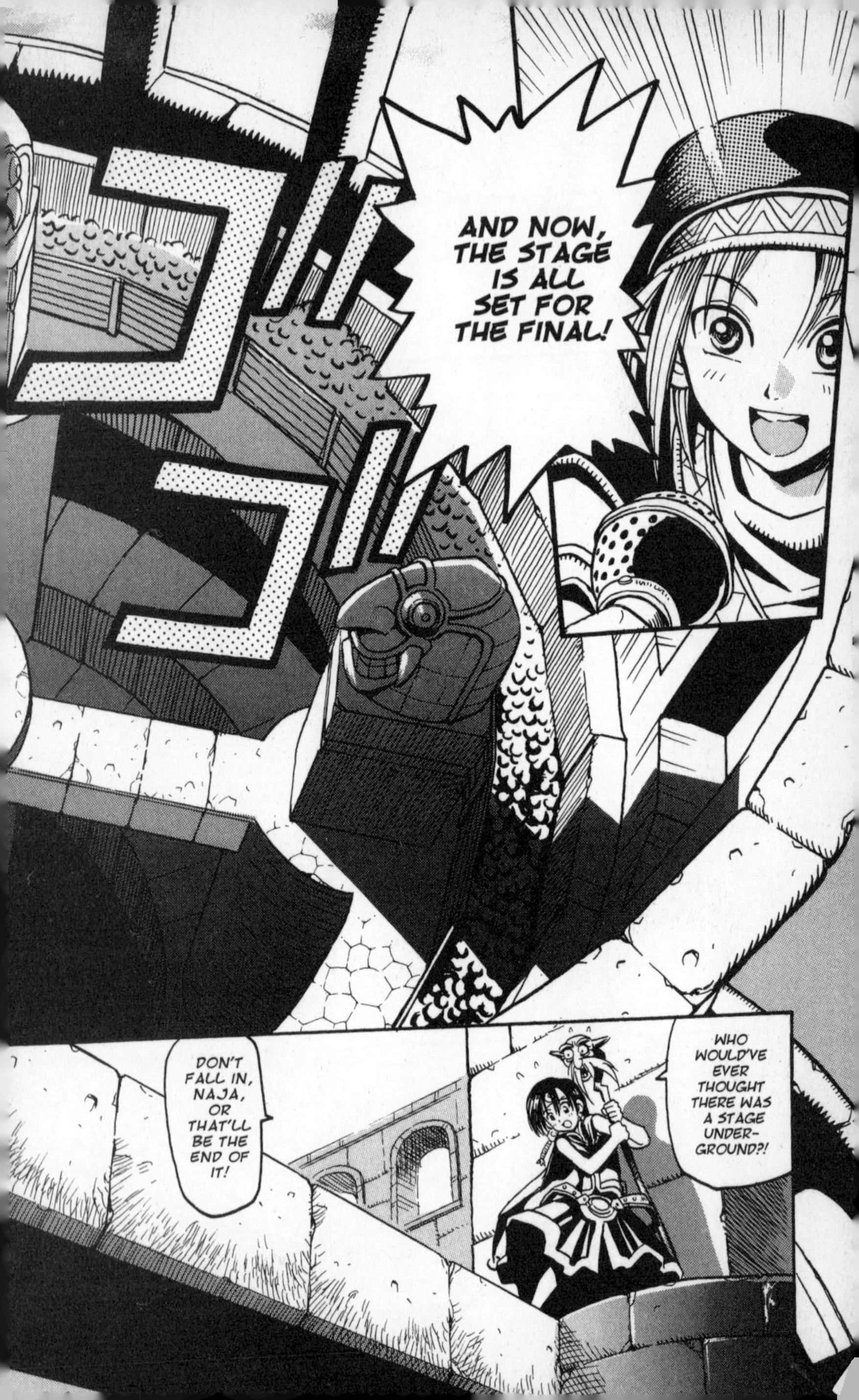
AND NOW, THE STAGE IS ALL SET FOR THE FINAL!
WHO WOULD'VE EVER THOUGHT THERE WAS A STAGE UNDER-GROUND?!
DON'T FALL IN, NAJA, OR THAT'LL BE THE END OF IT!

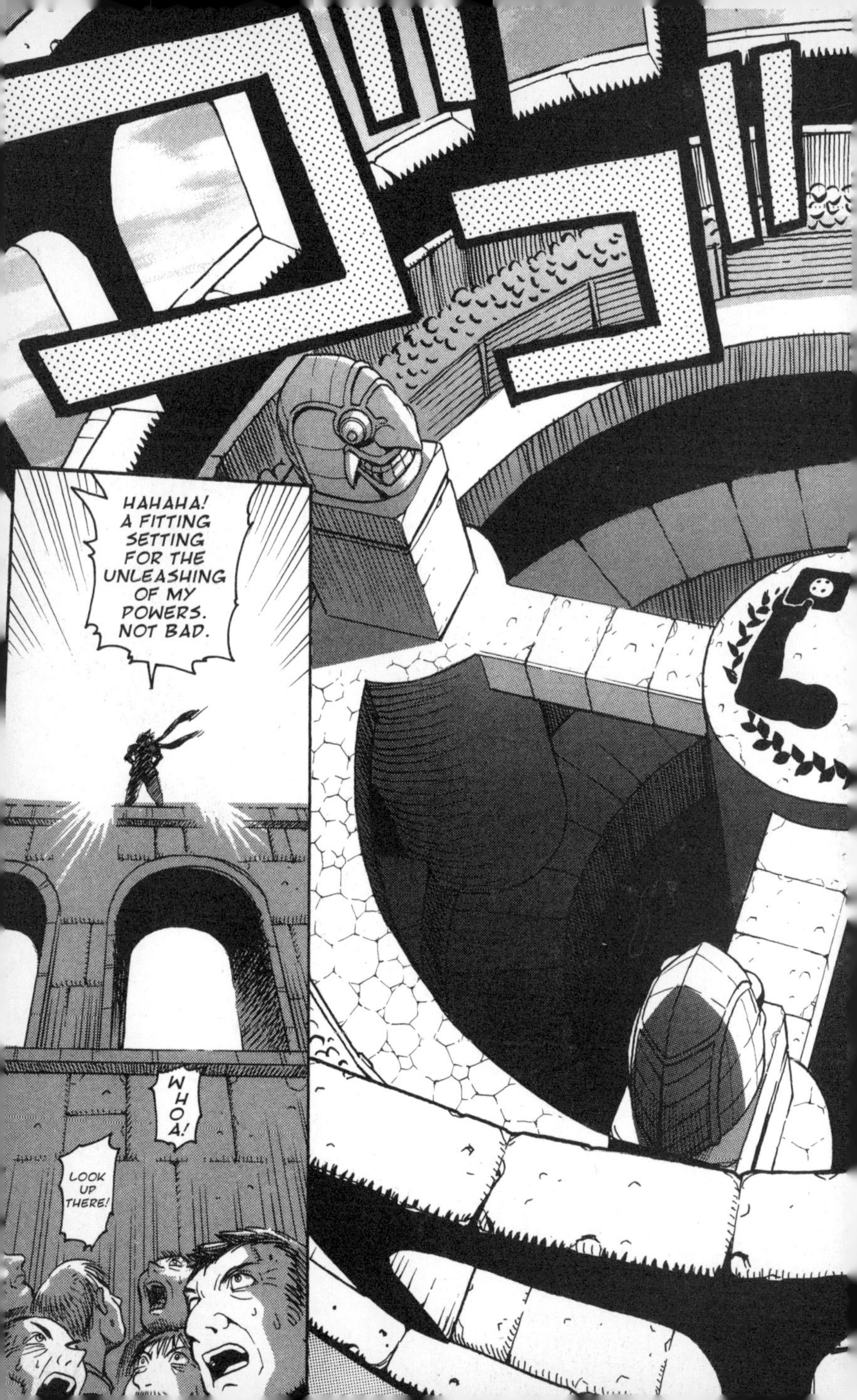
HAHAHA! A FITTING SETTING FOR THE UNLEASHING OF MY POWERS. NOT BAD.
WHOA!
LOOK UP THERE!

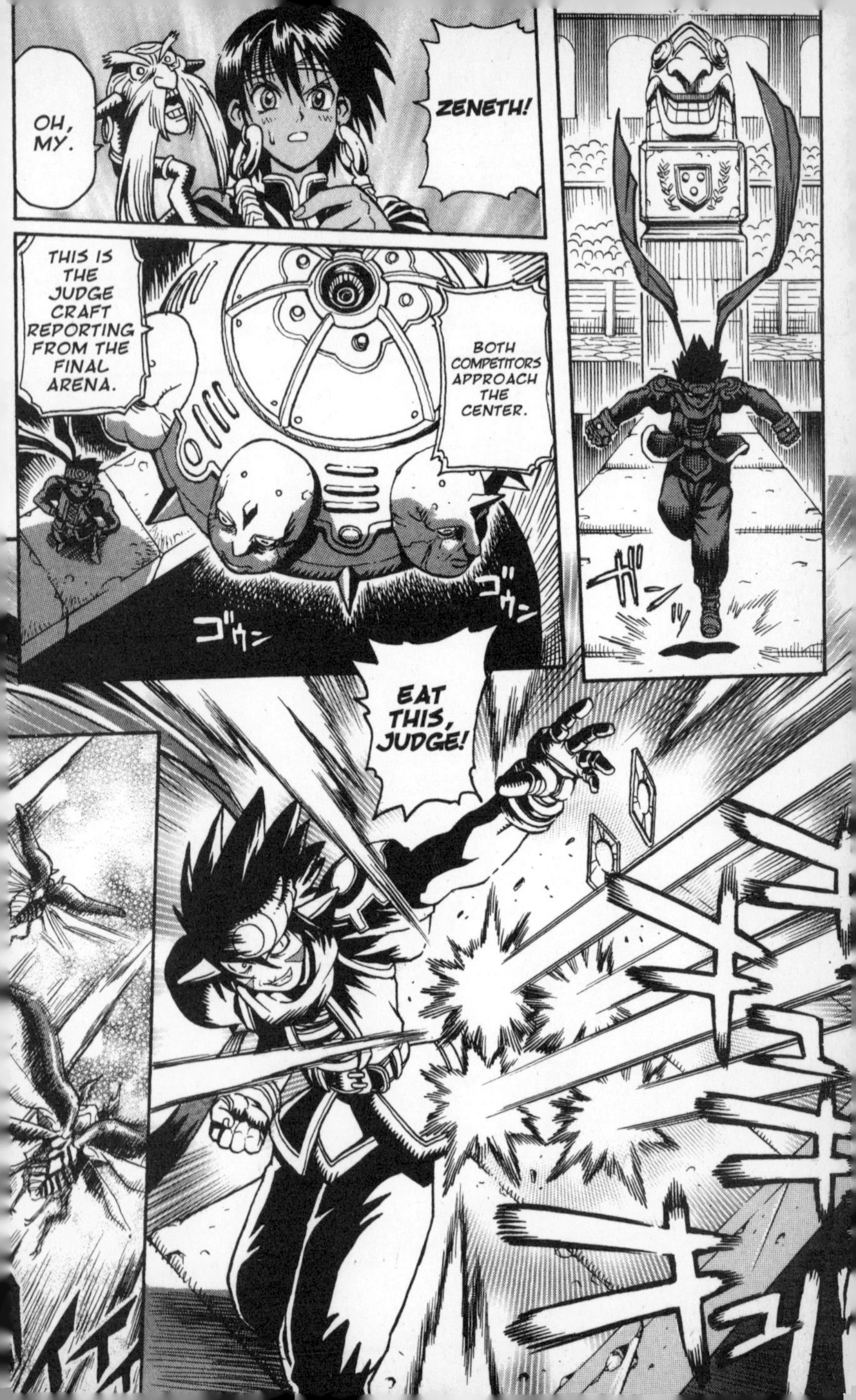
ZENETH!
OH, MY.
THIS IS THE JUDGE CRAFT REPORTING FROM THE FINAL ARENA.
BOTH COMPETITORS APPROACH THE CENTER.
EAT THIS, JUDGE!

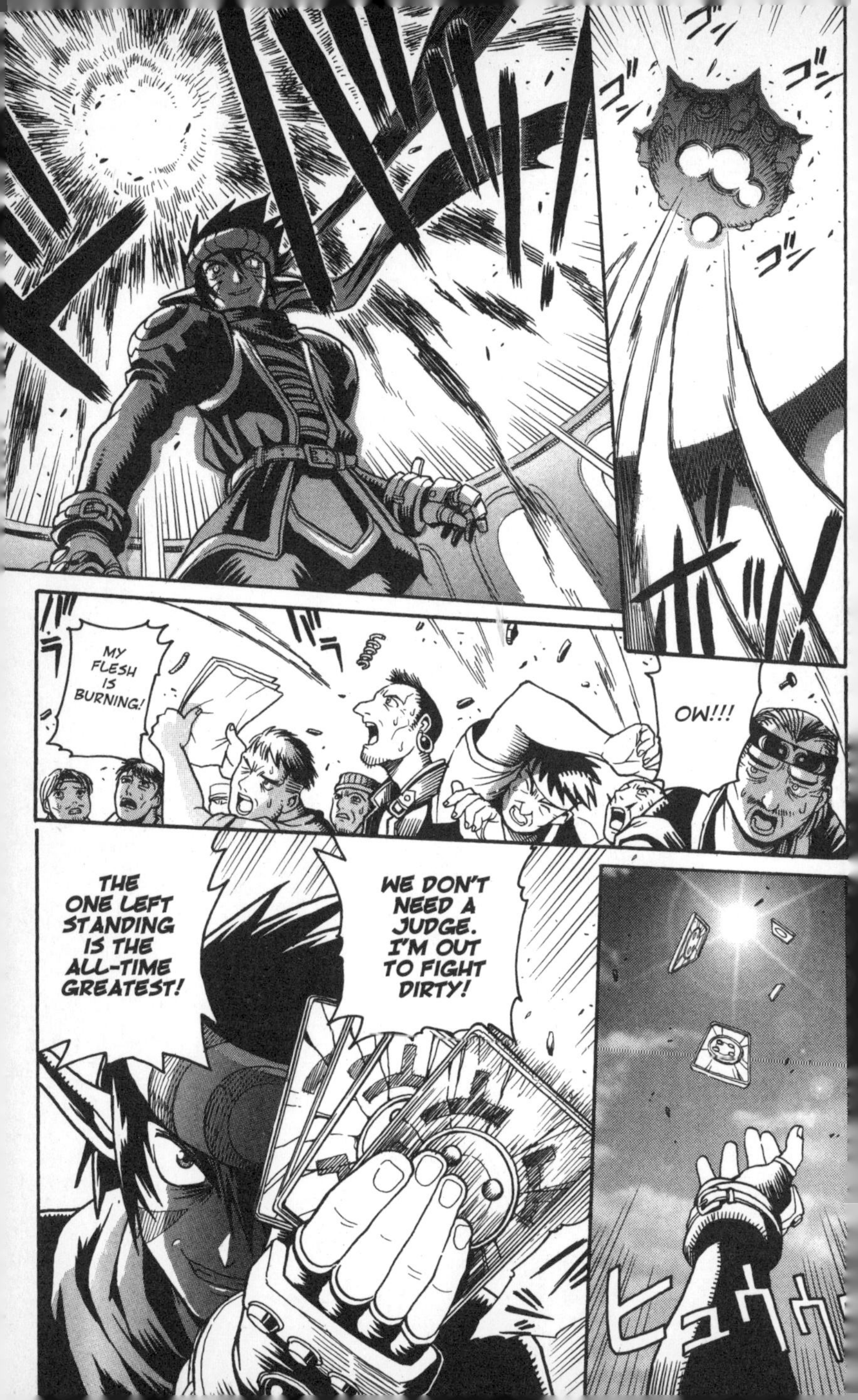
OW!!!
MY FLESH IS BURNING!
WE DON'T NEED A JUDGE. I'M OUT TO FIGHT DIRTY!
THE ONE LEFT STANDING IS THE ALL-TIME GREATEST!

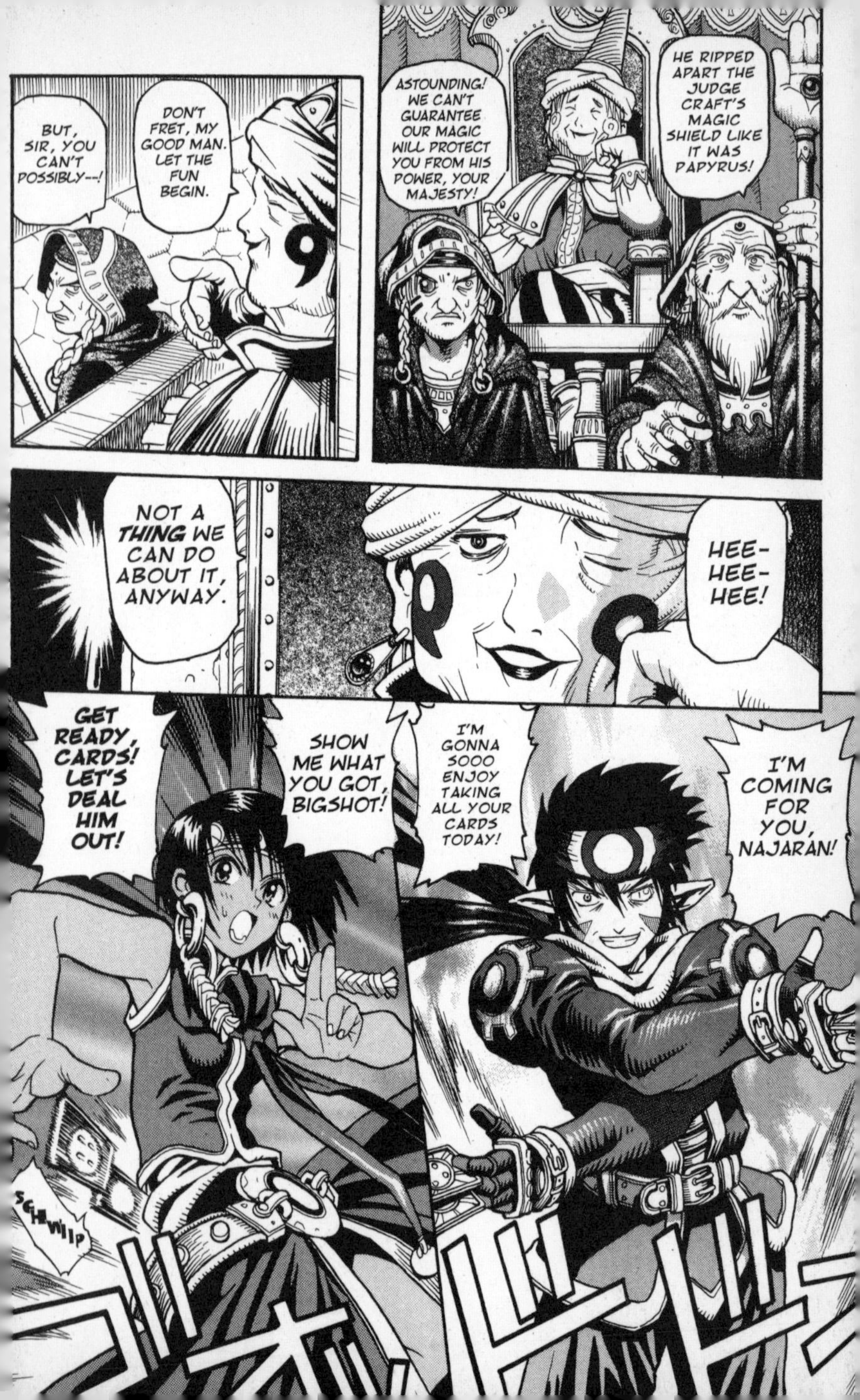
HE RIPPED APART THE JUDGE CRAFT'S MAGIC SHIELD LIKE IT WAS PAPYRUS!
ASTOUNDING! WE CAN'T GUARANTEE OUR MAGIC WILL PROTECT YOU FROM HIS POWER, YOUR MAJESTY!
DON'T FRET, MY GOOD MAN. LET THE FUN BEGIN.
BUT, SIR, YOU CAN'T POSSIBLY--!
HEE-HEE-HEE!
NOT A THING WE CAN DO ABOUT IT, ANYWAY.
I'M COMING FOR YOU, NAJARAN!
I'M GONNA SOOO ENJOY TAKING ALL YOUR CARDS TODAY!
SHOW ME WHAT YOU GOT, BIGSHOT!
GET READY, CARDS! LET'S DEAL HIM OUT!
SCHWIIIP

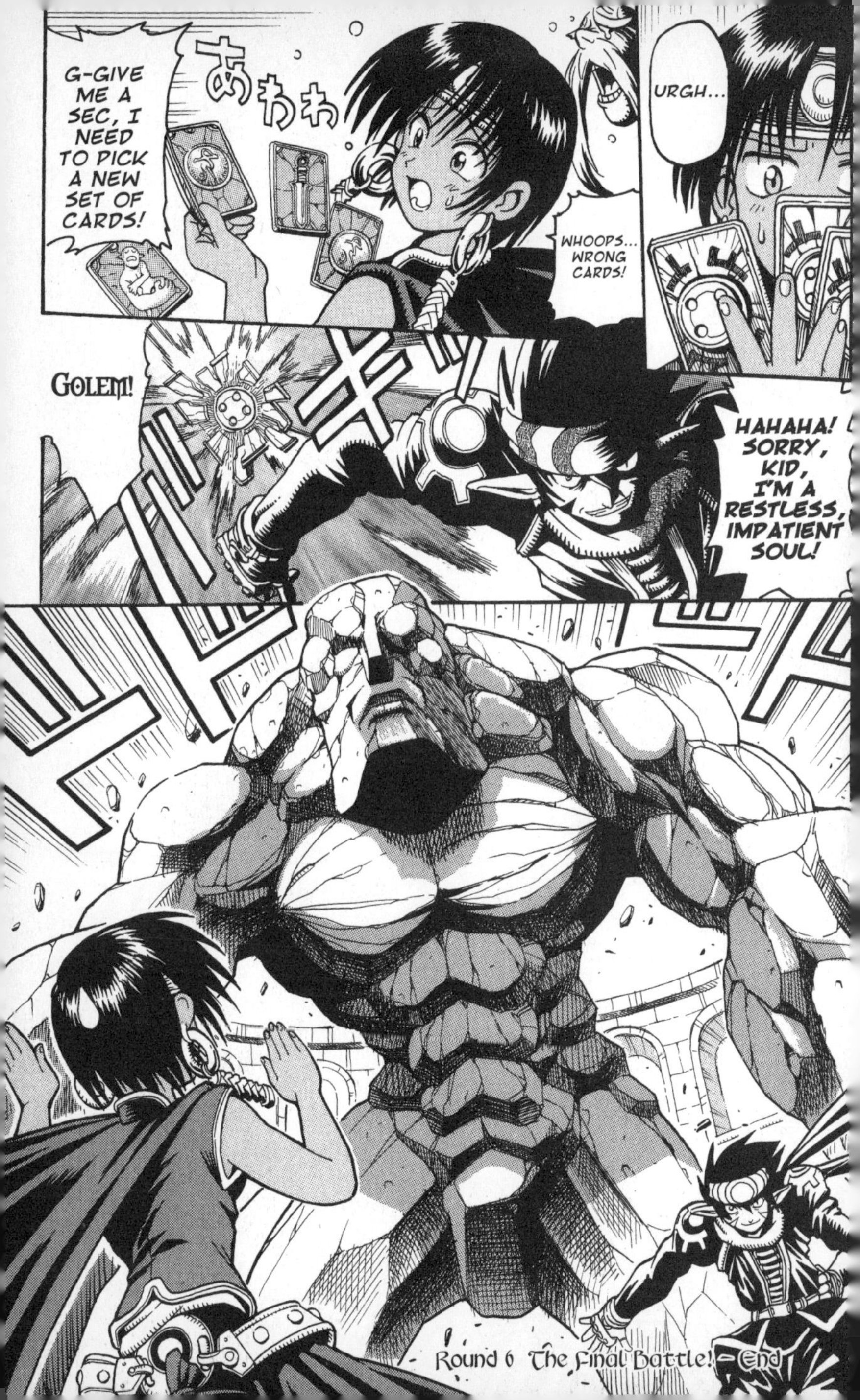
URGH...
WHOOPS... WRONG CARDS!
G-GIVE ME A SEC, I NEED TO PICK A NEW SET OF CARDS!
あわわ
HAHAHA! SORRY, KID, I'M A RESTLESS, IMPATIENT SOUL!
GOLEM!
Round 6 The Final Battle! - End

Neutral Creatures

A MAJOR CHARACTERISTIC OF NEUTRAL-CATEGORY CREATURES IS THAT THEY ARE NCAPABLE OF BEING EMPOWERED BY TERRESTRIAL EFFECTS (FIRE, WATER, AIR, EARTH) NO MATTER HOW FERTILE THEIR BATTLEGROUND. PRETTY INTENSE, EH? ALSO THEIR SUMMON COSTS ARE GENERALLY LOW, SO ALMOST ANYBODY--EVEN ME--CAN SUMMON NEUTRAL CREATURES FROM THEIR CARDS.

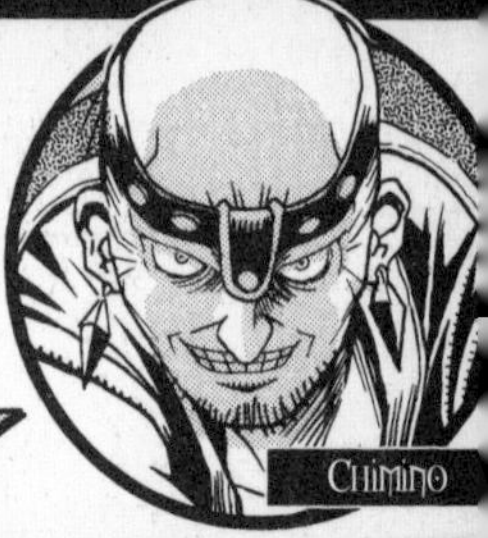

Chimino

Goblin

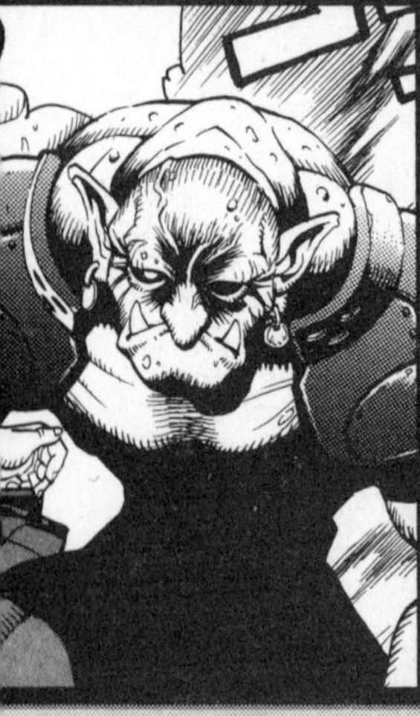

Attack Points
20
Defense Points
30
Summon Cost
10
Special Abilities
None.

GOBLIN IS A MUST-HAVE--BELIEVE ME! THEY SAY A CEPTER'S BATTLE BEGINS WITH A GOBLIN AND ENDS WITH A GOBLIN. YOU GET ME?

Decoy

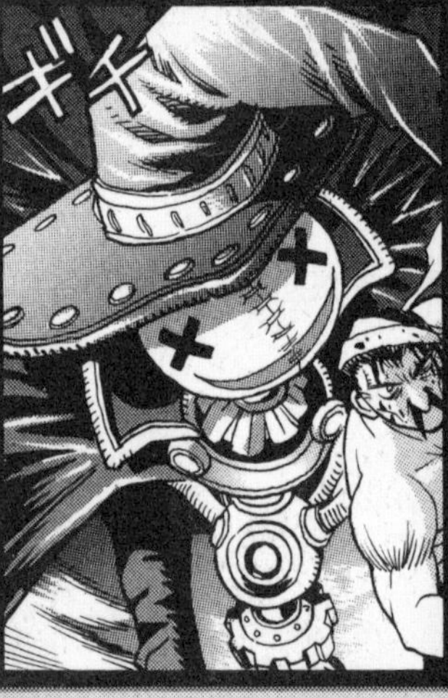
ギギ

Attack Points
0
Defense Points
20
Summon Cost
40
Special Abilities
Bounce opponent's attacks.

THIS IS A MAGIC DOLL UNDER A SPELL. EVERY SINGLE ATTACK LAUNCHED AT HIM WILL BE BOUNCED BACK AT YOUR OPPONENT. IF YOU USE HIM WISELY, YOU CAN EVEN BEAT A VERY POWERFUL OPPONENT WITH A SINGLE BLOW.

Sauriel

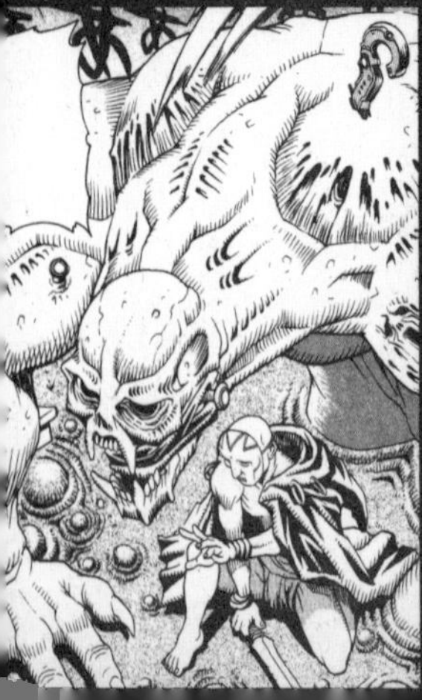

Attack Points
10
Defense Points
30
Summon Cost
55
Special Abilities
Instant lethal attack.

THIS IS A ZOMBIE WHO DEVOURS LIVING SOULS. NO MATTER HOW HIGH THE OPPONENT'S DEFENSE POINTS, HE CAN KILL THE OPPONENT INSTANTLY. SAURIEL IS ONE OF MANY POWERFUL NEUTRAL CREATURES.

Berserker

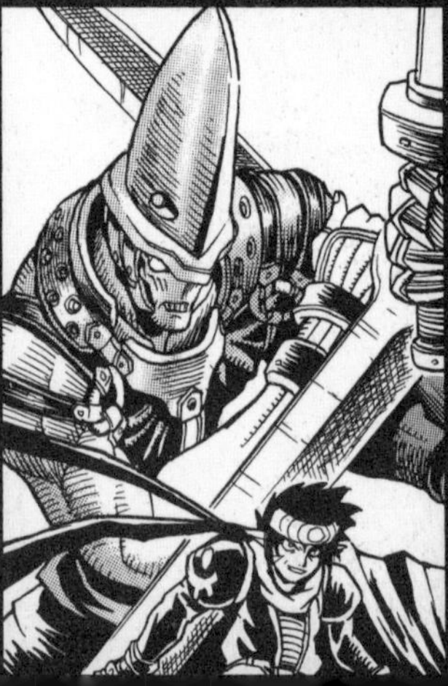

Attack Points
40
Defense Points
50
Summon Cost
60
Special Abilities
Self-damage.

A VERY CRAZY, DESTRUCTIVE CREATURE THAT ZENETH HANDLES. THE CREATURE OFTEN GOES NUTS DURING BATTLE. HE'LL INDISCRIMINATELY HARM ANYBODY NEARBY--EVEN HIMSELF.

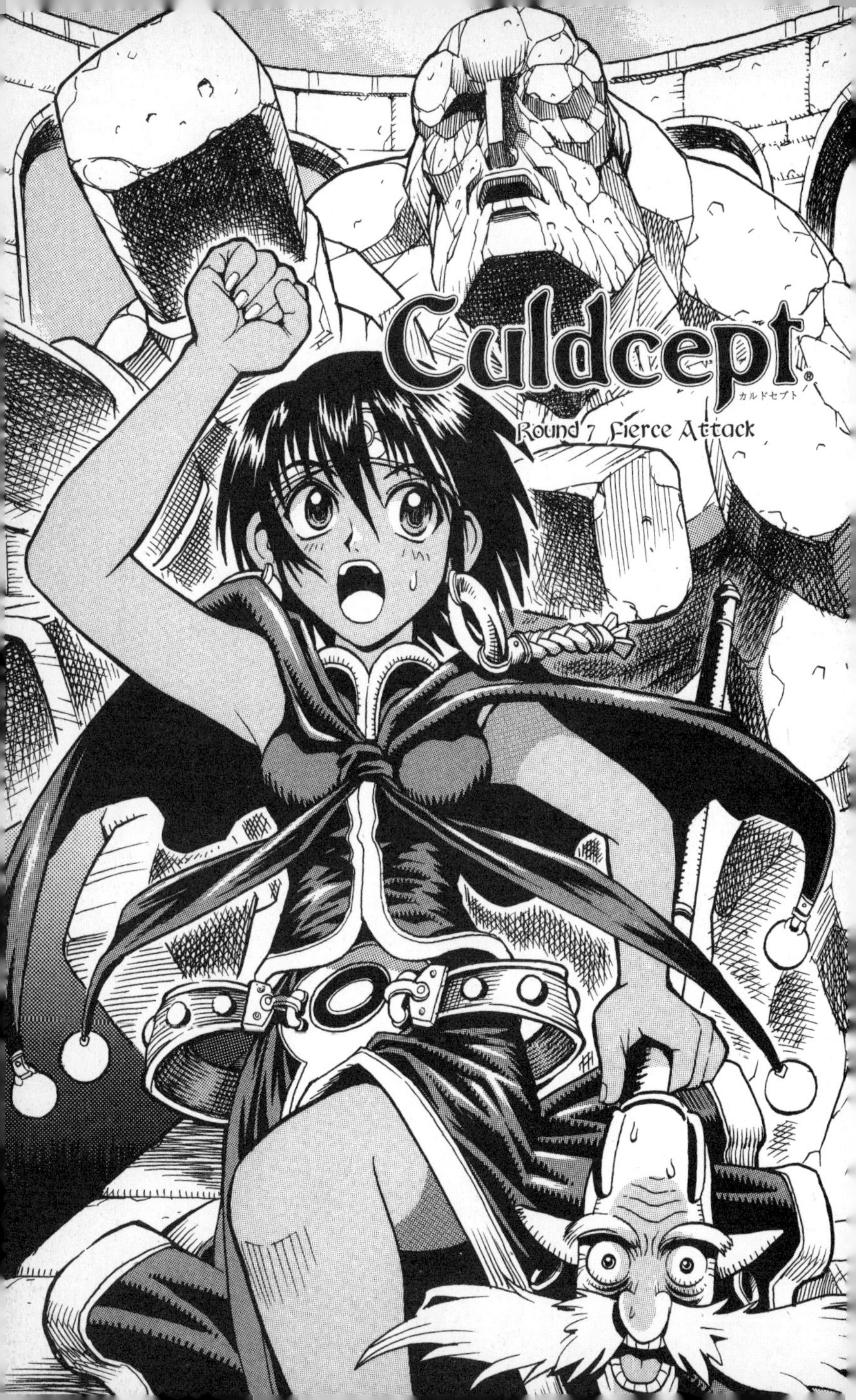
Culdcept®
カルドセプト
Round 7 Fierce Attack

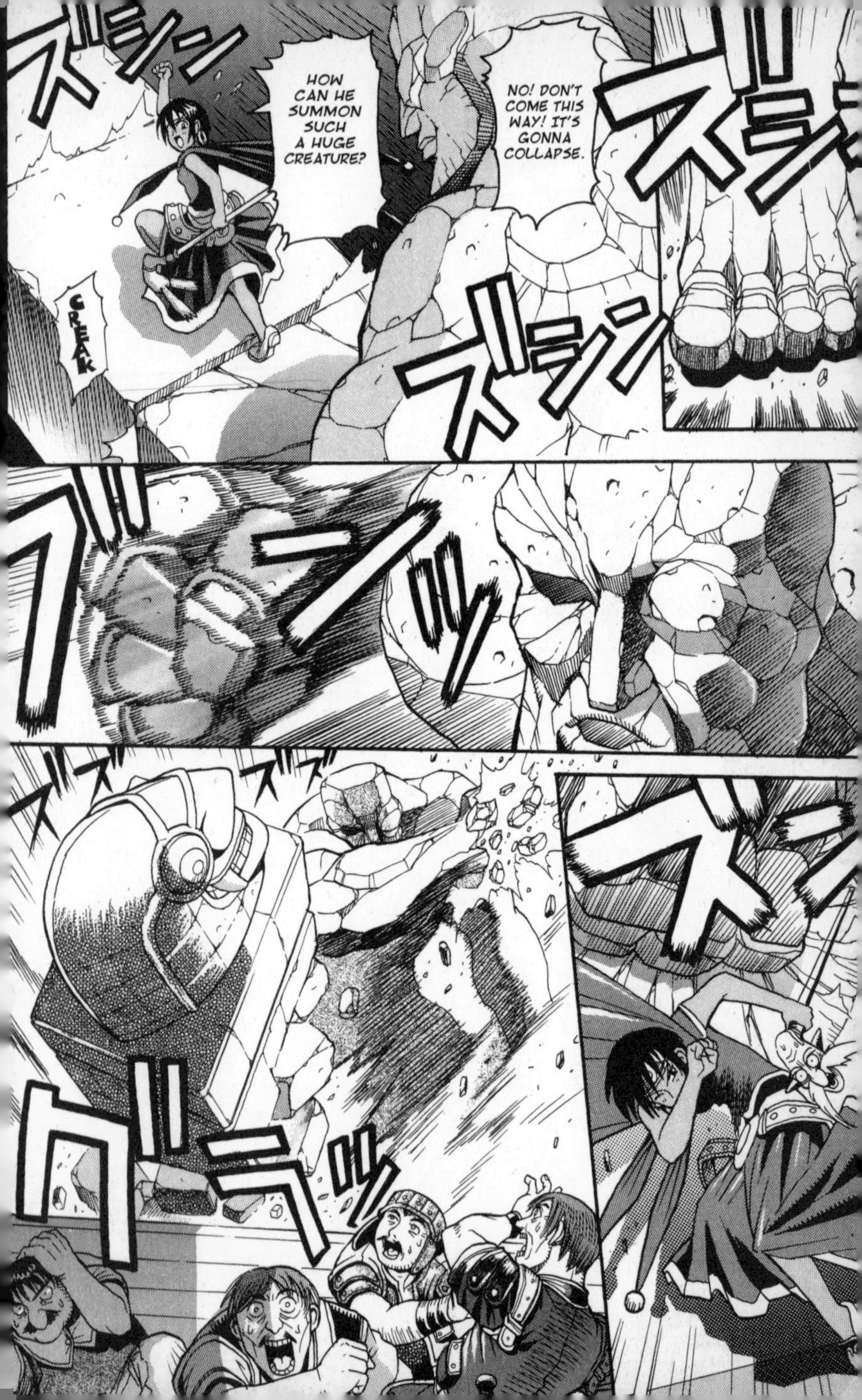
NO! DON'T COME THIS WAY! IT'S GONNA COLLAPSE.
HOW CAN HE SUMMON SUCH A HUGE CREATURE?
CREAK

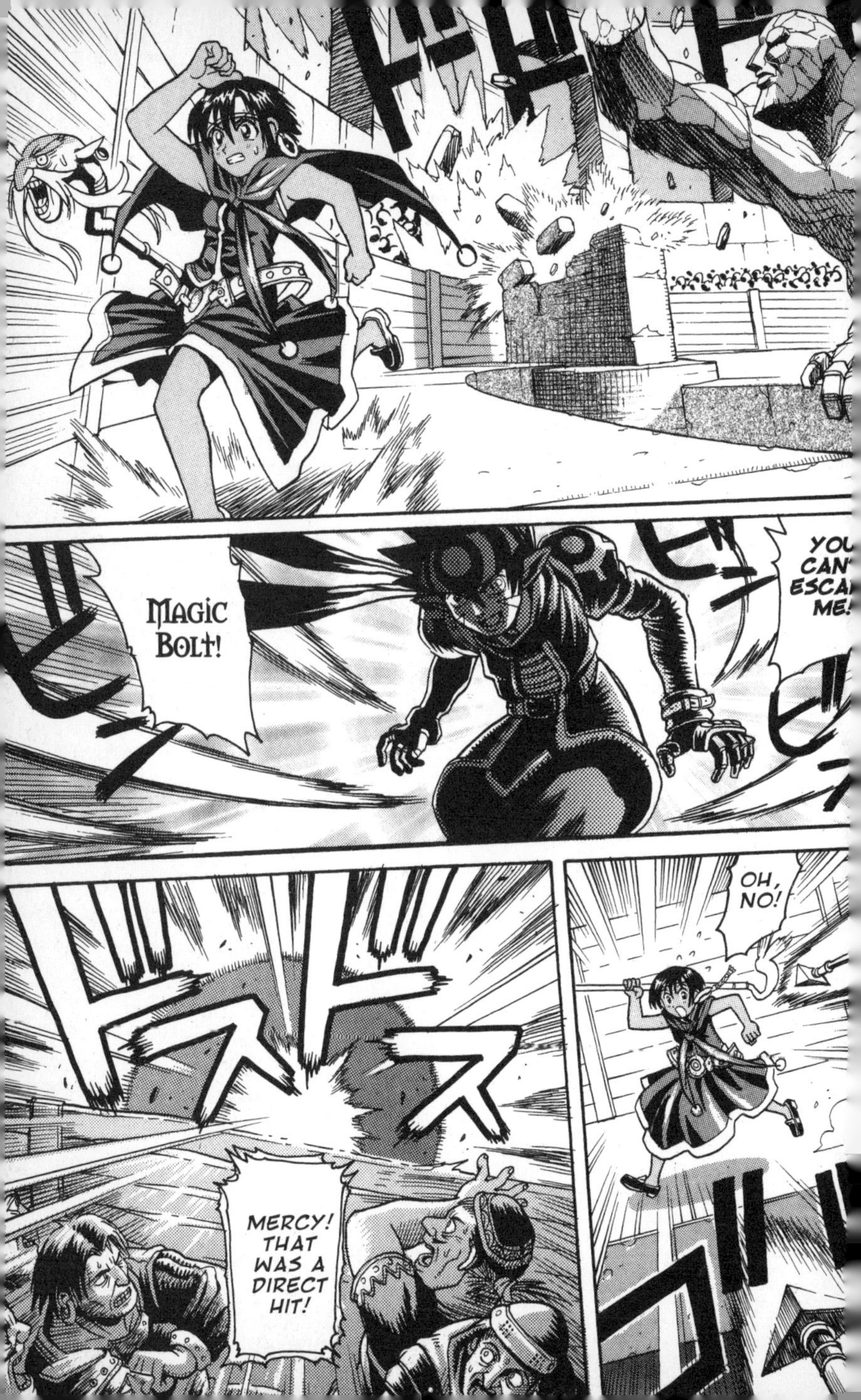
Magic Bolt!
OH, NO!
MERCY! THAT WAS A DIRECT HIT!

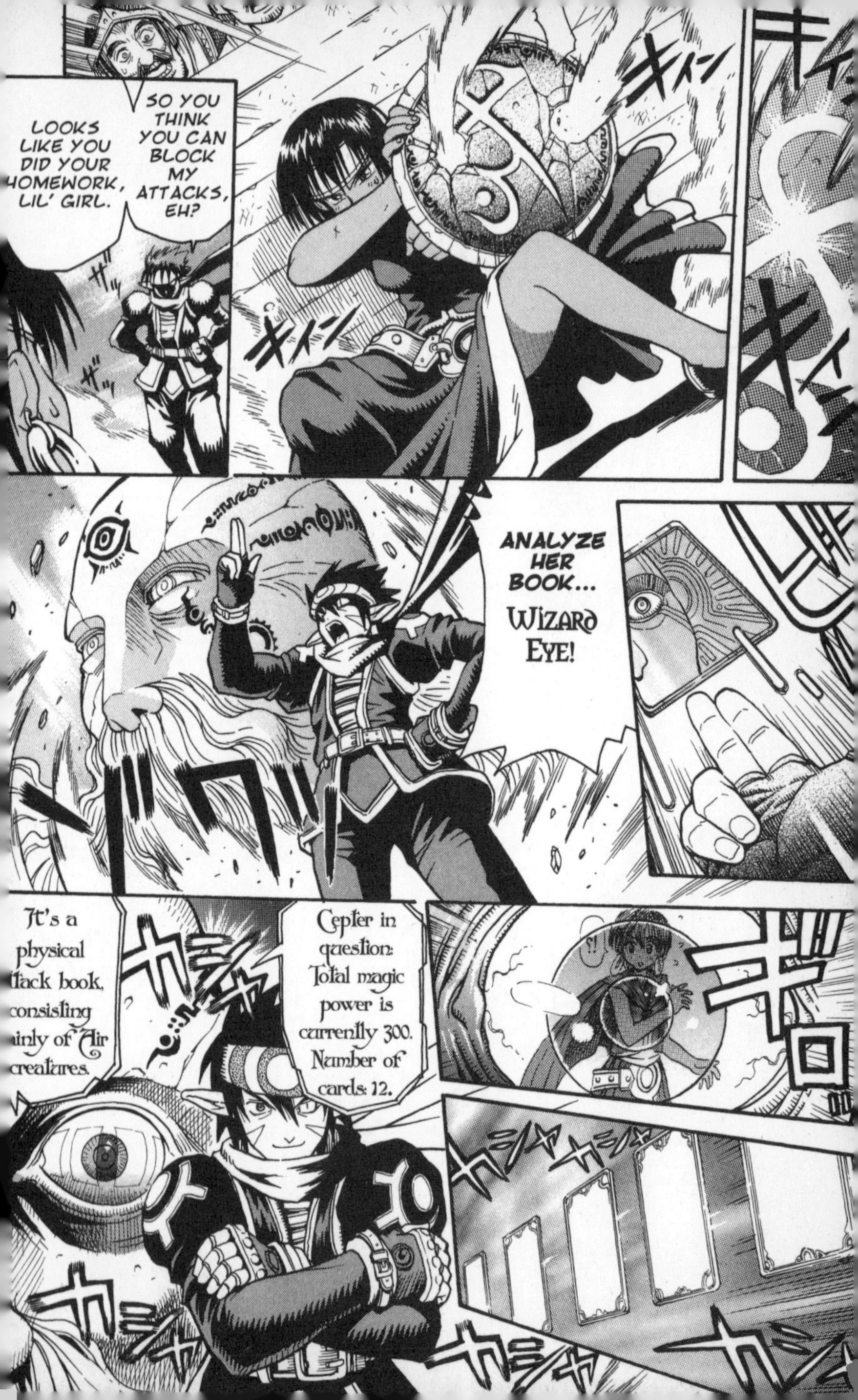
SO YOU THINK YOU CAN BLOCK MY ATTACKS, EH?
LOOKS LIKE YOU DID YOUR HOMEWORK, LIL' GIRL.
ANALYZE HER BOOK...
WIZARD EYE!
Cepter in question: Total magic power is currently 300. Number of cards: 12.
It's a physical ttack book, consisting ainly of Air creatures.

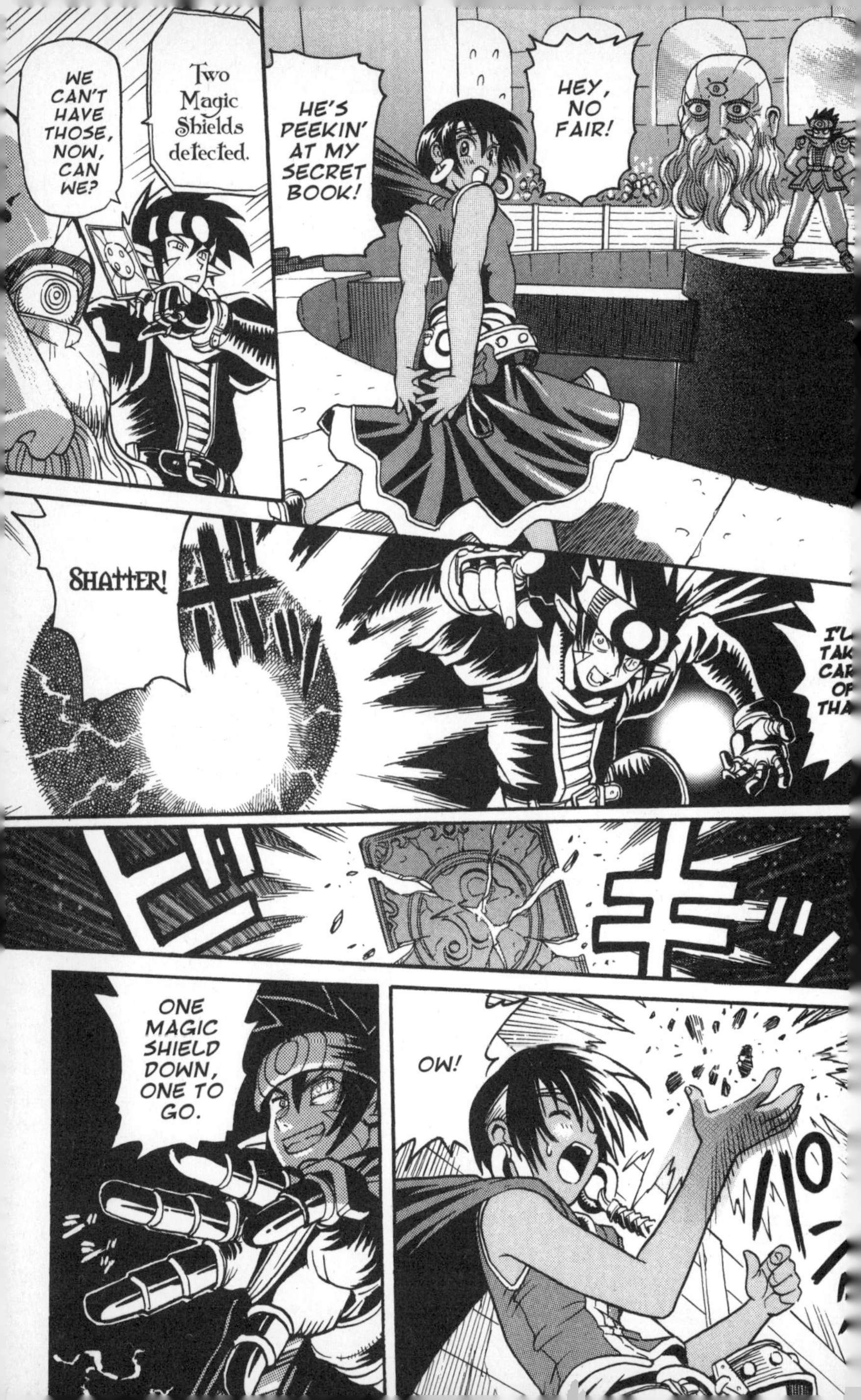
HEY, NO FAIR!
HE'S PEEKIN' AT MY SECRET BOOK!
Two Magic Shields detected.
WE CAN'T HAVE THOSE, NOW, CAN WE?
I'L TAK CAR OF THA
SHATTER!
OW!
ONE MAGIC SHIELD DOWN, ONE TO GO.

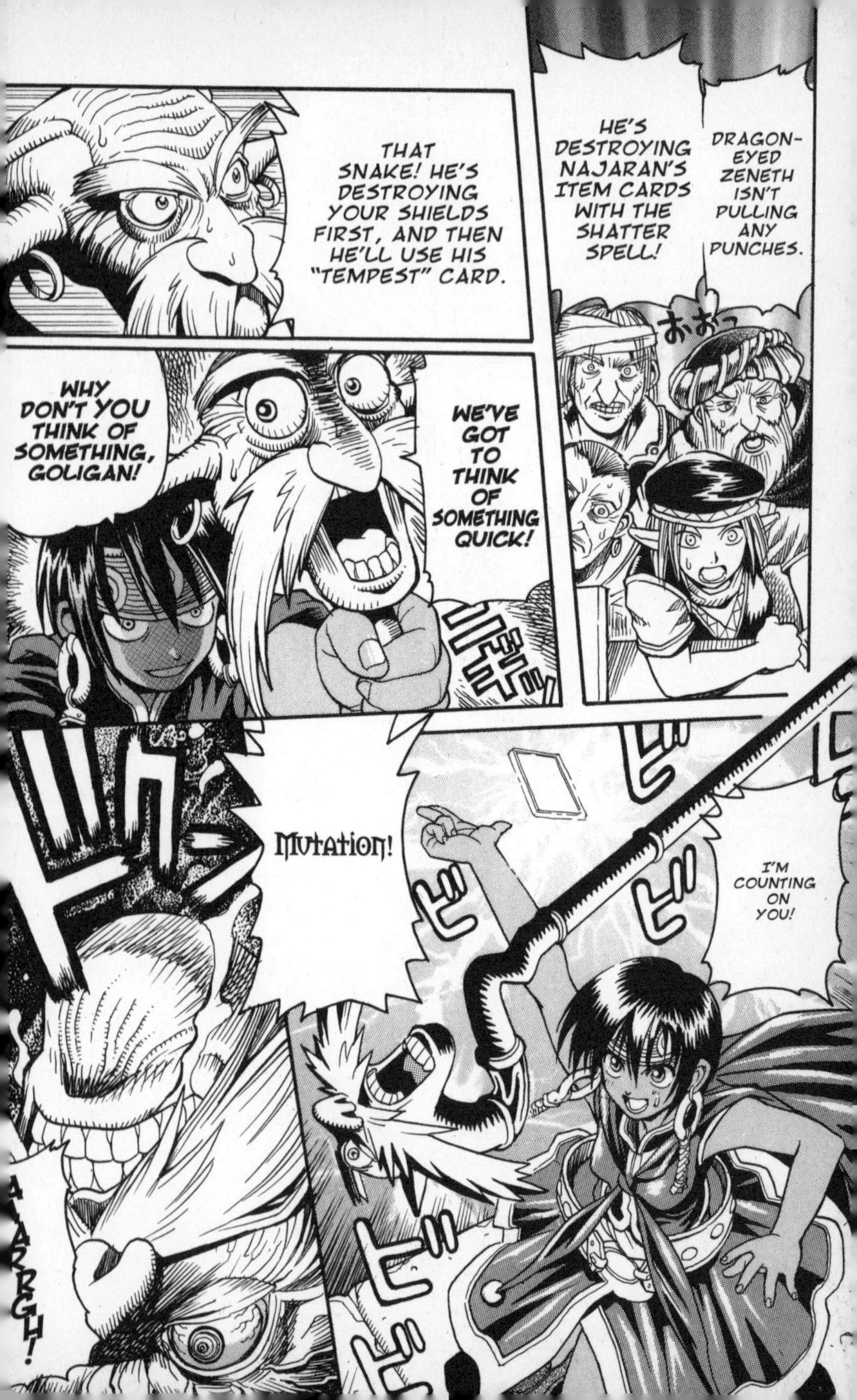
DRAGON-EYED ZENETH ISN'T PULLING ANY PUNCHES.
HE'S DESTROYING NAJARAN'S ITEM CARDS WITH THE SHATTER SPELL!
おおっ
THAT SNAKE! HE'S DESTROYING YOUR SHIELDS FIRST, AND THEN HE'LL USE HIS "TEMPEST" CARD.
WE'VE GOT TO THINK OF SOMETHING QUICK!
WHY DON'T YOU THINK OF SOMETHING, GOLIGAN!
I'M COUNTING ON YOU!
Mutation!
AAARGH!

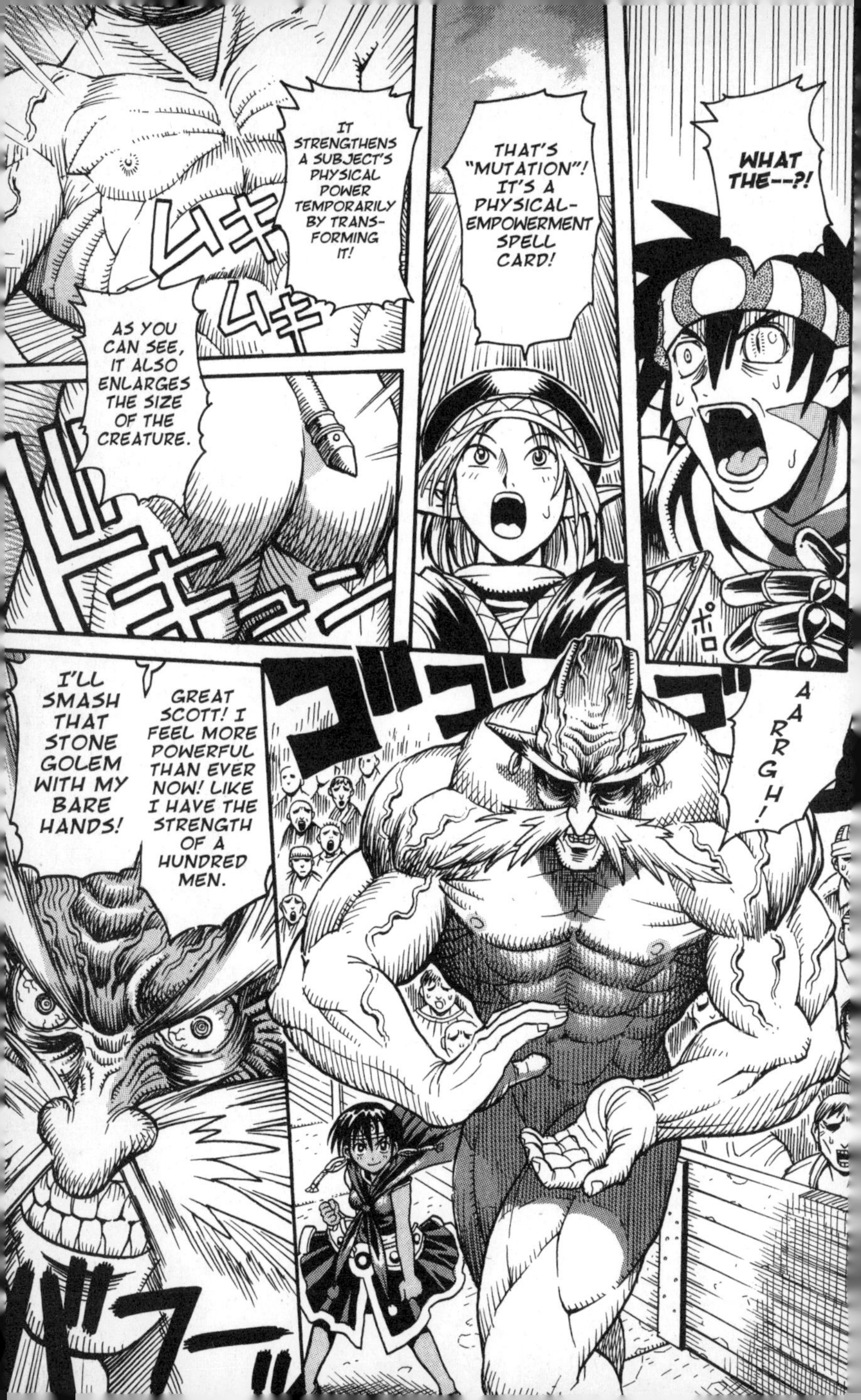
WHAT THE--?!
ポロ
THAT'S "MUTATION"! IT'S A PHYSICAL-EMPOWERMENT SPELL CARD!
IT STRENGTHENS A SUBJECT'S PHYSICAL POWER TEMPORARILY BY TRANS-FORMING IT!
ムキ
ムキ
AS YOU CAN SEE, IT ALSO ENLARGES THE SIZE OF THE CREATURE.
AARRGH!
GREAT SCOTT! I FEEL MORE POWERFUL THAN EVER NOW! LIKE I HAVE THE STRENGTH OF A HUNDRED MEN.
I'LL SMASH THAT STONE GOLEM WITH MY BARE HANDS!

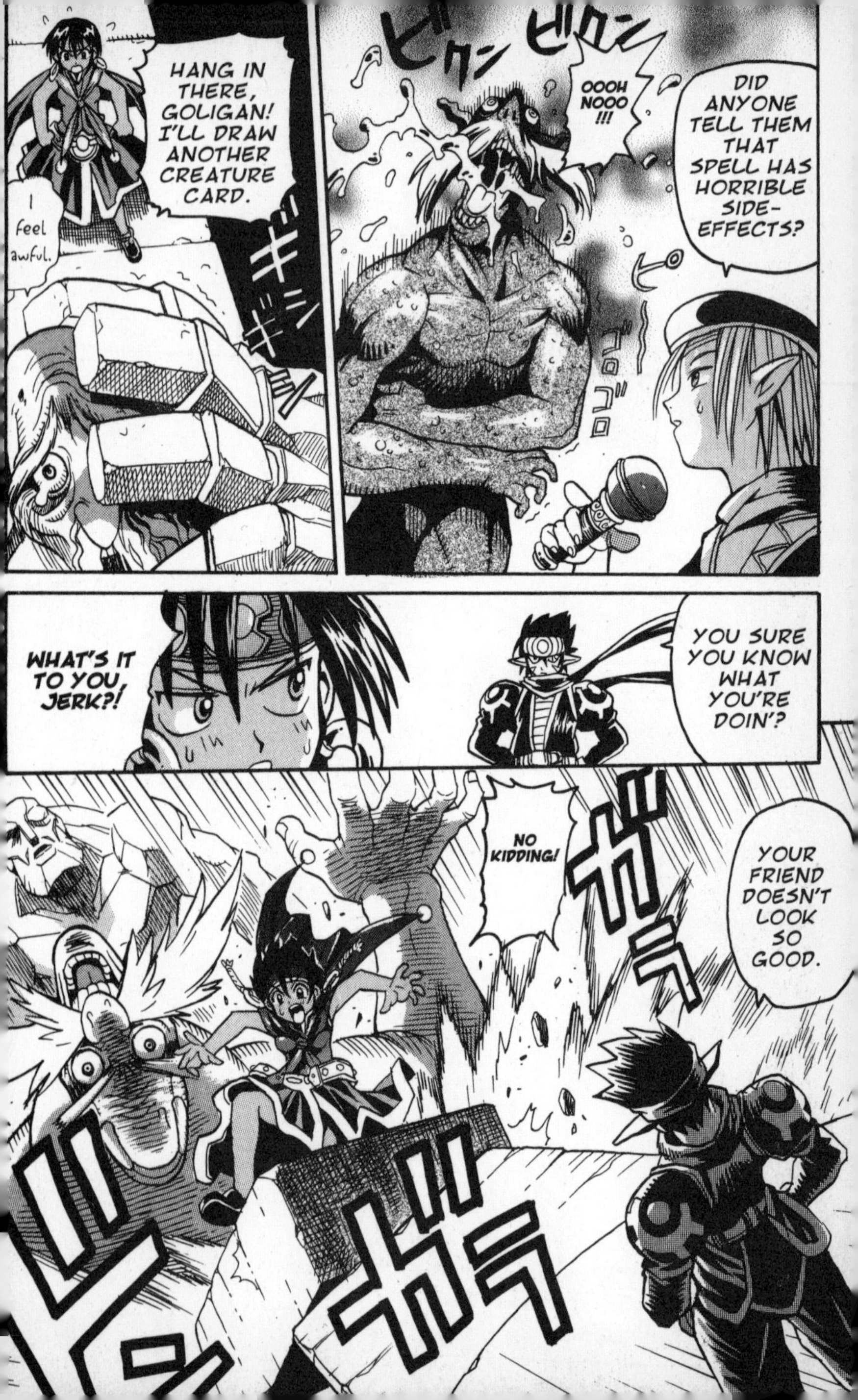
DID ANYONE TELL THEM THAT SPELL HAS HORRIBLE SIDE-EFFECTS?
OOOH NOOO !!!
HANG IN THERE, GOLIGAN! I'LL DRAW ANOTHER CREATURE CARD.
I feel awful.
YOU SURE YOU KNOW WHAT YOU'RE DOIN'?
WHAT'S IT TO YOU, JERK?!
YOUR FRIEND DOESN'T LOOK SO GOOD.
NO KIDDING!

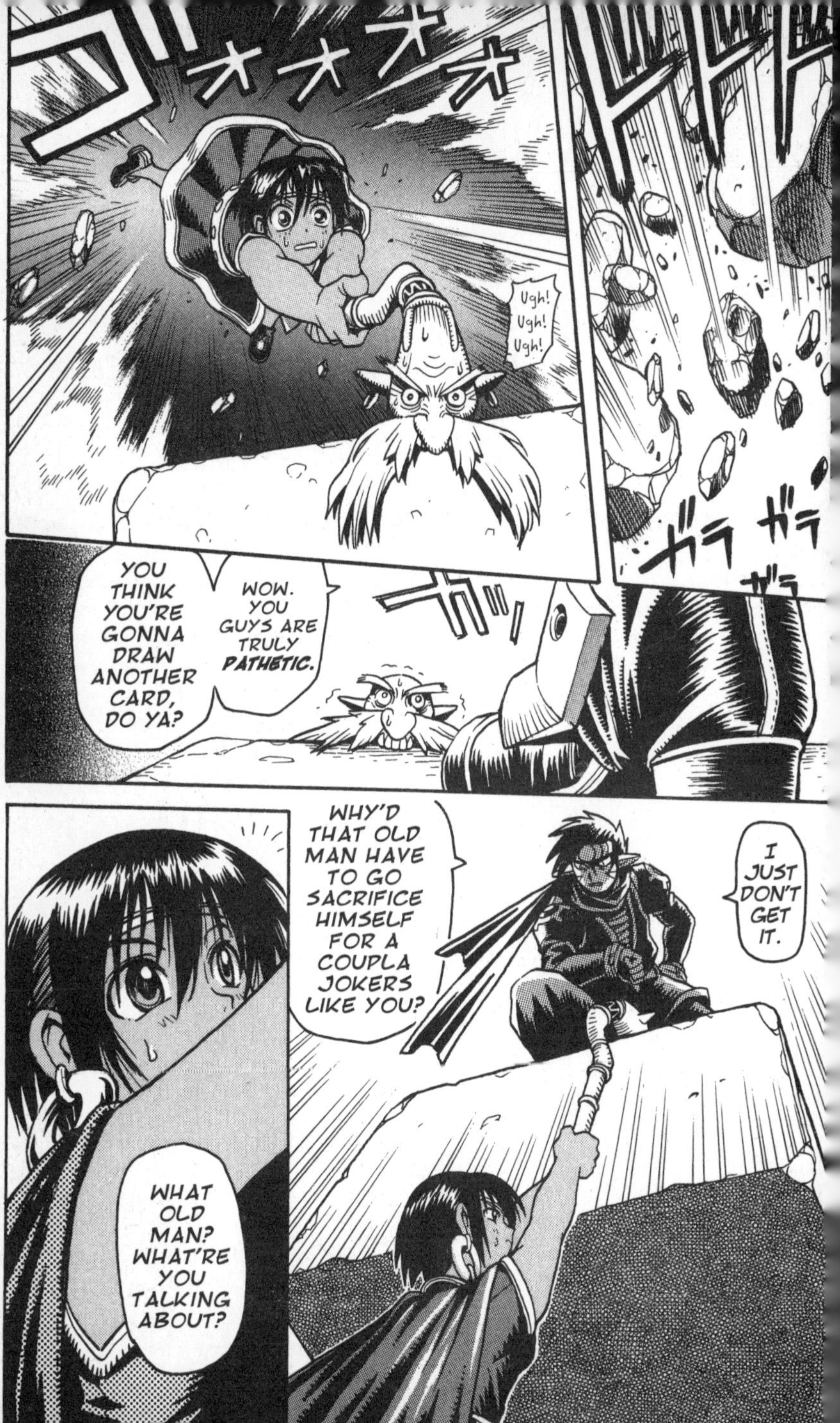
ガラ ガラ ガラ
ゴオオオオ
Ugh! Ugh! Ugh!
ガッ
WOW. YOU GUYS ARE TRULY **PATHETIC.**
YOU THINK YOU'RE GONNA DRAW ANOTHER CARD, DO YA?
I JUST DON'T GET IT.
WHY'D THAT OLD MAN HAVE TO GO SACRIFICE HIMSELF FOR A COUPLA JOKERS LIKE YOU?
WHAT OLD MAN? WHAT'RE YOU TALKING ABOUT?

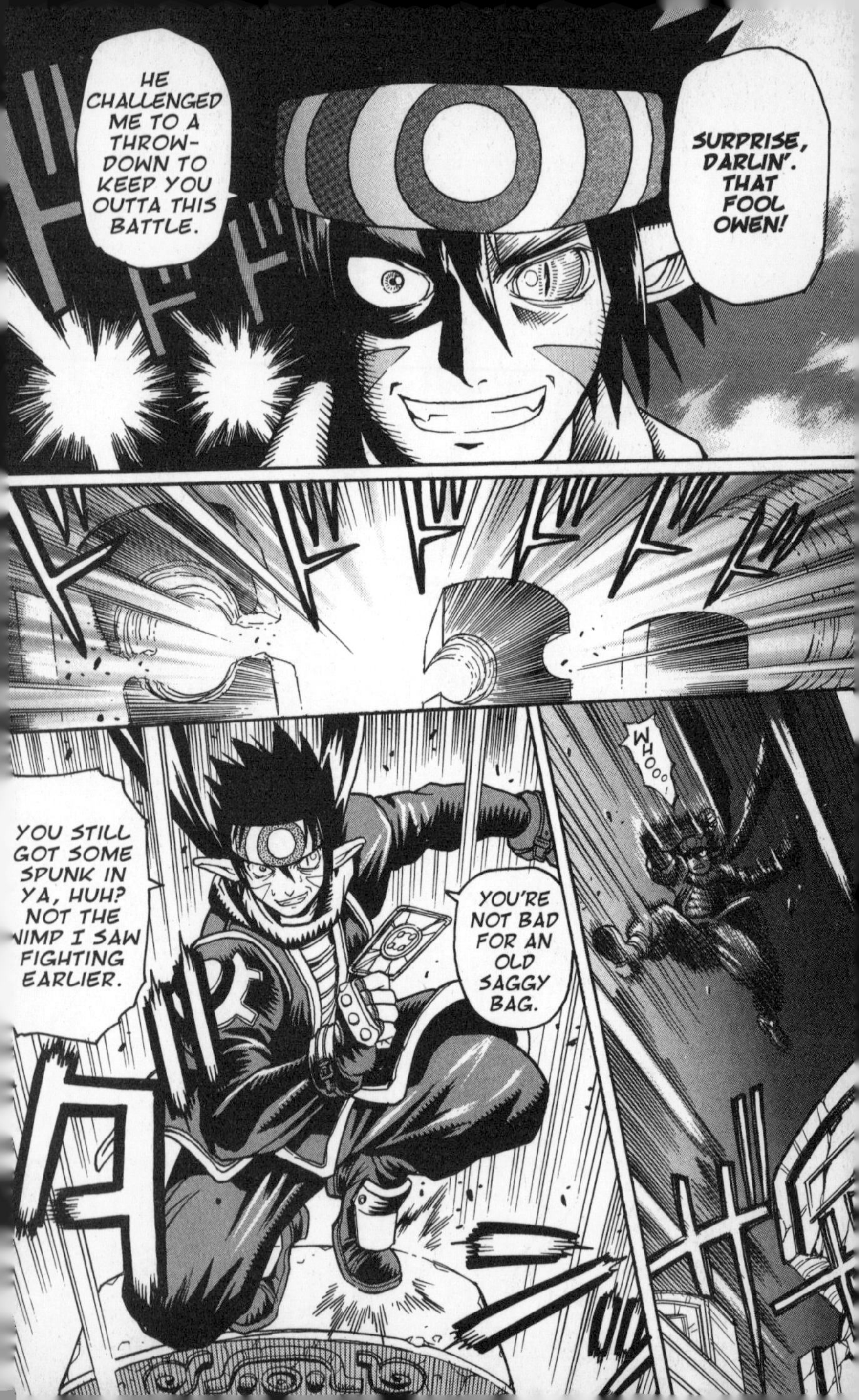
SURPRISE, DARLIN'. THAT FOOL OWEN!
HE CHALLENGED ME TO A THROW-DOWN TO KEEP YOU OUTTA THIS BATTLE.
WHOOO!
YOU'RE NOT BAD FOR AN OLD SAGGY BAG.
YOU STILL GOT SOME SPUNK IN YA, HUH? NOT THE WIMP I SAW FIGHTING EARLIER.

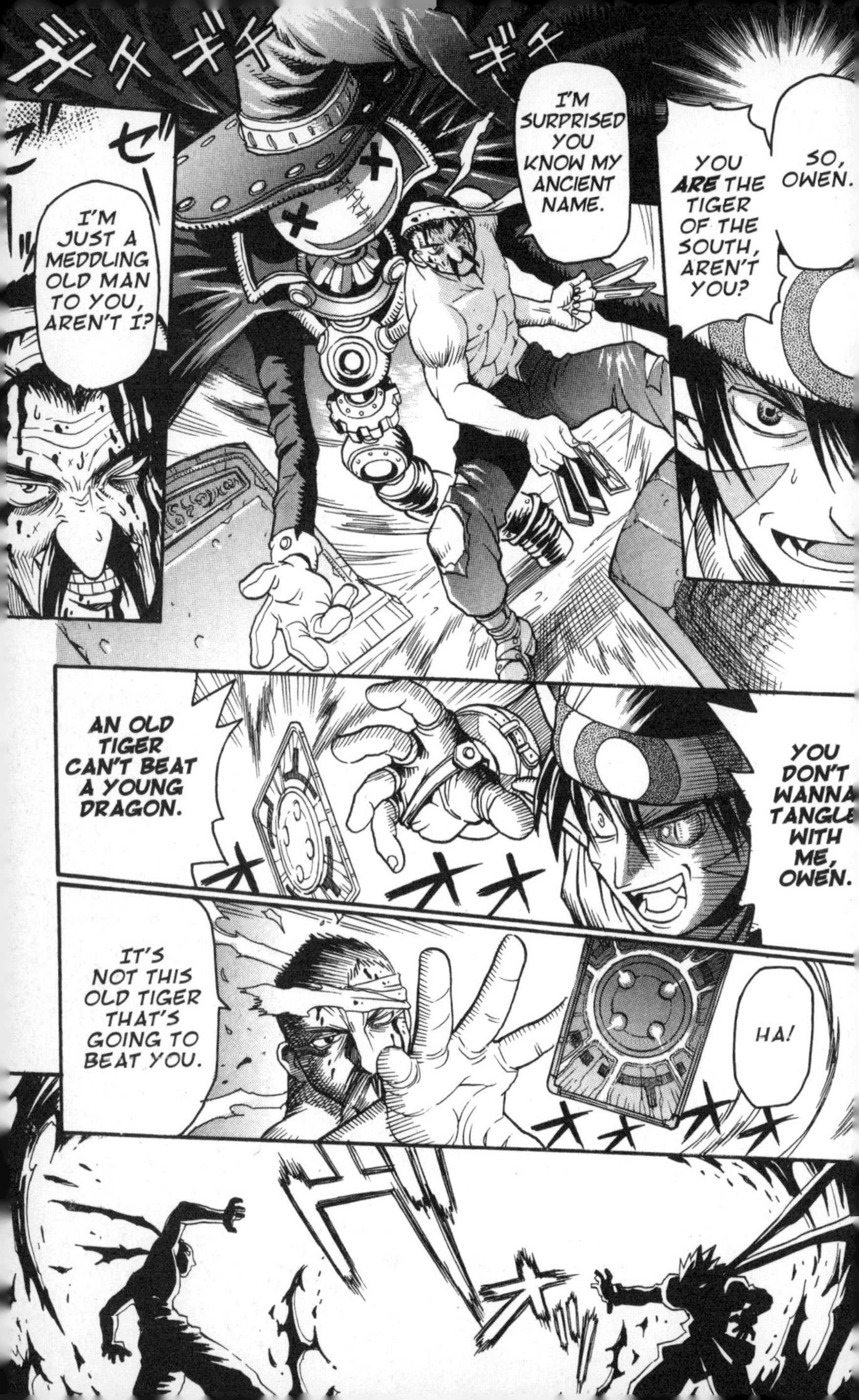

SO, OWEN.
YOU ARE THE TIGER OF THE SOUTH, AREN'T YOU?
I'M SURPRISED YOU KNOW MY ANCIENT NAME.
I'M JUST A MEDDLING OLD MAN TO YOU, AREN'T I?
YOU DON'T WANNA TANGLE WITH ME, OWEN.
AN OLD TIGER CAN'T BEAT A YOUNG DRAGON.
HA!
IT'S NOT THIS OLD TIGER THAT'S GOING TO BEAT YOU.

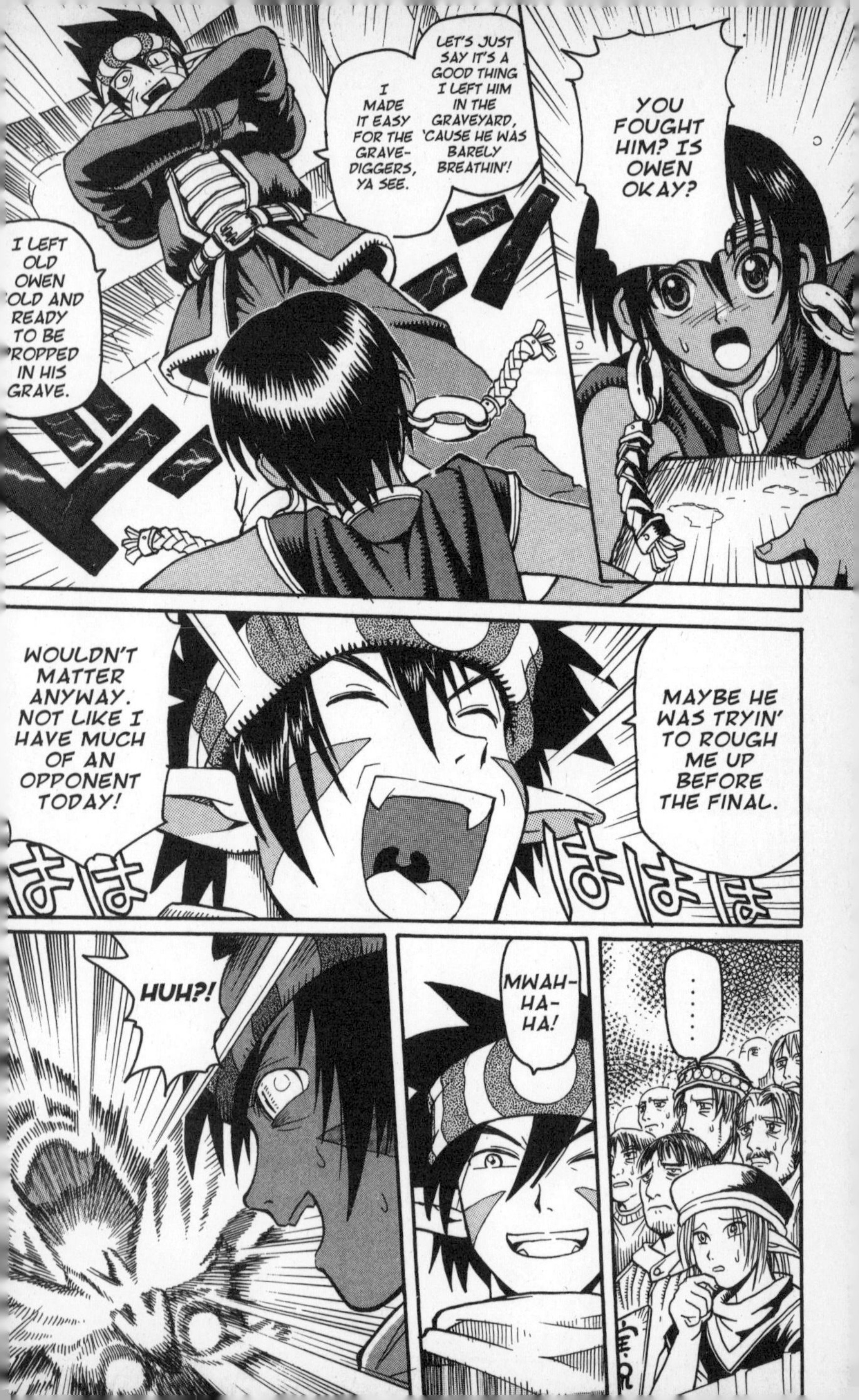
YOU FOUGHT HIM? IS OWEN OKAY?
LET'S JUST SAY IT'S A GOOD THING I LEFT HIM IN THE GRAVEYARD, 'CAUSE HE WAS BARELY BREATHIN'!
I MADE IT EASY FOR THE GRAVE-DIGGERS, YA SEE.
I LEFT OLD OWEN COLD AND READY TO BE PROPPED IN HIS GRAVE.
MAYBE HE WAS TRYIN' TO ROUGH ME UP BEFORE THE FINAL.
WOULDN'T MATTER ANYWAY. NOT LIKE I HAVE MUCH OF AN OPPONENT TODAY!
ははは
はは
......
MWAH-HA-HA!
HUH?!

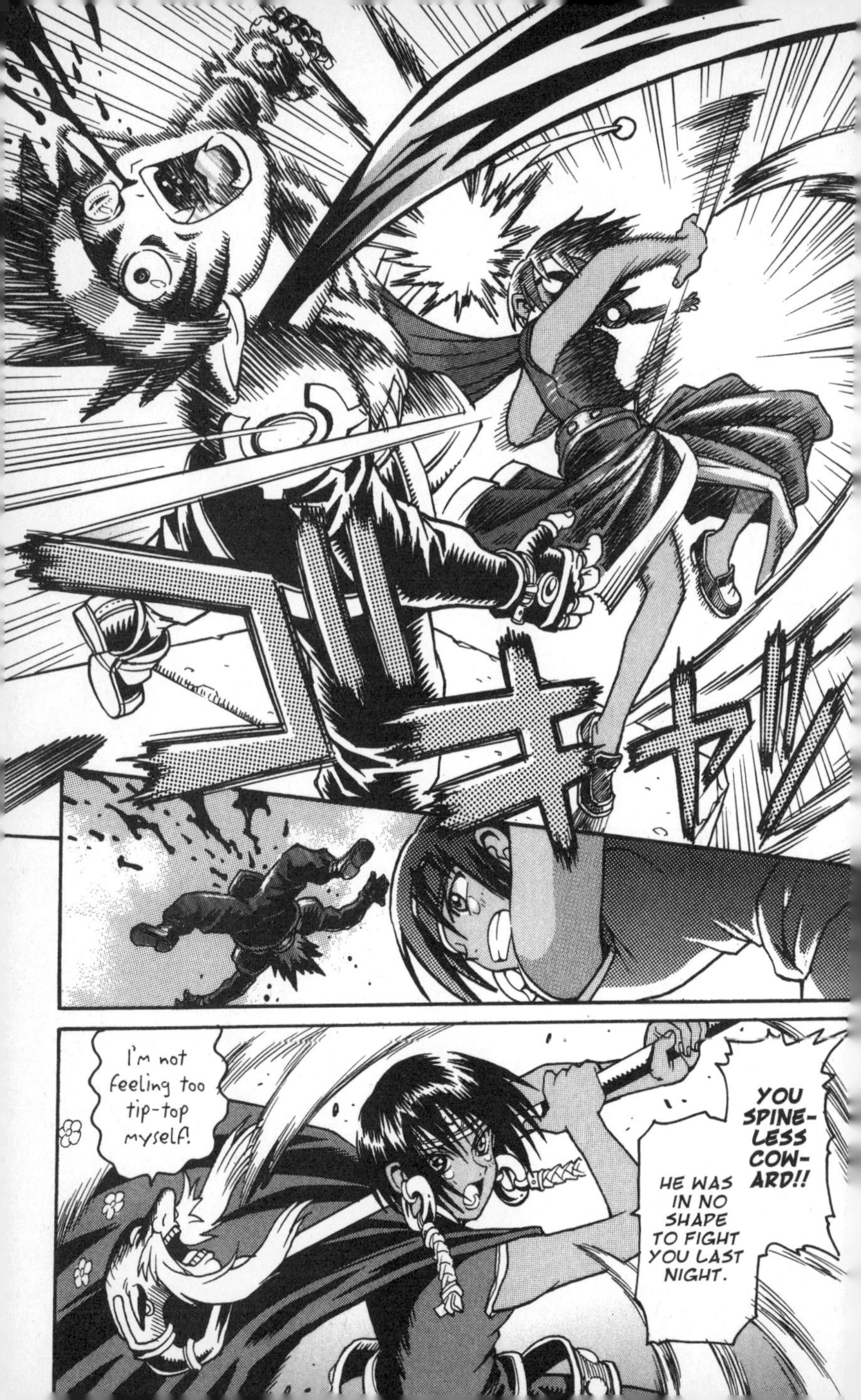
YOU SPINE-LESS COW-ARD!!
HE WAS IN NO SHAPE TO FIGHT YOU LAST NIGHT.
I'm not feeling too tip-top myself!

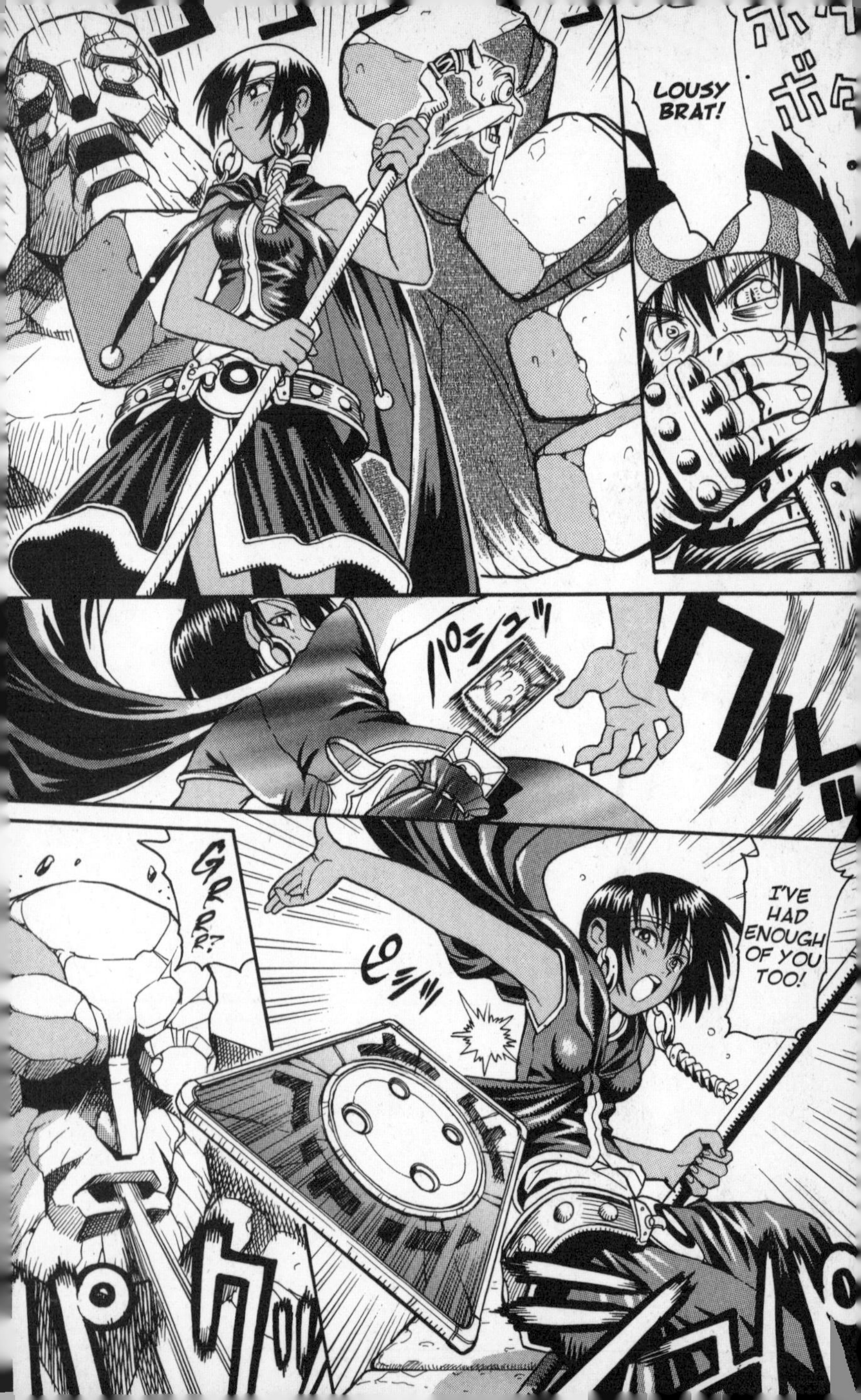
LOUSY BRAT!
I'VE HAD ENOUGH OF YOU TOO!
GRRR?!

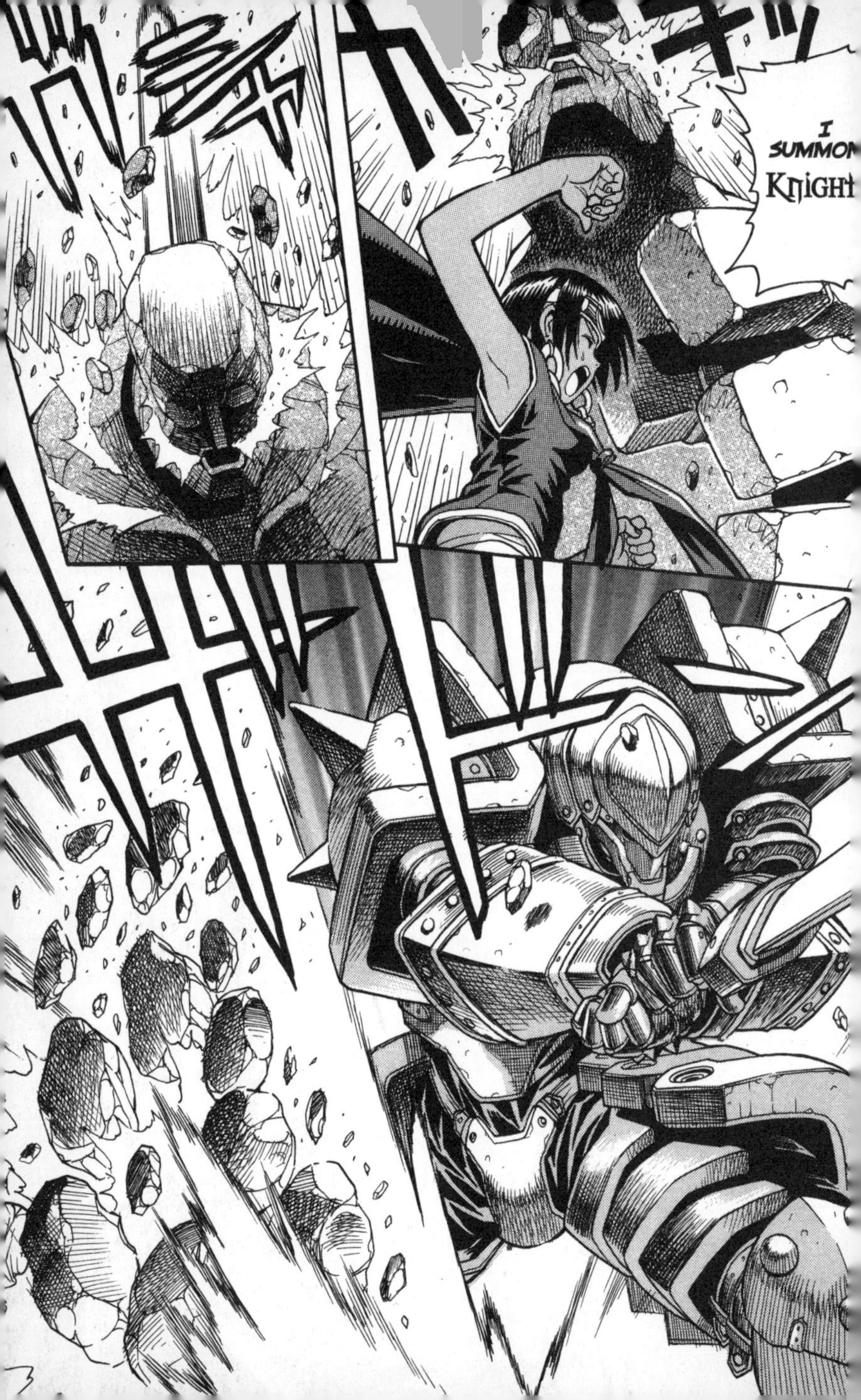
I SUMMON
Knight

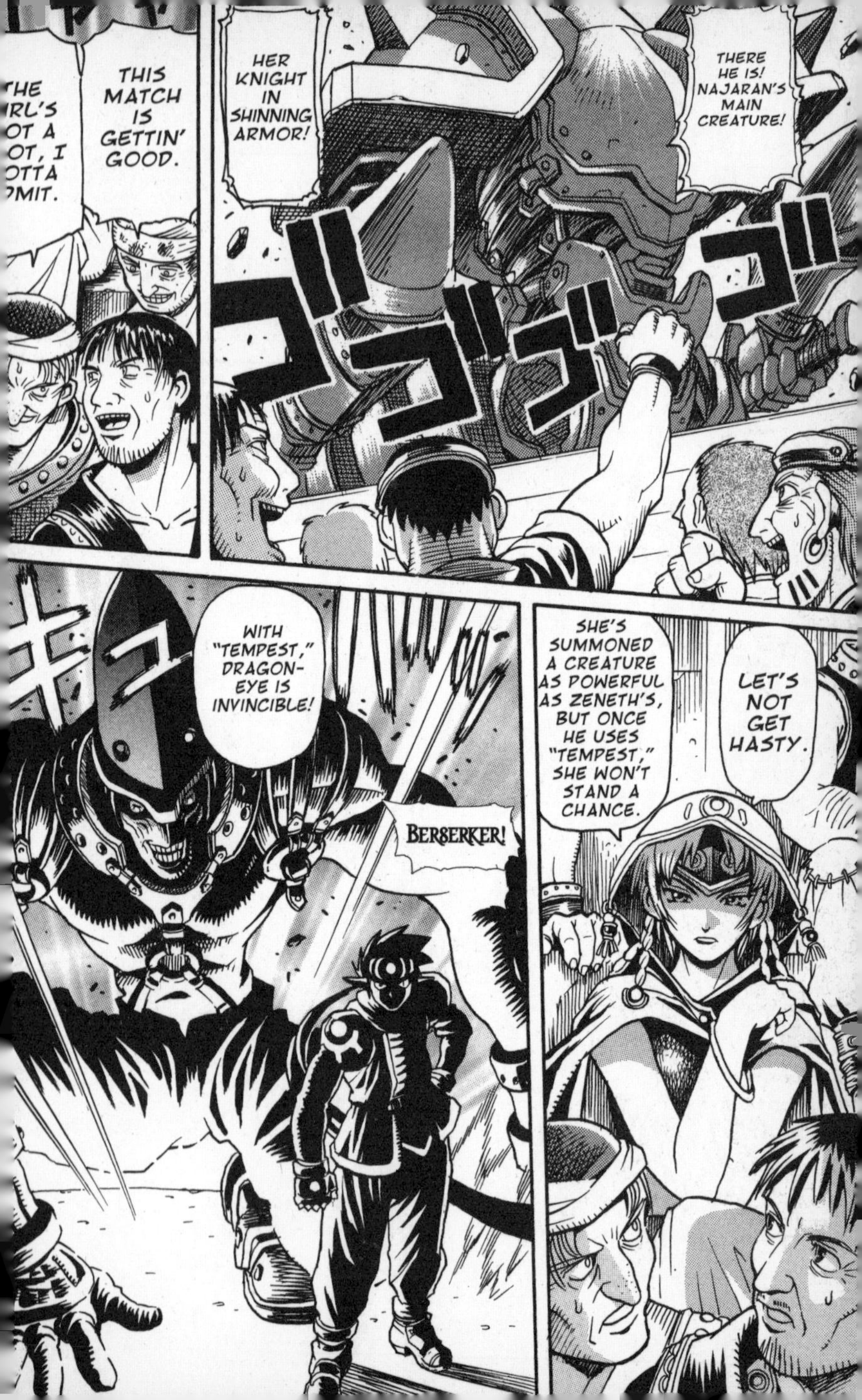
THERE HE IS! NAJARAN'S MAIN CREATURE!
HER KNIGHT IN SHINNING ARMOR!
ゴゴゴゴ
THIS MATCH IS GETTIN' GOOD.
THE IRL'S OT A OT, I OTTA DMIT.
LET'S NOT GET HASTY.
SHE'S SUMMONED A CREATURE AS POWERFUL AS ZENETH'S, BUT ONCE HE USES "TEMPEST," SHE WON'T STAND A CHANCE.
WITH "TEMPEST," DRAGON-EYE IS INVINCIBLE!
BERSERKER!
キ

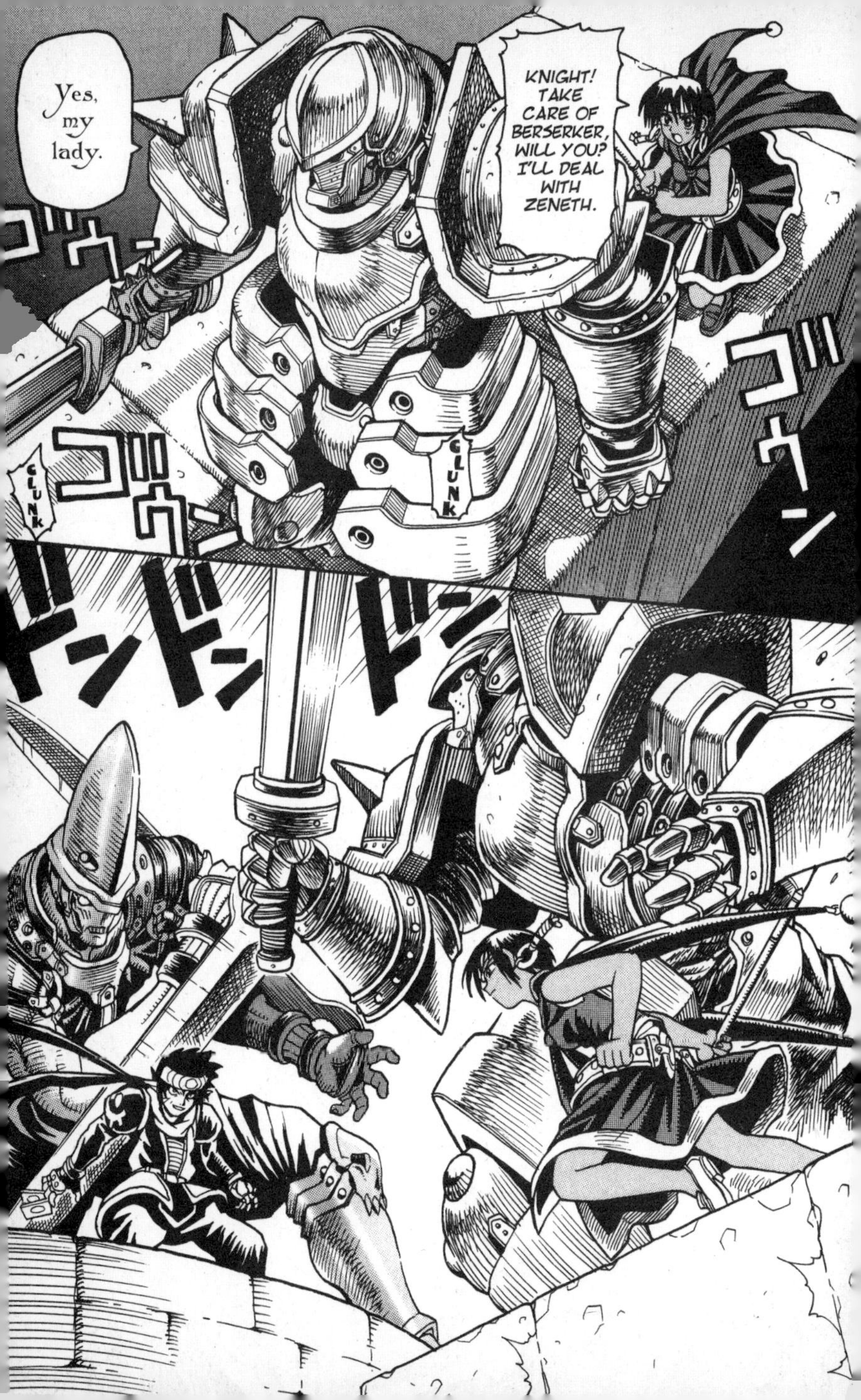
KNIGHT! TAKE CARE OF BERSERKER, WILL YOU? I'LL DEAL WITH ZENETH.
Yes, my lady.
ゴウン
GLUNK
GLUNK
ゴウン
ゴウー
ドン
ドンドン

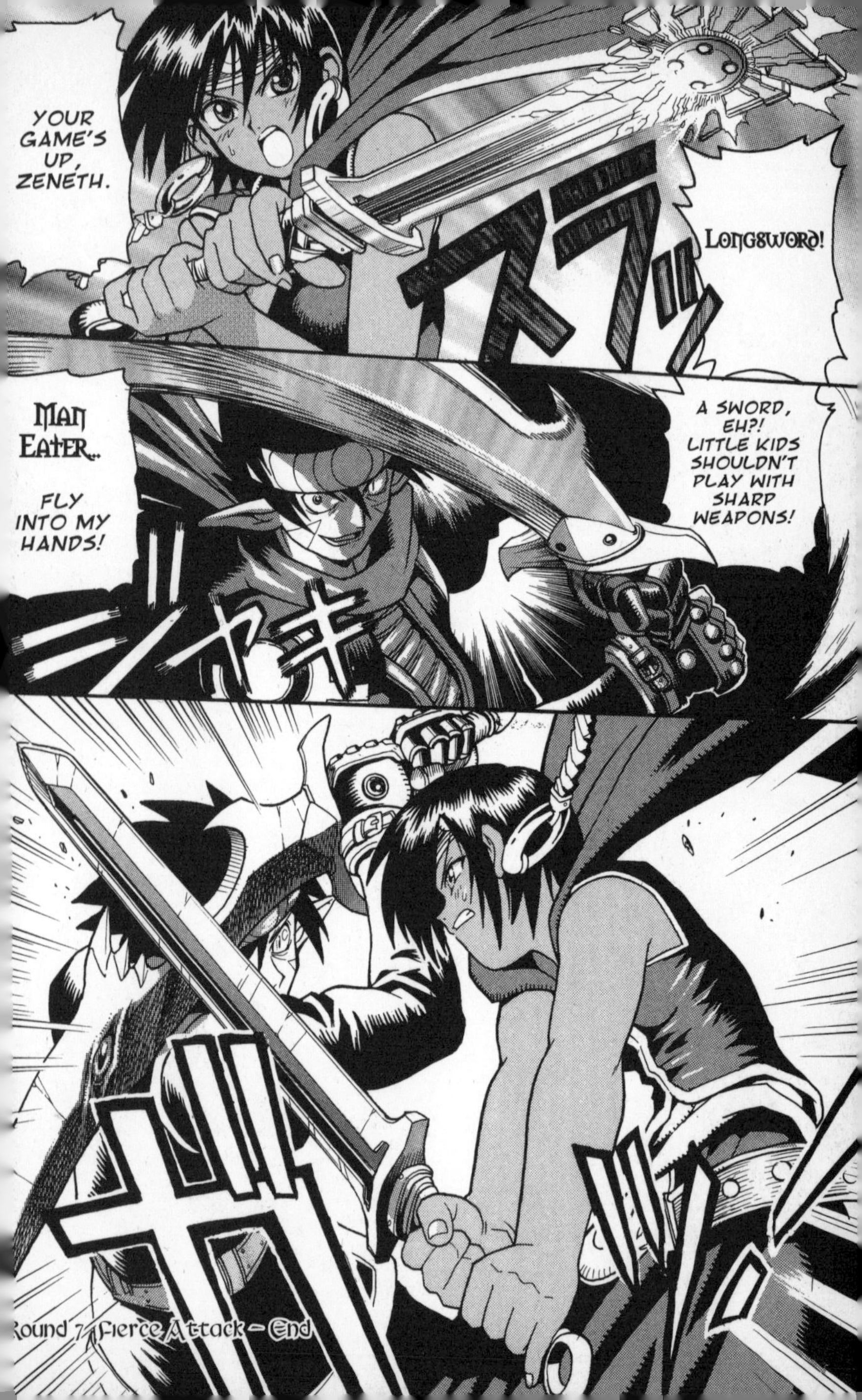
YOUR GAME'S UP, ZENETH.
LONGSWORD!
A SWORD, EH?! LITTLE KIDS SHOULDN'T PLAY WITH SHARP WEAPONS!
MAN EATER...
FLY INTO MY HANDS!
Round 7 Fierce Attack - End

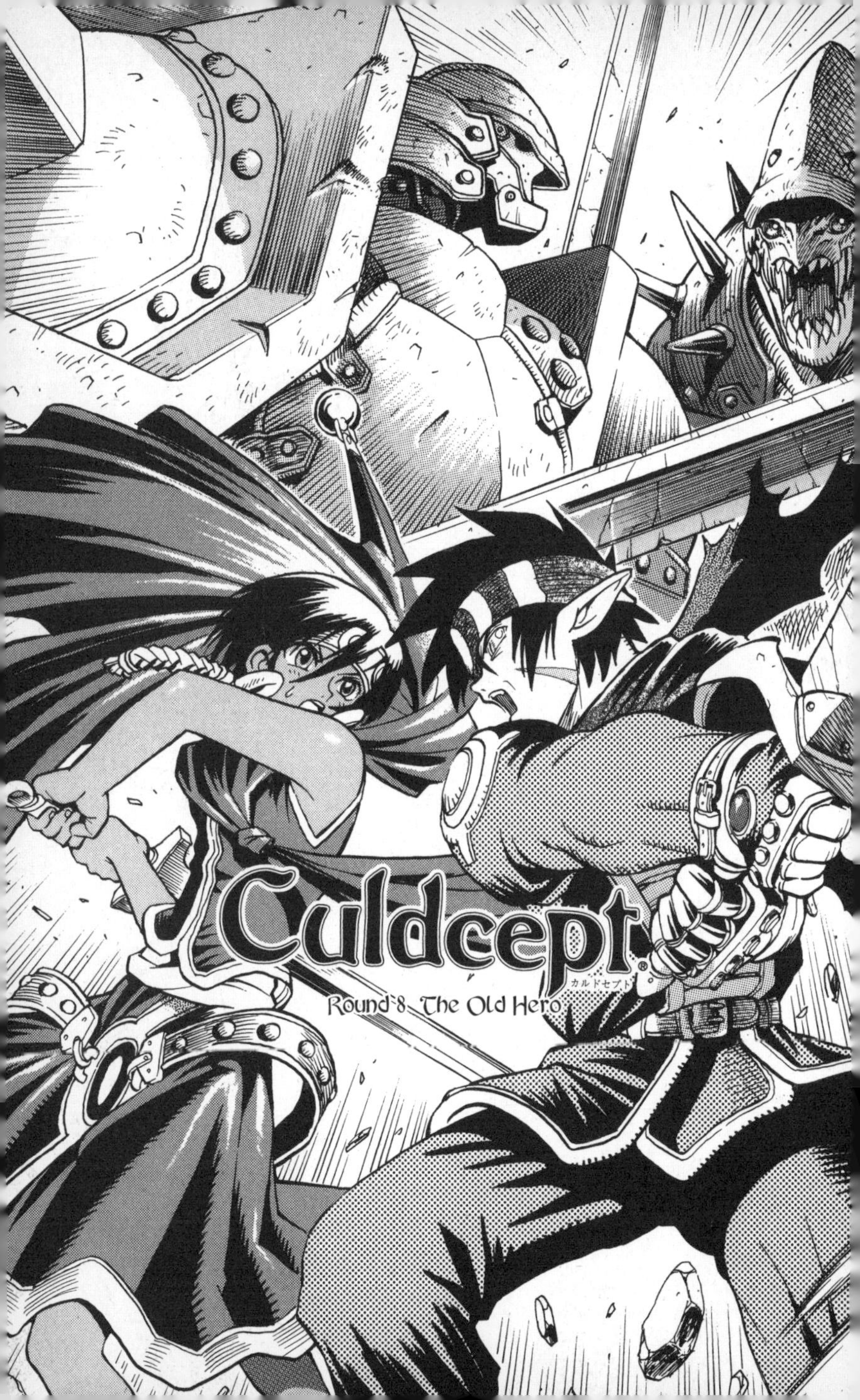
Culdcept
カルドセプト
Round 8 The Old Hero

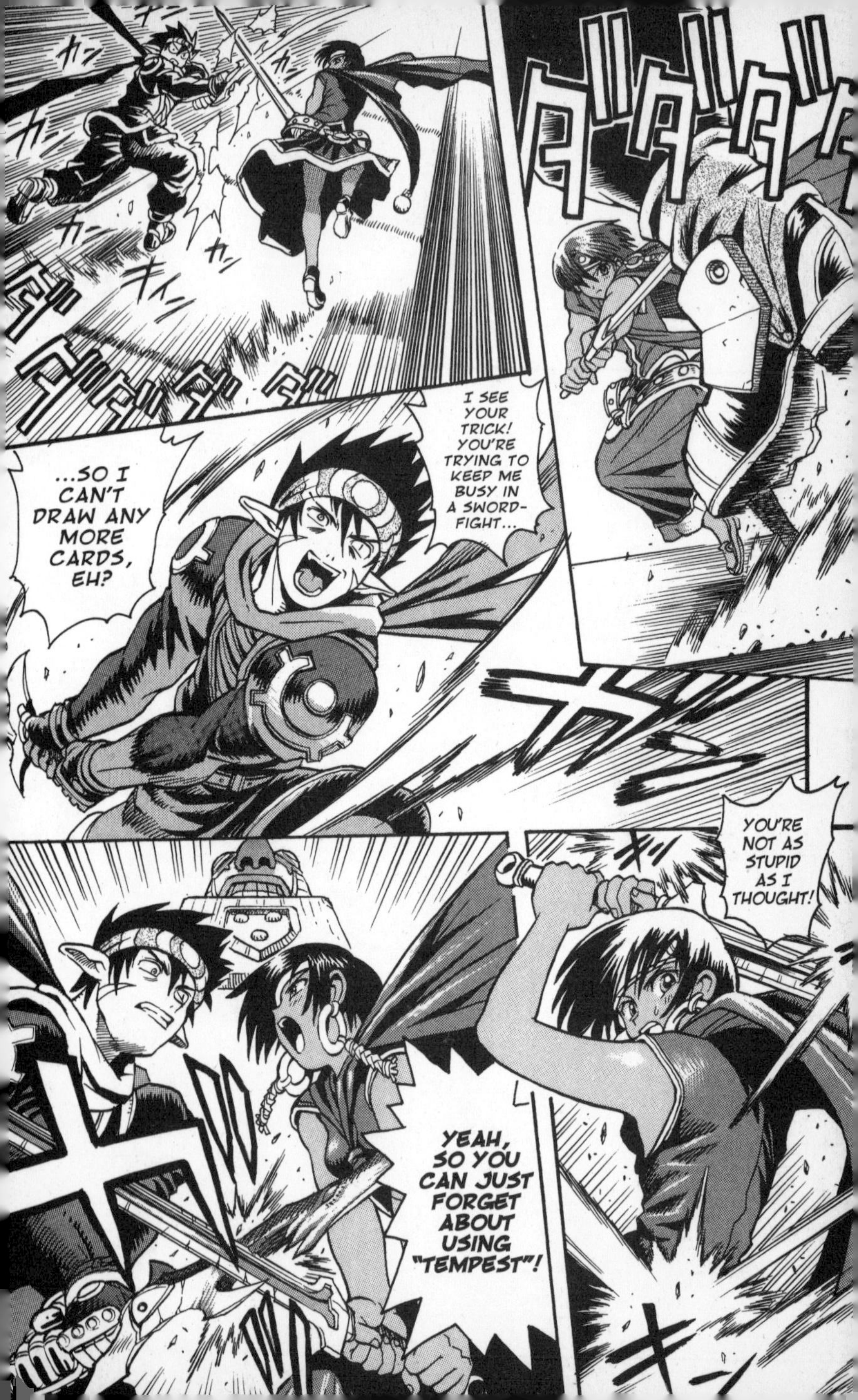
I SEE YOUR TRICK! YOU'RE TRYING TO KEEP ME BUSY IN A SWORD-FIGHT...
...SO I CAN'T DRAW ANY MORE CARDS, EH?
YOU'RE NOT AS STUPID AS I THOUGHT!
YEAH, SO YOU CAN JUST FORGET ABOUT USING "TEMPEST"!

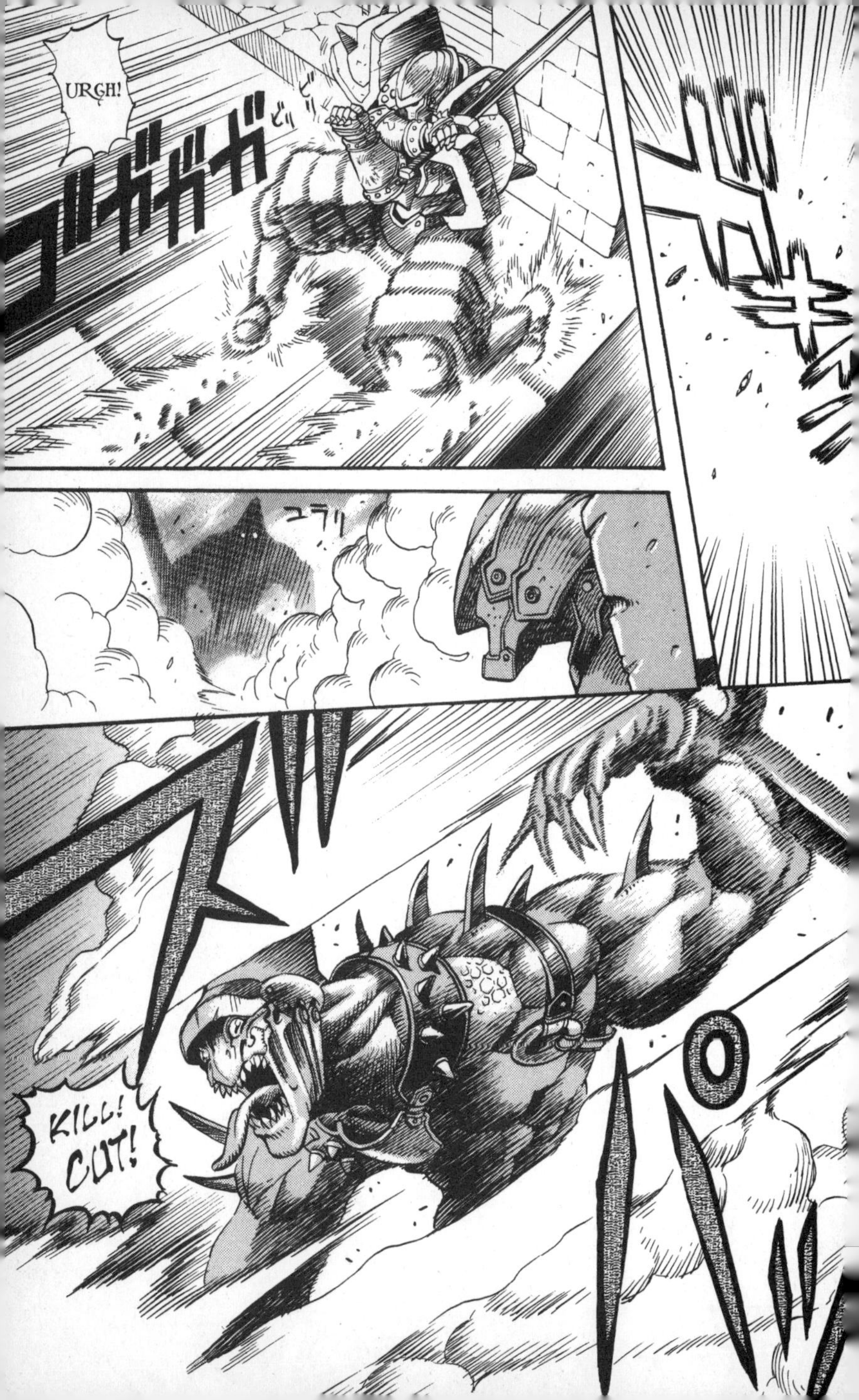
URGH!
KILL! CUT!

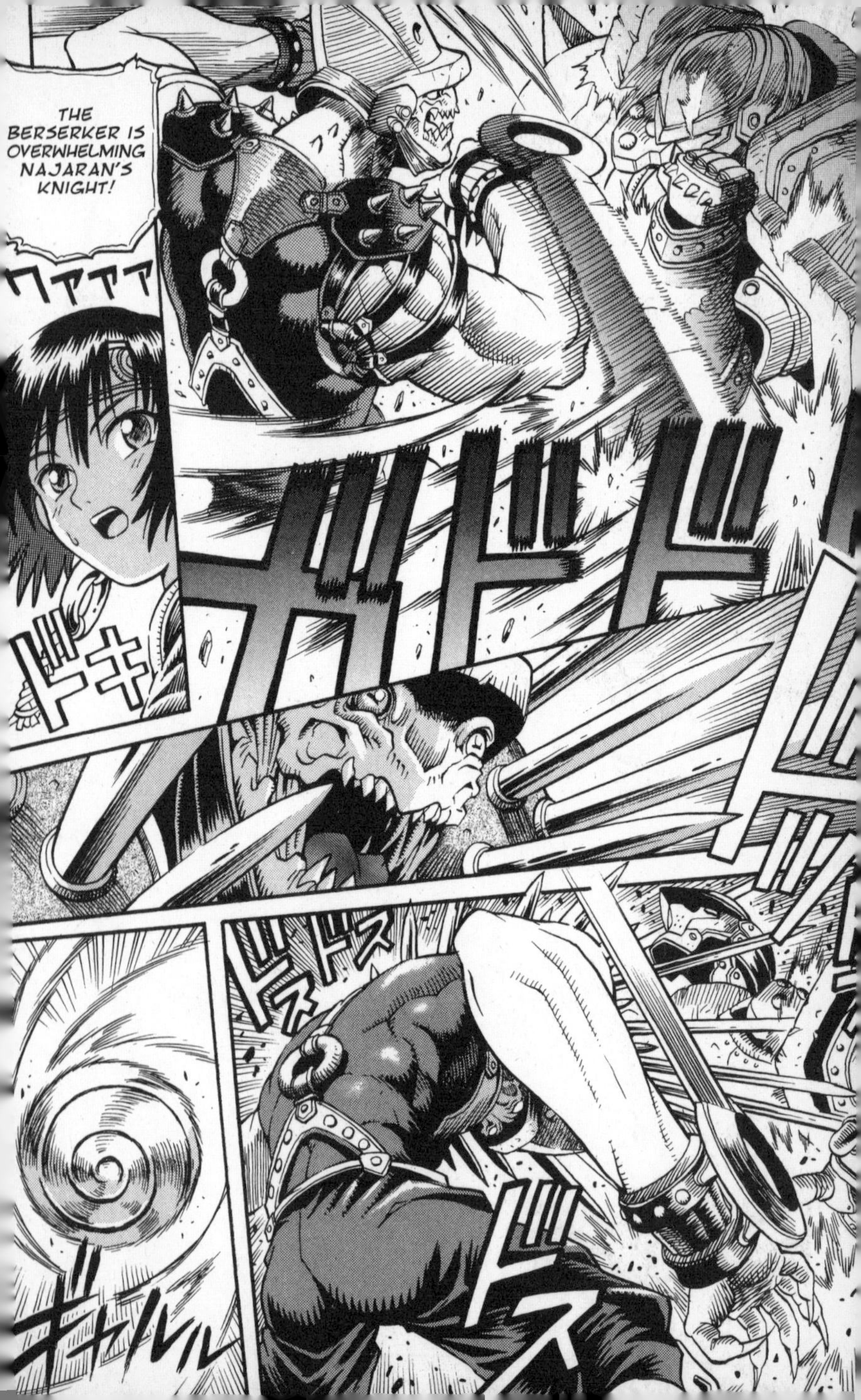
THE BERSERKER IS OVERWHELMING NAJARAN'S KNIGHT!

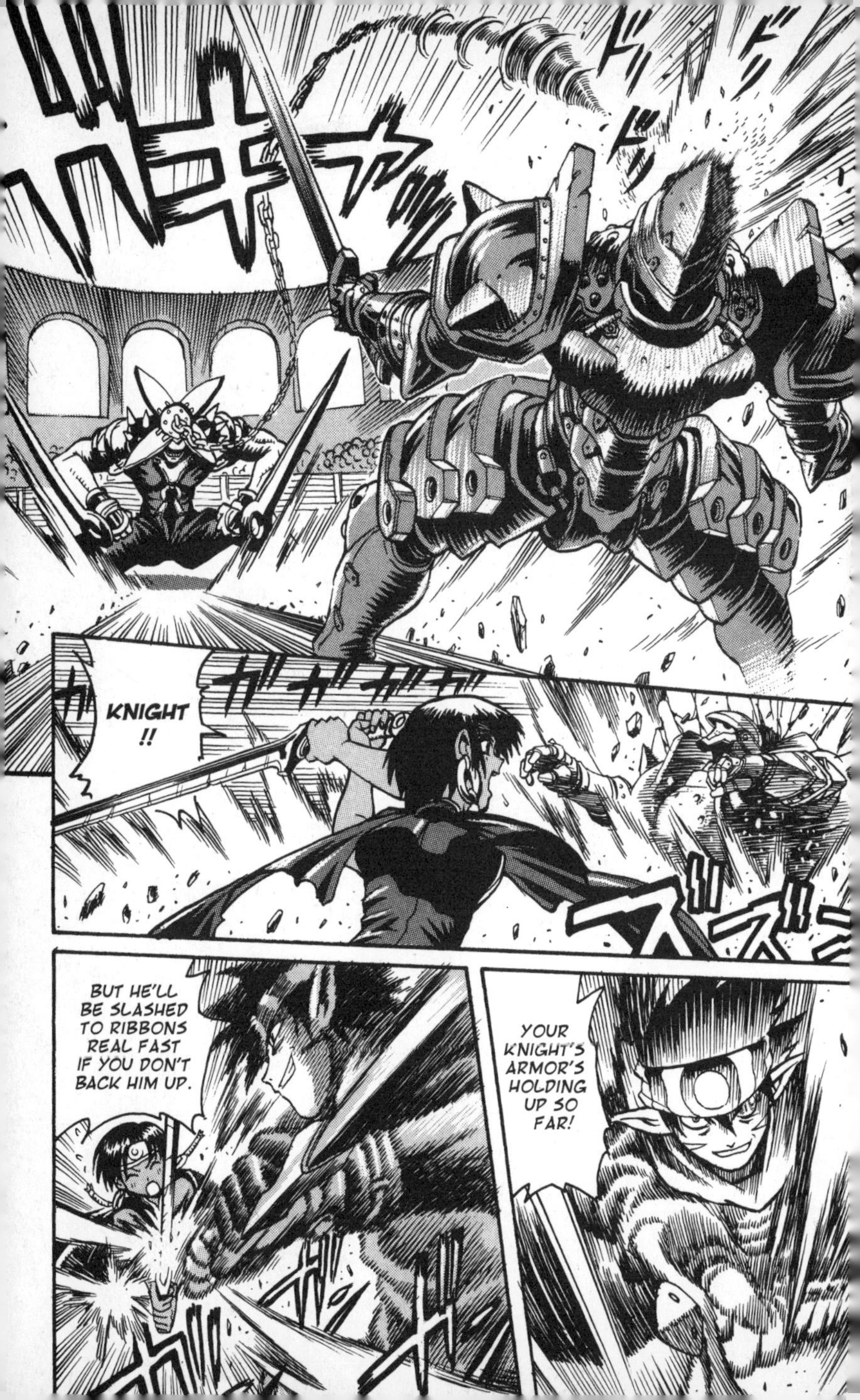
KNIGHT !!
YOUR KNIGHT'S ARMOR'S HOLDING UP SO FAR!
BUT HE'LL BE SLASHED TO RIBBONS REAL FAST IF YOU DON'T BACK HIM UP.

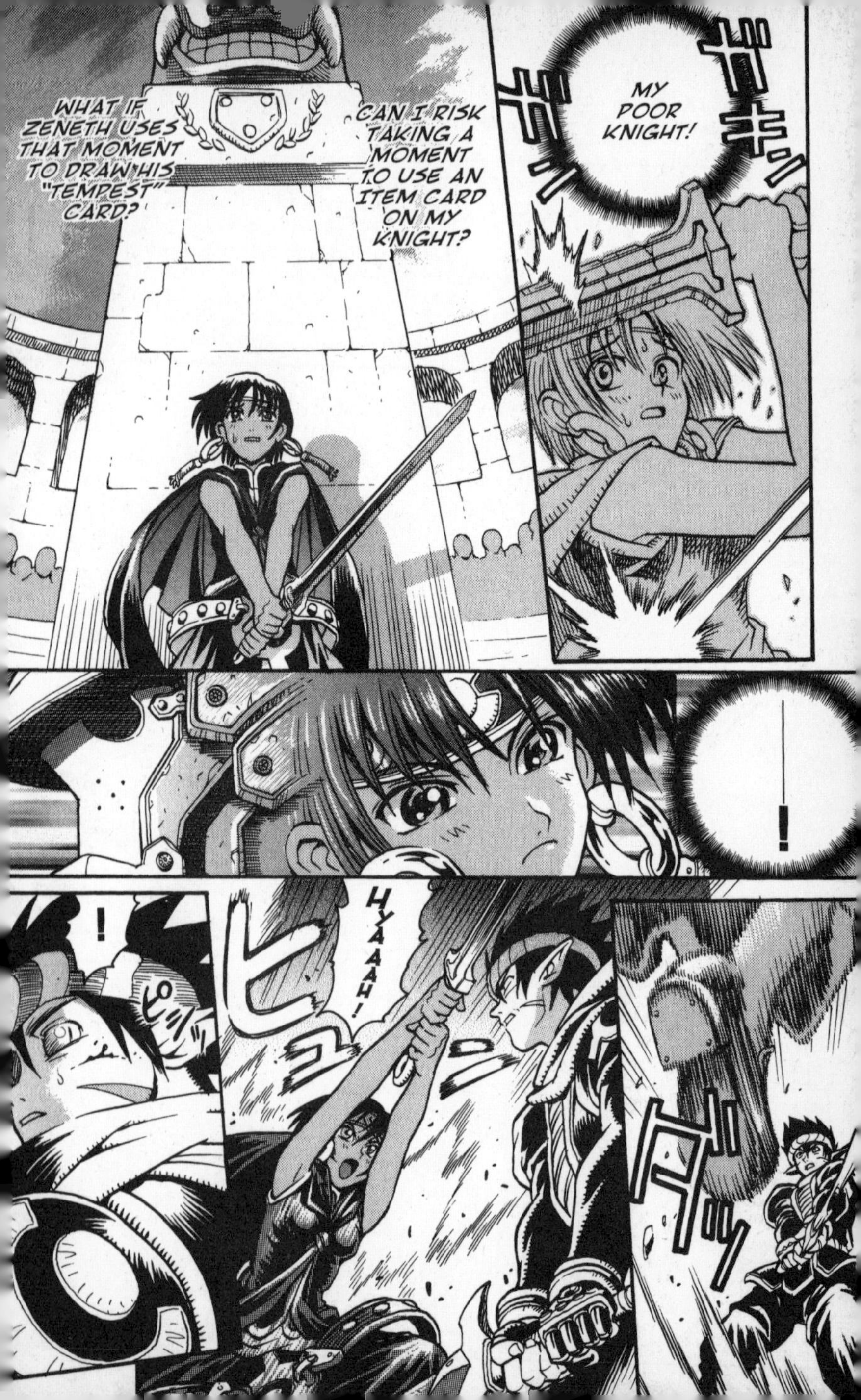
MY POOR KNIGHT!
CAN I RISK TAKING A MOMENT TO USE AN ITEM CARD ON MY KNIGHT?
WHAT IF ZENETH USES THAT MOMENT TO DRAW HIS "TEMPEST" CARD?
!
HYAAAAH!
!

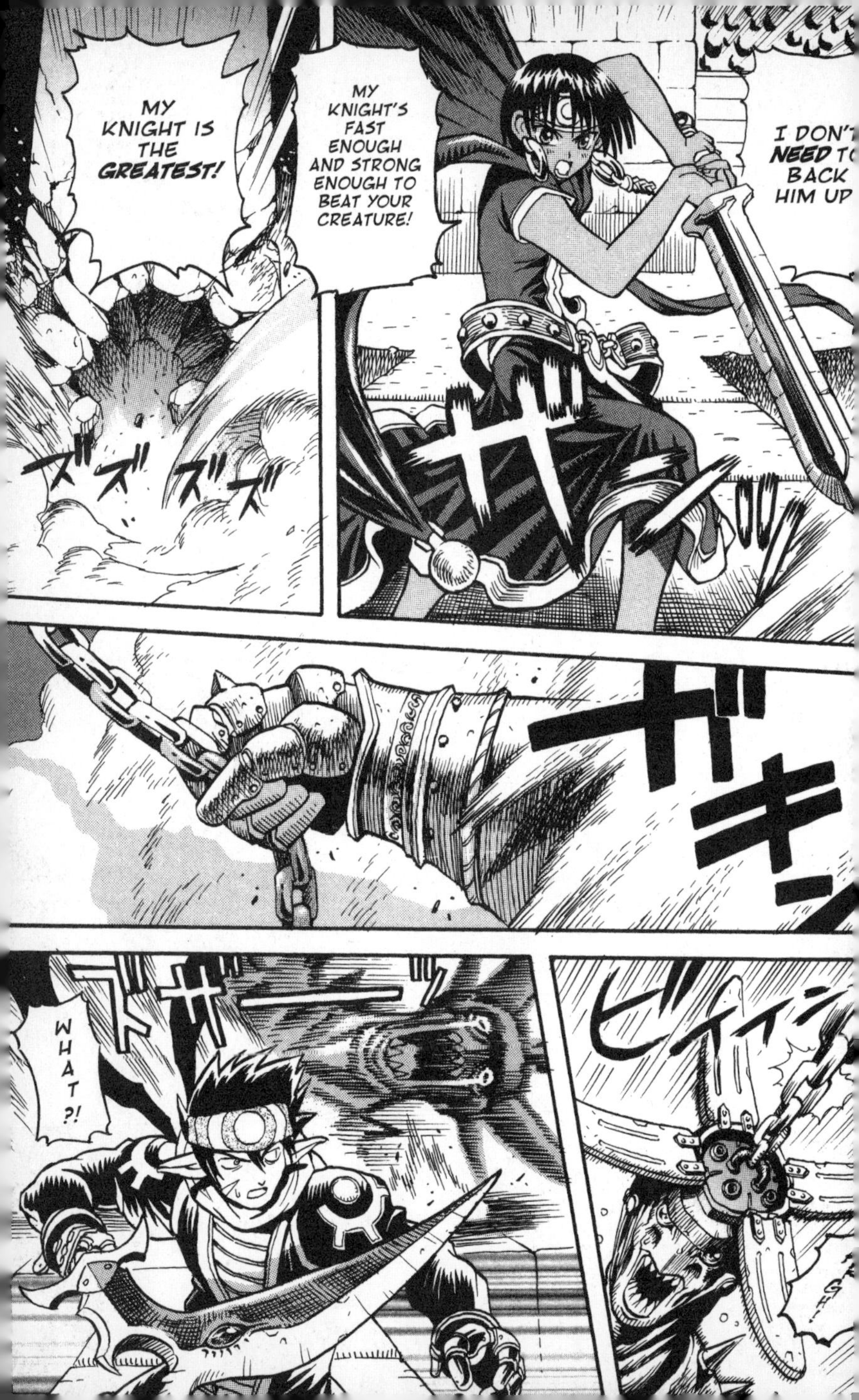

I DON'T NEED T BACK HIM UP
MY KNIGHT'S FAST ENOUGH AND STRONG ENOUGH TO BEAT YOUR CREATURE!
MY KNIGHT IS THE GREATEST!
WHAT?!

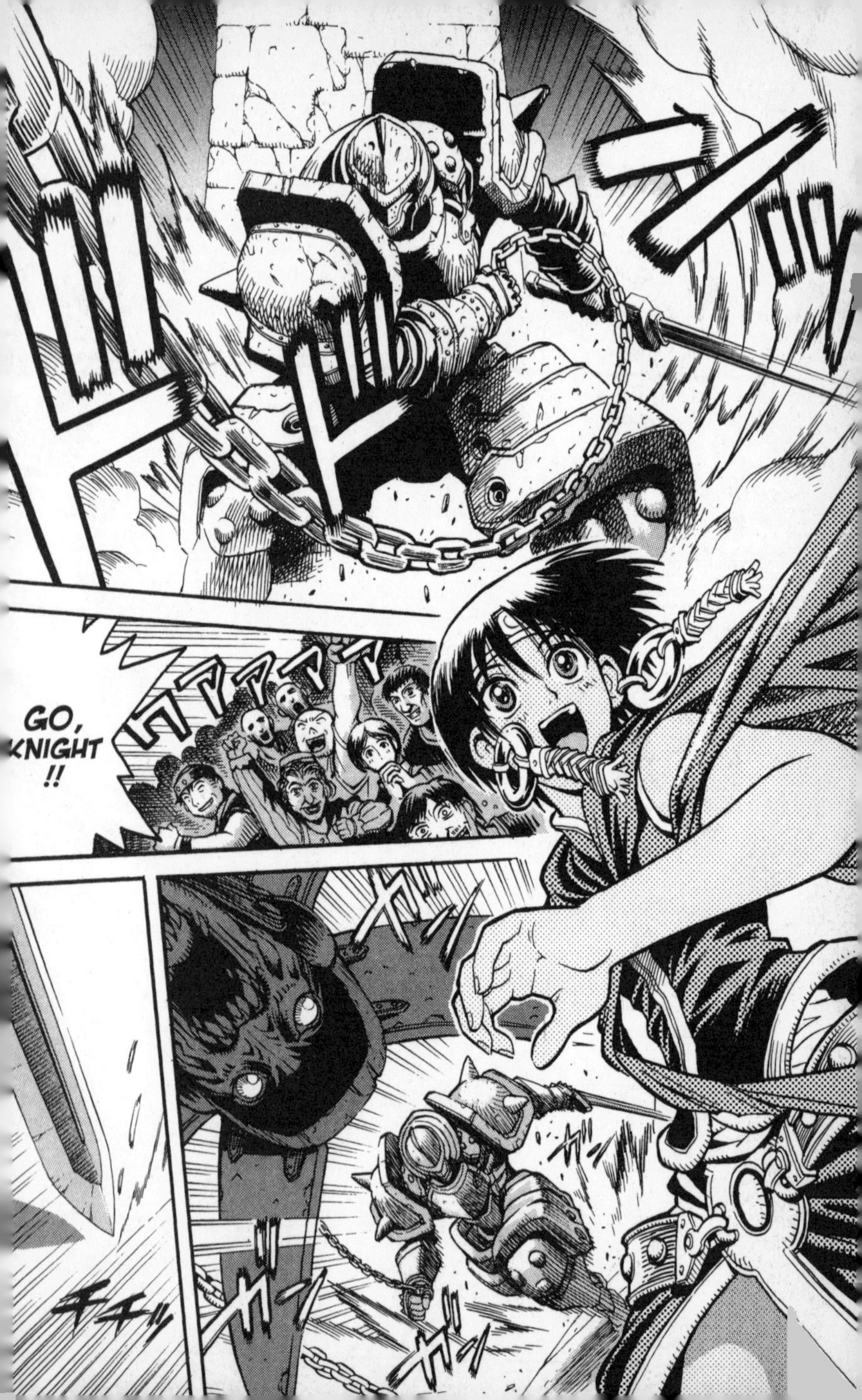
GO, KNIGHT !!

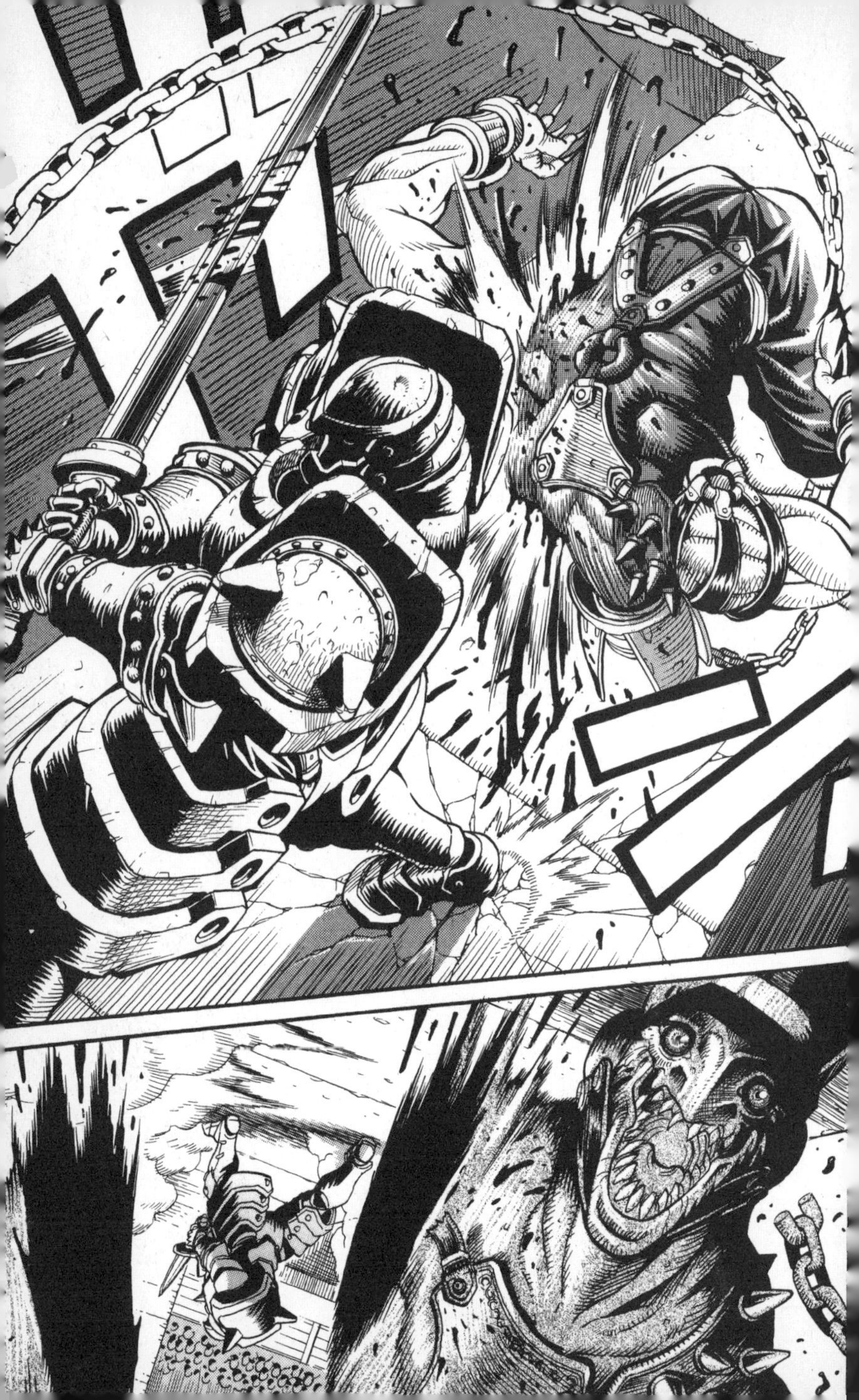

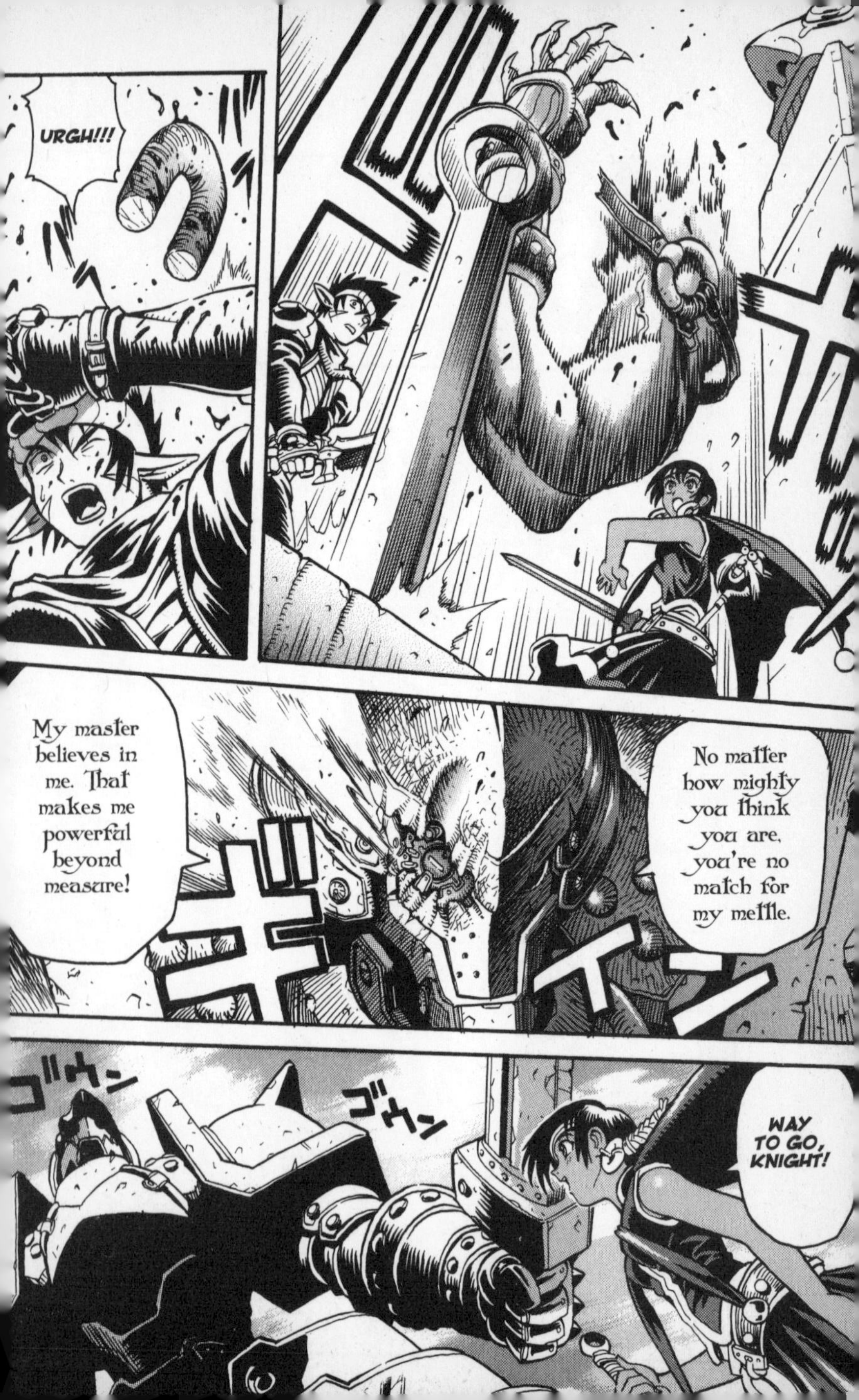
URGH!!!
No matter how mighty you think you are, you're no match for my mettle.
My master believes in me. That makes me powerful beyond measure!
WAY TO GO, KNIGHT!

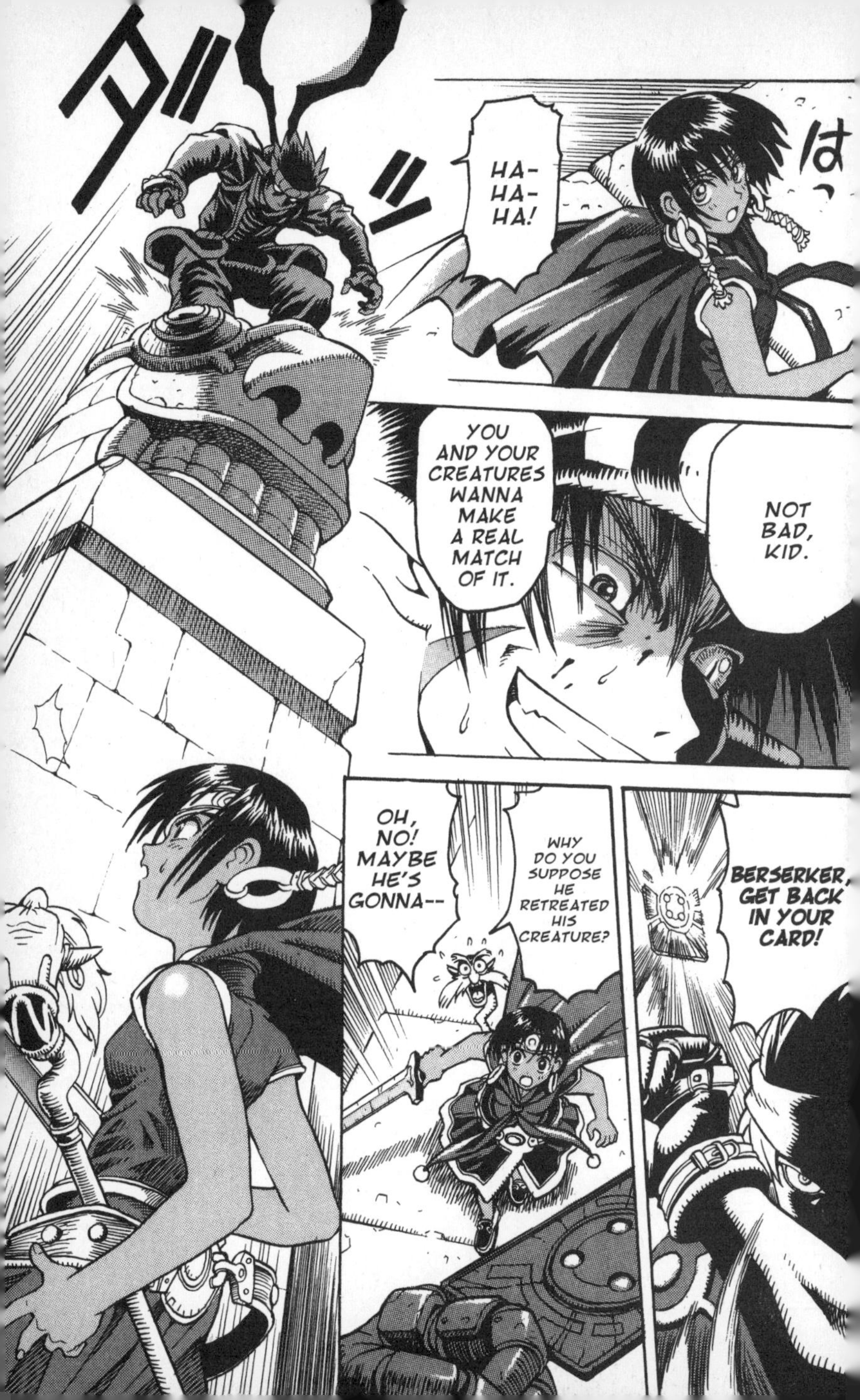

はっ
HA-HA-HA!
NOT BAD, KID.
YOU AND YOUR CREATURES WANNA MAKE A REAL MATCH OF IT.
ダッ
BERSERKER, GET BACK IN YOUR CARD!
WHY DO YOU SUPPOSE HE RETREATED HIS CREATURE?
OH, NO! MAYBE HE'S GONNA--

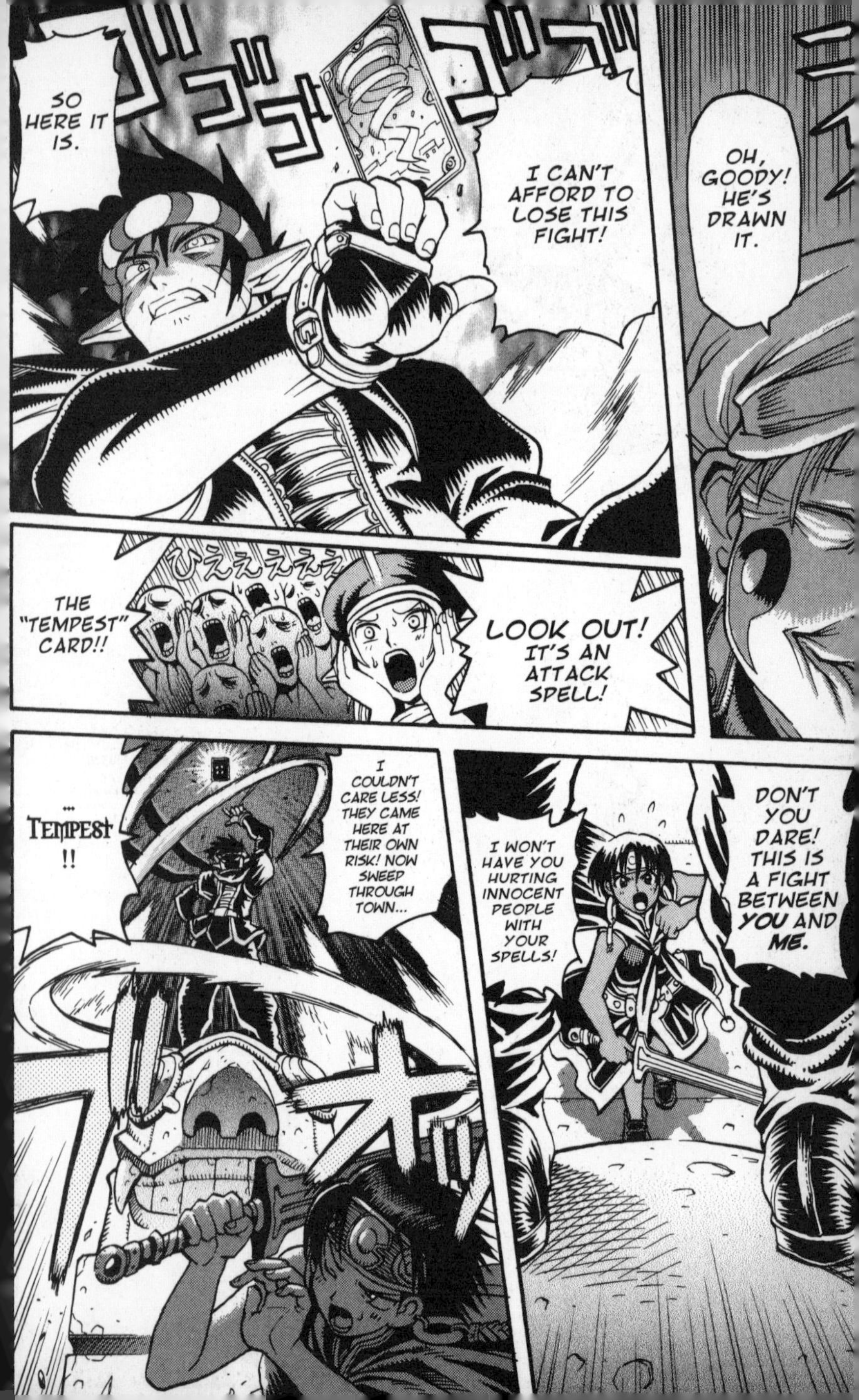

OH, GOODY! HE'S DRAWN IT.
I CAN'T AFFORD TO LOSE THIS FIGHT!
SO HERE IT IS.
LOOK OUT! IT'S AN ATTACK SPELL!
ひえええええ
THE "TEMPEST" CARD!!
DON'T YOU DARE! THIS IS A FIGHT BETWEEN YOU AND ME.
I WON'T HAVE YOU HURTING INNOCENT PEOPLE WITH YOUR SPELLS!
I COULDN'T CARE LESS! THEY CAME HERE AT THEIR OWN RISK! NOW SWEEP THROUGH TOWN...
...TEMPEST!!

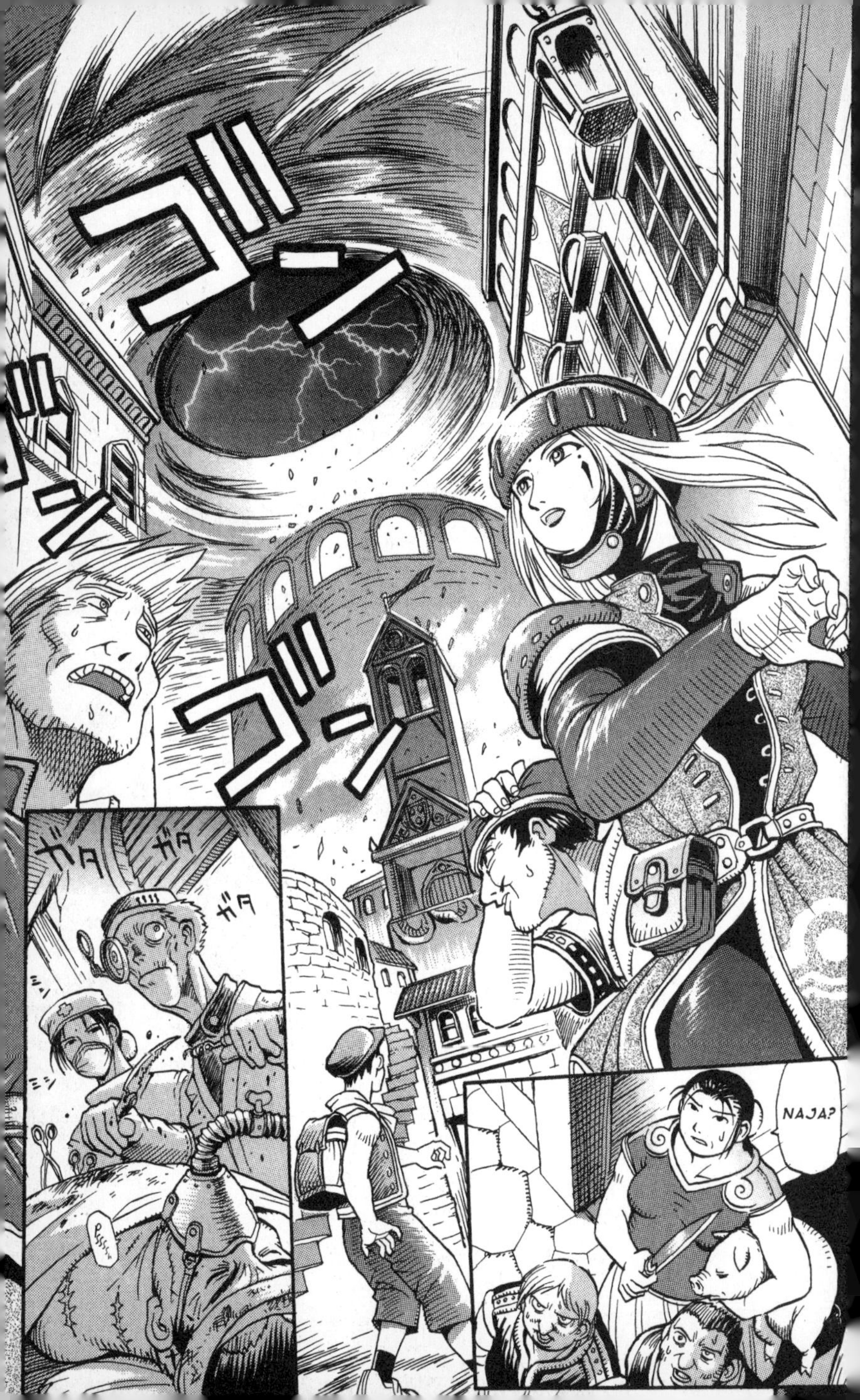
NAJA?
ガタ ガタ
ガタ

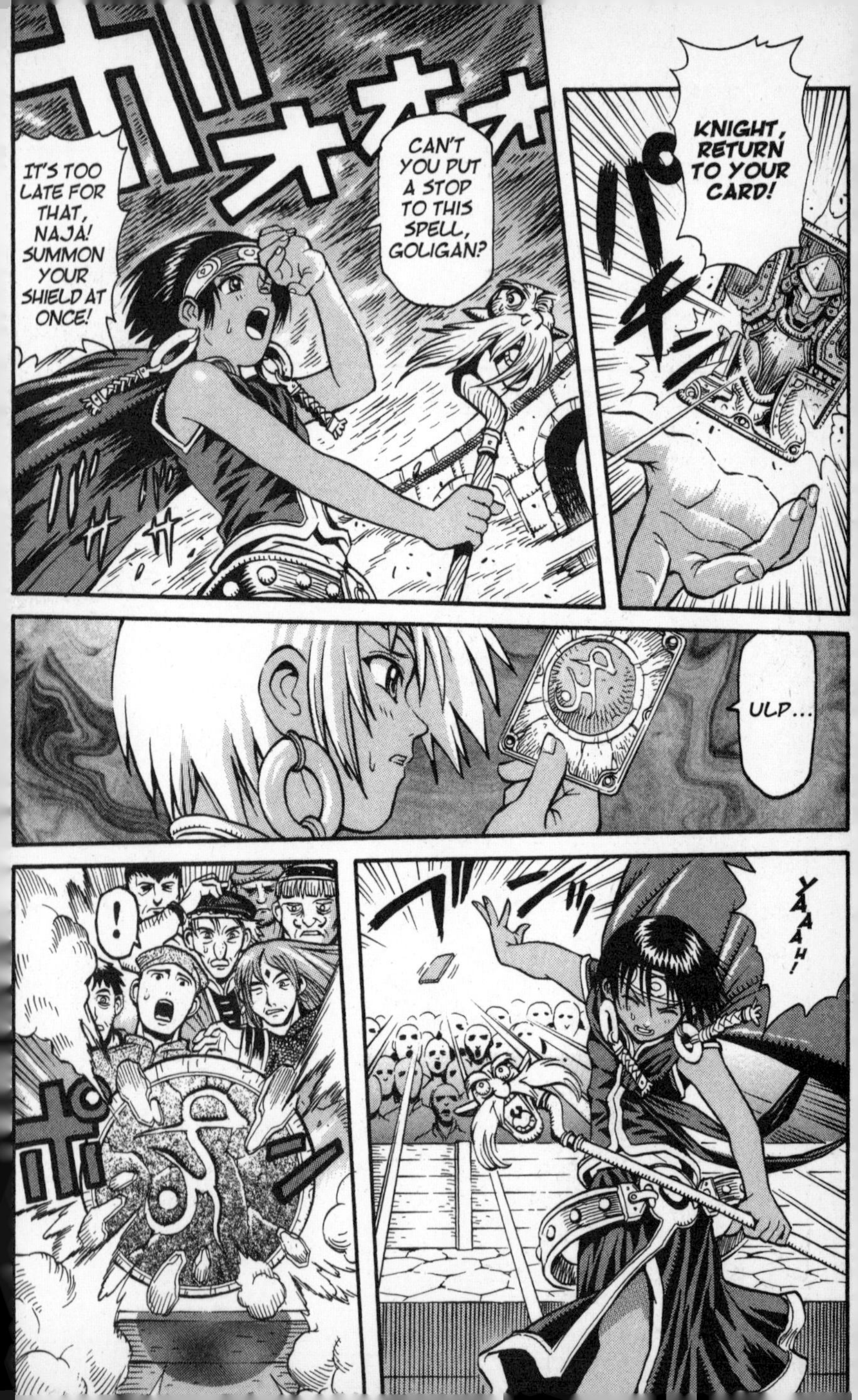
KNIGHT, RETURN TO YOUR CARD!
CAN'T YOU PUT A STOP TO THIS SPELL, GOLIGAN?
IT'S TOO LATE FOR THAT, NAJÁ! SUMMON YOUR SHIELD AT ONCE!
ULP...
YAAAAH!
!

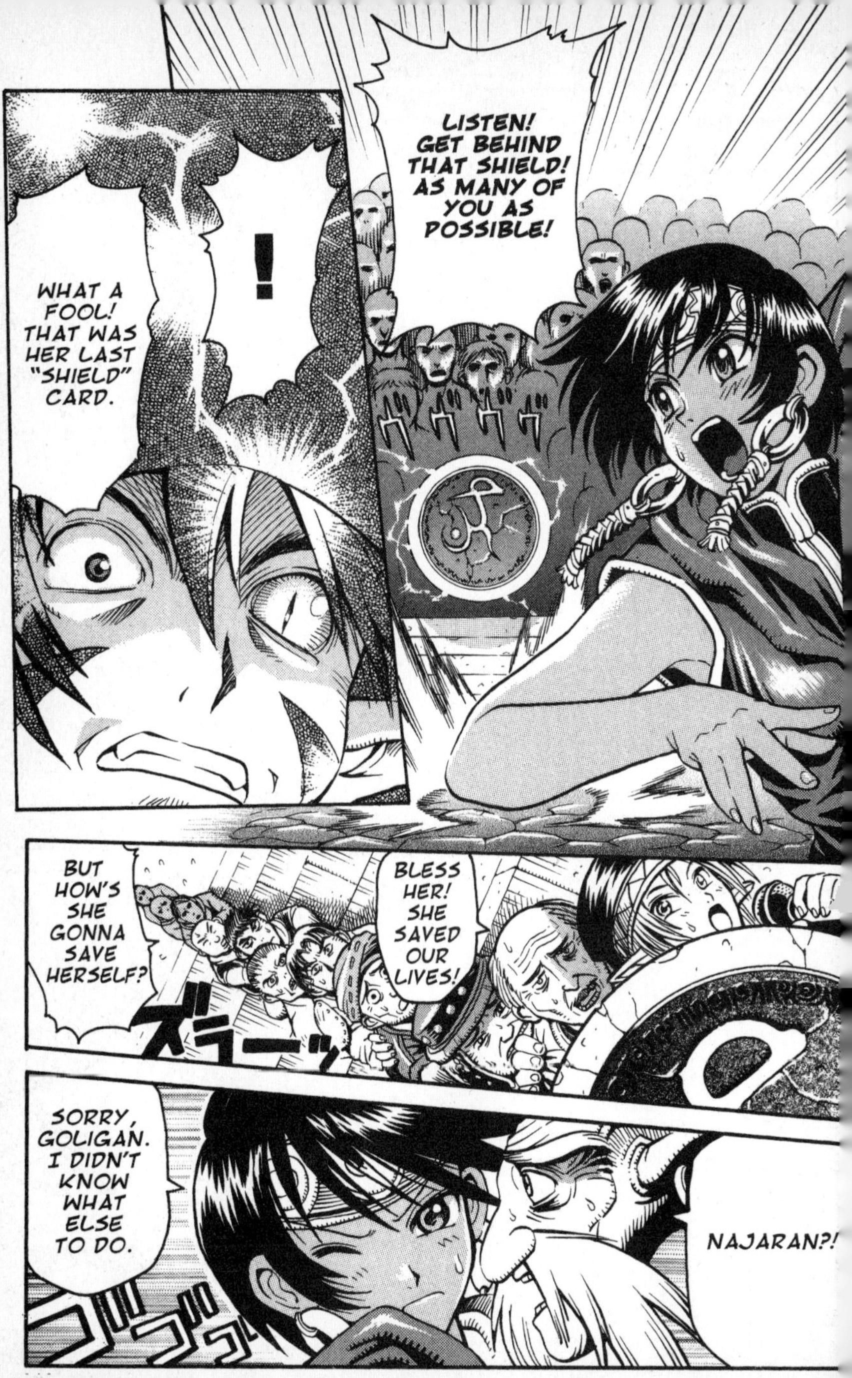
LISTEN! GET BEHIND THAT SHIELD! AS MANY OF YOU AS POSSIBLE!
!
WHAT A FOOL! THAT WAS HER LAST "SHIELD" CARD.
BLESS HER! SHE SAVED OUR LIVES!
BUT HOW'S SHE GONNA SAVE HERSELF?
NAJARAN?!
SORRY, GOLIGAN. I DIDN'T KNOW WHAT ELSE TO DO.

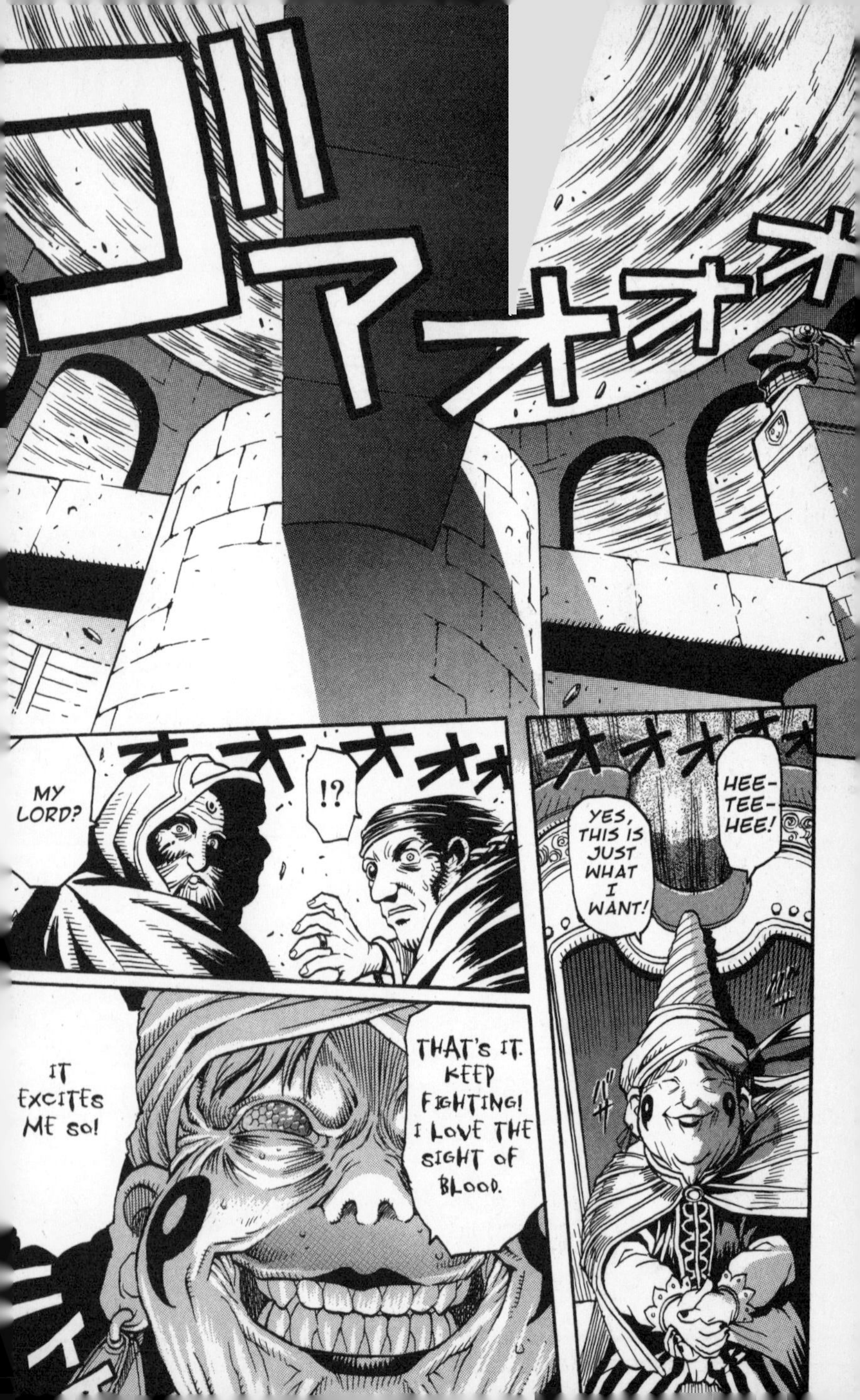
ゴアーオオオ
HEE-TEE-HEE!
YES, THIS IS JUST WHAT I WANT!
!?
MY LORD?
THAT'S IT. KEEP FIGHTING! I LOVE THE SIGHT OF BLOOD.
IT EXCITES ME SO!

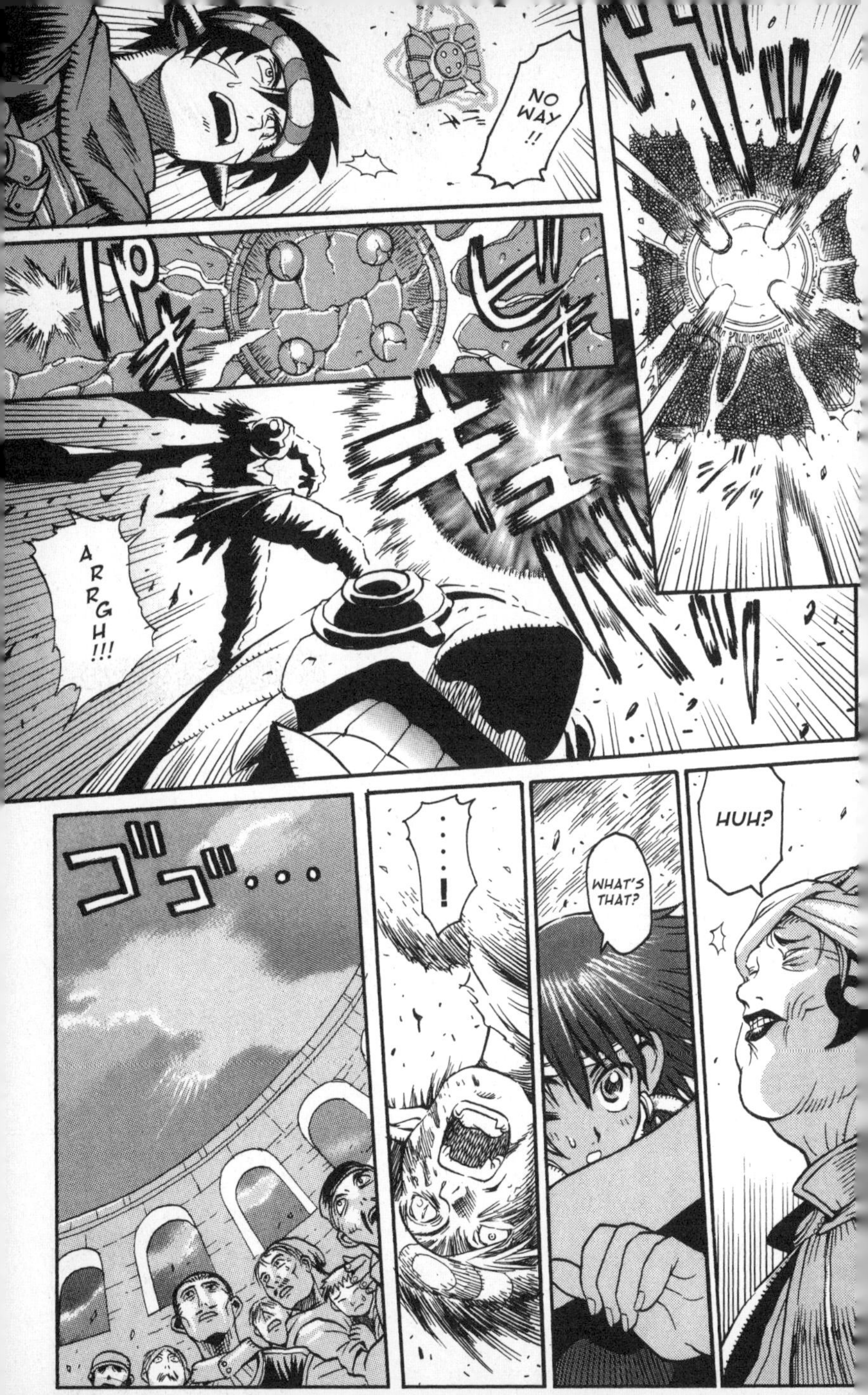

NO WAY !!
ARRGH!!!
HUH?
WHAT'S THAT?
.....!

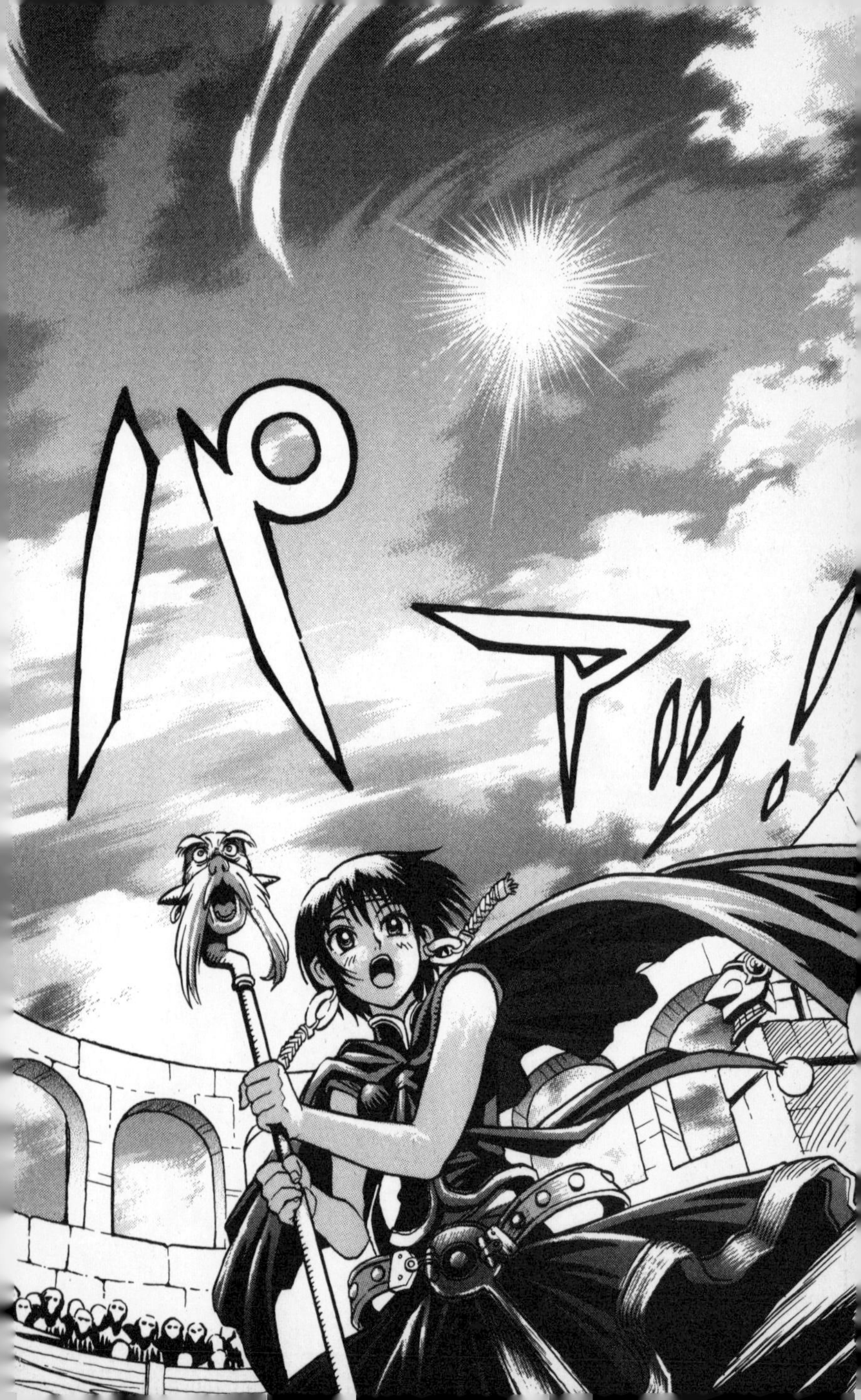
パアッ!

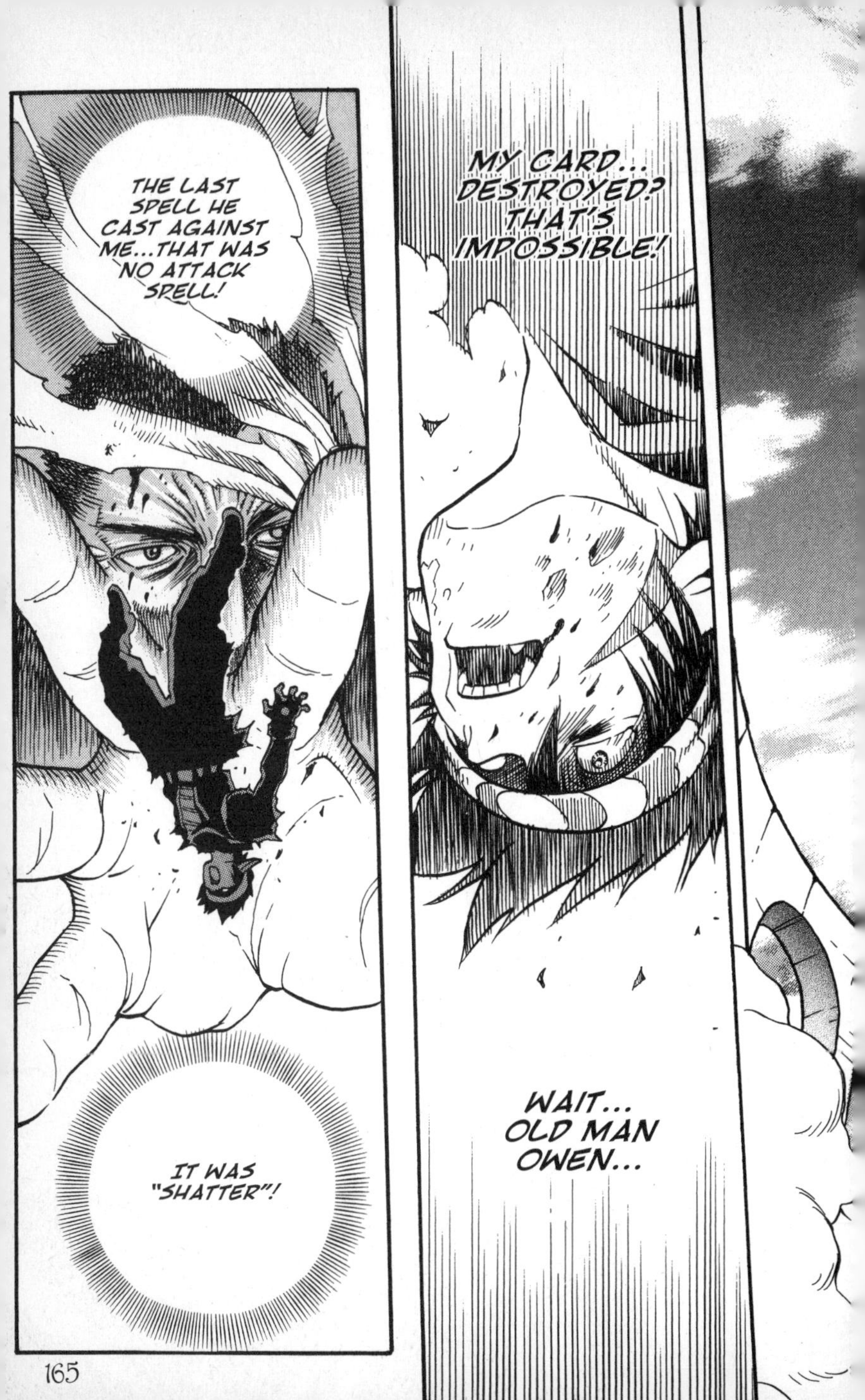
MY CARD... DESTROYED? THAT'S IMPOSSIBLE!
WAIT... OLD MAN OWEN...
THE LAST SPELL HE CAST AGAINST ME...THAT WAS NO ATTACK SPELL!
IT WAS "SHATTER"!

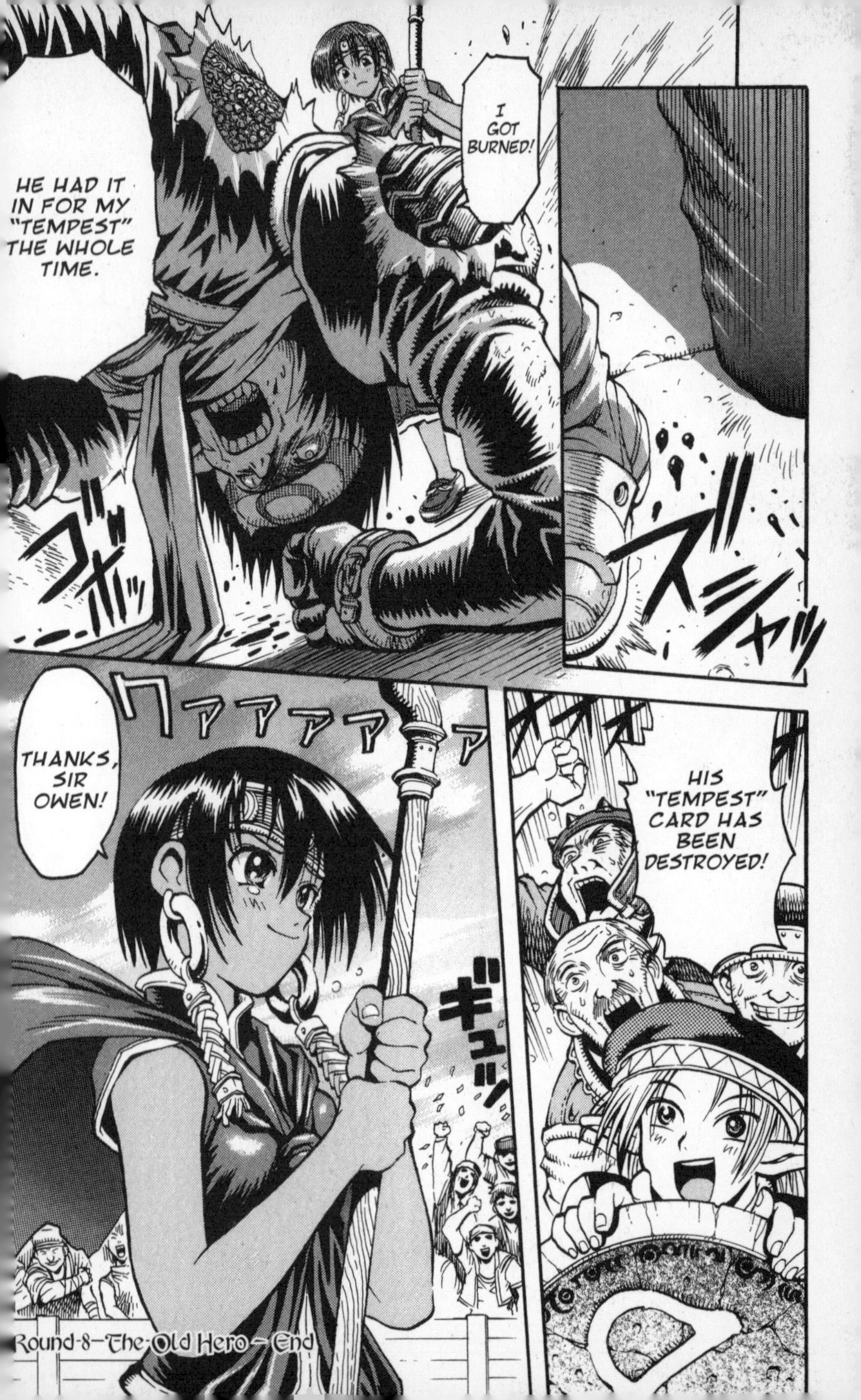
ズシャッ
I GOT BURNED!
HE HAD IT IN FOR MY "TEMPEST" THE WHOLE TIME.
ゴボッ
オオオ
HIS "TEMPEST" CARD HAS BEEN DESTROYED!
ワァアアアア
THANKS, SIR OWEN!
ギュッ
Round 8 — The Old Hero — End

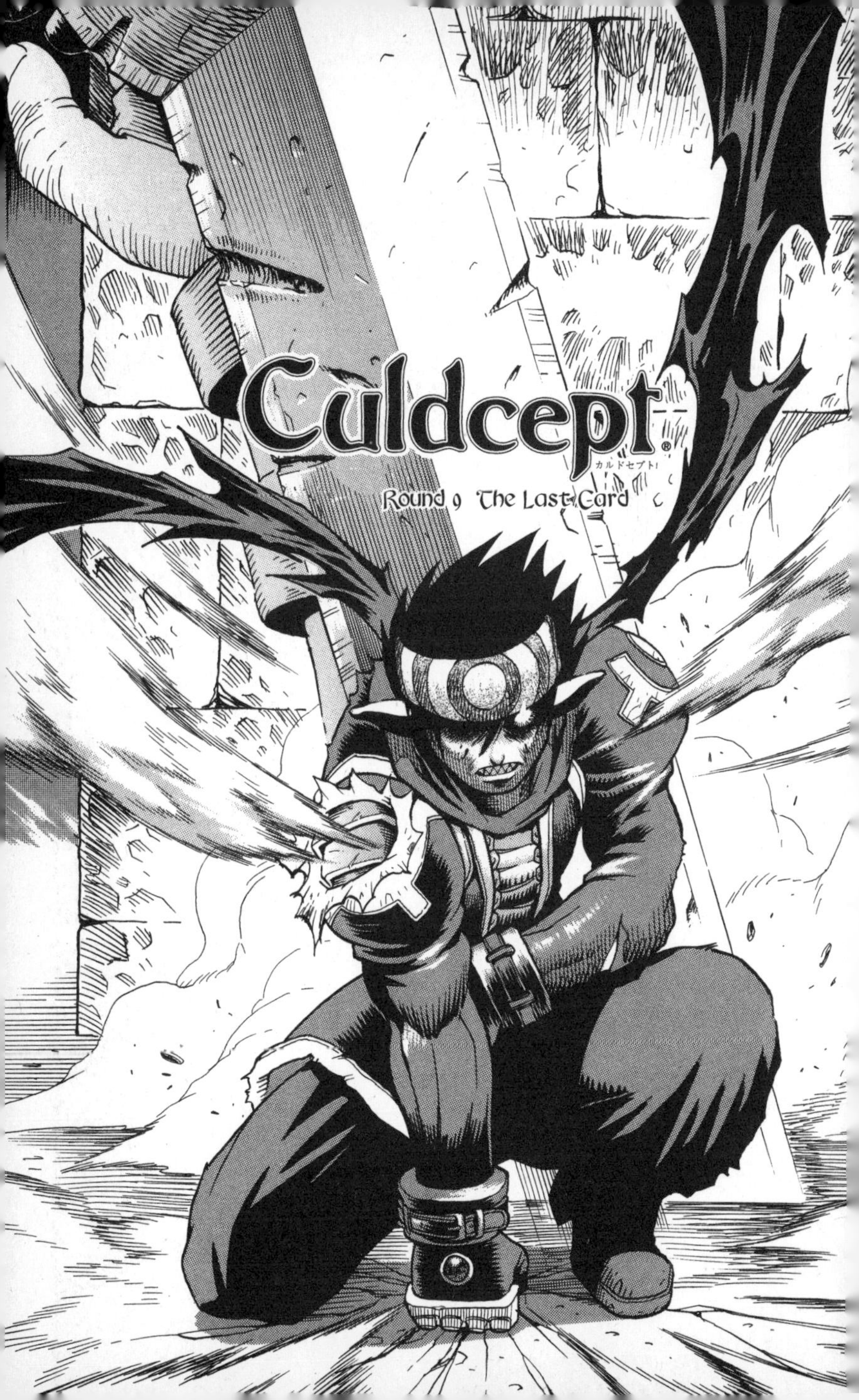
Culdcept
カルドセプト
Round 9 The Last Card

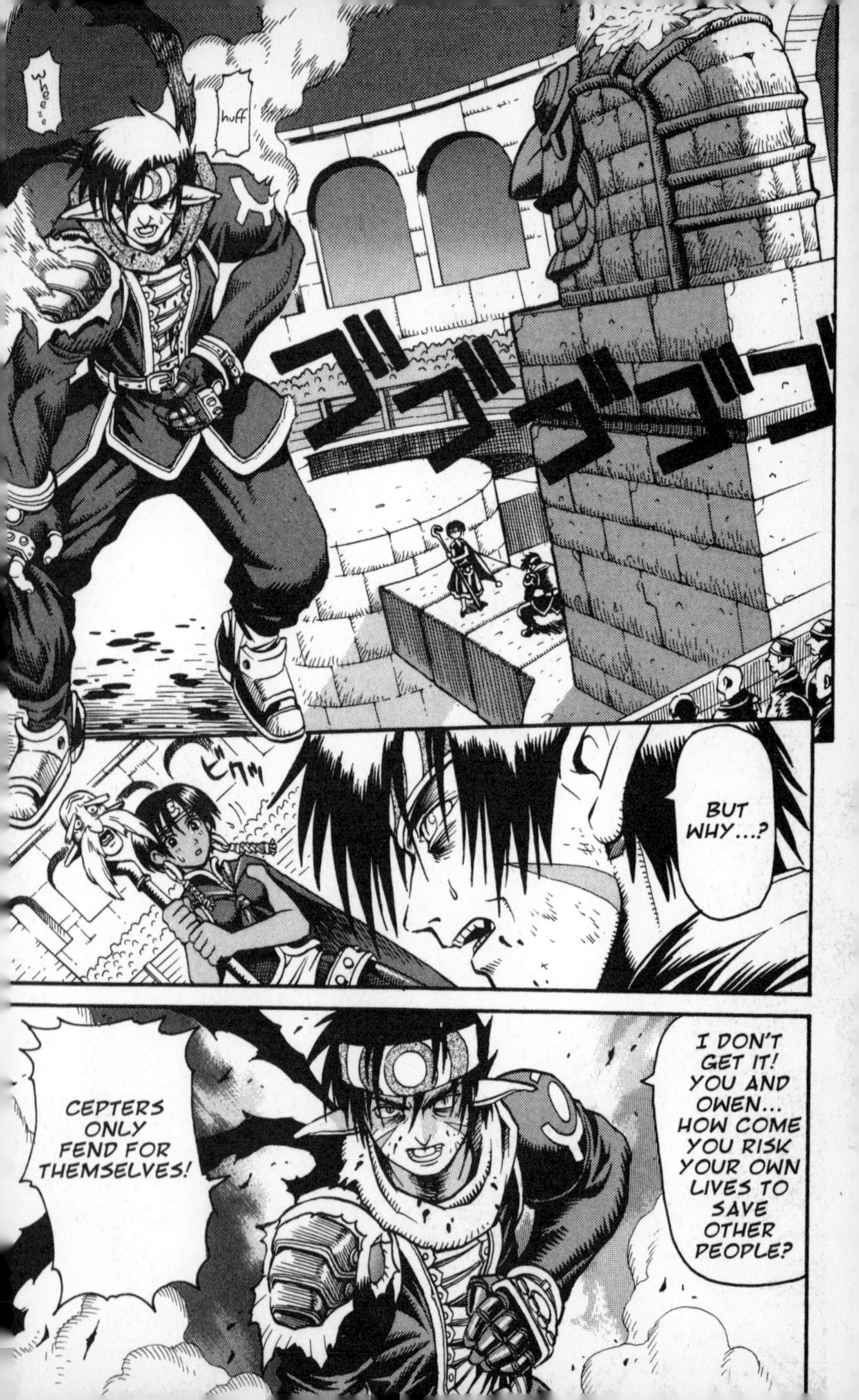
huff
wheeze
ゴゴゴゴ
BUT WHY...?
ビクッ
I DON'T GET IT! YOU AND OWEN... HOW COME YOU RISK YOUR OWN LIVES TO SAVE OTHER PEOPLE?
CEPTERS ONLY FEND FOR THEMSELVES!

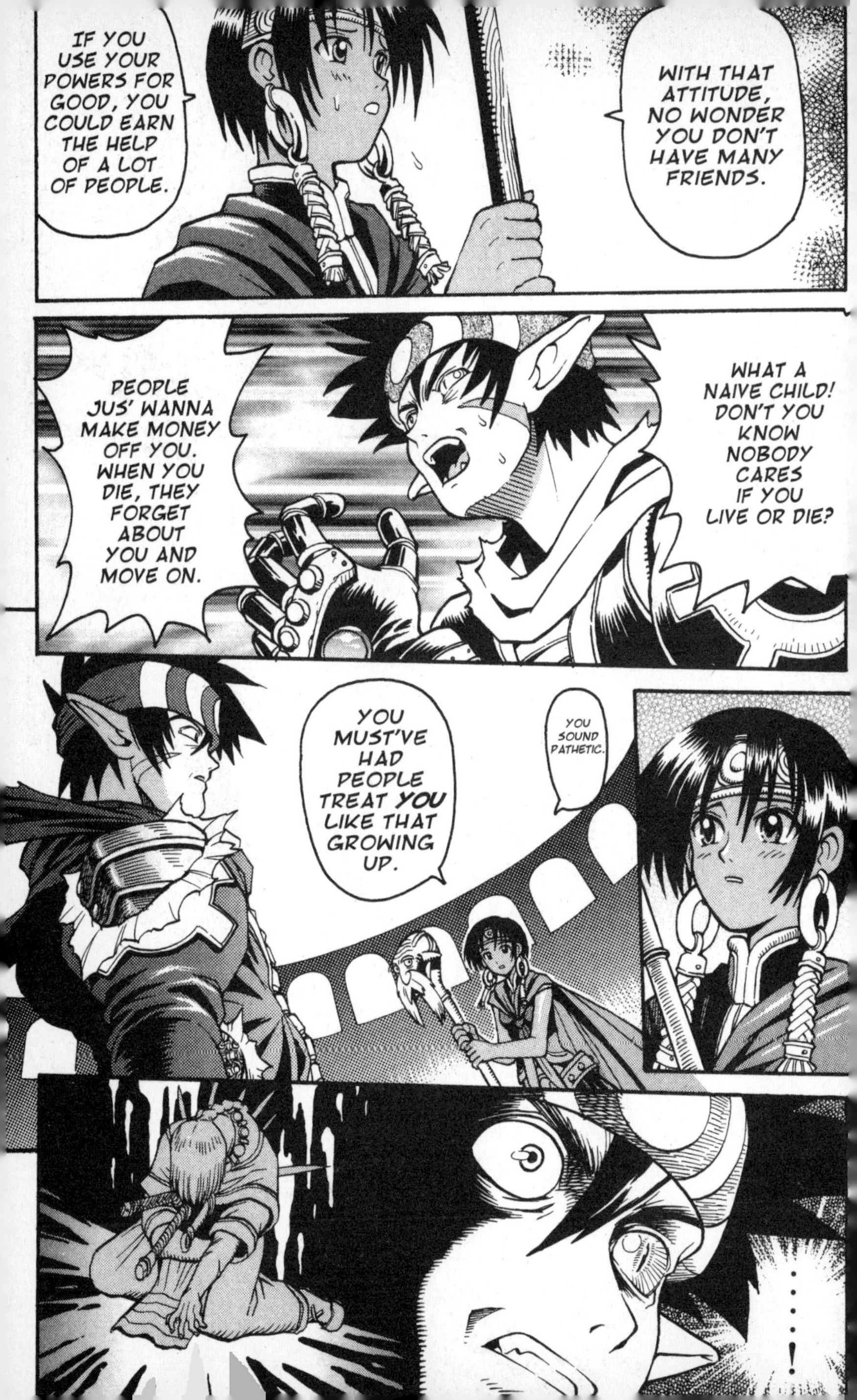
WITH THAT ATTITUDE, NO WONDER YOU DON'T HAVE MANY FRIENDS.
IF YOU USE YOUR POWERS FOR GOOD, YOU COULD EARN THE HELP OF A LOT OF PEOPLE.
WHAT A NAIVE CHILD! DON'T YOU KNOW NOBODY CARES IF YOU LIVE OR DIE?
PEOPLE JUS' WANNA MAKE MONEY OFF YOU. WHEN YOU DIE, THEY FORGET ABOUT YOU AND MOVE ON.
YOU SOUND PATHETIC.
YOU MUST'VE HAD PEOPLE TREAT *YOU* LIKE THAT GROWING UP.
......!

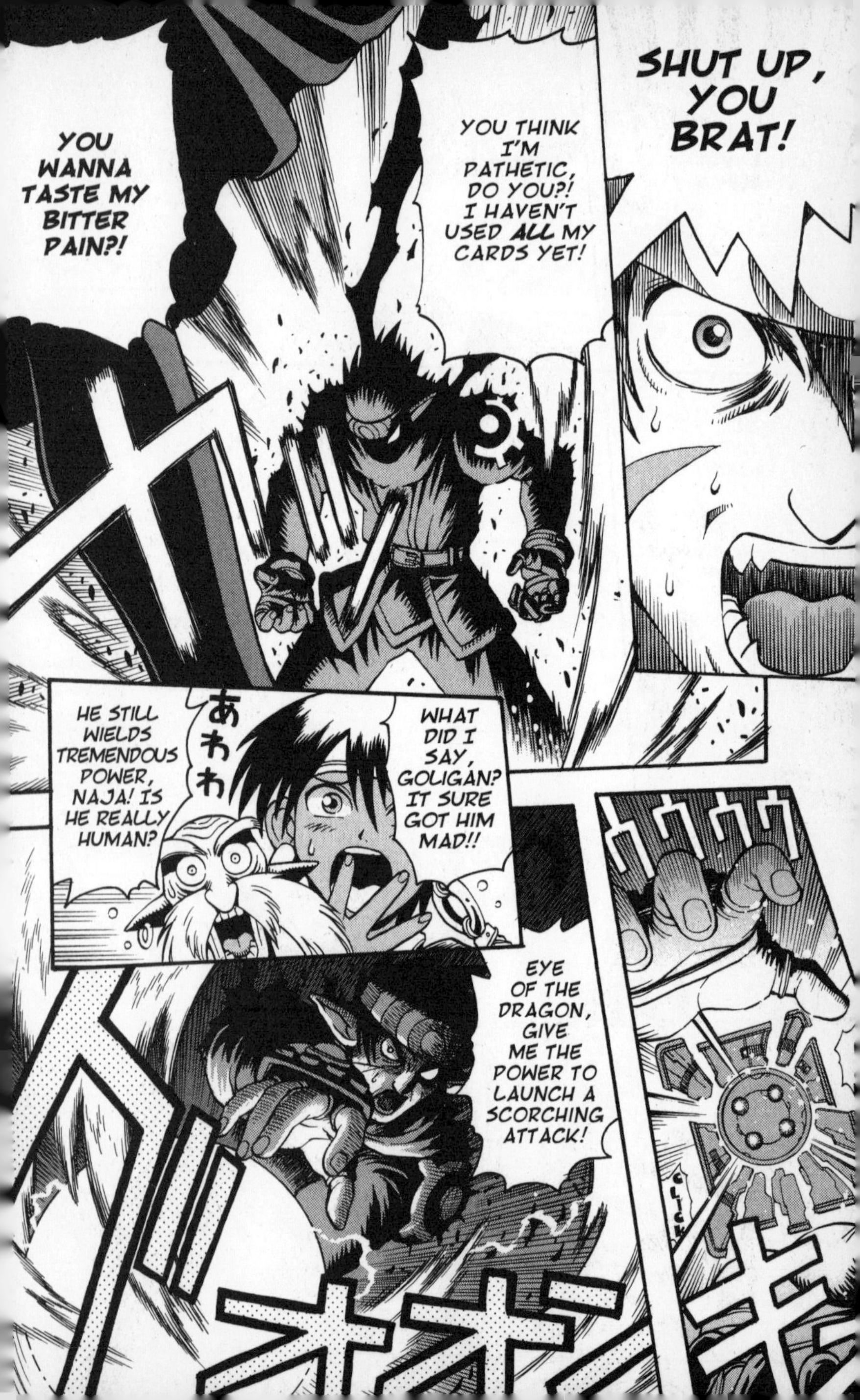
SHUT UP, YOU BRAT!
YOU THINK I'M PATHETIC, DO YOU?! I HAVEN'T USED ALL MY CARDS YET!
YOU WANNA TASTE MY BITTER PAIN?!
WHAT DID I SAY, GOLIGAN? IT SURE GOT HIM MAD!!
あわわ
HE STILL WIELDS TREMENDOUS POWER, NAJA! IS HE REALLY HUMAN?
ウウウウ
CLICK
EYE OF THE DRAGON, GIVE ME THE POWER TO LAUNCH A SCORCHING ATTACK!

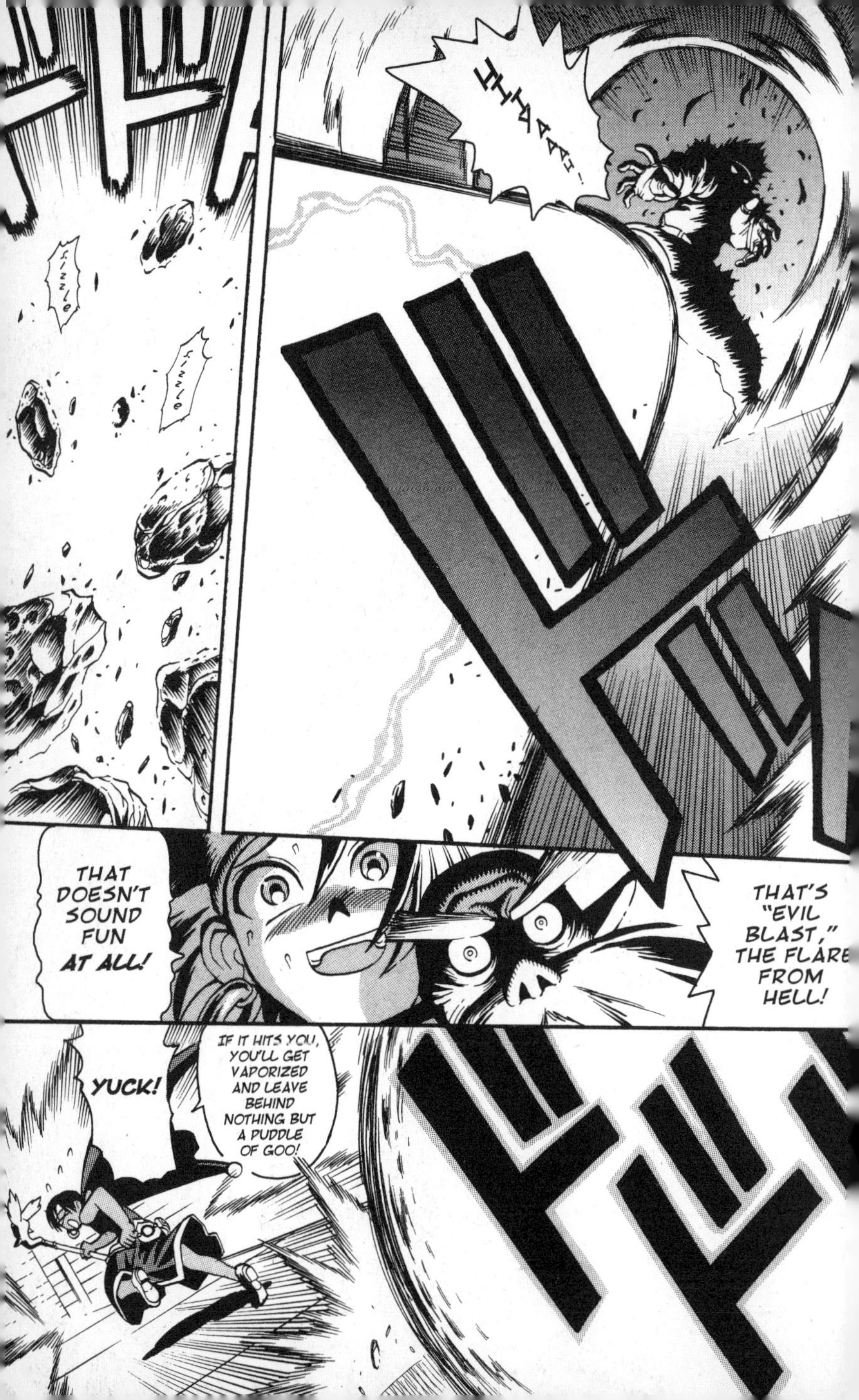
sizzle
sizzle
THAT'S "EVIL BLAST," THE FLARE FROM HELL!
THAT DOESN'T SOUND FUN AT ALL!
IF IT HITS YOU, YOU'LL GET VAPORIZED AND LEAVE BEHIND NOTHING BUT A PUDDLE OF GOO!
YUCK!

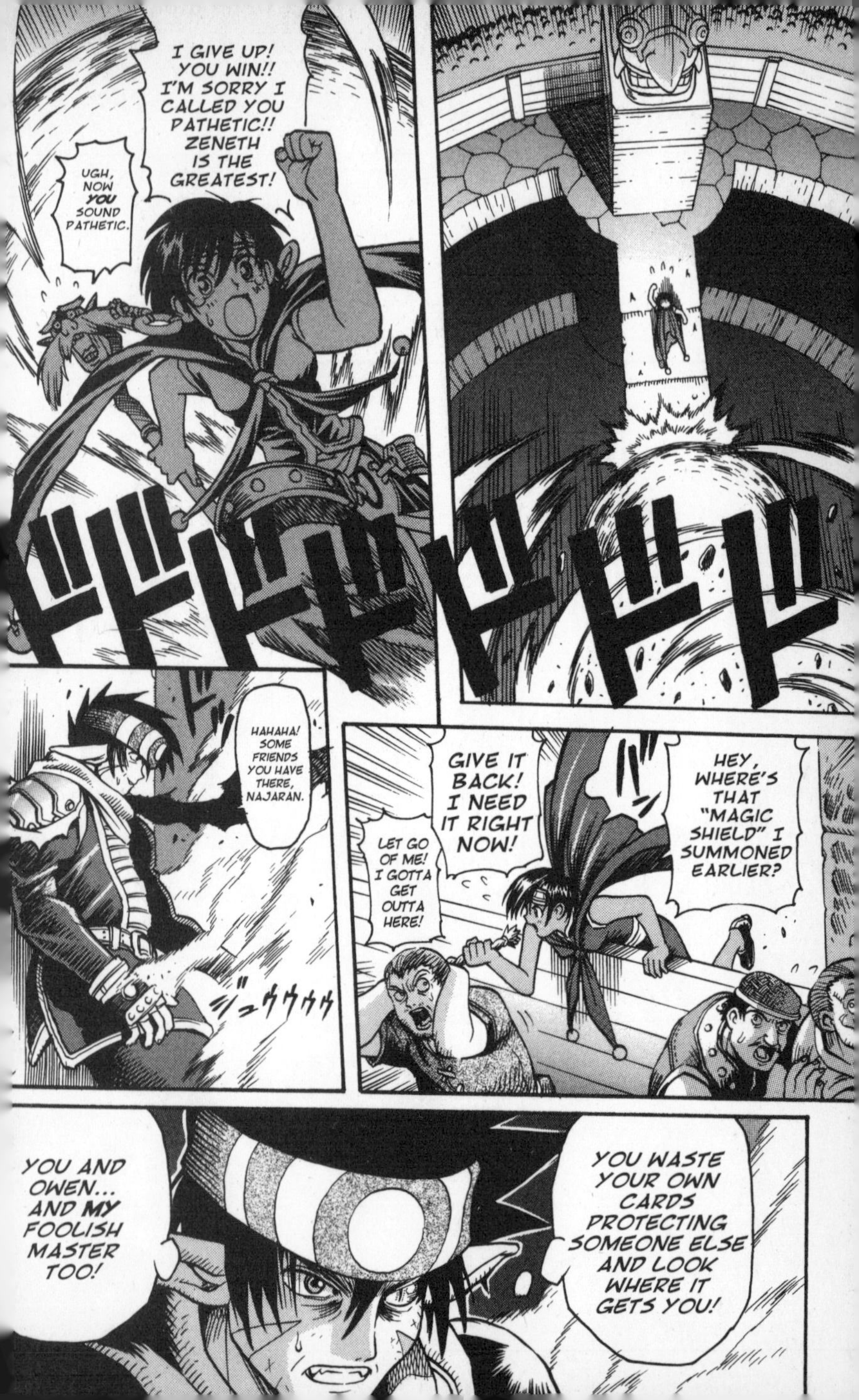
I GIVE UP! YOU WIN!! I'M SORRY I CALLED YOU PATHETIC!! ZENETH IS THE GREATEST!
UGH, NOW **YOU** SOUND PATHETIC.
HEY, WHERE'S THAT "MAGIC SHIELD" I SUMMONED EARLIER?
GIVE IT BACK! I NEED IT RIGHT NOW!
LET GO OF ME! I GOTTA GET OUTTA HERE!
HAHAHA! SOME FRIENDS YOU HAVE THERE, NAJARAN.
YOU WASTE YOUR OWN CARDS PROTECTING SOMEONE ELSE AND LOOK WHERE IT GETS YOU!
YOU AND OWEN... AND **MY** FOOLISH MASTER TOO!

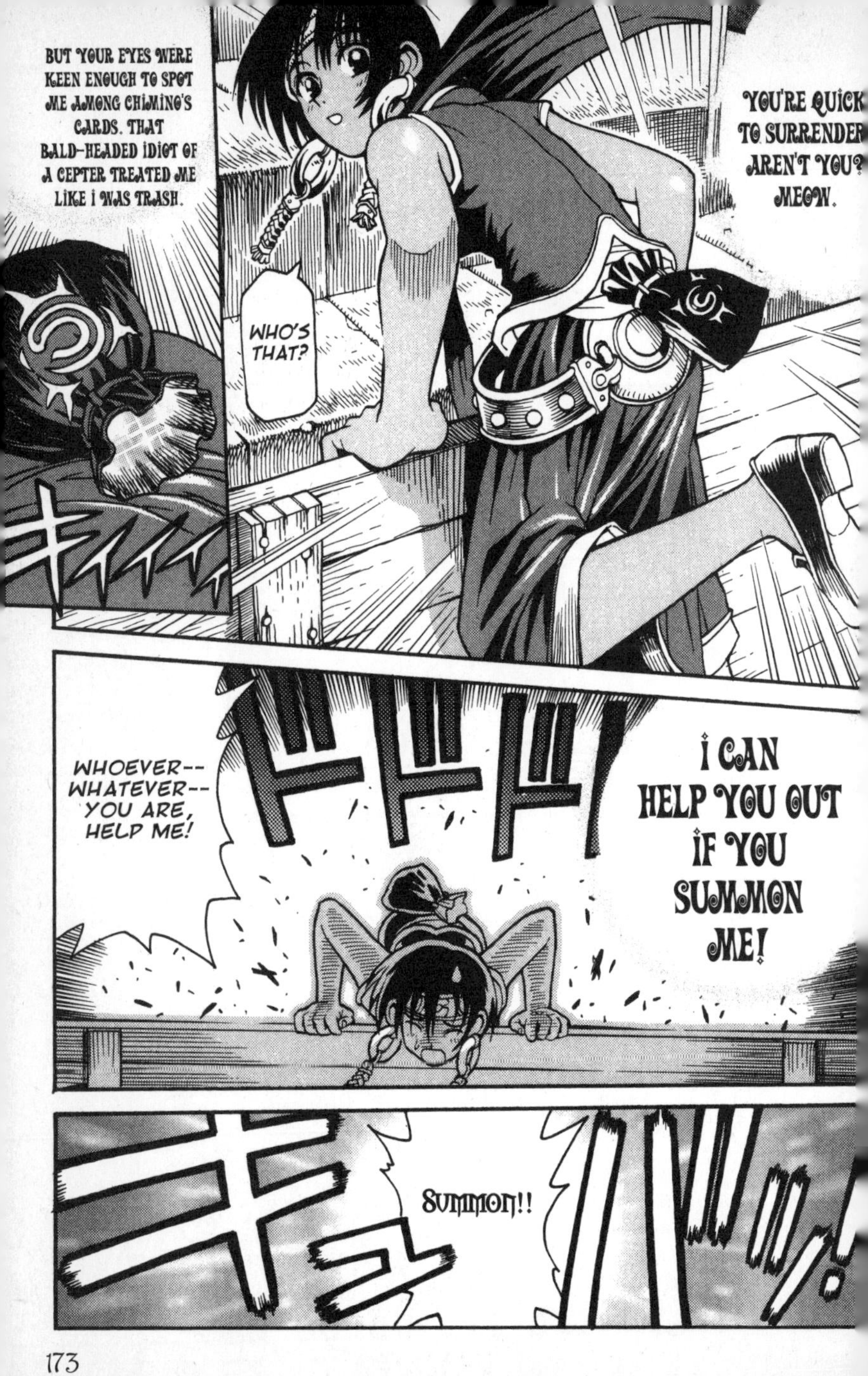
YOU'RE QUICK TO SURRENDER AREN'T YOU? MEOW.
WHO'S THAT?
BUT YOUR EYES WERE KEEN ENOUGH TO SPOT ME AMONG CHIMING'S CARDS. THAT BALD-HEADED IDIOT OF A CEPTER TREATED ME LIKE I WAS TRASH.
I CAN HELP YOU OUT IF YOU SUMMON ME!
WHOEVER-- WHATEVER-- YOU ARE, HELP ME!
SUMMON!!

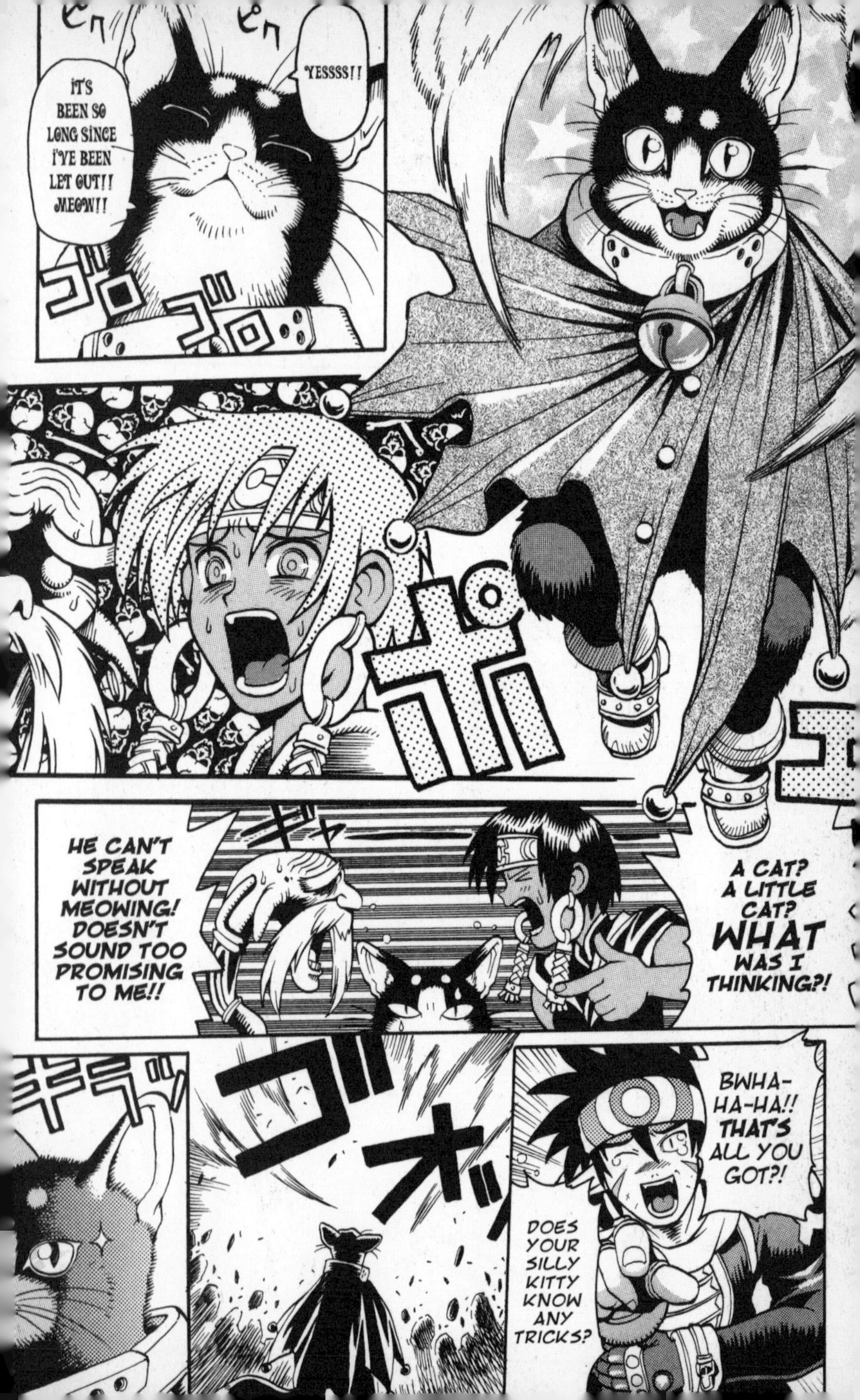
YESSSS!!
IT'S BEEN SO LONG SINCE I'VE BEEN LET OUT!! MEOW!!
A CAT? A LITTLE CAT? WHAT WAS I THINKING?!
HE CAN'T SPEAK WITHOUT MEOWING! DOESN'T SOUND TOO PROMISING TO ME!!
BWHA-HA-HA!! THAT'S ALL YOU GOT?!
DOES YOUR SILLY KITTY KNOW ANY TRICKS?

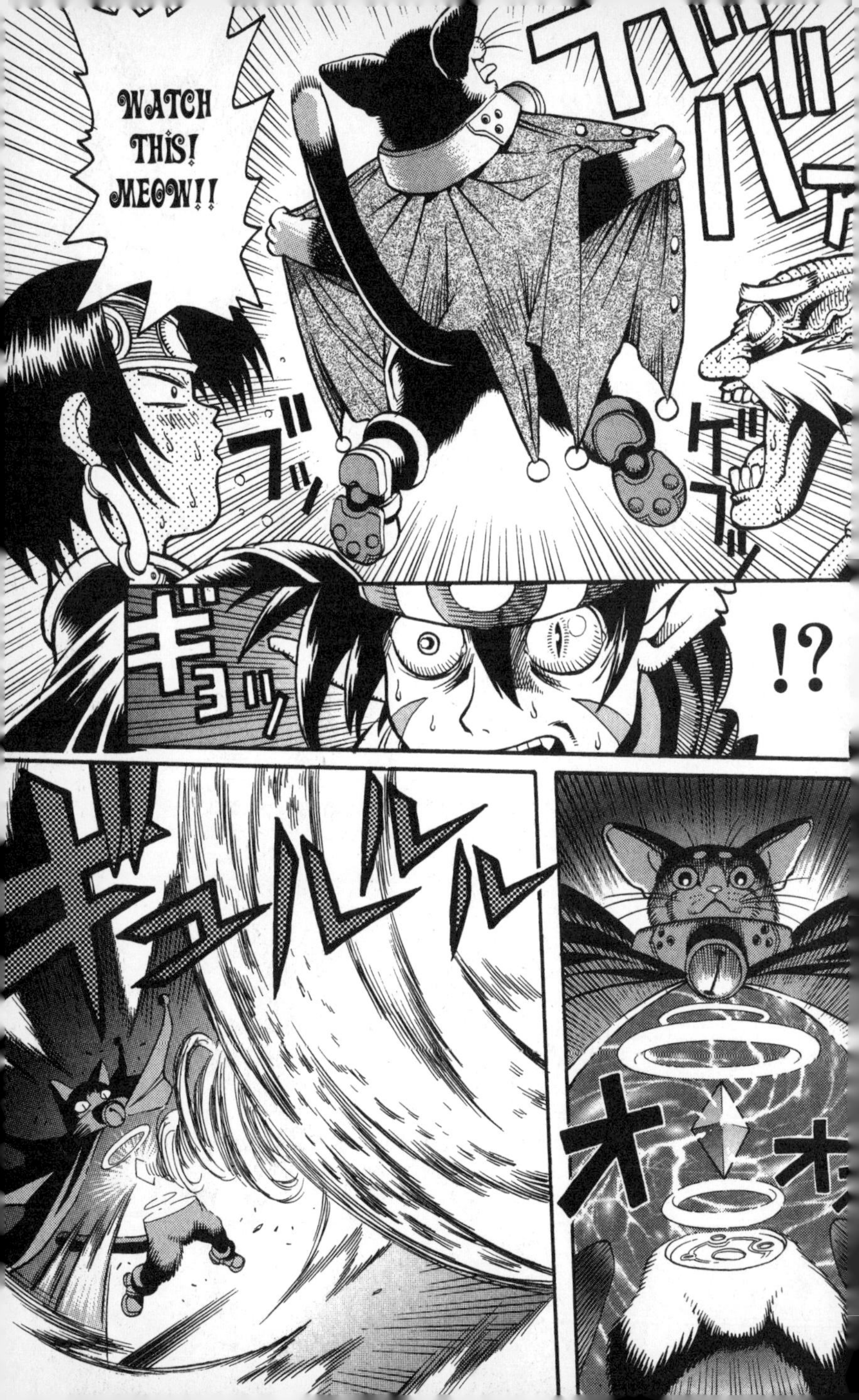
WATCH THIS! MEOW!!
!?

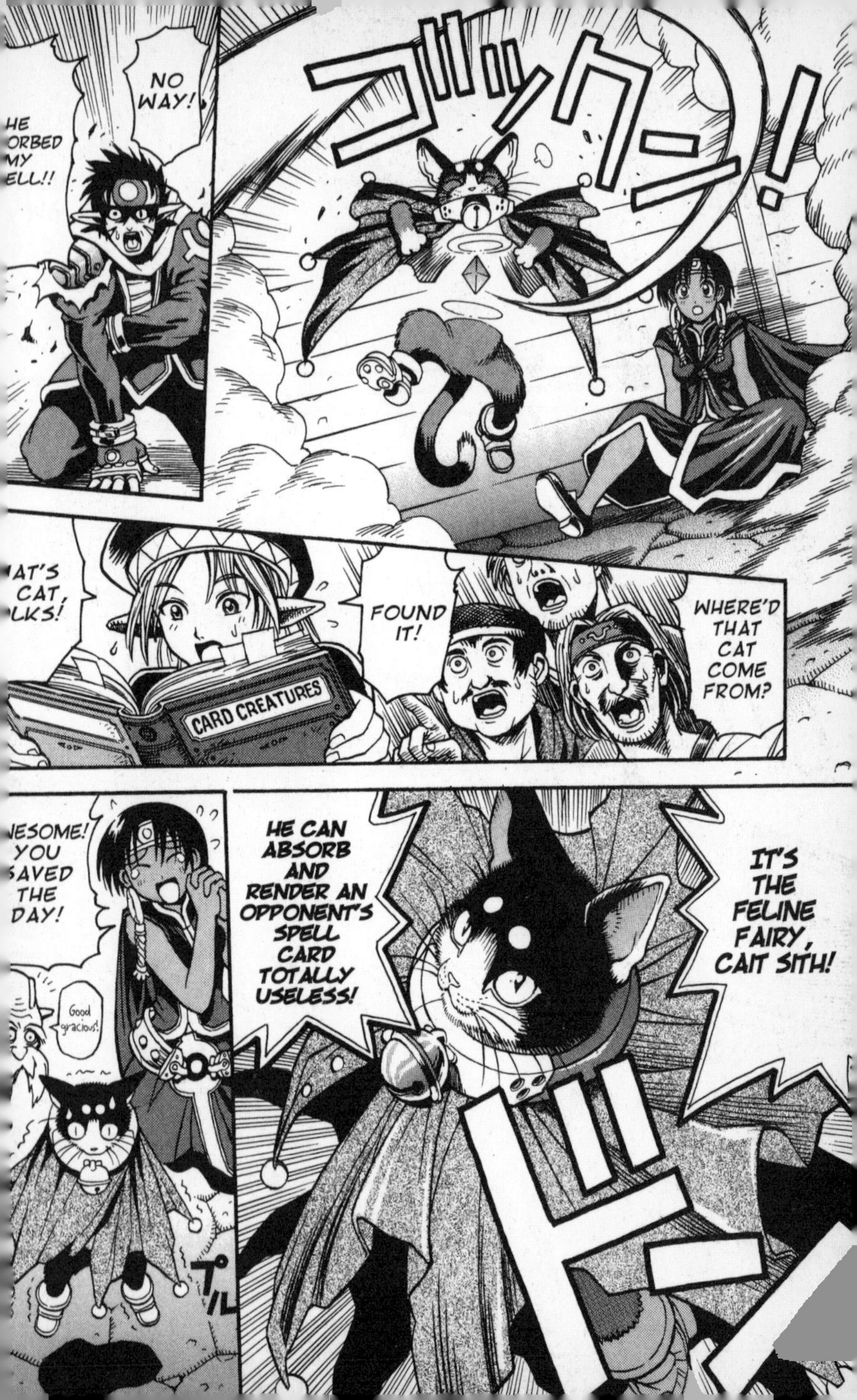

NO WAY!
HE ORBED MY ELL!!
WHERE'D THAT CAT COME FROM?
FOUND IT!
CARD CREATURES
AT'S CAT, LKS!
IT'S THE FELINE FAIRY, CAIT SITH!
HE CAN ABSORB AND RENDER AN OPPONENT'S SPELL CARD TOTALLY USELESS!
ドーン
ESOME! YOU SAVED THE DAY!
Good gracious!

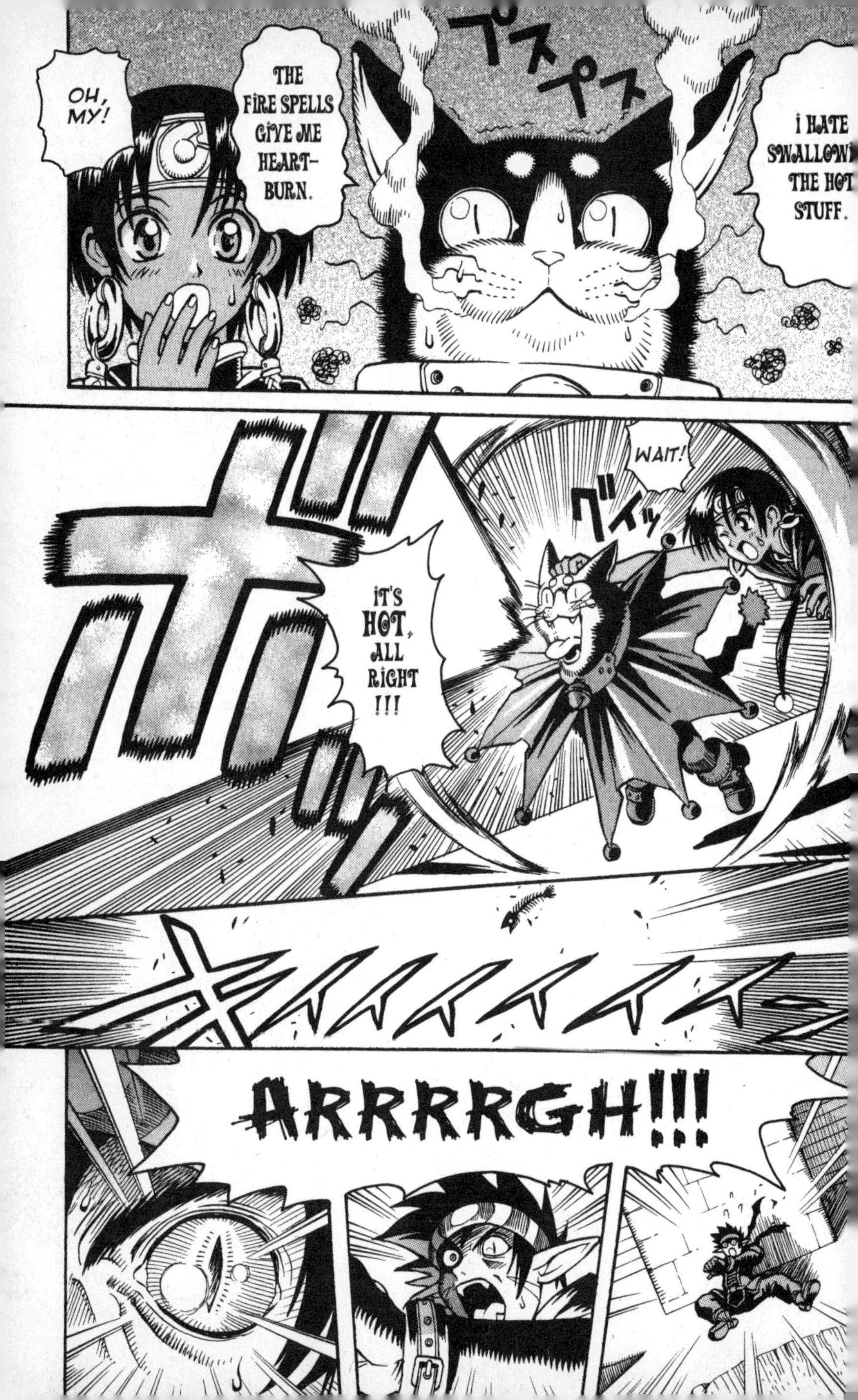
プスプス
I HATE SWALLOWI THE HOT STUFF.
THE FIRE SPELLS GIVE ME HEART-BURN.
OH, MY!
WAIT!
グイッ
IT'S HOT, ALL RIGHT!!!
ARRRRGH!!!

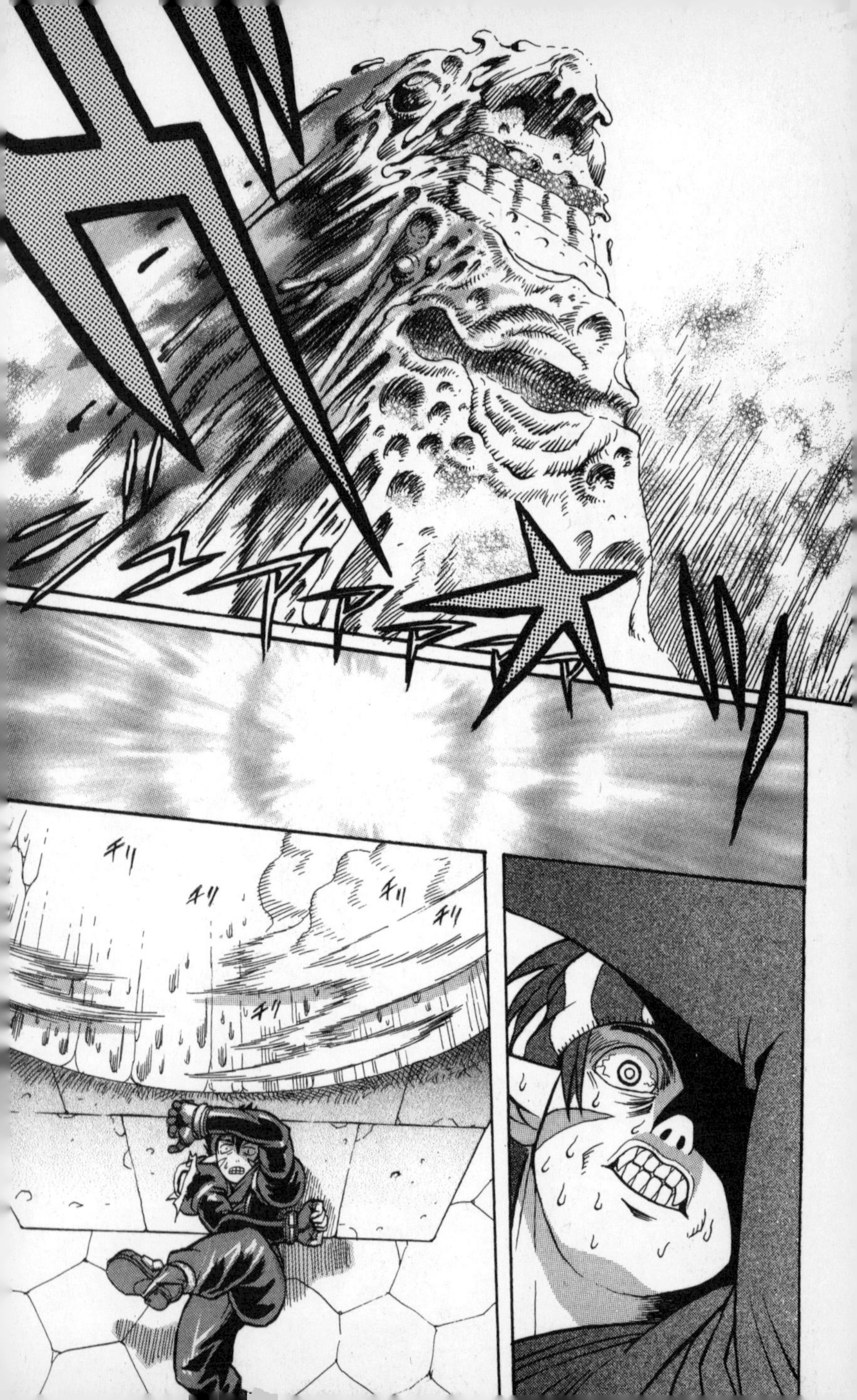
チリ
チリ
チリ
チリ
チリ

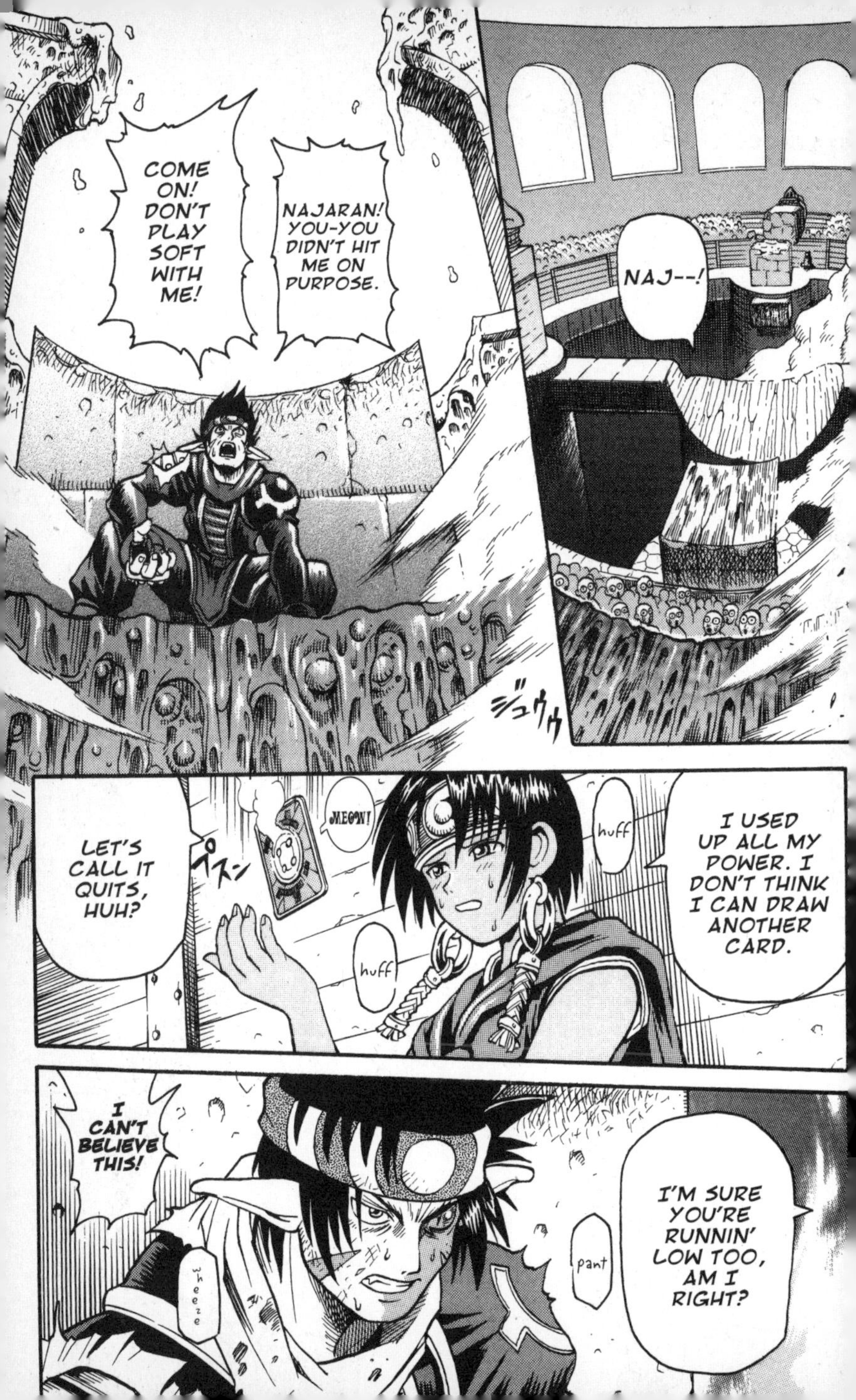
NAJ--!
NAJARAN! YOU-YOU DIDN'T HIT ME ON PURPOSE.
COME ON! DON'T PLAY SOFT WITH ME!
ジュウウ
I USED UP ALL MY POWER. I DON'T THINK I CAN DRAW ANOTHER CARD.
huff
MEOW!
huff
LET'S CALL IT QUITS, HUH?
I'M SURE YOU'RE RUNNIN' LOW TOO, AM I RIGHT?
pant
wheeze
I CAN'T BELIEVE THIS!

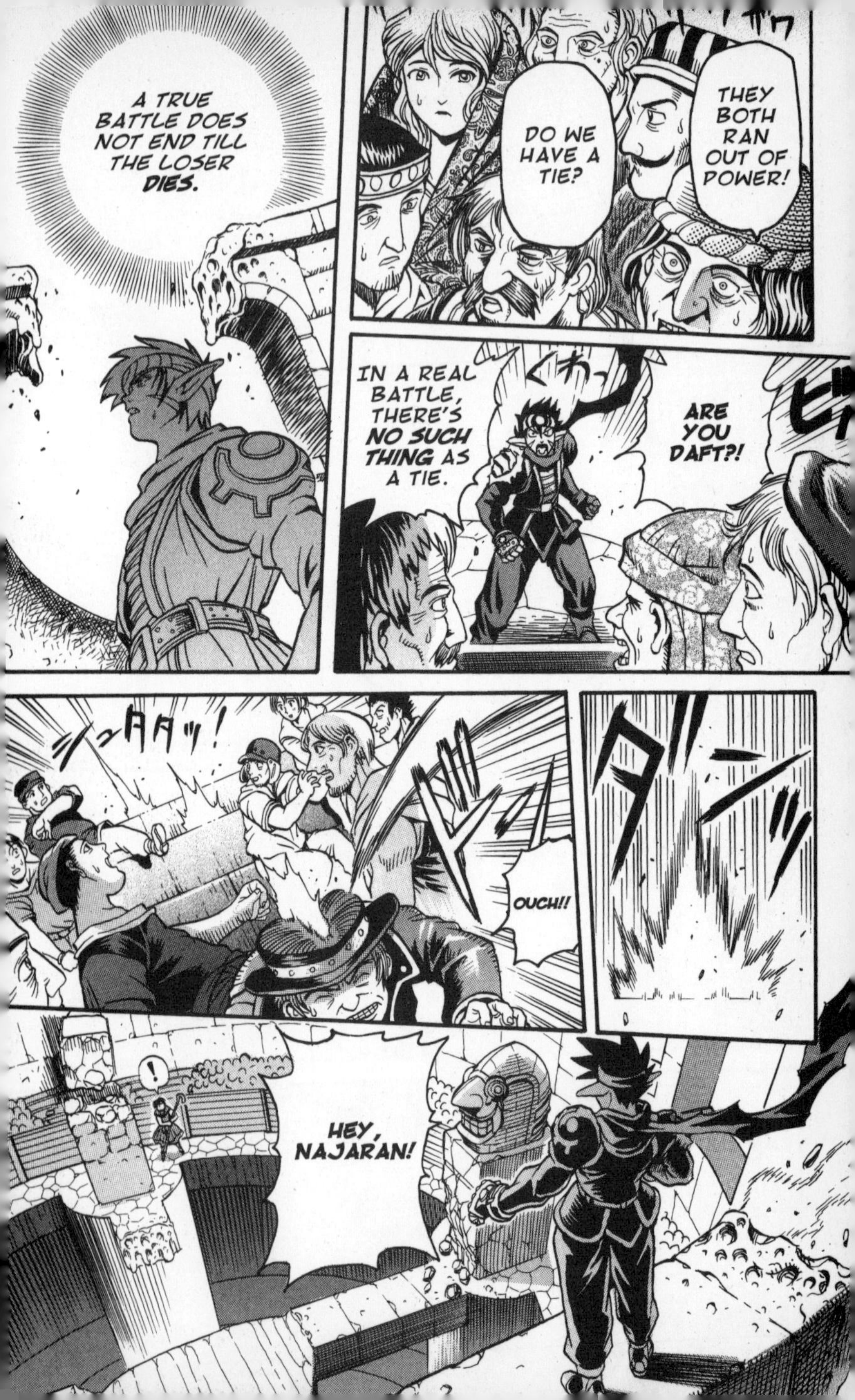
THEY BOTH RAN OUT OF POWER!
DO WE HAVE A TIE?
ARE YOU DAFT?!
くわっ
IN A REAL BATTLE, THERE'S NO SUCH THING AS A TIE.
A TRUE BATTLE DOES NOT END TILL THE LOSER DIES.
OUCH!!
シュタタッ!
!
HEY, NAJARAN!

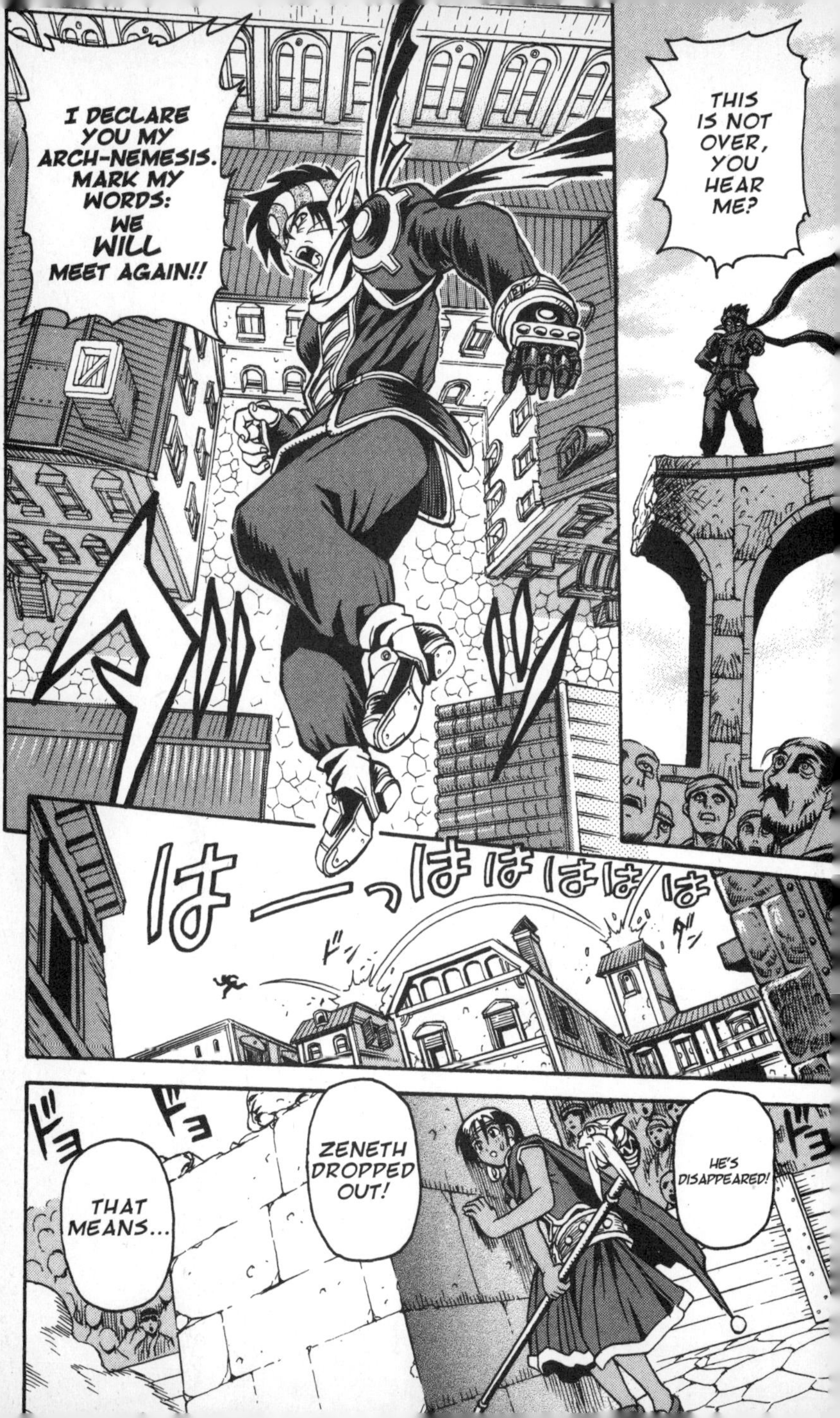
THIS IS NOT OVER, YOU HEAR ME?
I DECLARE YOU MY ARCH-NEMESIS. MARK MY WORDS: WE WILL MEET AGAIN!!
はーっははははは
ダン
ドン
HE'S DISAPPEARED!
ZENETH DROPPED OUT!
THAT MEANS...

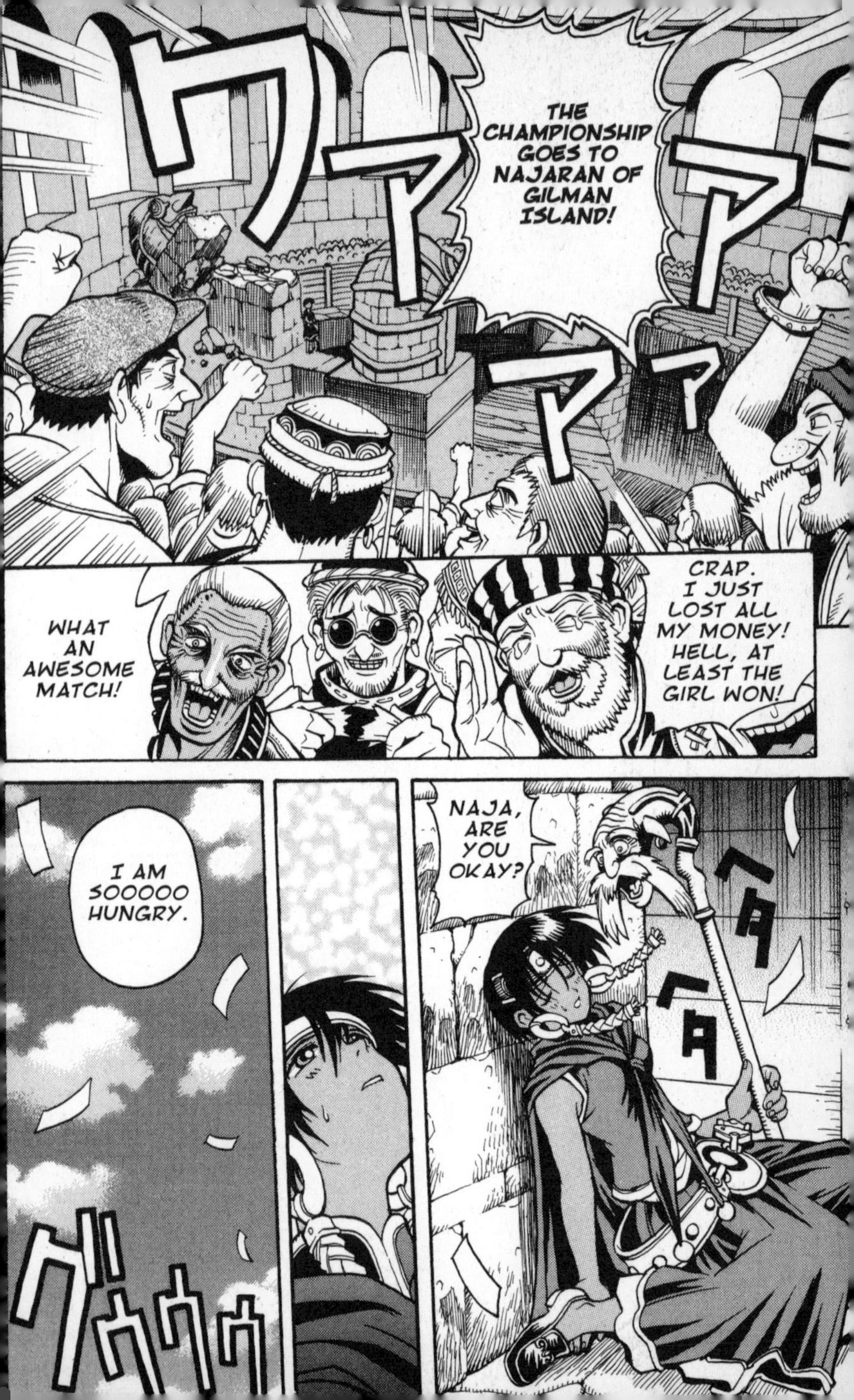
THE CHAMPIONSHIP GOES TO NAJARAN OF GILMAN ISLAND!
CRAP. I JUST LOST ALL MY MONEY! HELL, AT LEAST THE GIRL WON!
WHAT AN AWESOME MATCH!
NAJA, ARE YOU OKAY?
I AM SOOOOO HUNGRY.

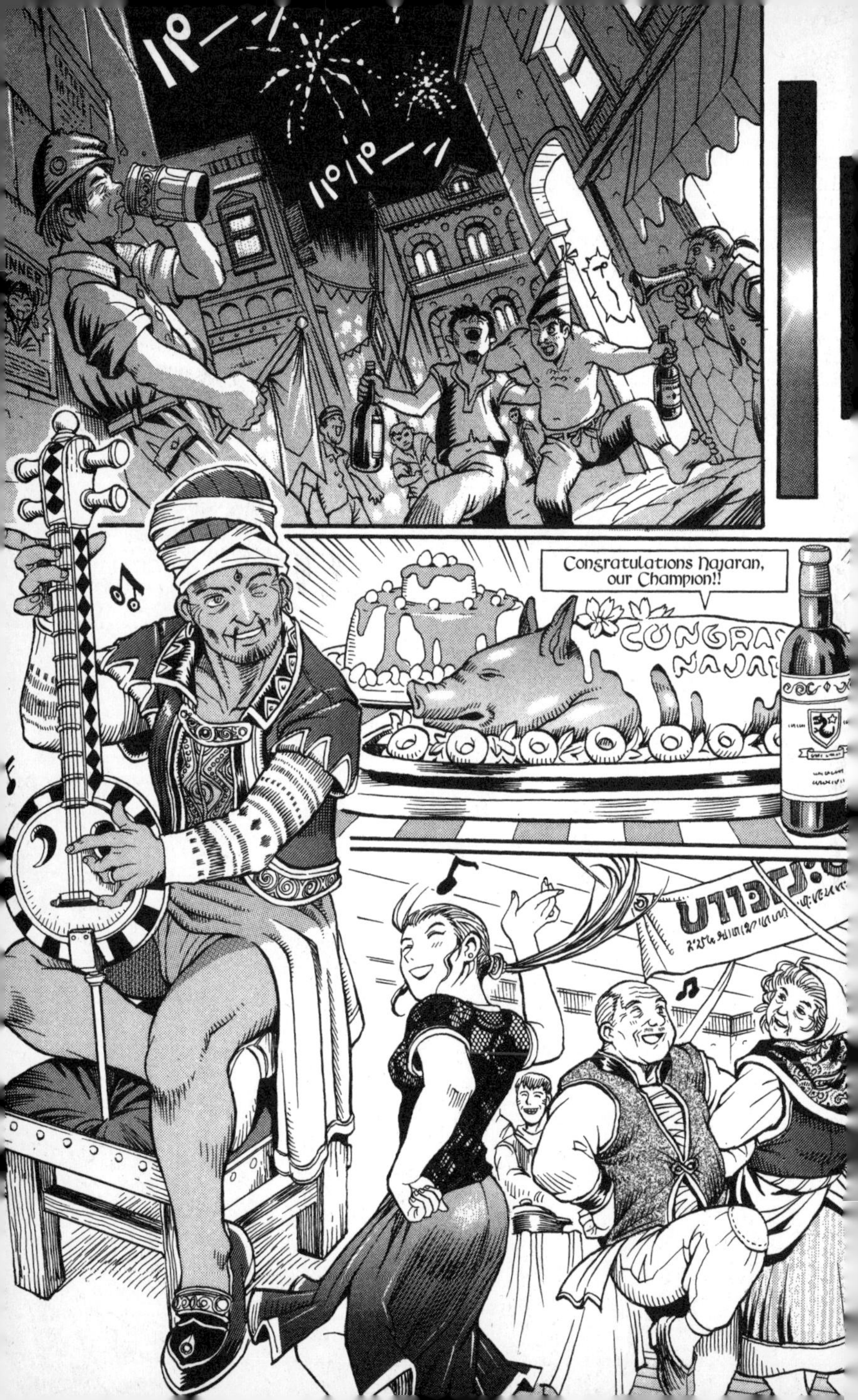
パーン
パパーン
Congratulations Najaran, our Champion!!

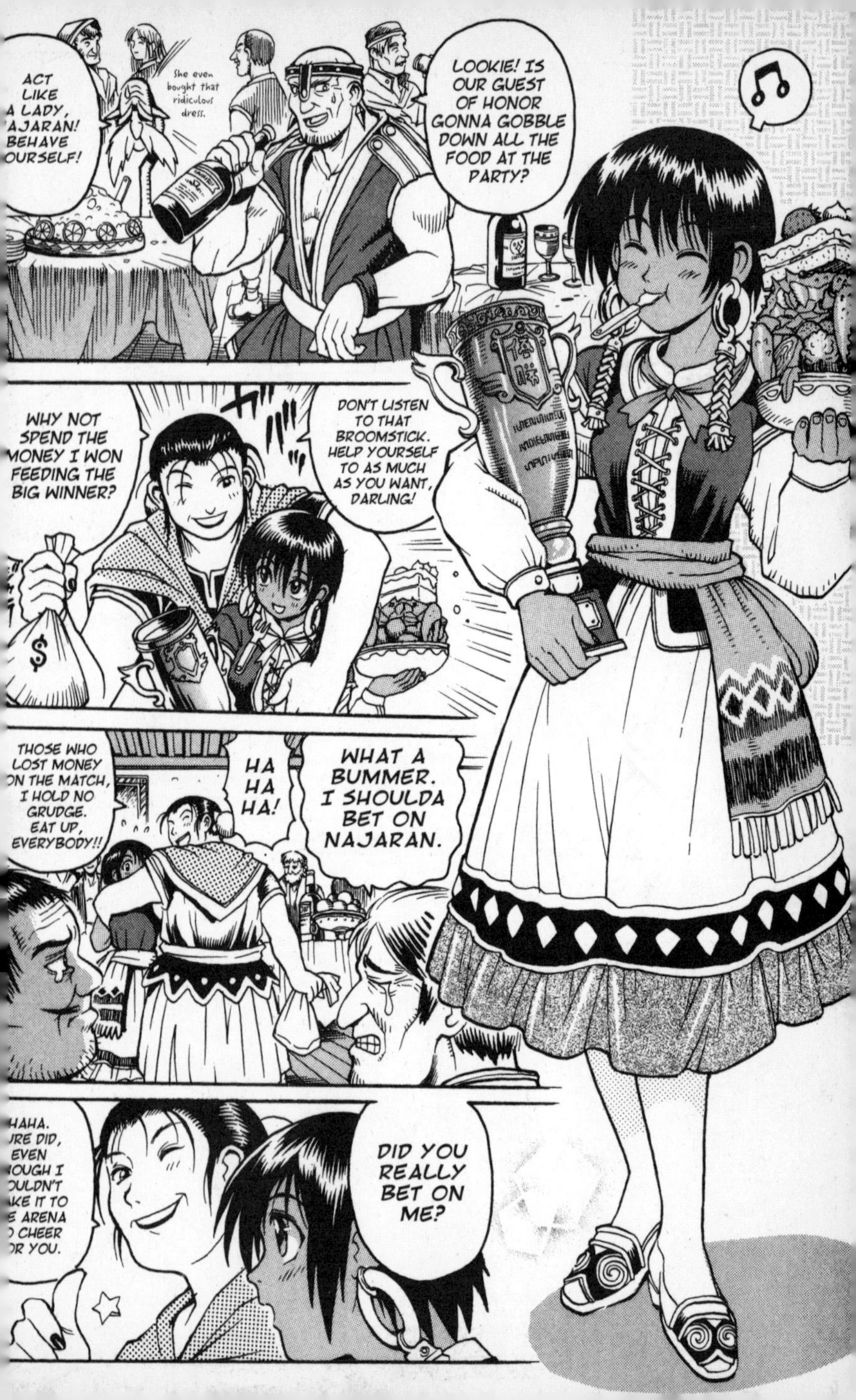
♪
LOOKIE! IS OUR GUEST OF HONOR GONNA GOBBLE DOWN ALL THE FOOD AT THE PARTY?
She even bought that ridiculous dress.
ACT LIKE A LADY, AJARAN! BEHAVE OURSELF!
DON'T LISTEN TO THAT BROOMSTICK. HELP YOURSELF TO AS MUCH AS YOU WANT, DARLING!
WHY NOT SPEND THE MONEY I WON FEEDING THE BIG WINNER?
$
WHAT A BUMMER. I SHOULDA BET ON NAJARAN.
HA HA HA!
THOSE WHO LOST MONEY ON THE MATCH, I HOLD NO GRUDGE. EAT UP, EVERYBODY!!
DID YOU REALLY BET ON ME?
HAHA. URE DID, EVEN HOUGH I OULDN'T AKE IT TO E ARENA O CHEER OR YOU.

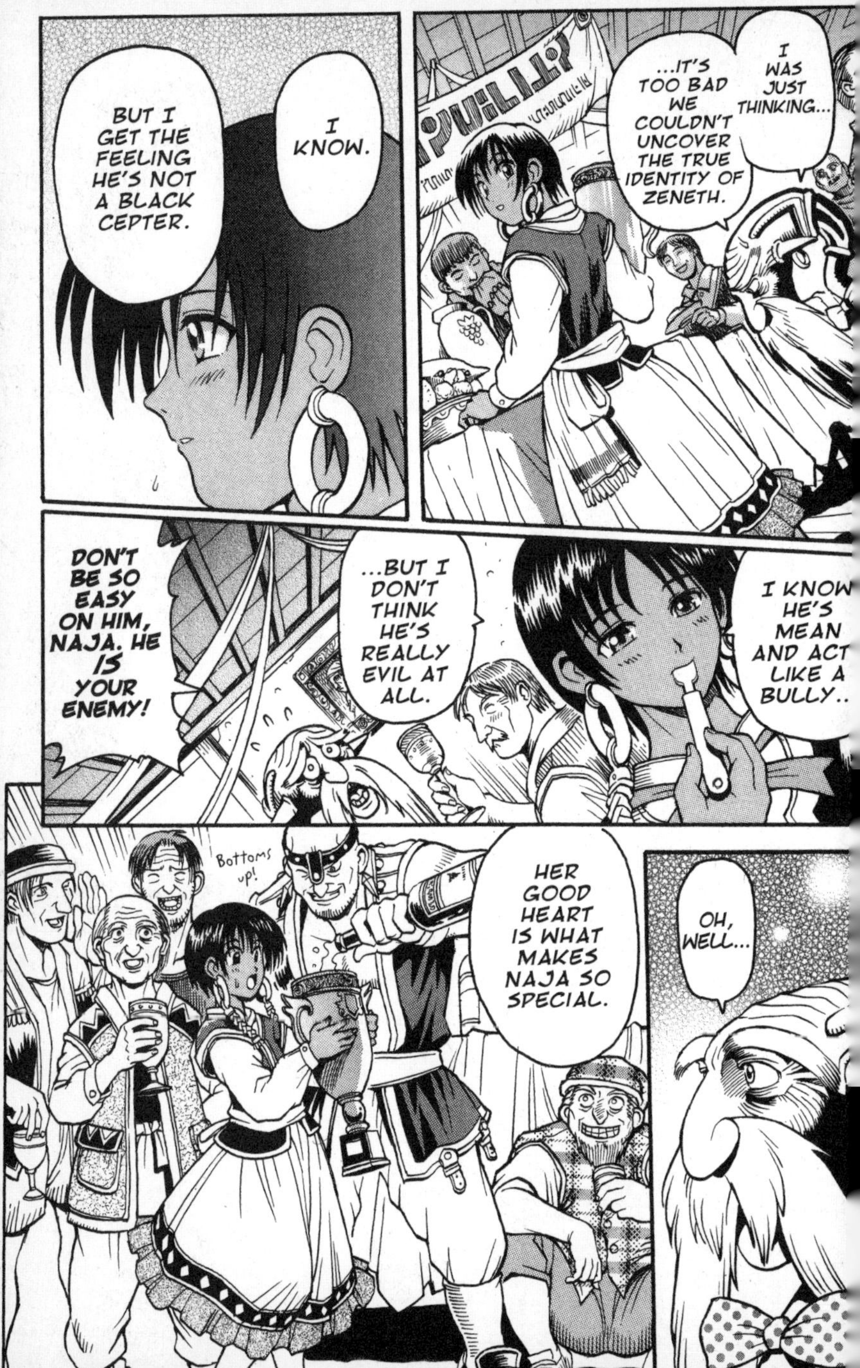
I WAS JUST THINKING...
...IT'S TOO BAD WE COULDN'T UNCOVER THE TRUE IDENTITY OF ZENETH.
I KNOW.
BUT I GET THE FEELING HE'S NOT A BLACK CEPTER.
I KNOW HE'S MEAN AND ACT LIKE A BULLY..
...BUT I DON'T THINK HE'S REALLY EVIL AT ALL.
DON'T BE SO EASY ON HIM, NAJA. HE IS YOUR ENEMY!
OH, WELL...
HER GOOD HEART IS WHAT MAKES NAJA SO SPECIAL.
Bottoms up!

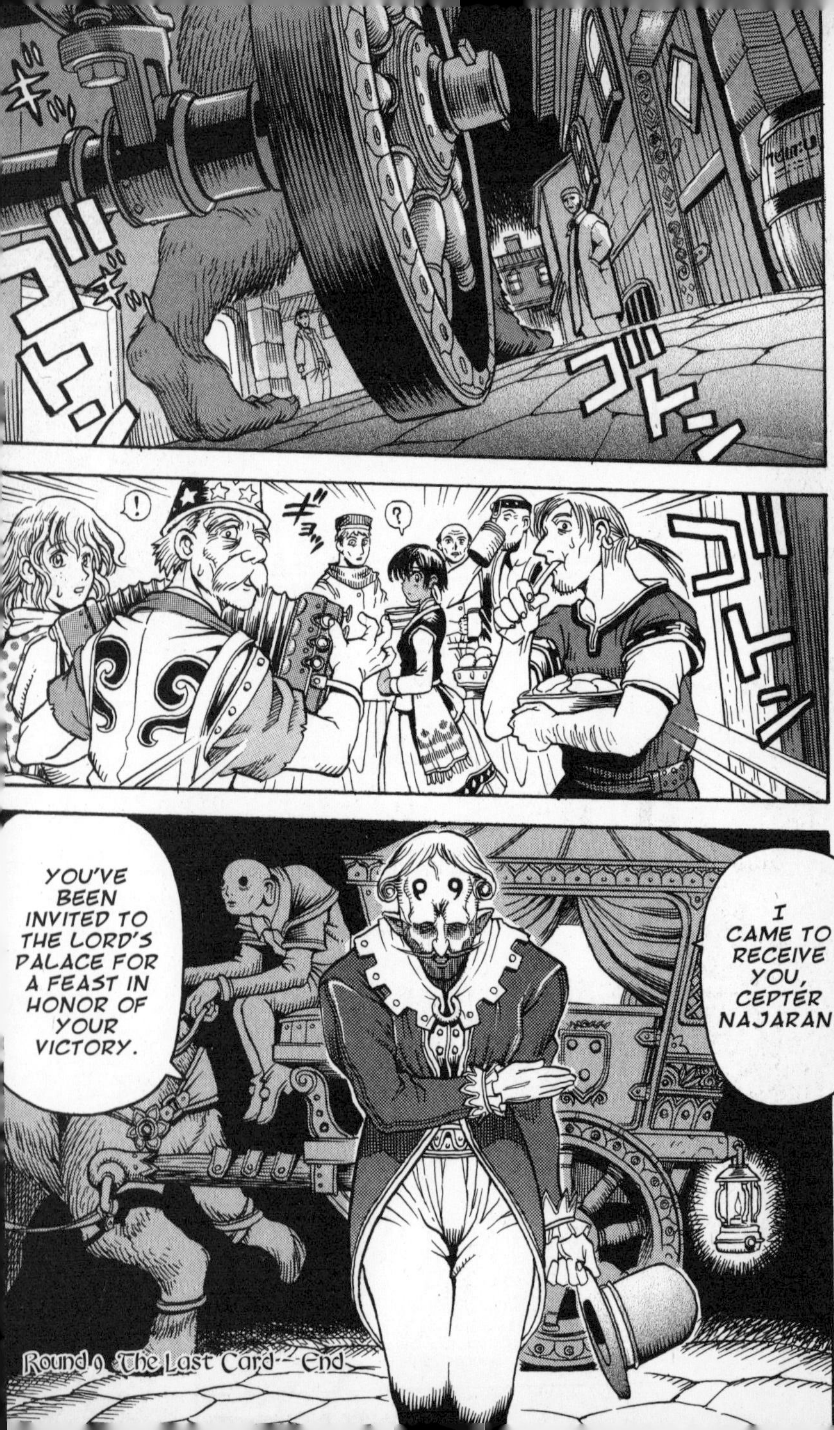
?
ギョッ
!
I CAME TO RECEIVE YOU, CEPTER NAJARAN.
YOU'VE BEEN INVITED TO THE LORD'S PALACE FOR A FEAST IN HONOR OF YOUR VICTORY.
Round 9 The Last Card -- End

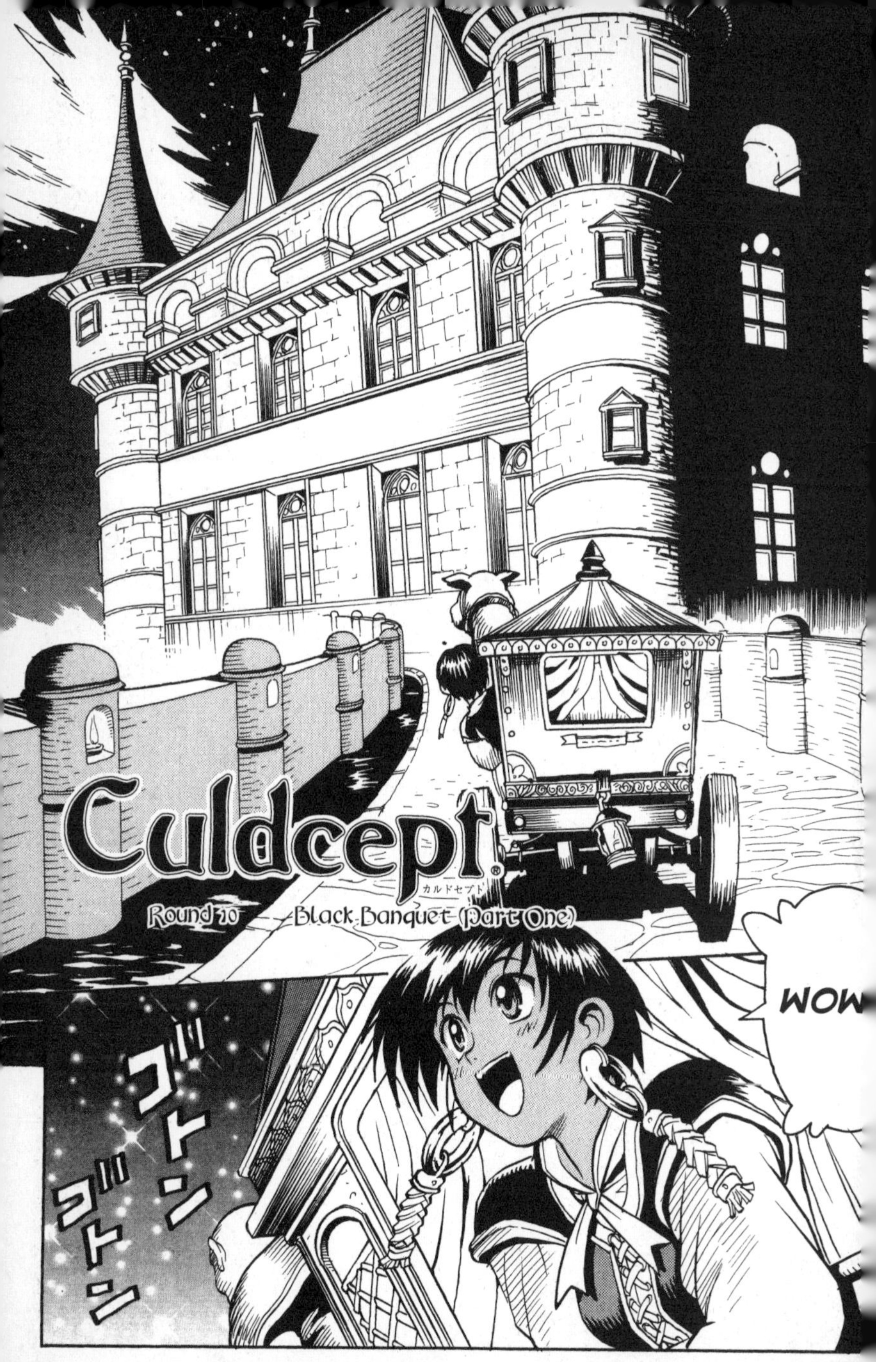
Culdcept®
カルドセプト
Round 10 Black Banquet (Part One)
WOW
ゴトン
ゴトン

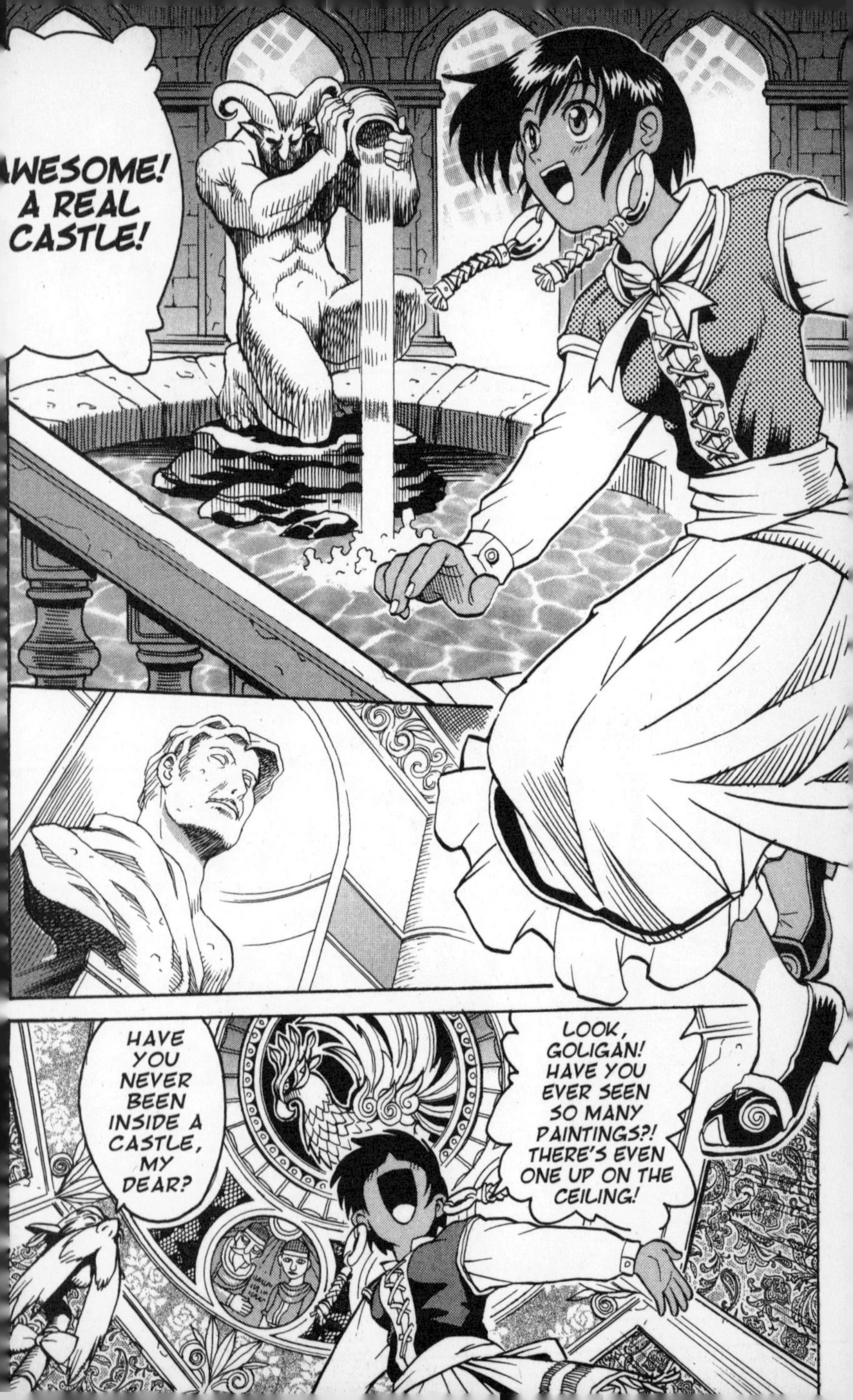
AWESOME! A REAL CASTLE!
LOOK, GOLIGAN! HAVE YOU EVER SEEN SO MANY PAINTINGS?! THERE'S EVEN ONE UP ON THE CEILING!
HAVE YOU NEVER BEEN INSIDE A CASTLE, MY DEAR?

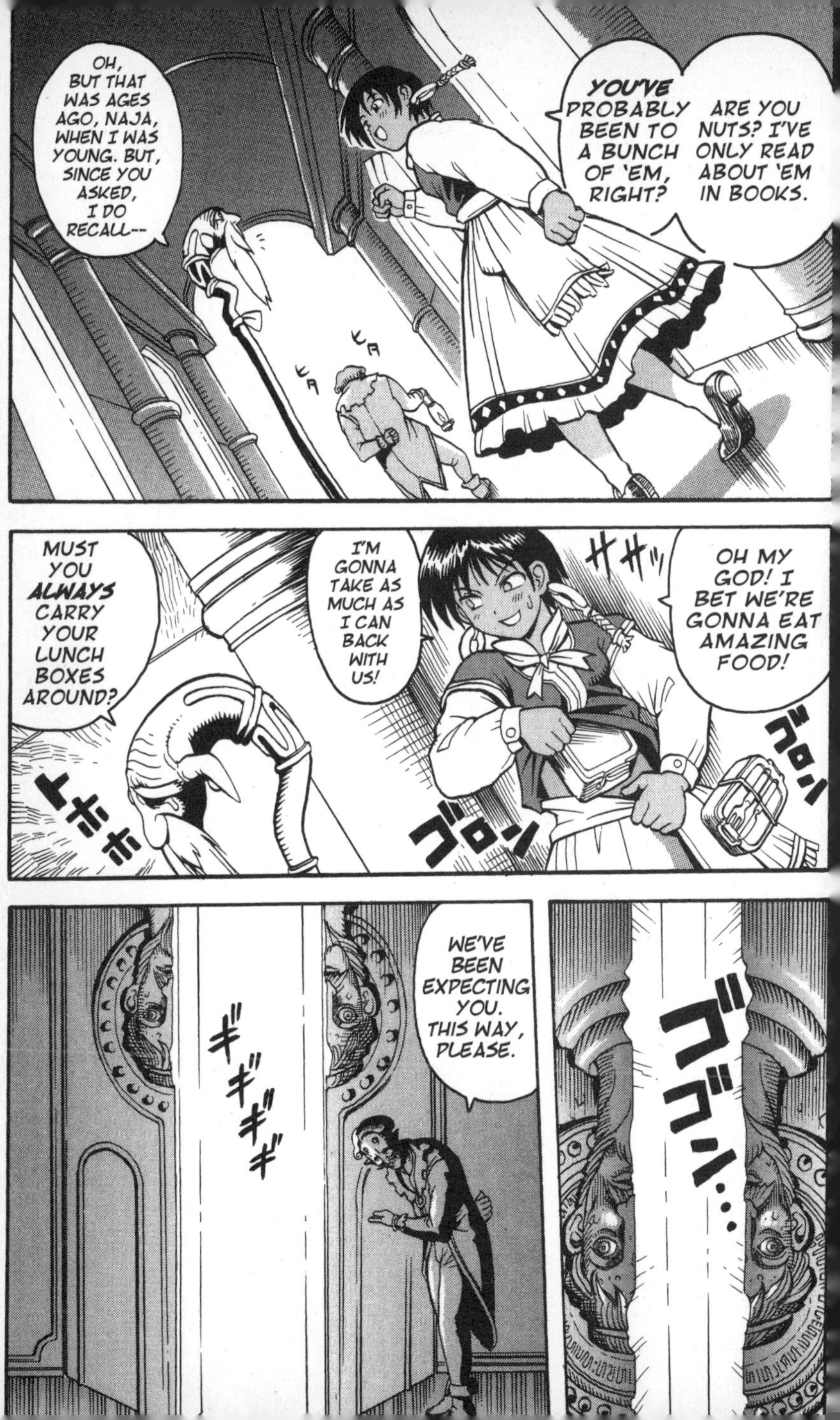
ARE YOU NUTS? I'VE ONLY READ ABOUT 'EM IN BOOKS.
YOU'VE PROBABLY BEEN TO A BUNCH OF 'EM, RIGHT?
OH, BUT THAT WAS AGES AGO, NAJA, WHEN I WAS YOUNG. BUT, SINCE YOU ASKED, I DO RECALL--
ヒタ ヒタ
OH MY GOD! I BET WE'RE GONNA EAT AMAZING FOOD!
ザザッ
I'M GONNA TAKE AS MUCH AS I CAN BACK WITH US!
ゴロンッ
ゴロンッ
MUST YOU *ALWAYS* CARRY YOUR LUNCH BOXES AROUND?
トホホ
ゴゴンッ…
WE'VE BEEN EXPECTING YOU. THIS WAY, PLEASE.
ギギギギ

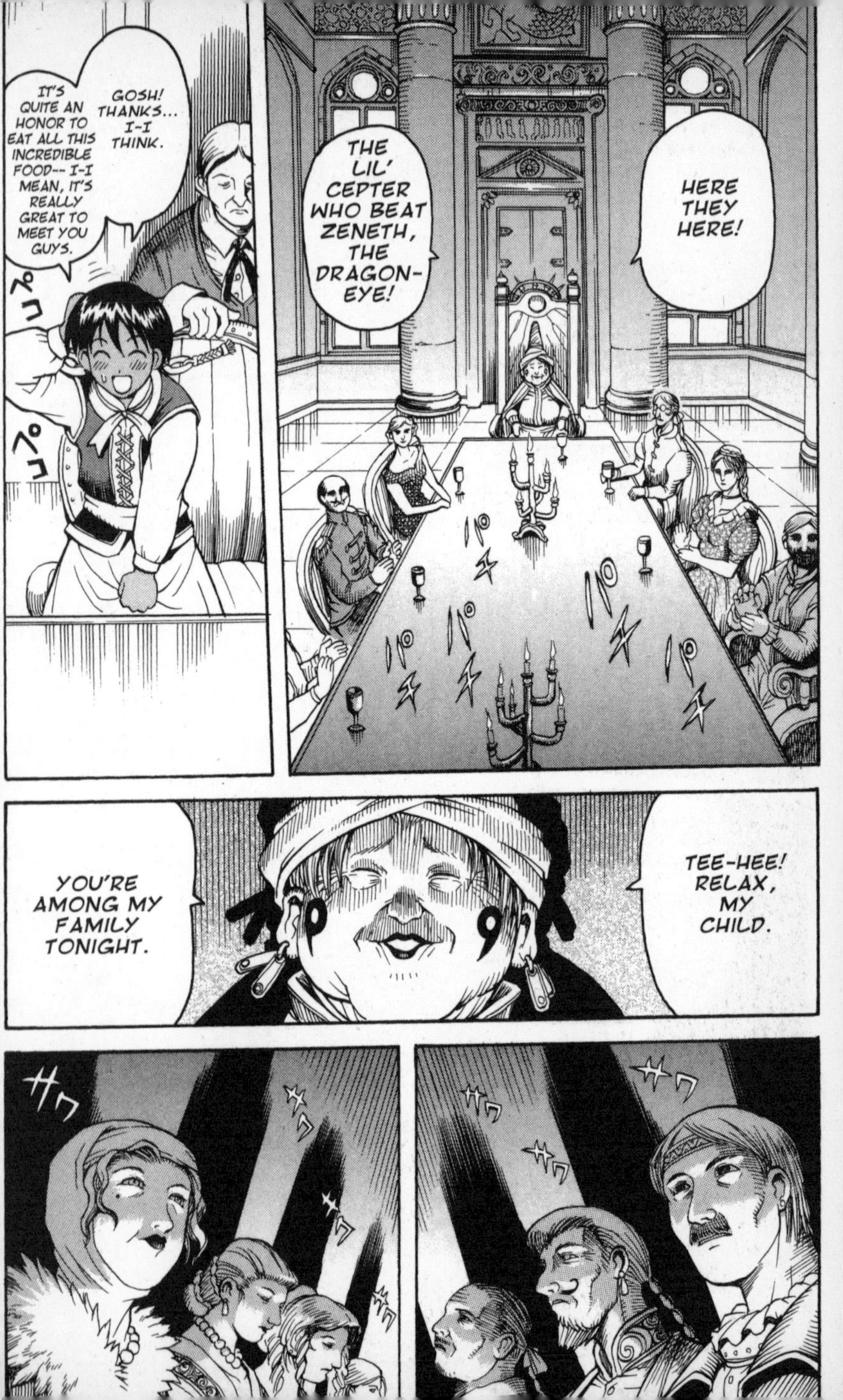

HERE THEY HERE!
THE LIL' CEPTER WHO BEAT ZENETH, THE DRAGON-EYE!
パチ パチ パチ パチ パチ
GOSH! THANKS... I-I THINK.
IT'S QUITE AN HONOR TO EAT ALL THIS INCREDIBLE FOOD-- I-I MEAN, IT'S REALLY GREAT TO MEET YOU GUYS.
ペコ ペコ
TEE-HEE! RELAX, MY CHILD.
YOU'RE AMONG MY FAMILY TONIGHT.
ザワ ザワ ザワ
ザワ ザワ ザワ ザワ

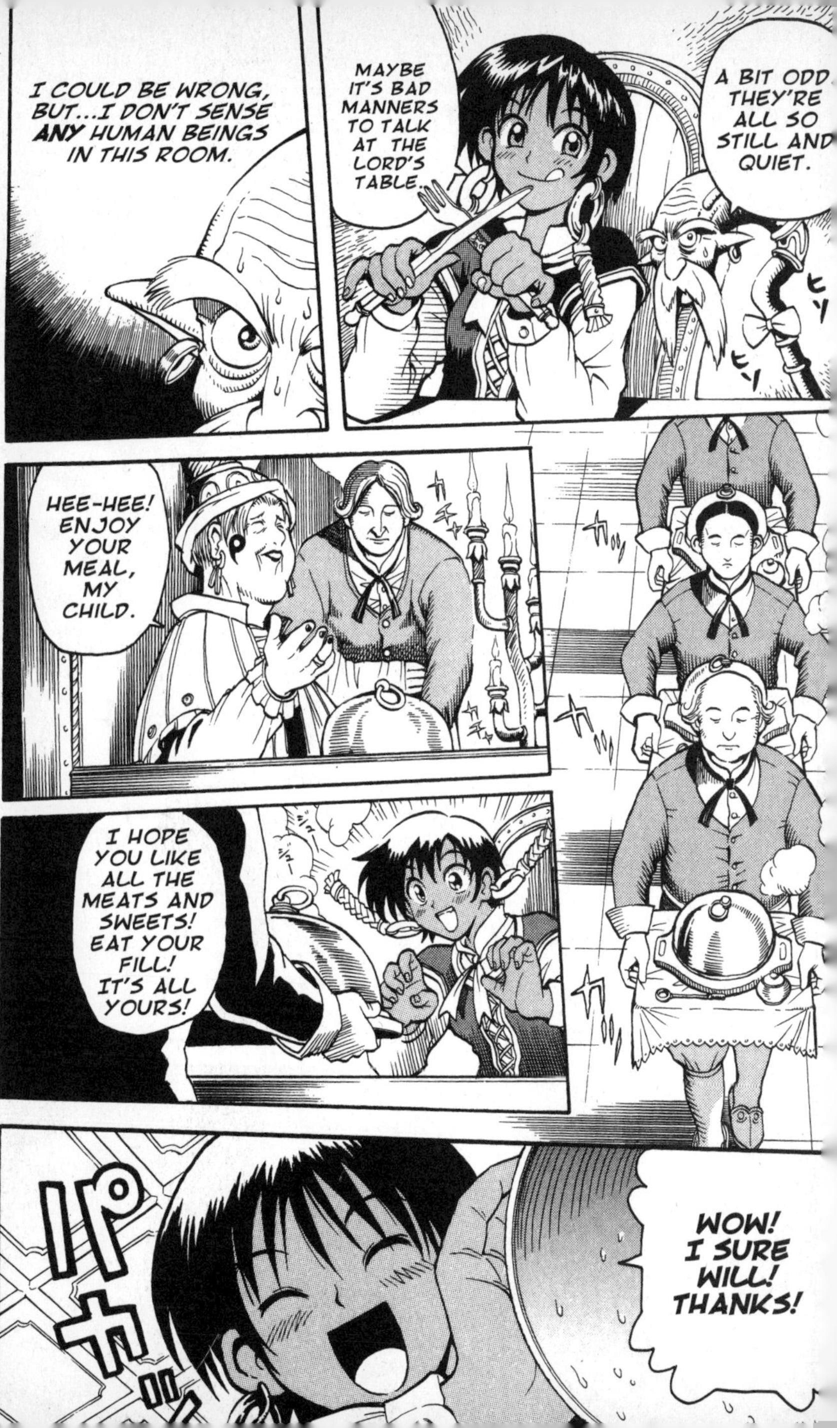
A BIT ODD THEY'RE ALL SO STILL AND QUIET.
MAYBE IT'S BAD MANNERS TO TALK AT THE LORD'S TABLE.
I COULD BE WRONG, BUT...I DON'T SENSE **ANY** HUMAN BEINGS IN THIS ROOM.
HEE-HEE! ENJOY YOUR MEAL, MY CHILD.
I HOPE YOU LIKE ALL THE MEATS AND SWEETS! EAT YOUR FILL! IT'S ALL YOURS!
WOW! I SURE WILL! THANKS!

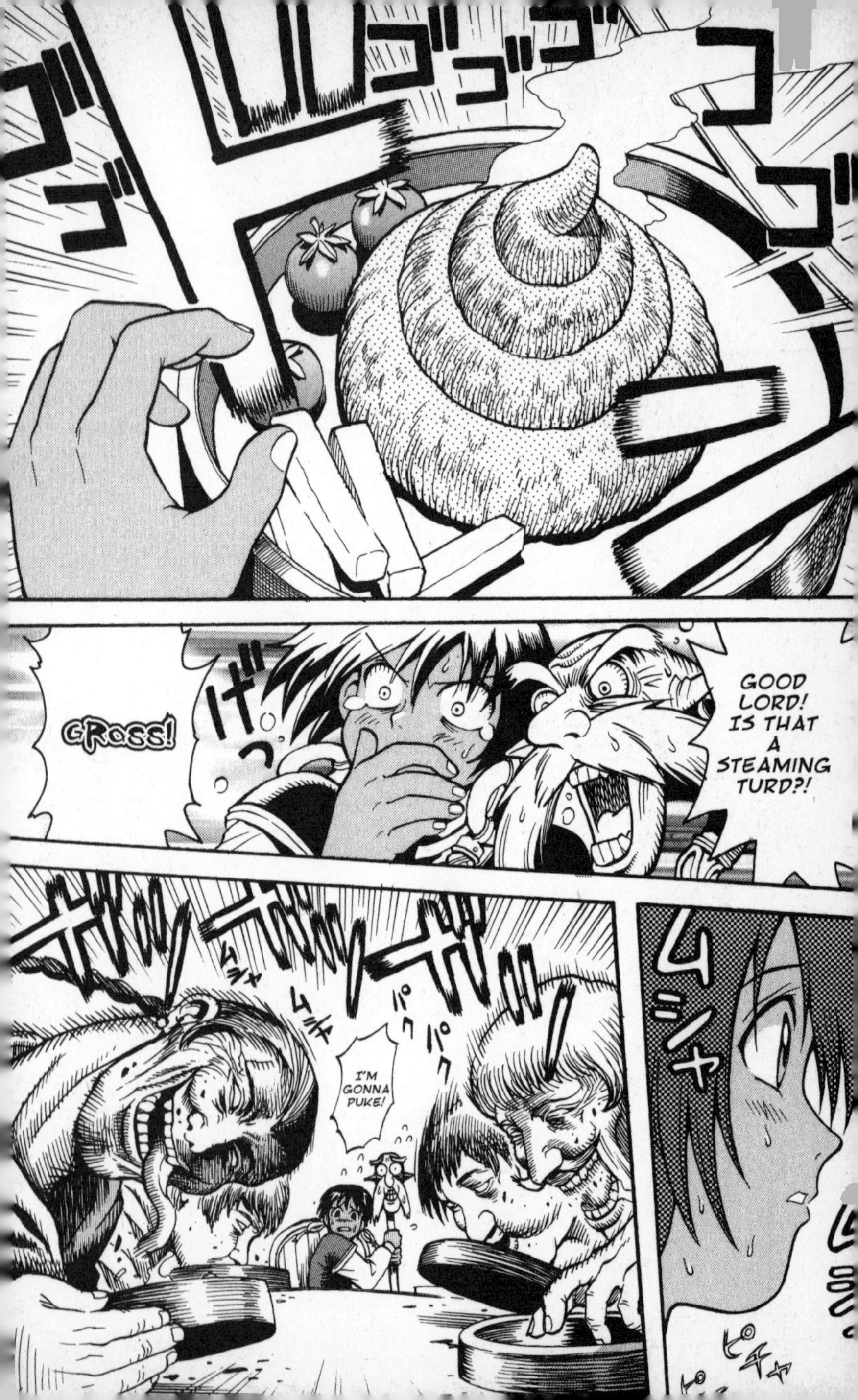
GOOD LORD! IS THAT A STEAMING TURD?!
GROSS!
I'M GONNA PUKE!

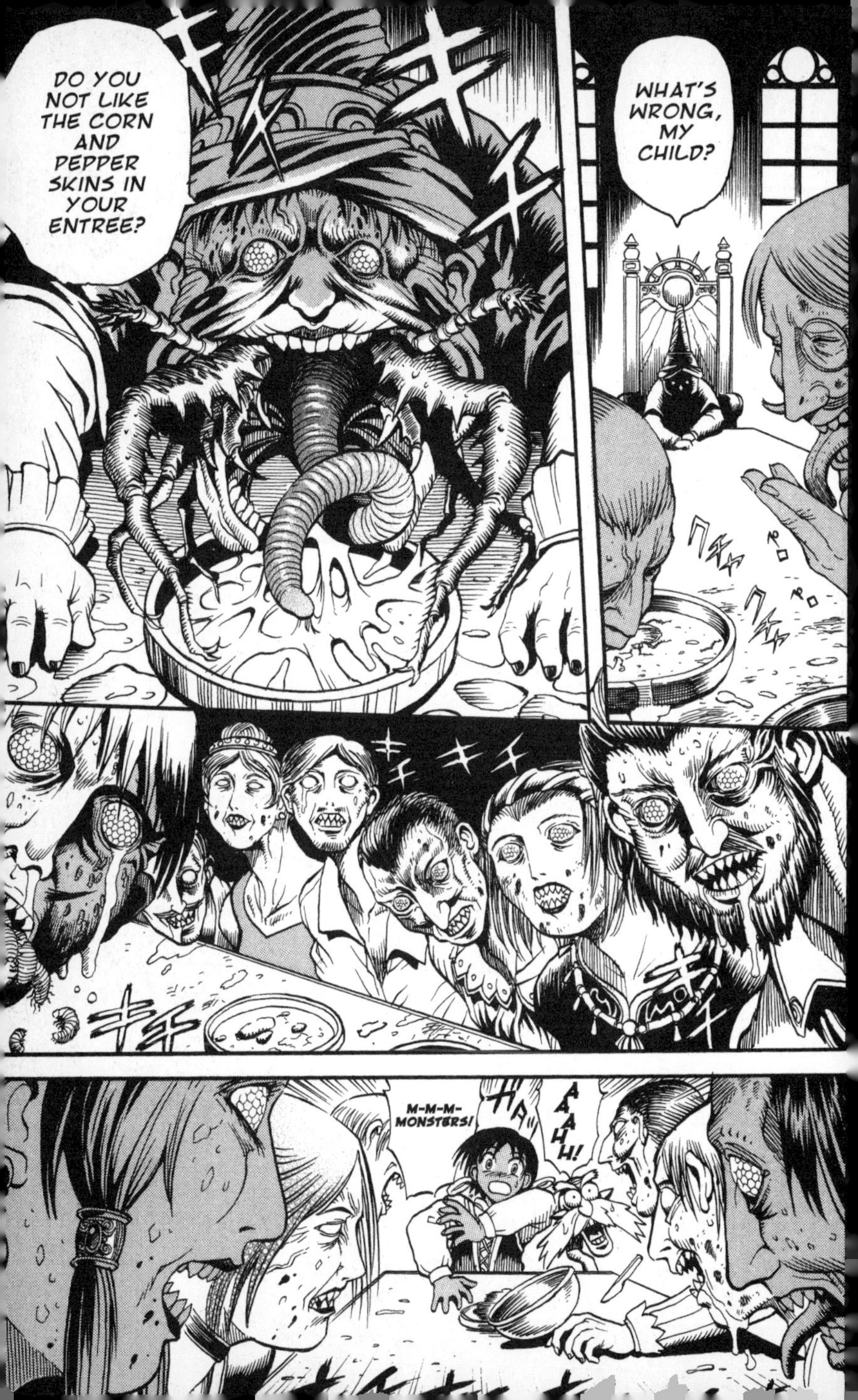
WHAT'S WRONG, MY CHILD?
DO YOU NOT LIKE THE CORN AND PEPPER SKINS IN YOUR ENTREE?
AAAHH!
HA
M-M-M-MONSTERS!

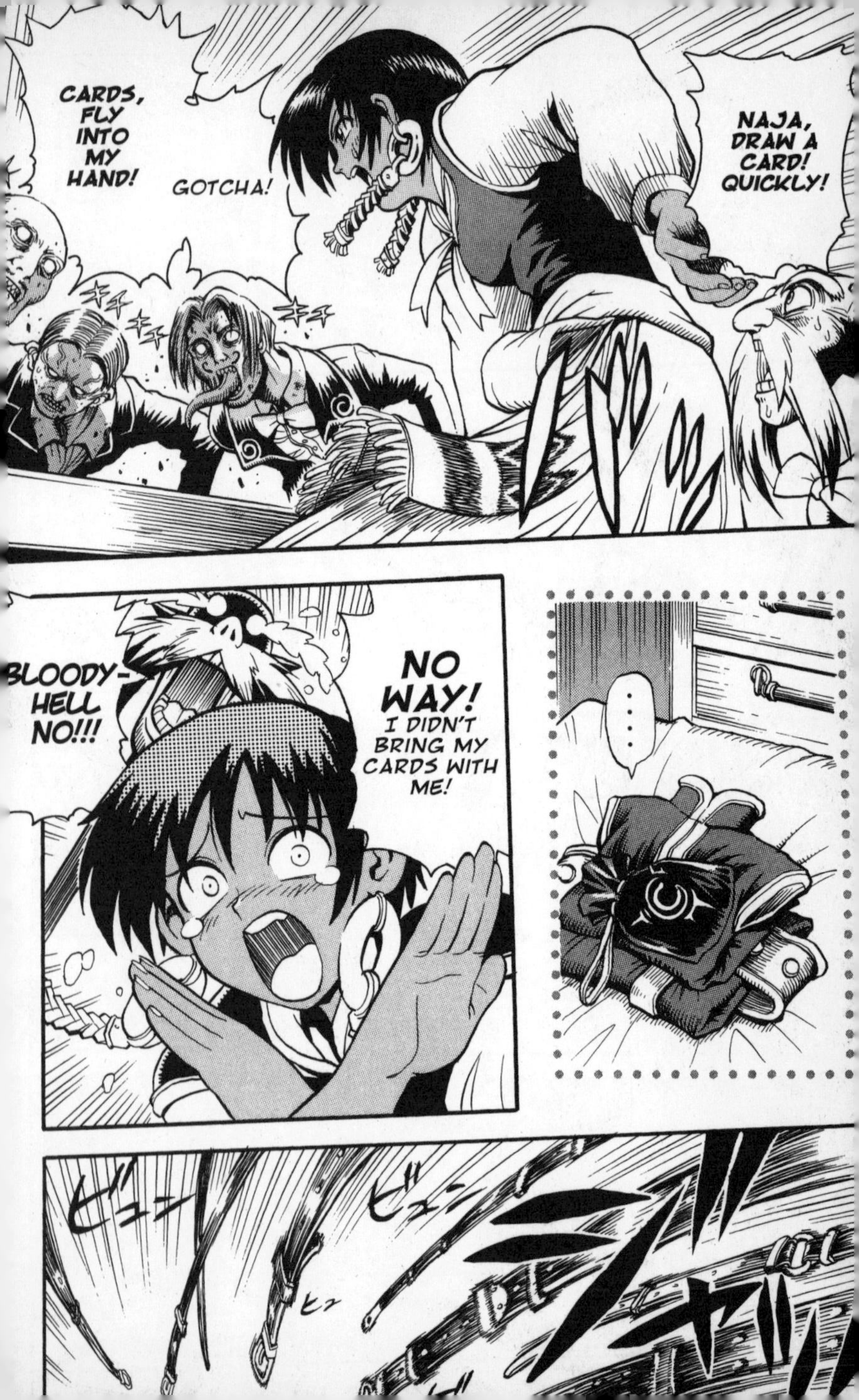
NAJA, DRAW A CARD! QUICKLY!
CARDS, FLY INTO MY HAND!
GOTCHA!
...
NO WAY! I DIDN'T BRING MY CARDS WITH ME!
BLOODY-HELL NO!!!

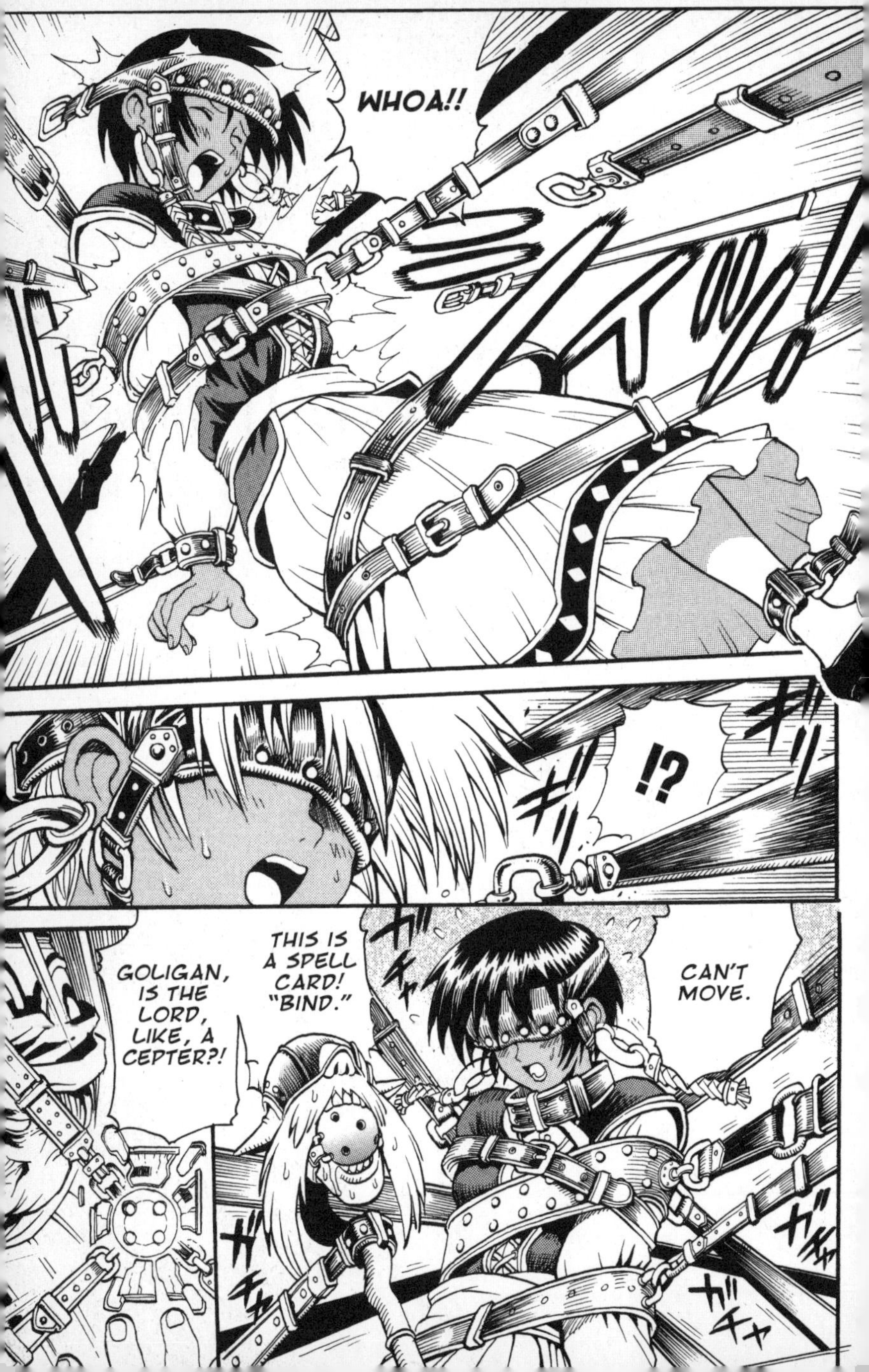
WHOA!!
!?
CAN'T MOVE.
THIS IS A SPELL CARD! "BIND."
GOLIGAN, IS THE LORD, LIKE, A CEPTER?!

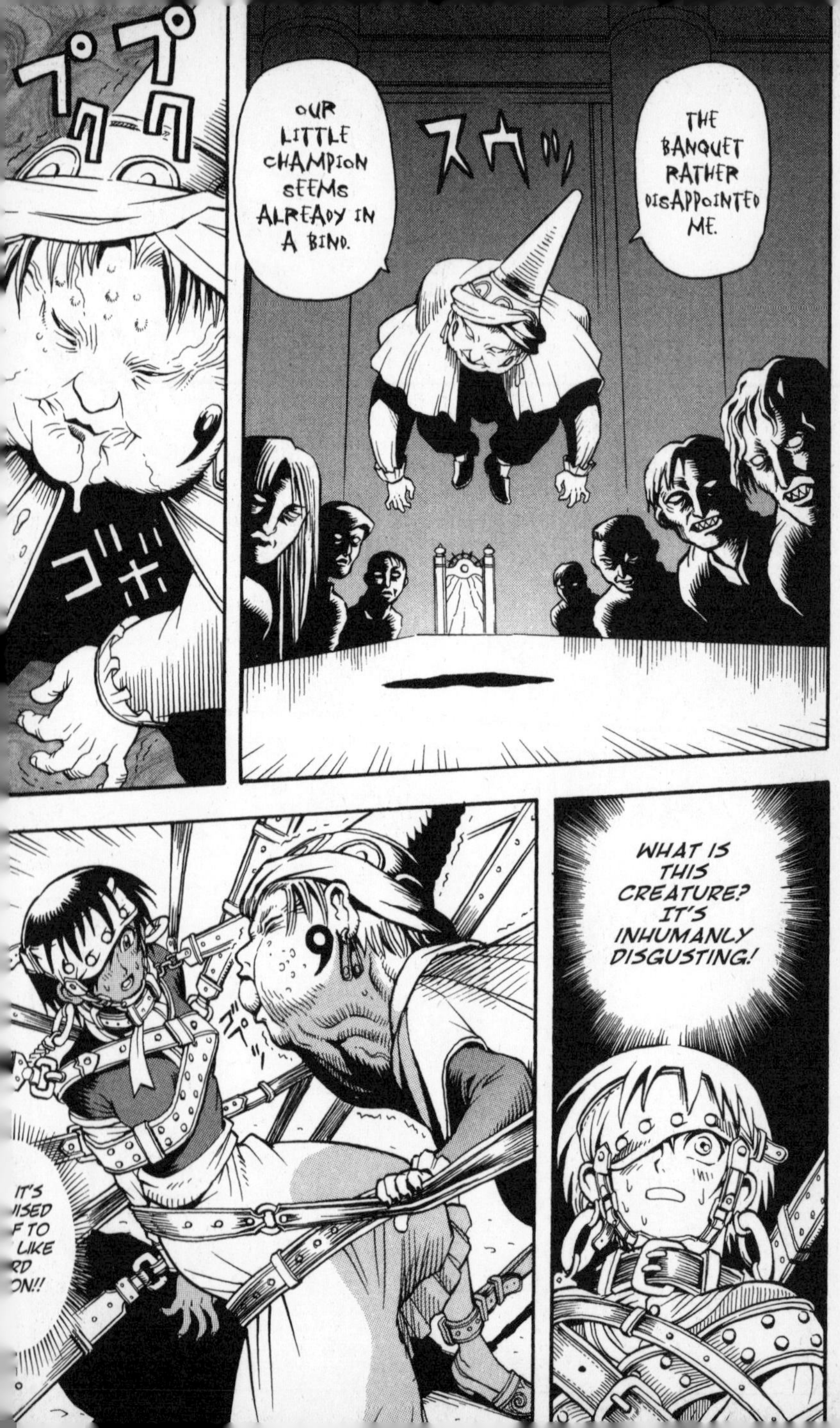
THE BANQUET RATHER DISAPPOINTED ME.
OUR LITTLE CHAMPION SEEMS ALREADY IN A BIND.
WHAT IS THIS CREATURE? IT'S INHUMANLY DISGUSTING!
IT'S

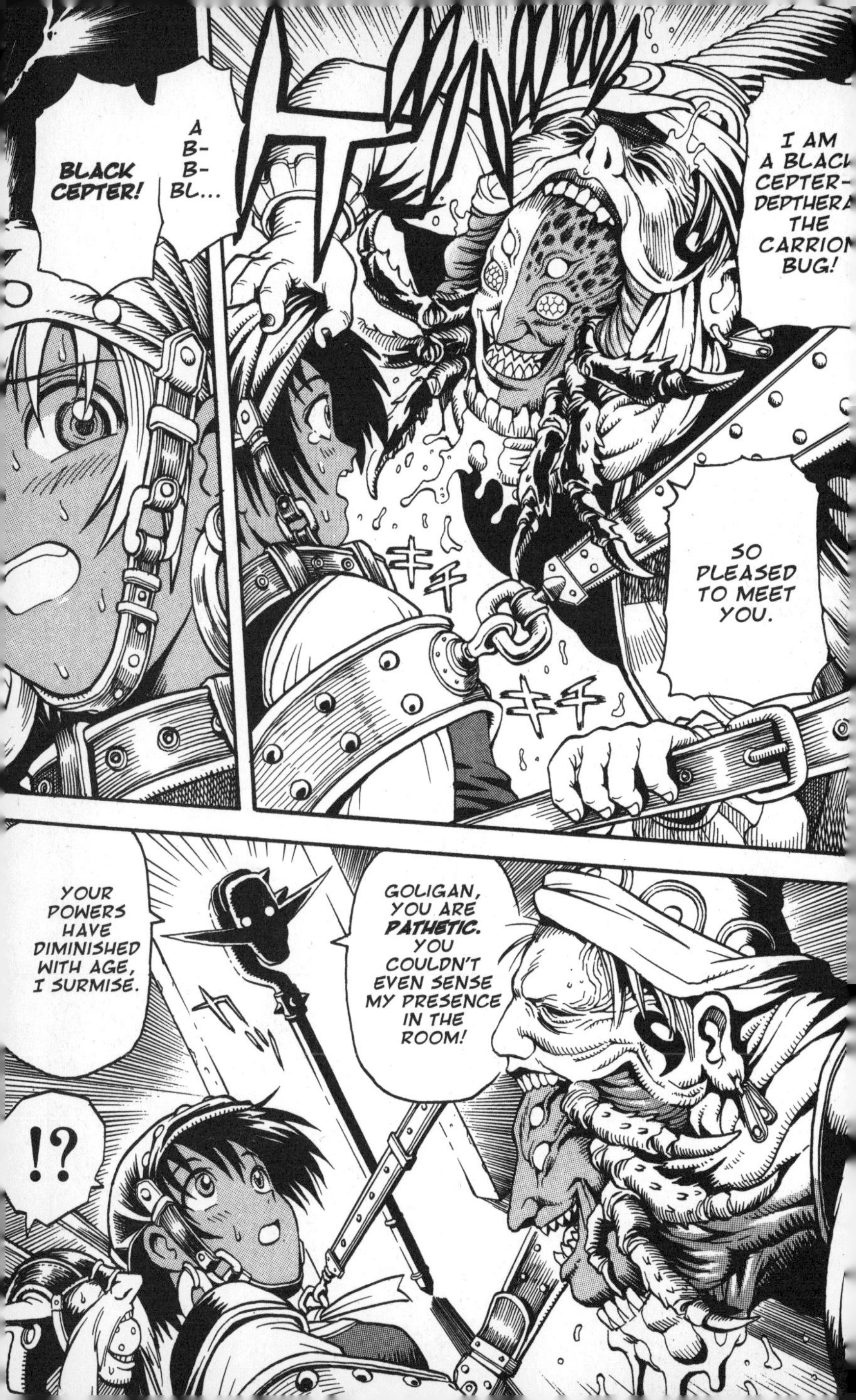
I AM A BLACK CEPTER-DEPTHERA THE CARRION BUG!
SO PLEASED TO MEET YOU.
キチ
キチ
A B- B- BL...
BLACK CEPTER!
GOLIGAN, YOU ARE PATHETIC. YOU COULDN'T EVEN SENSE MY PRESENCE IN THE ROOM!
YOUR POWERS HAVE DIMINISHED WITH AGE, I SURMISE.
!?

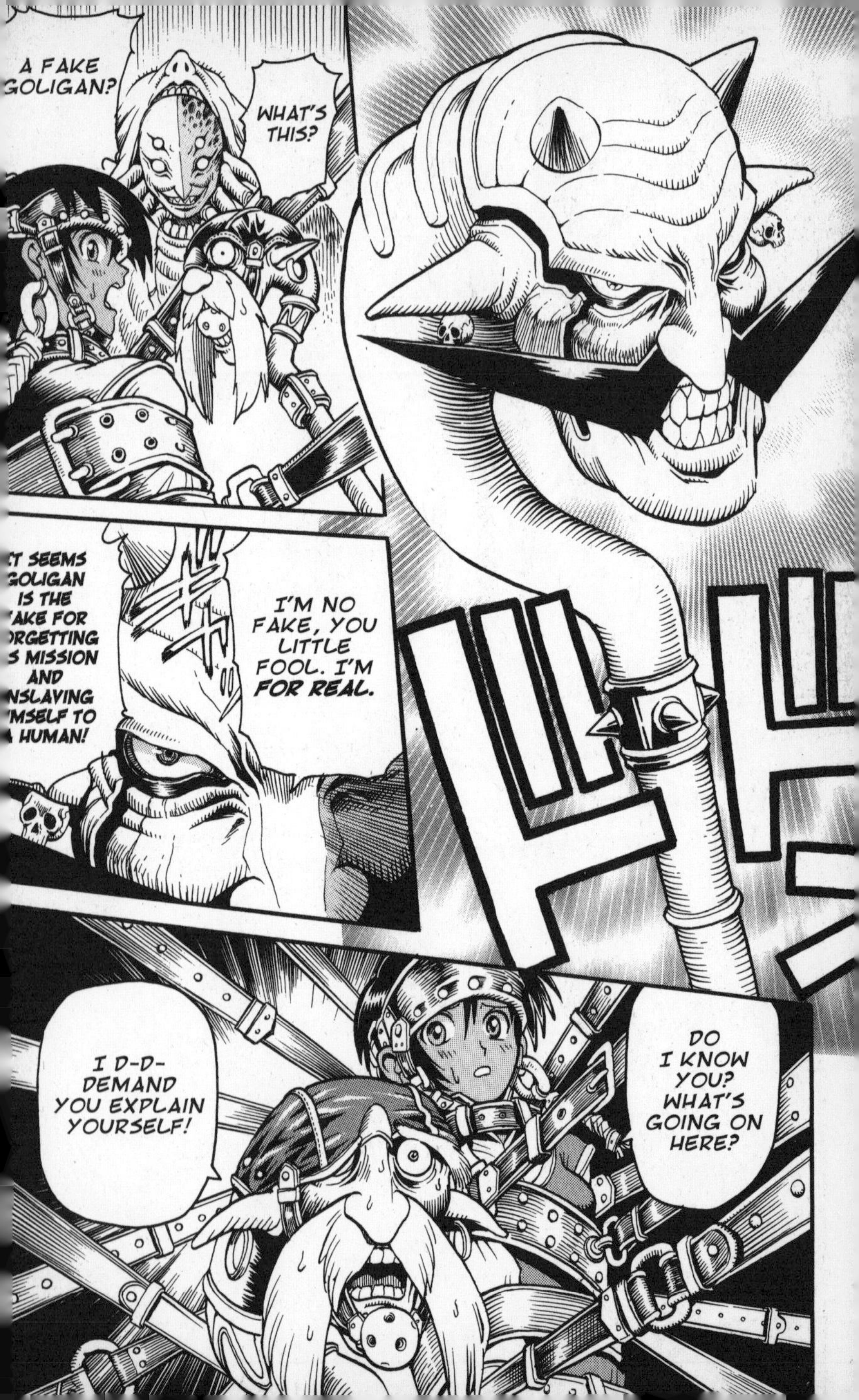
WHAT'S THIS?
A FAKE GOLIGAN?
I'M NO FAKE, YOU LITTLE FOOL. I'M FOR REAL.
T SEEMS GOLIGAN IS THE AKE FOR ORGETTING S MISSION AND NSLAVING IMSELF TO A HUMAN!
DO I KNOW YOU? WHAT'S GOING ON HERE?
I D-D-DEMAND YOU EXPLAIN YOURSELF!

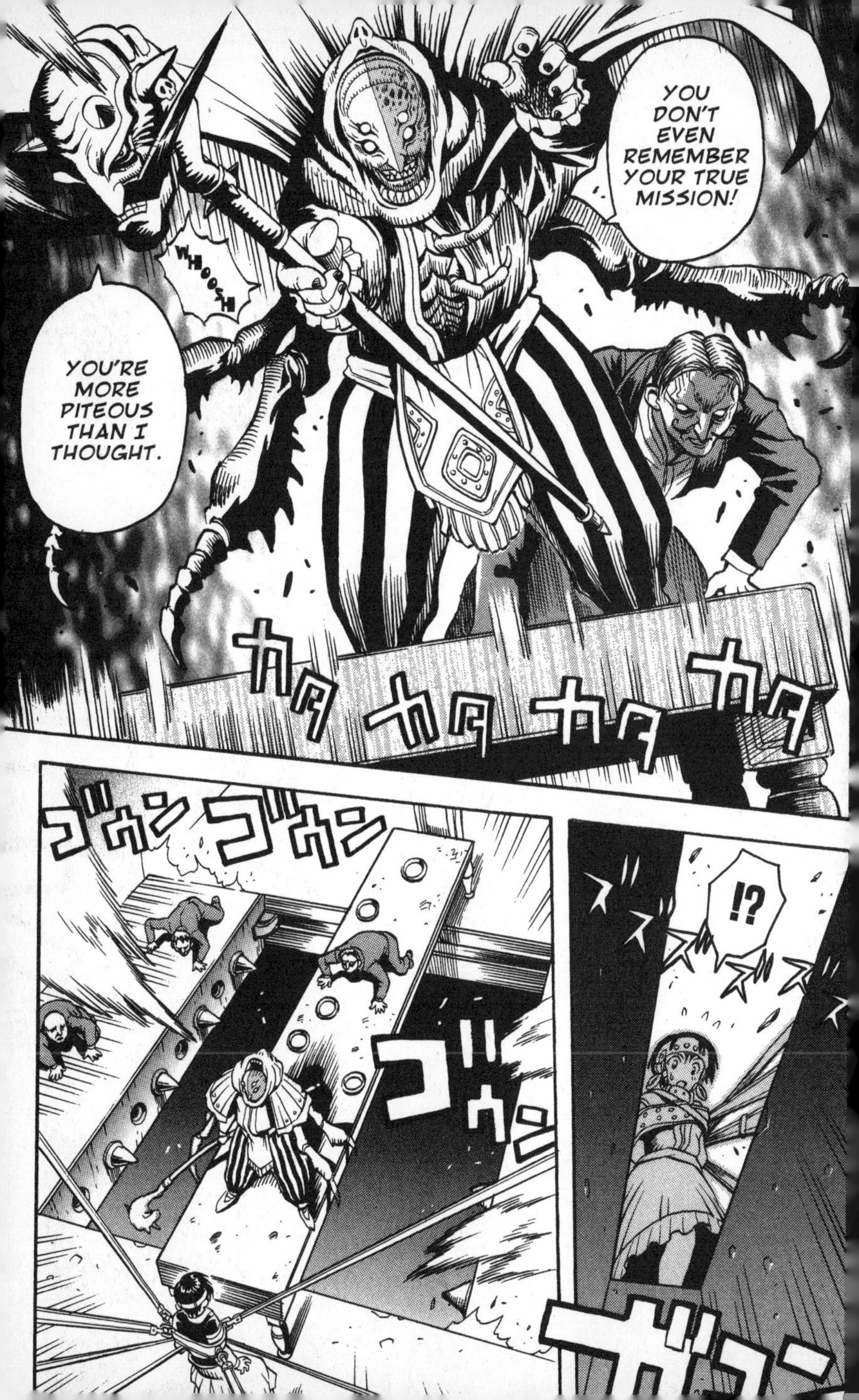
YOU DON'T EVEN REMEMBER YOUR TRUE MISSION!
WHOOSH
YOU'RE MORE PITEOUS THAN I THOUGHT.
カタ カタ カタ カタ
!?
ゴウン ゴウン
ゴウン

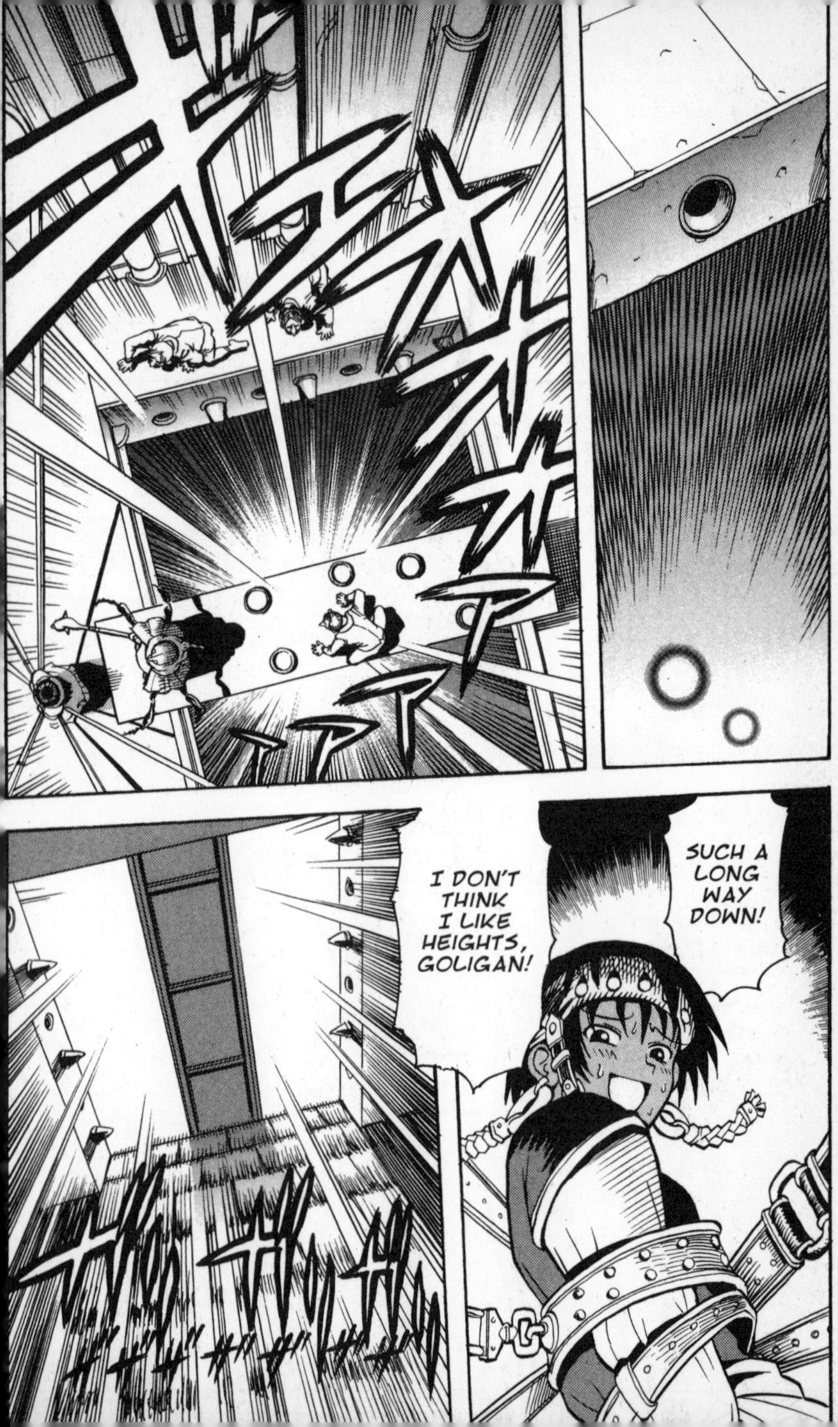
SUCH A LONG WAY DOWN!
I DON'T THINK I LIKE HEIGHTS, GOLIGAN!

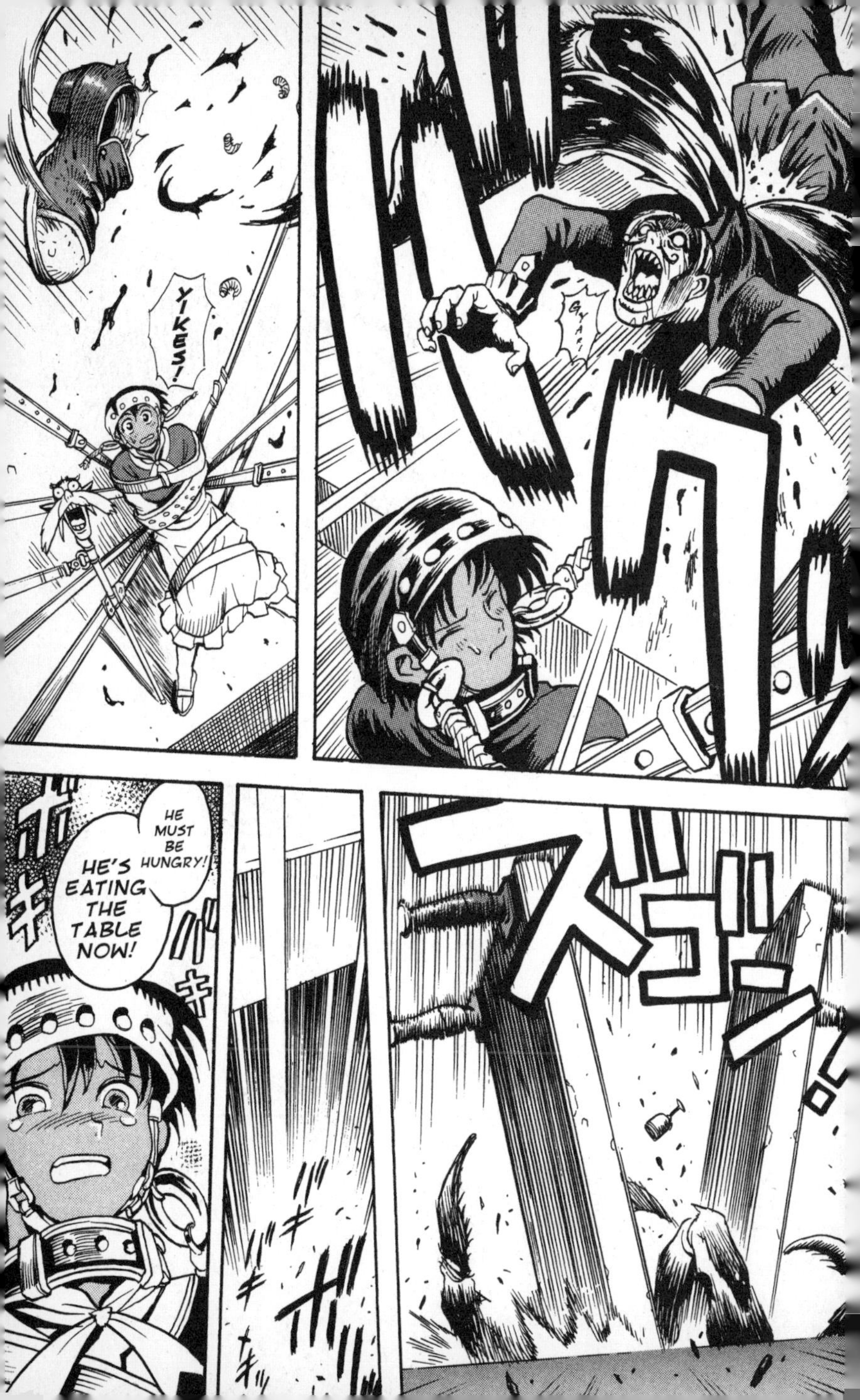
GYAA!
YIKES!
HE MUST BE HUNGRY!
HE'S EATING THE TABLE NOW!

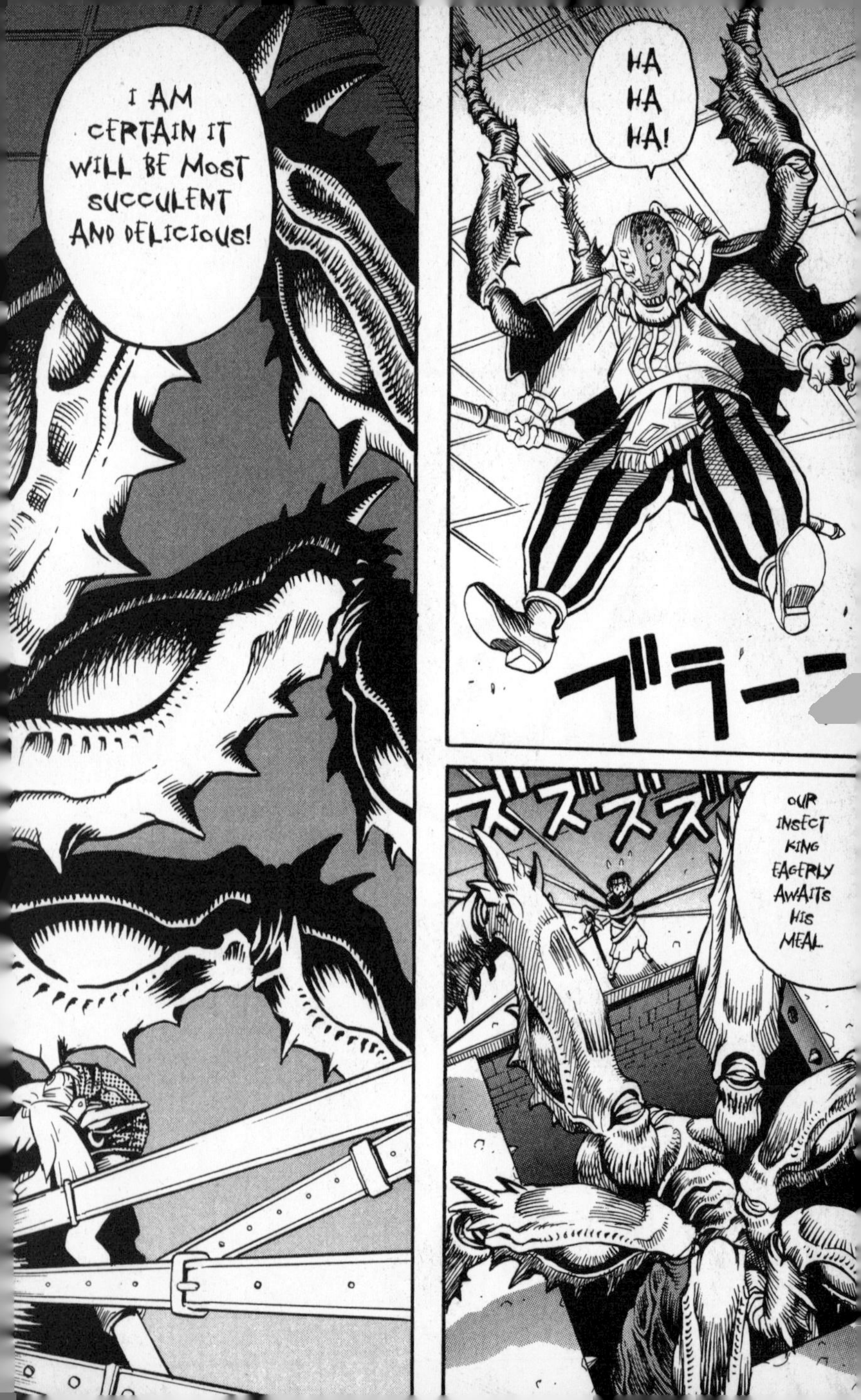
HA HA HA!
ブラー
ズズズズ
OUR INSECT KING EAGERLY AWAITS HIS MEAL
I AM CERTAIN IT WILL BE MOST SUCCULENT AND DELICIOUS!

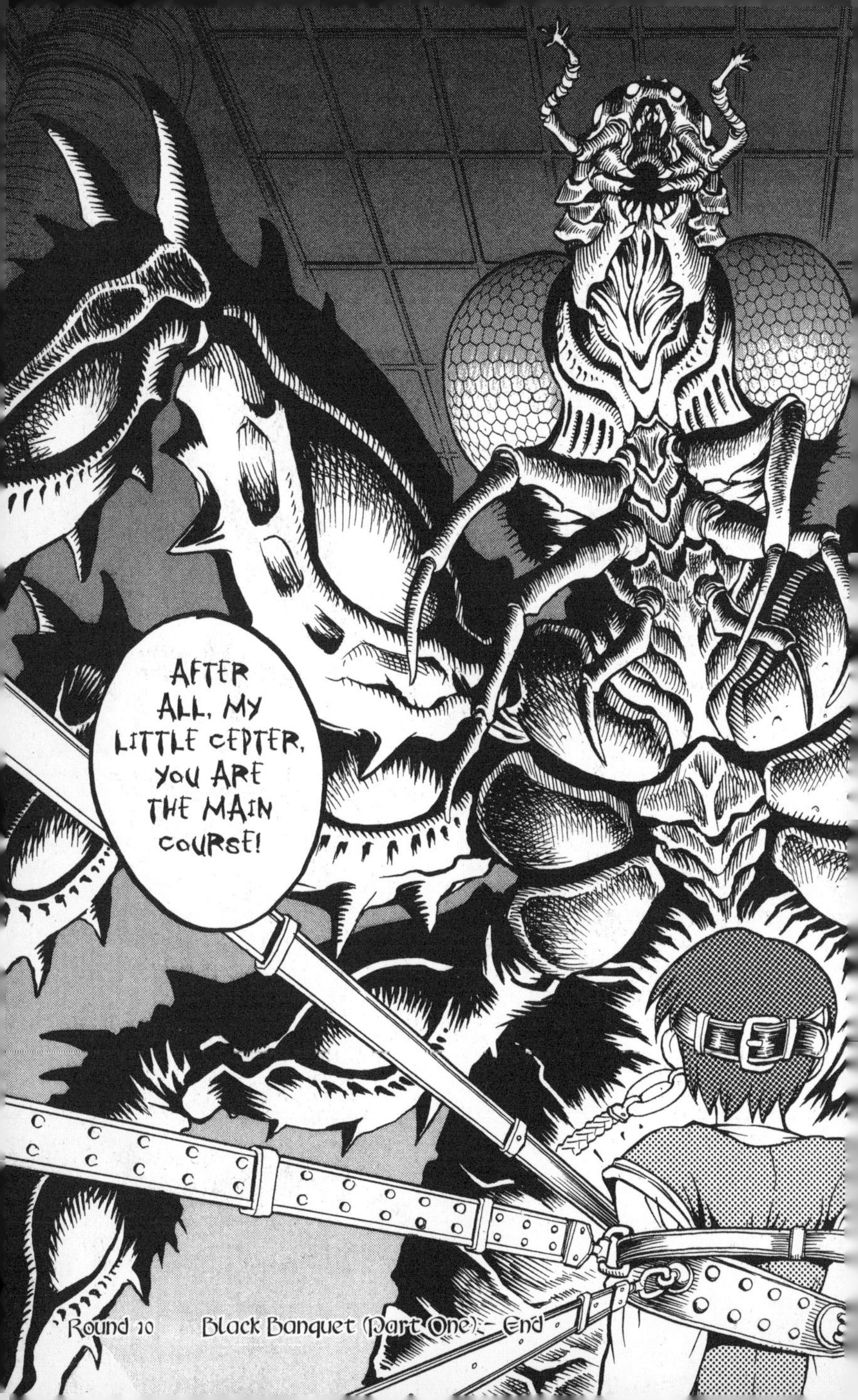
AFTER ALL, MY LITTLE CEPTER, YOU ARE THE MAIN COURSE!
Round 10 Black Banquet (Part One) - End

FIRE CREATURES

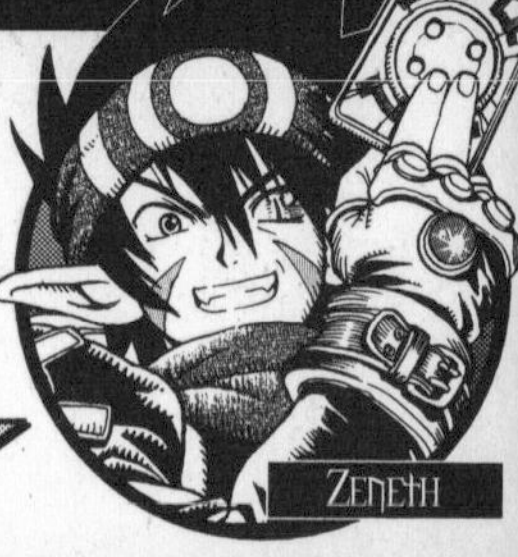
ZENETH

IRE CREATURES POSSESS GREAT ATTACK POWER. IT ISN'T
WORTH THE TROUBLE FOR YOUR OPPONENT TO USE CHEAP
RICKS ON THEM. FIERY CREATURES BURN UP ANYTHING
HAT GETS IN THE WAY! THEY ARE INDISPENSABLE IN CEPTER
BATTLES!

GOLEM

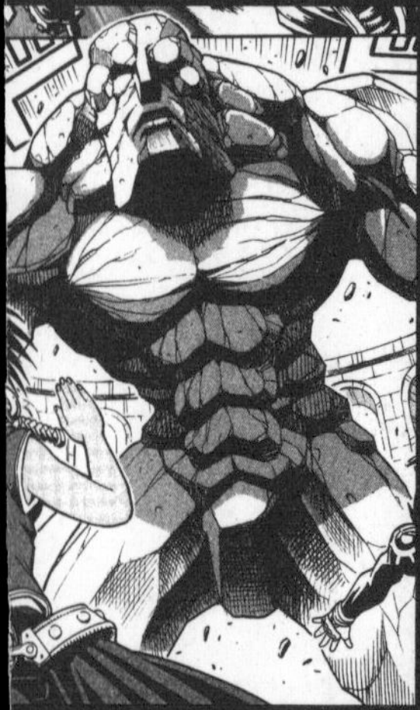

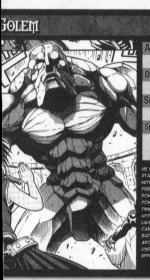

Attack Points
40
Defense Points
40
Summon Cost
60
Special Abilities
His power degenerates over time.

HE IS A HUGE STONE STATUE EMPOWERED WITH MAGIC SPELLS. PRETTY COOL, EH? HIS DOWNSIDE IS THAT HIS POWER WEAKENS OVER TIME. WITH A HYPERACTIVE OPPONENT LIKE NAJARAN WHO CAN PROLONG THE BATTLE BY RUNNING AROUND, IT'S HARD TO USE THIS CREATURE EFFECTIVELY.

CAIT SITH

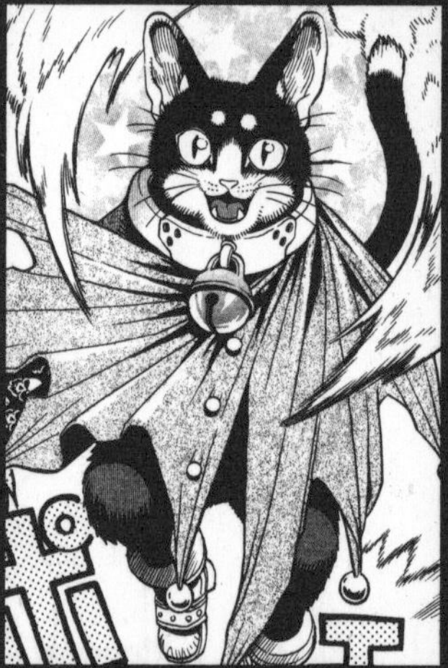

Attack Points
20
Defense Points
30
Summon Cost
75
Special Abilities
Curbing spells, etc.

HE MAY LOOK LIKE A CAT, BUT HE CLAIMS TO BE A FAIRY. HE EVEN DEFLECTED MY MOST LETHAL ATTACK! THIS IS ONE YOU DON'T UNDERESTIMATE!

I'M NOT A CAT. MEOW.

LAME WEEVIL

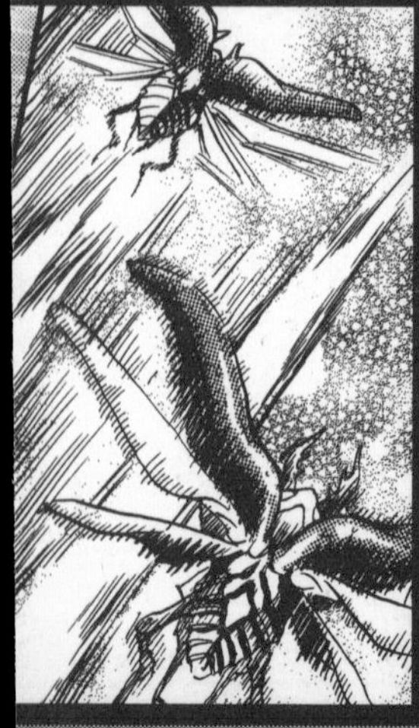

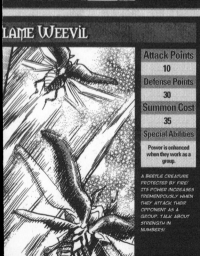

Attack Points
10
Defense Points
30
Summon Cost
35
Special Abilities
Power is enhanced when they work as a group.

A BEETLE CREATURE PROTECTED BY FIRE! ITS POWER INCREASES TREMENDOUSLY WHEN THEY ATTACK THEIR OPPONENT AS A GROUP. TALK ABOUT STRENGTH IN NUMBERS!

GOLIGANA

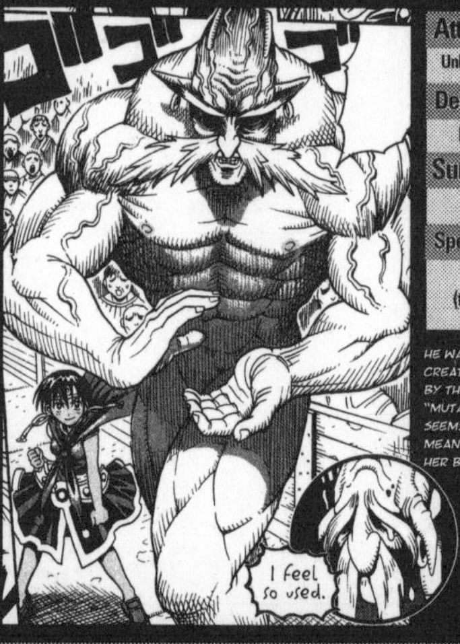
I feel so used.

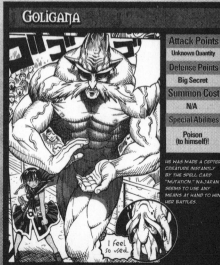

Attack Points
Unknown Quantity
Defense Points
Big Secret
Summon Cost
N/A
Special Abilities
Poison (to himself)!

HE WAS MADE A CEPTER CREATURE INSTANTLY BY THE SPELL CARD "MUTATION." NAJARAN SEEMS TO USE ANY MEANS AT HAND TO WIN HER BATTLES.

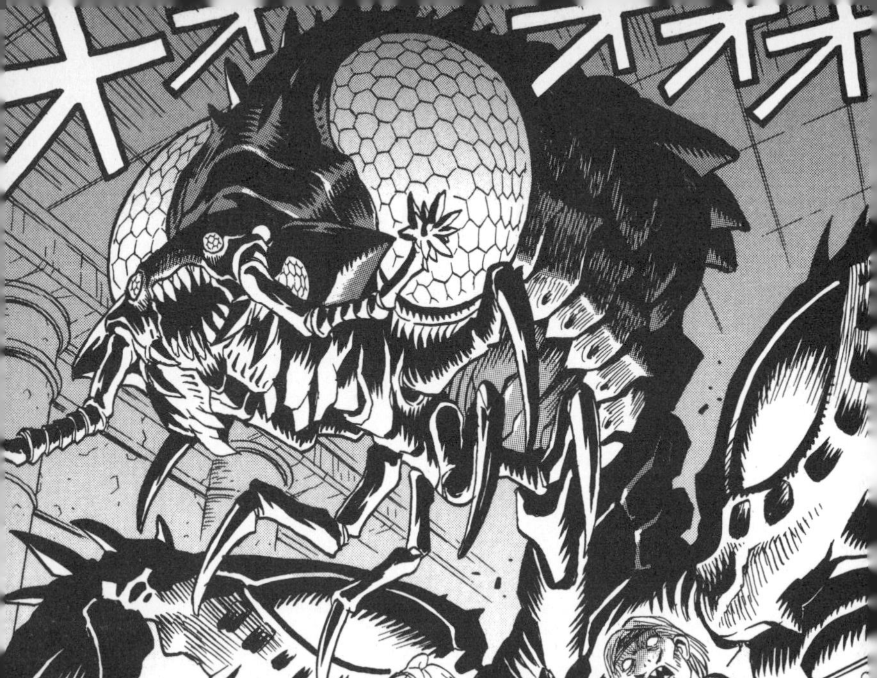
Culdcept
カルドセプト
Round 11 Black Banquet (Part Two)

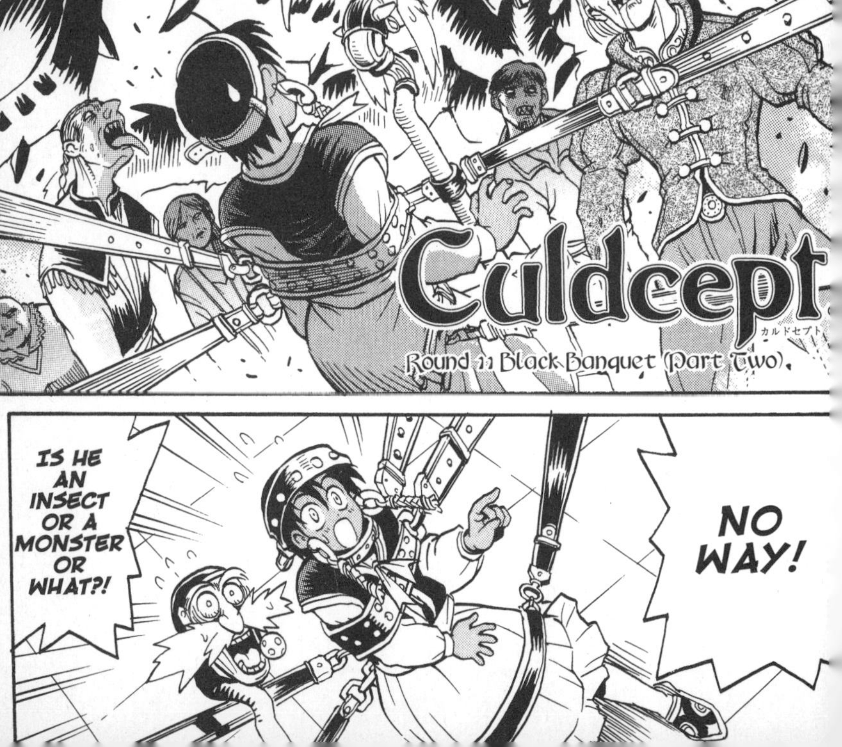
NO WAY!
IS HE AN INSECT OR A MONSTER OR WHAT?!

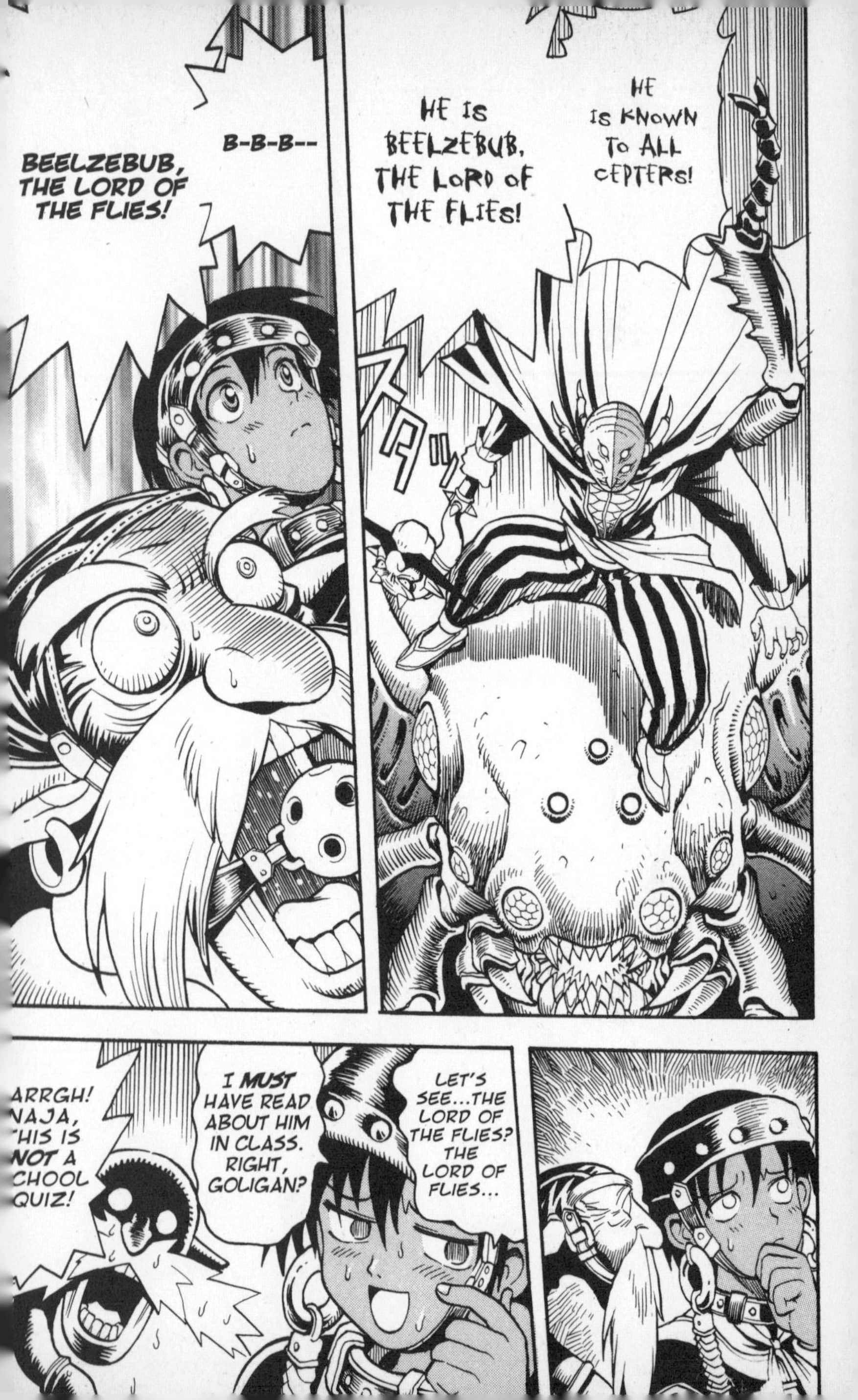
HE IS KNOWN TO ALL CEPTERS!
HE IS BEELZEBUB, THE LORD OF THE FLIES!
B-B-B--
BEELZEBUB, THE LORD OF THE FLIES!
LET'S SEE...THE LORD OF THE FLIES? THE LORD OF FLIES...
I *MUST* HAVE READ ABOUT HIM IN CLASS. RIGHT, GOLIGAN?
ARRGH! NAJA, THIS IS *NOT* A CHOOL QUIZ!

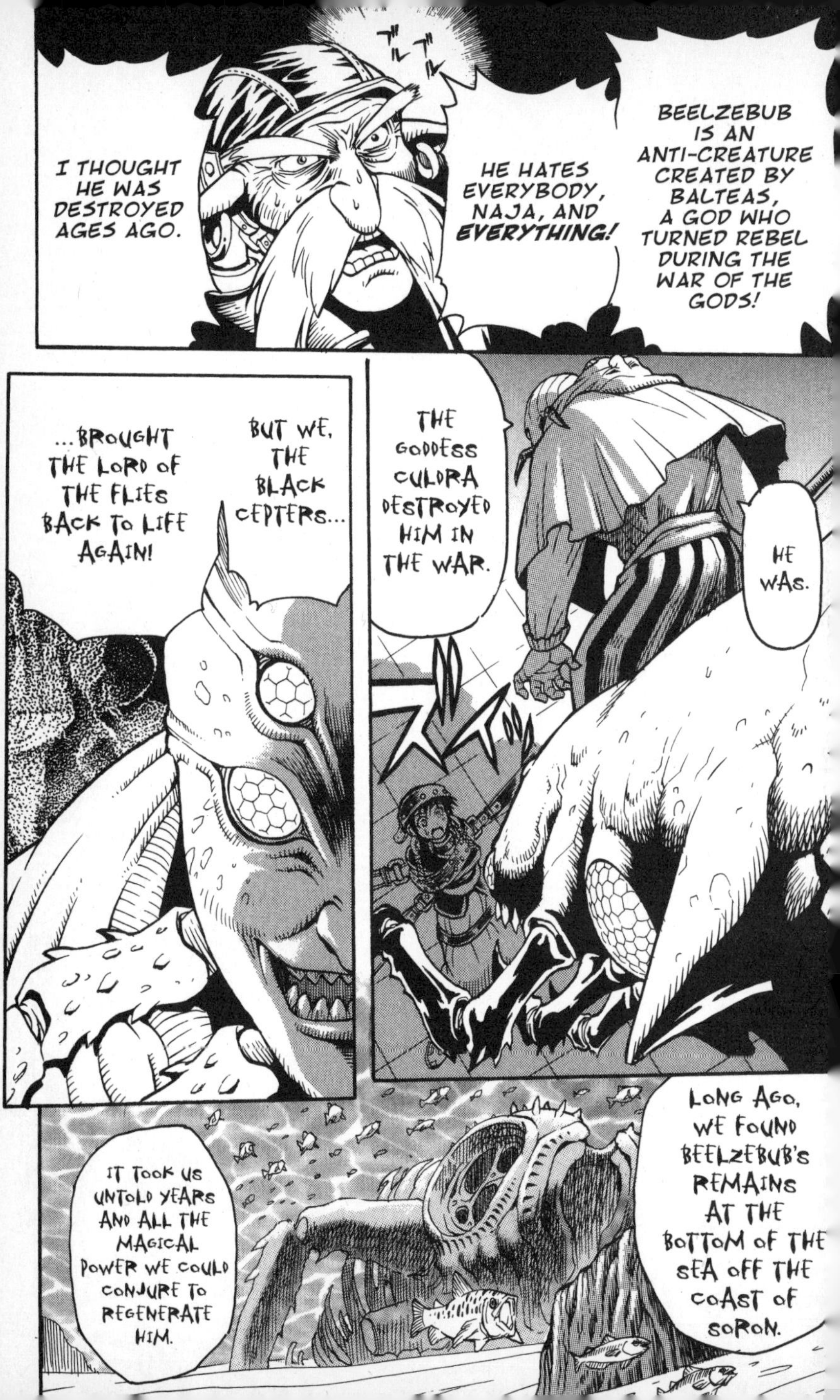
ブルブル
BEELZEBUB IS AN ANTI-CREATURE CREATED BY BALTEAS, A GOD WHO TURNED REBEL DURING THE WAR OF THE GODS!
HE HATES EVERYBODY, NAJA, AND **EVERYTHING!**
I THOUGHT HE WAS DESTROYED AGES AGO.
THE GODDESS CULORA DESTROYED HIM IN THE WAR.
HE WAS.
BUT WE, THE BLACK CEPTERS...
...BROUGHT THE LORD OF THE FLIES BACK TO LIFE AGAIN!
LONG AGO, WE FOUND BEELZEBUB'S REMAINS AT THE BOTTOM OF THE SEA OFF THE COAST OF SORON.
IT TOOK US UNTOLD YEARS AND ALL THE MAGICAL POWER WE COULD CONJURE TO REGENERATE HIM.

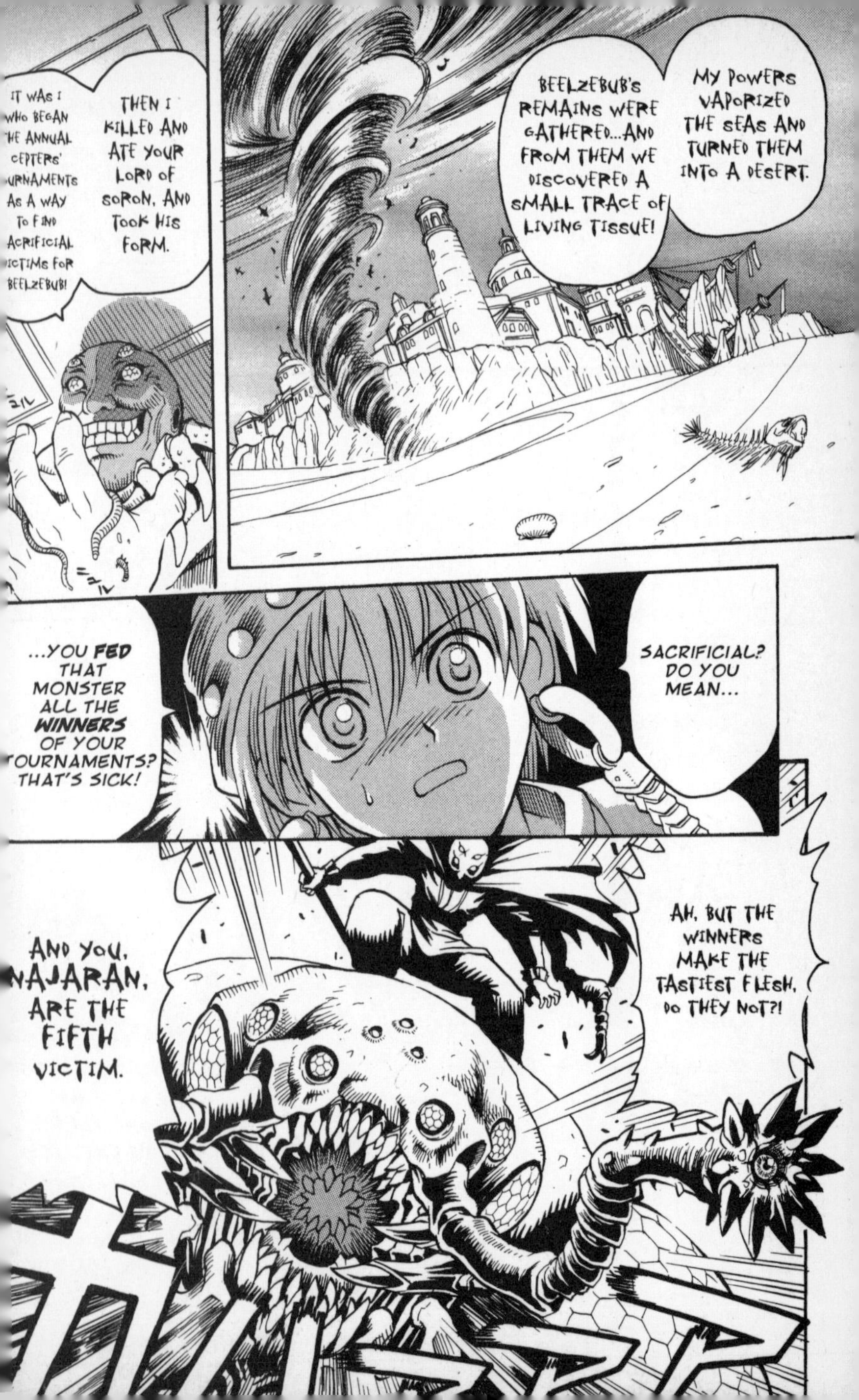
MY POWERS VAPORIZED THE SEAS AND TURNED THEM INTO A DESERT.
BEELZEBUB'S REMAINS WERE GATHERED...AND FROM THEM WE DISCOVERED A SMALL TRACE OF LIVING TISSUE!
THEN I KILLED AND ATE YOUR LORD OF SORON, AND TOOK HIS FORM.
IT WAS I WHO BEGAN HE ANNUAL CEPTERS' URNAMENTS AS A WAY TO FIND ACRIFICIAL ICTIMS FOR BEELZEBUB!
SACRIFICIAL? DO YOU MEAN...
...YOU FED THAT MONSTER ALL THE WINNERS OF YOUR TOURNAMENTS? THAT'S SICK!
AH, BUT THE WINNERS MAKE THE TASTIEST FLESH, DO THEY NOT?!
AND YOU, NAJARAN, ARE THE FIFTH VICTIM.

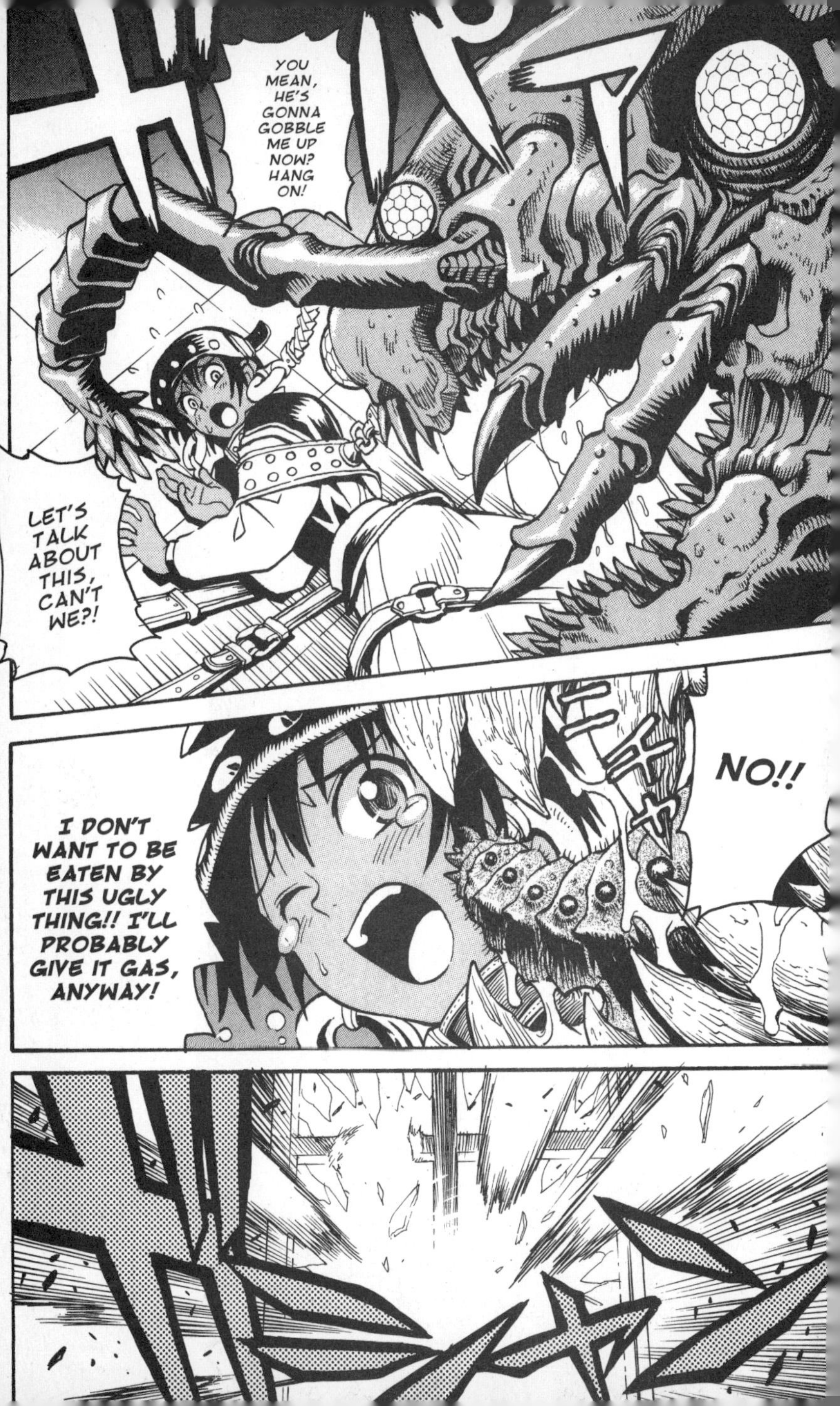
YOU MEAN, HE'S GONNA GOBBLE ME UP NOW? HANG ON!
LET'S TALK ABOUT THIS, CAN'T WE?!
NO!!
I DON'T WANT TO BE EATEN BY THIS UGLY THING!! I'LL PROBABLY GIVE IT GAS, ANYWAY!

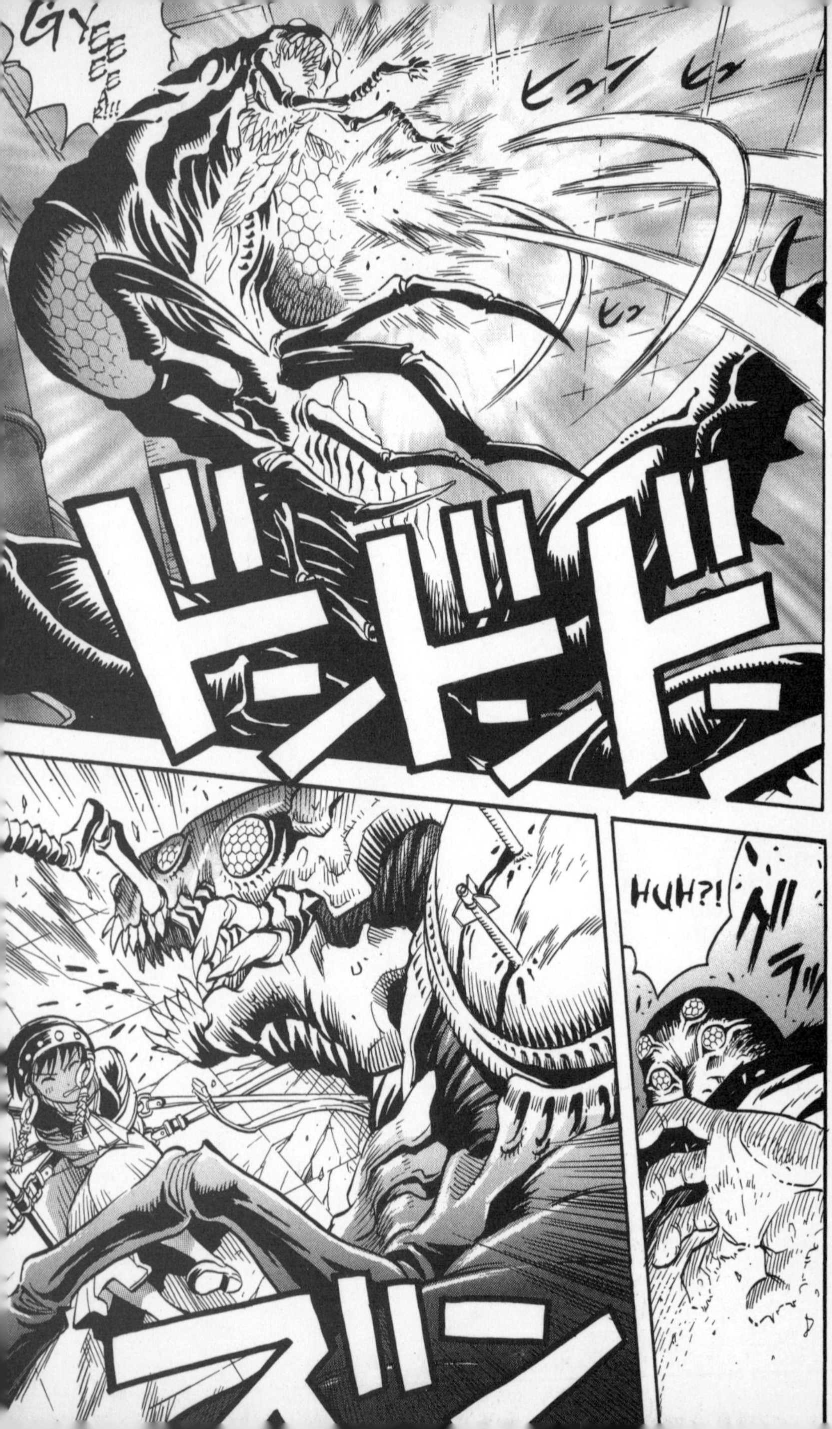

GYEEEEEAR!!!
ヒュン ヒュ
ヒュ
ドドドド
HUH?!
バッ
ズー

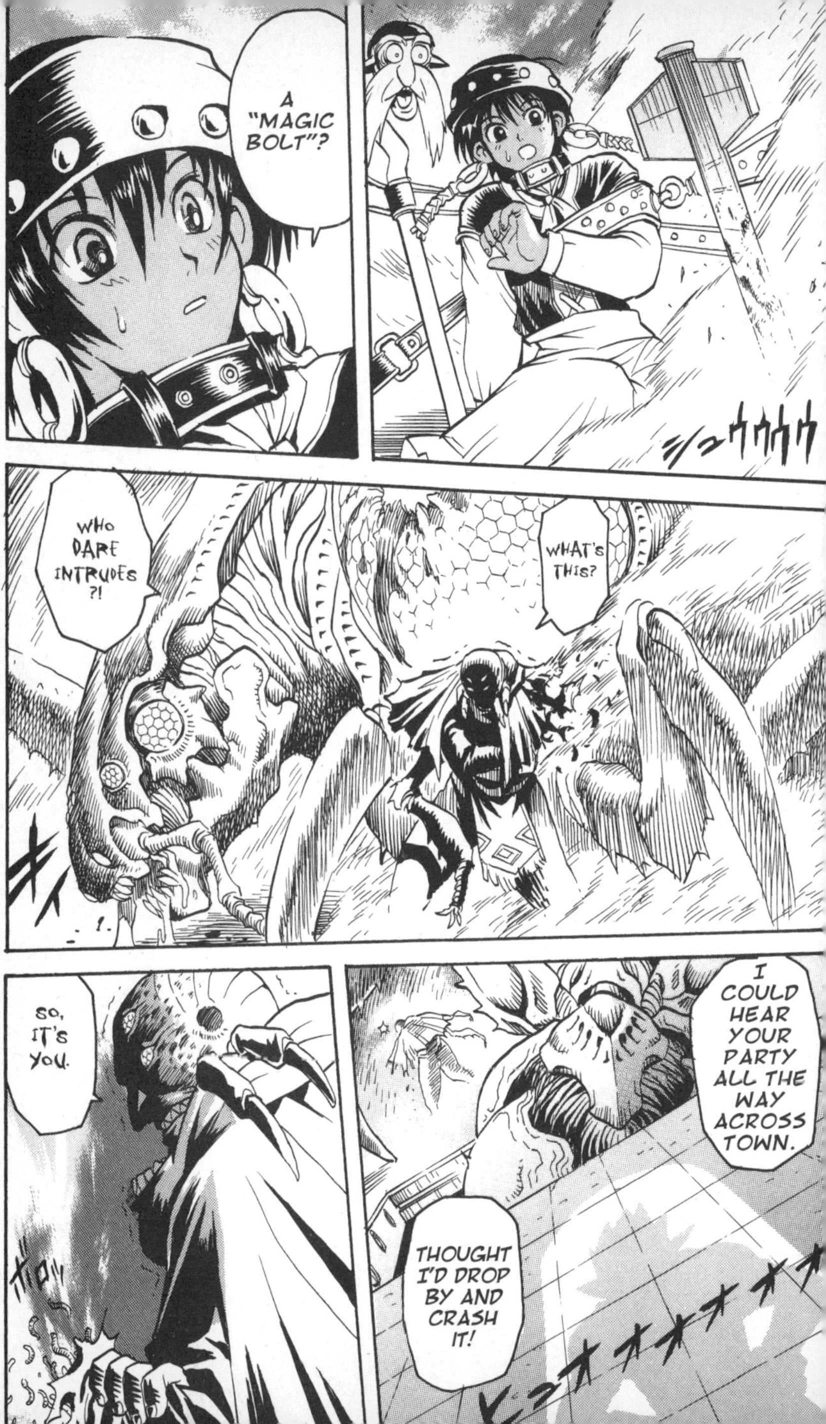
シュウウウウ
A "MAGIC BOLT"?
WHAT'S THIS?
WHO DARE INTRUDES?!
I COULD HEAR YOUR PARTY ALL THE WAY ACROSS TOWN.
THOUGHT I'D DROP BY AND CRASH IT!
ヒュオオオオオ
SO, IT'S YOU.

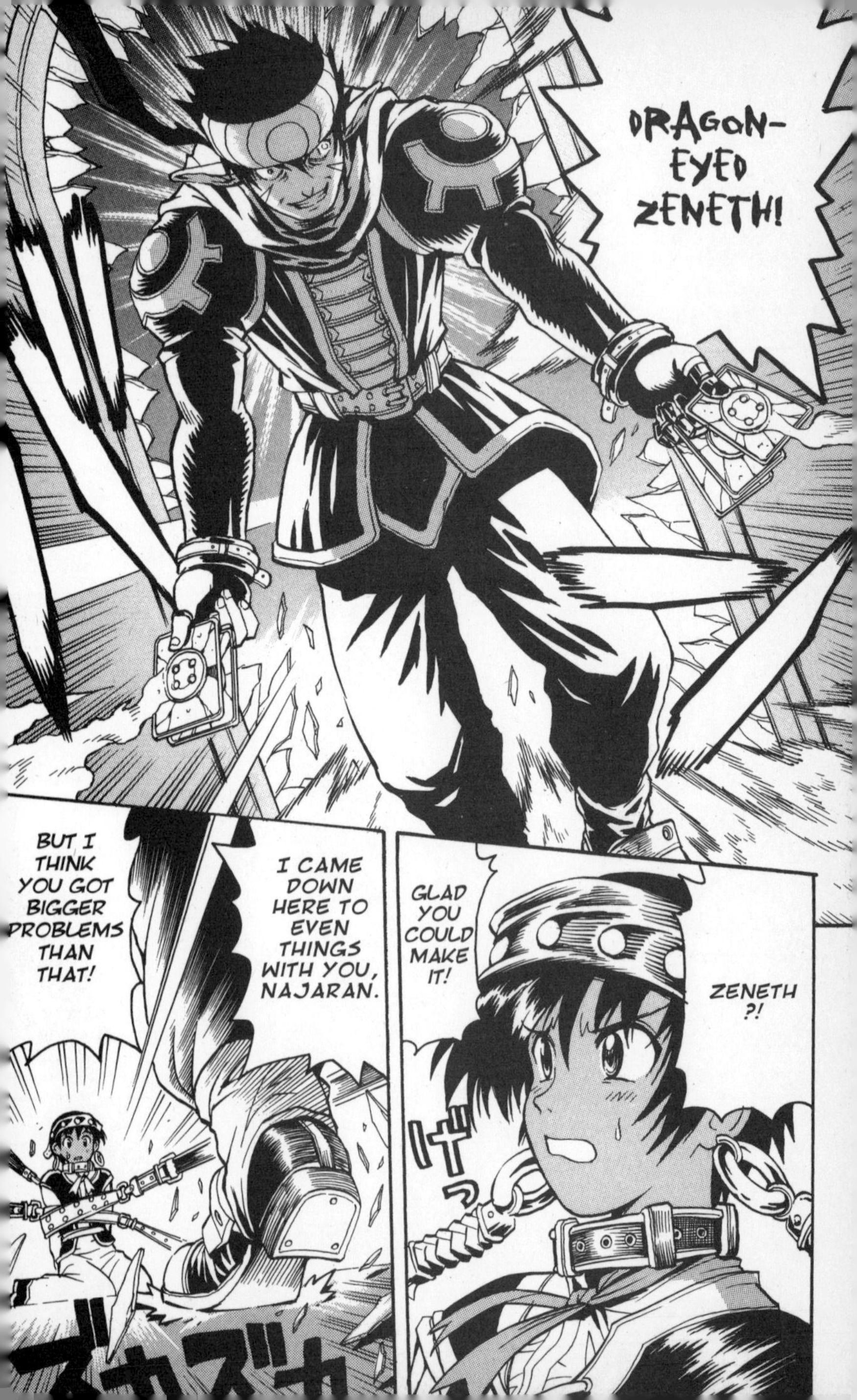
DRAGON-EYED ZENETH!
ZENETH?!
GLAD YOU COULD MAKE IT!
I CAME DOWN HERE TO EVEN THINGS WITH YOU, NAJARAN.
BUT I THINK YOU GOT BIGGER PROBLEMS THAN THAT!

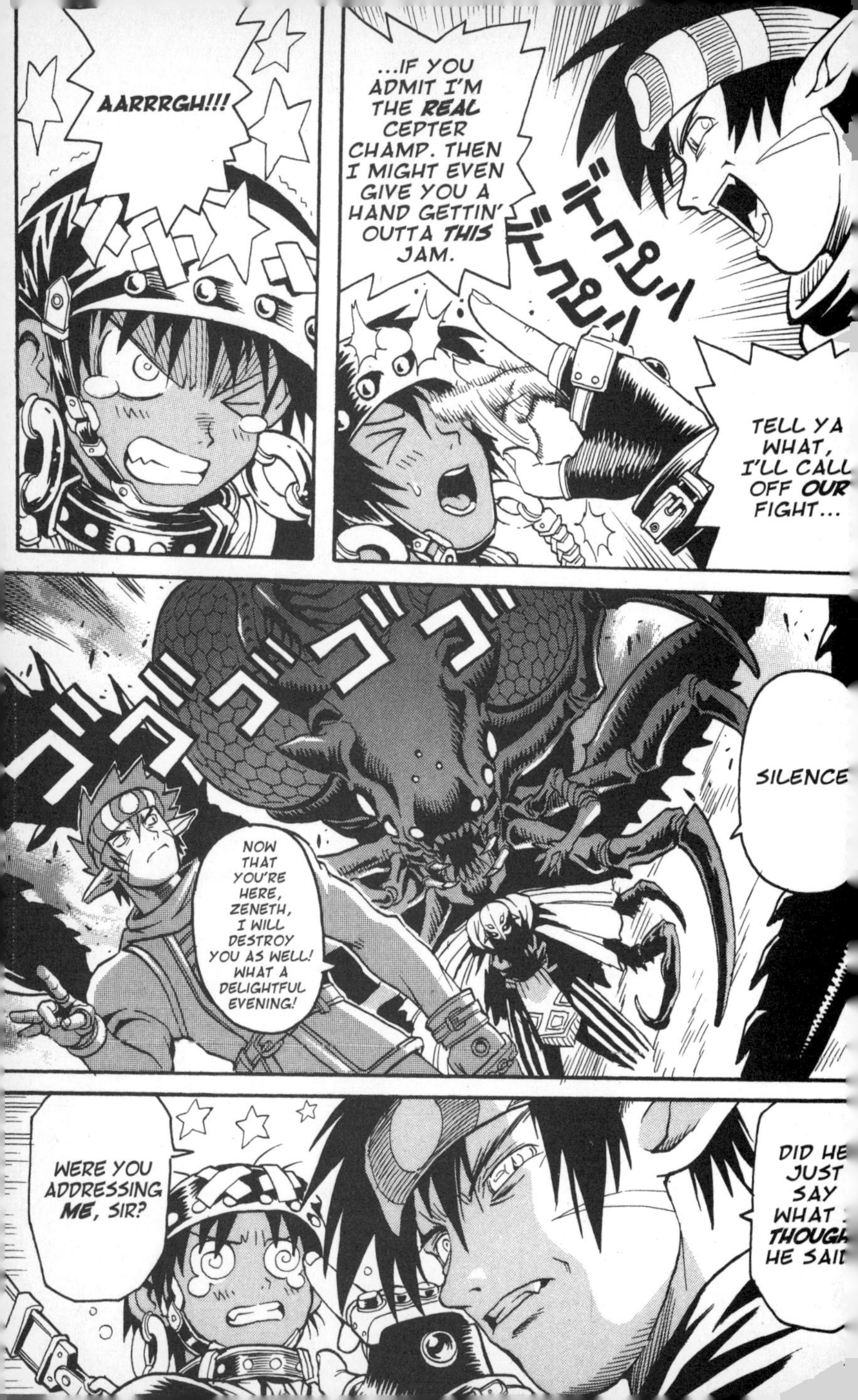
TELL YA WHAT, I'LL CALL OFF **OUR** FIGHT...
...IF YOU ADMIT I'M THE **REAL** CEPTER CHAMP. THEN I MIGHT EVEN GIVE YOU A HAND GETTIN' OUTTA **THIS** JAM.
デコピッ
デコピッ
AARRRGH!!!
SILENCE
NOW THAT YOU'RE HERE, ZENETH, I WILL DESTROY YOU AS WELL! WHAT A DELIGHTFUL EVENING!
ゴゴゴゴ
DID HE JUST SAY WHAT **THOUGH** HE SAI
WERE YOU ADDRESSING **ME**, SIR?

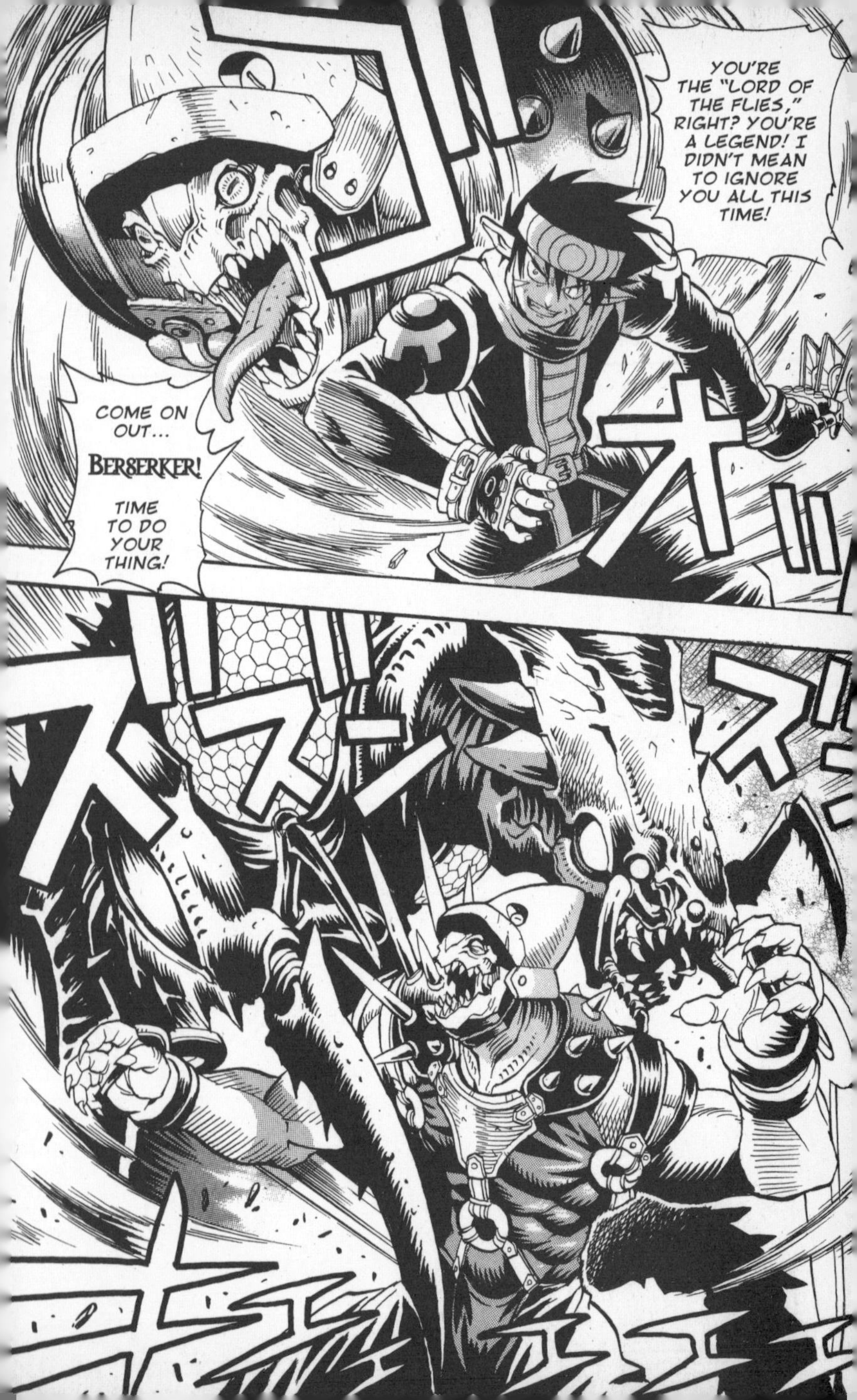
YOU'RE THE "LORD OF THE FLIES," RIGHT? YOU'RE A LEGEND! I DIDN'T MEAN TO IGNORE YOU ALL THIS TIME!
COME ON OUT... BERSERKER! TIME TO DO YOUR THING!

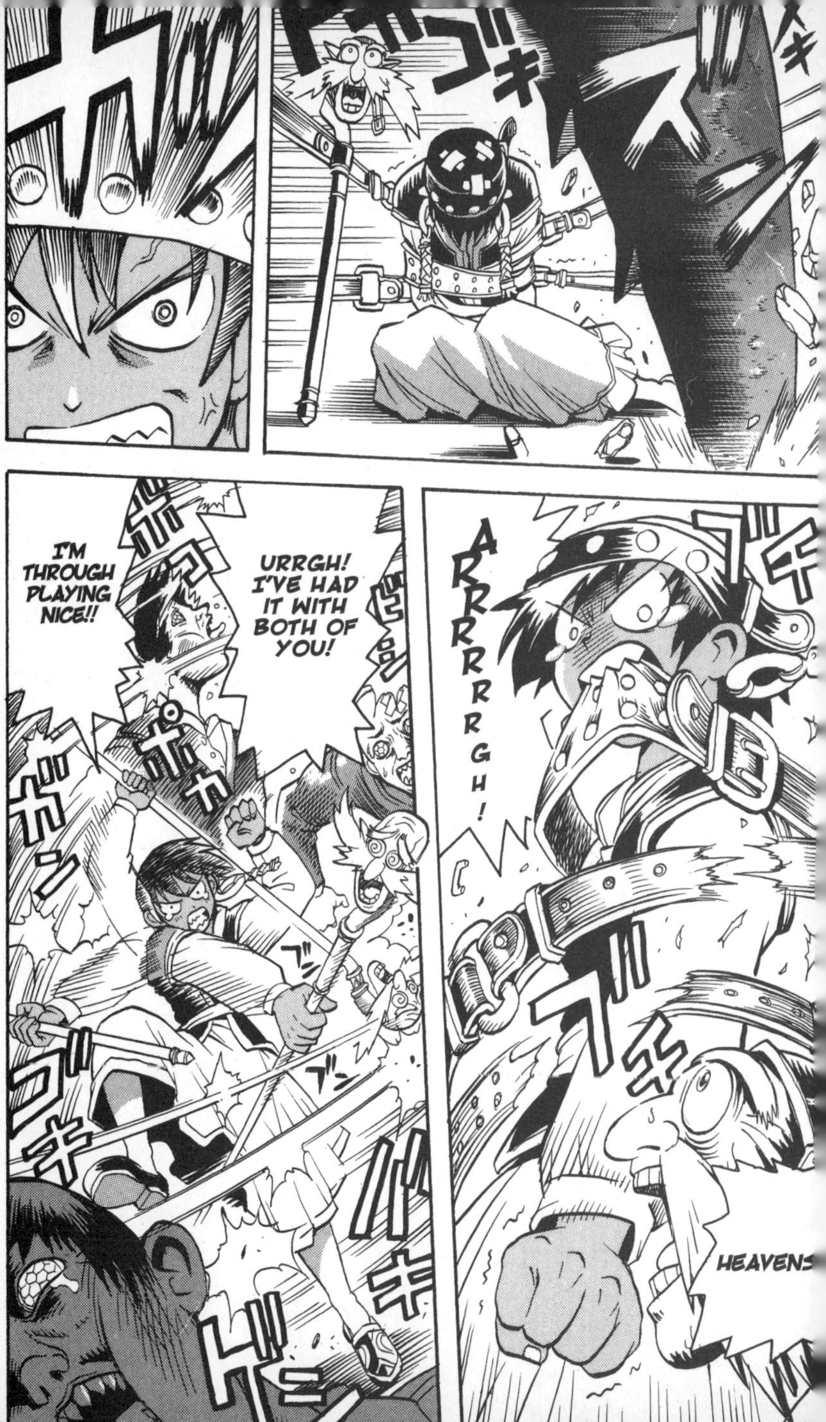
ARRRRRRRGH!
HEAVENS
URRGH! I'VE HAD IT WITH BOTH OF YOU!
I'M THROUGH PLAYING NICE!!

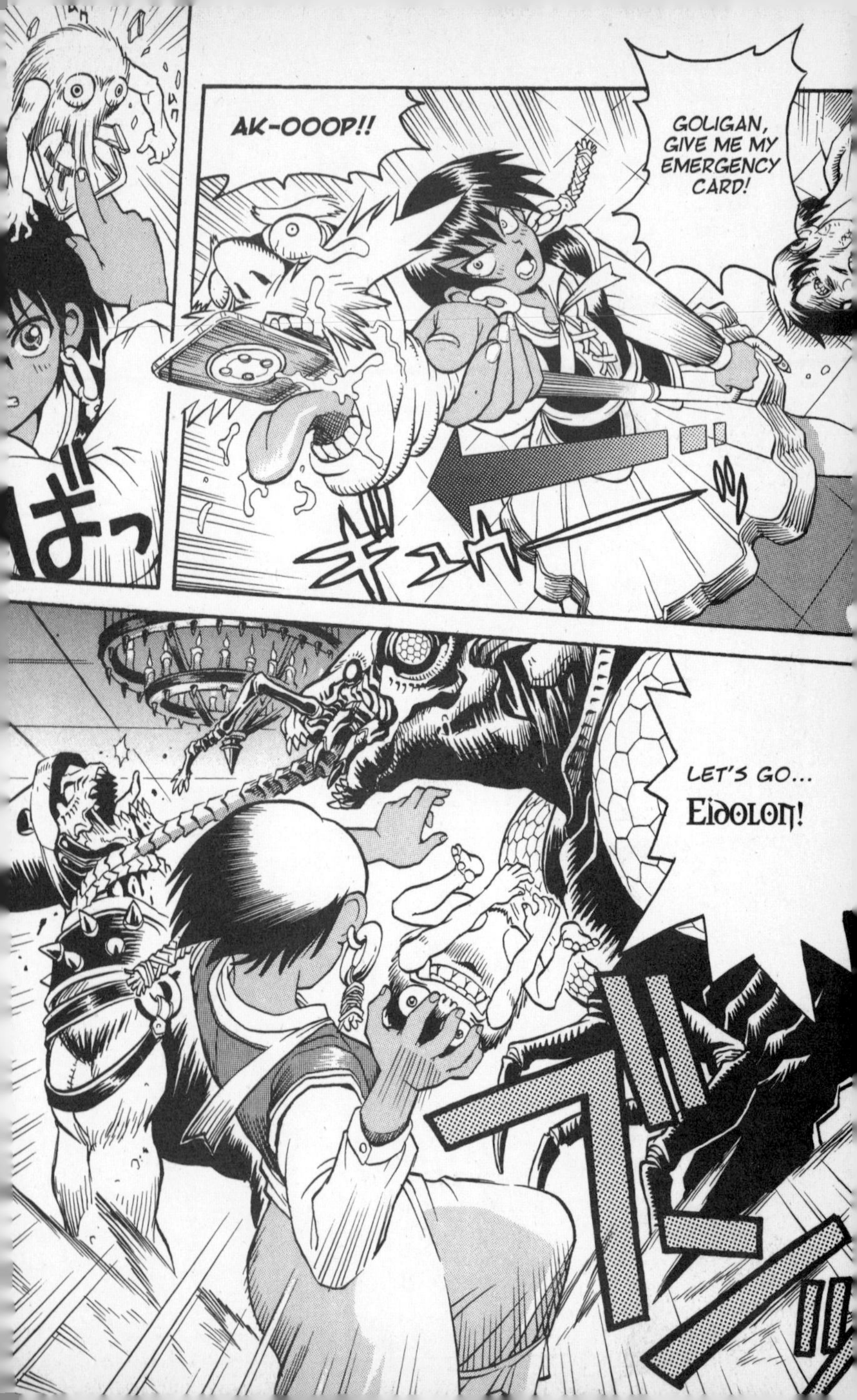
GOLIGAN, GIVE ME MY EMERGENCY CARD!
AK-OOOP!!
ばっ
LET'S GO... Eidolon!

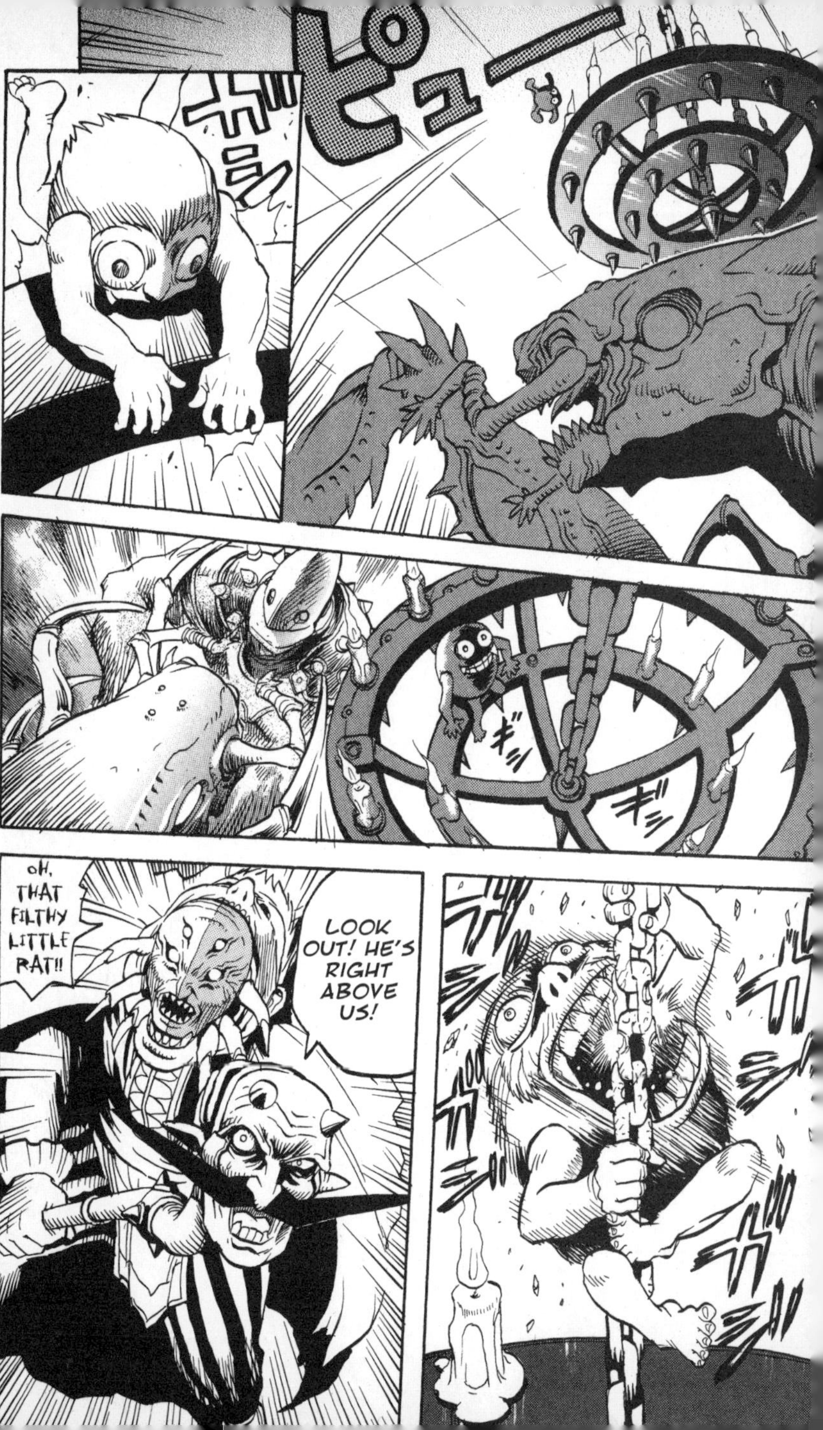
ピュー
ギシ
ギシ
LOOK OUT! HE'S RIGHT ABOVE US!
OH, THAT FILTHY LITTLE RAT!!

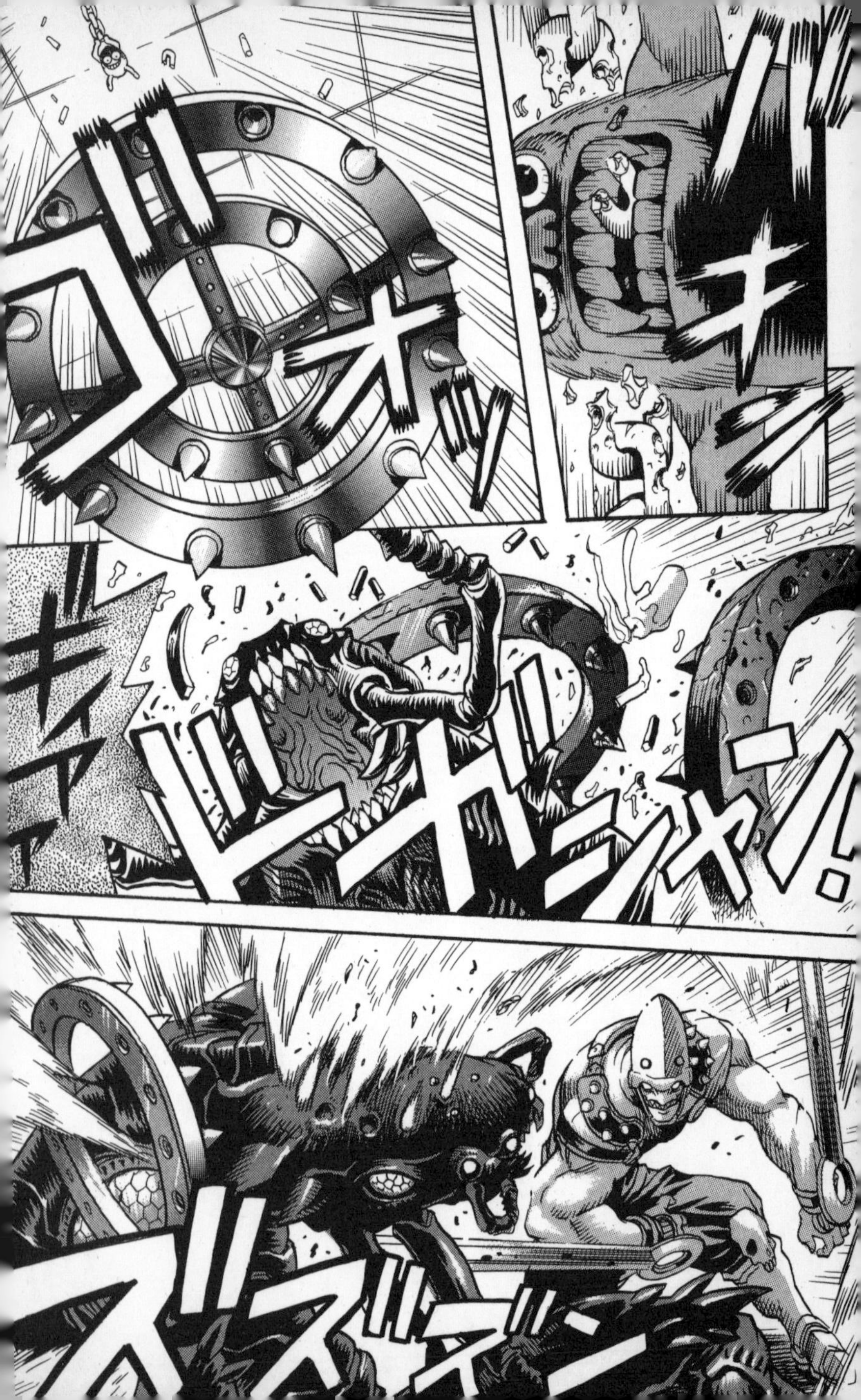
バキッ
ゴオッ
ドガシャーン!
ギイヤァ
ズズズーン

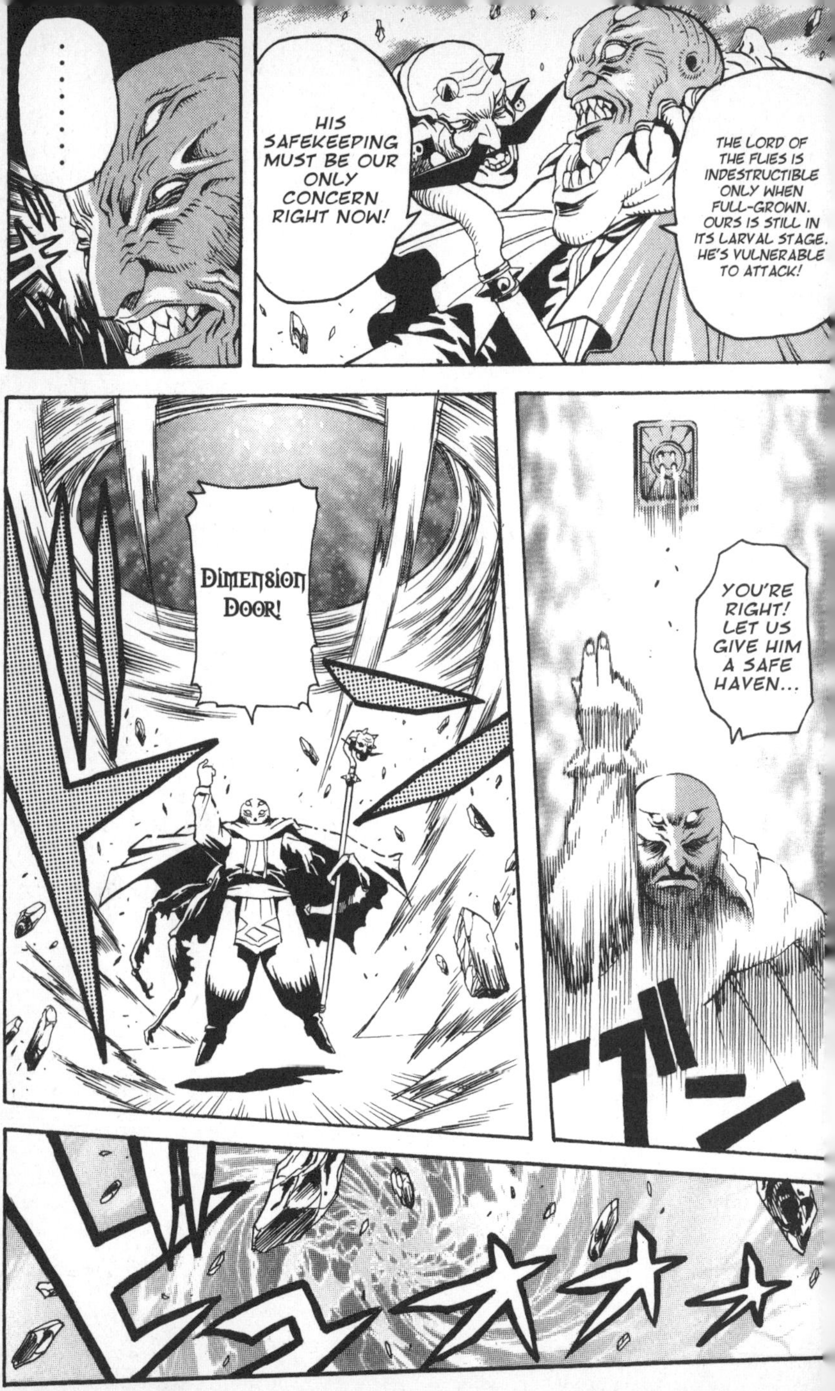
THE LORD OF THE FLIES IS INDESTRUCTIBLE ONLY WHEN FULL-GROWN. OURS IS STILL IN ITS LARVAL STAGE. HE'S VULNERABLE TO ATTACK!
HIS SAFEKEEPING MUST BE OUR ONLY CONCERN RIGHT NOW!
......
YOU'RE RIGHT! LET US GIVE HIM A SAFE HAVEN...
Dimension Door!

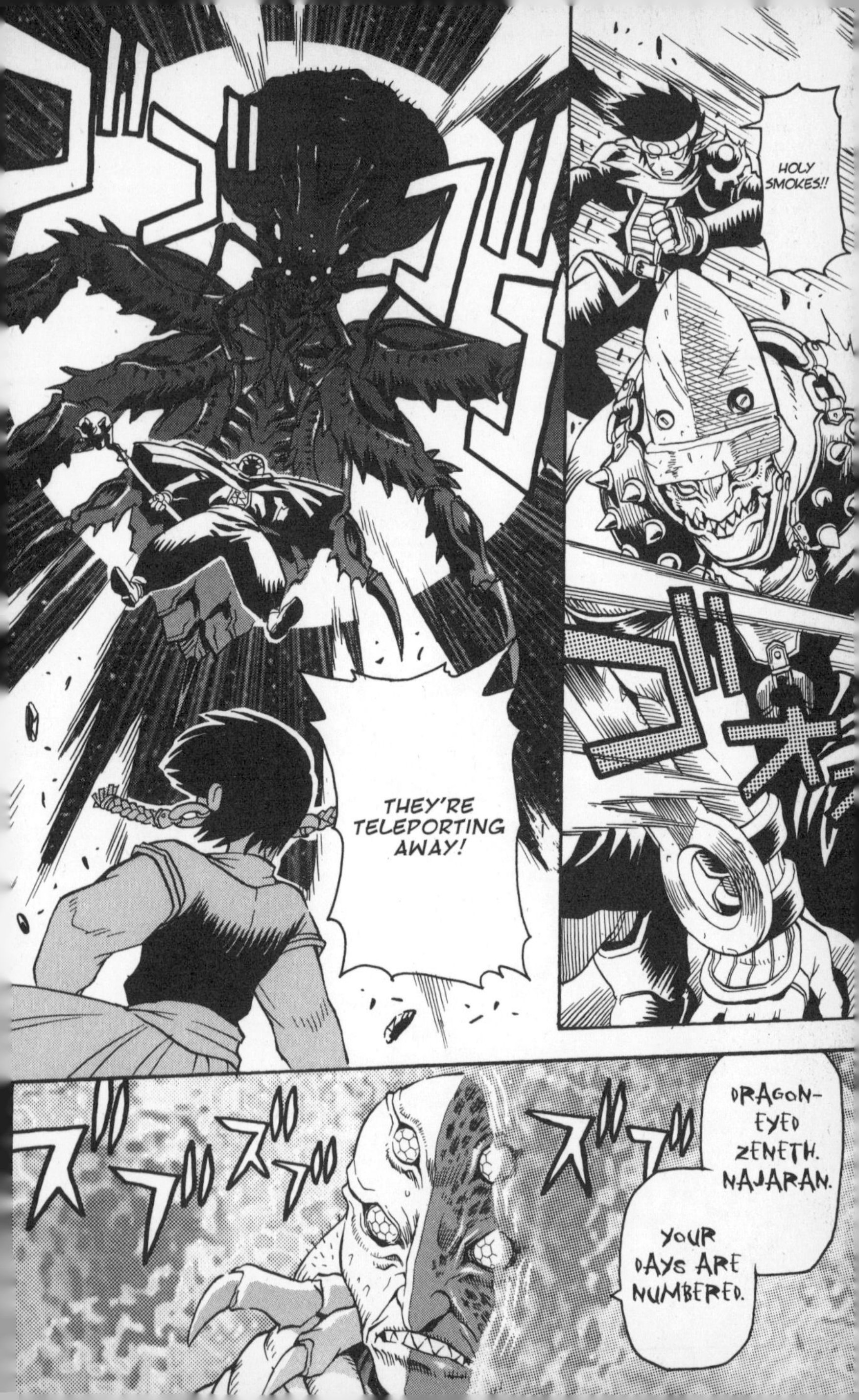
HOLY SMOKES!!
THEY'RE TELEPORTING AWAY!
DRAGON-EYED ZENETH. NAJARAN.
YOUR DAYS ARE NUMBERED.

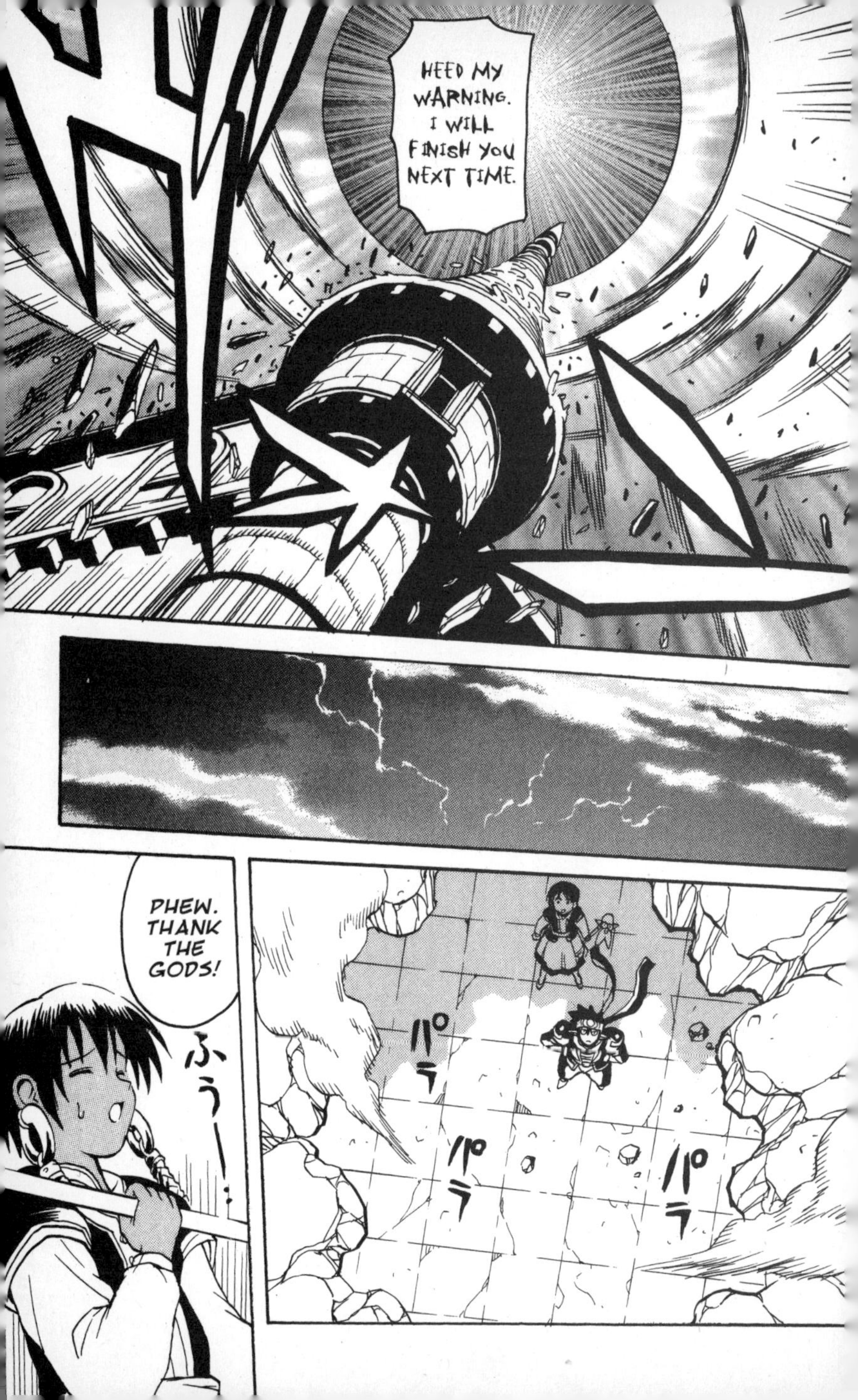
HEED MY WARNING. I WILL FINISH YOU NEXT TIME.
パラ
パラ
パラ
PHEW. THANK THE GODS!
ふうー!

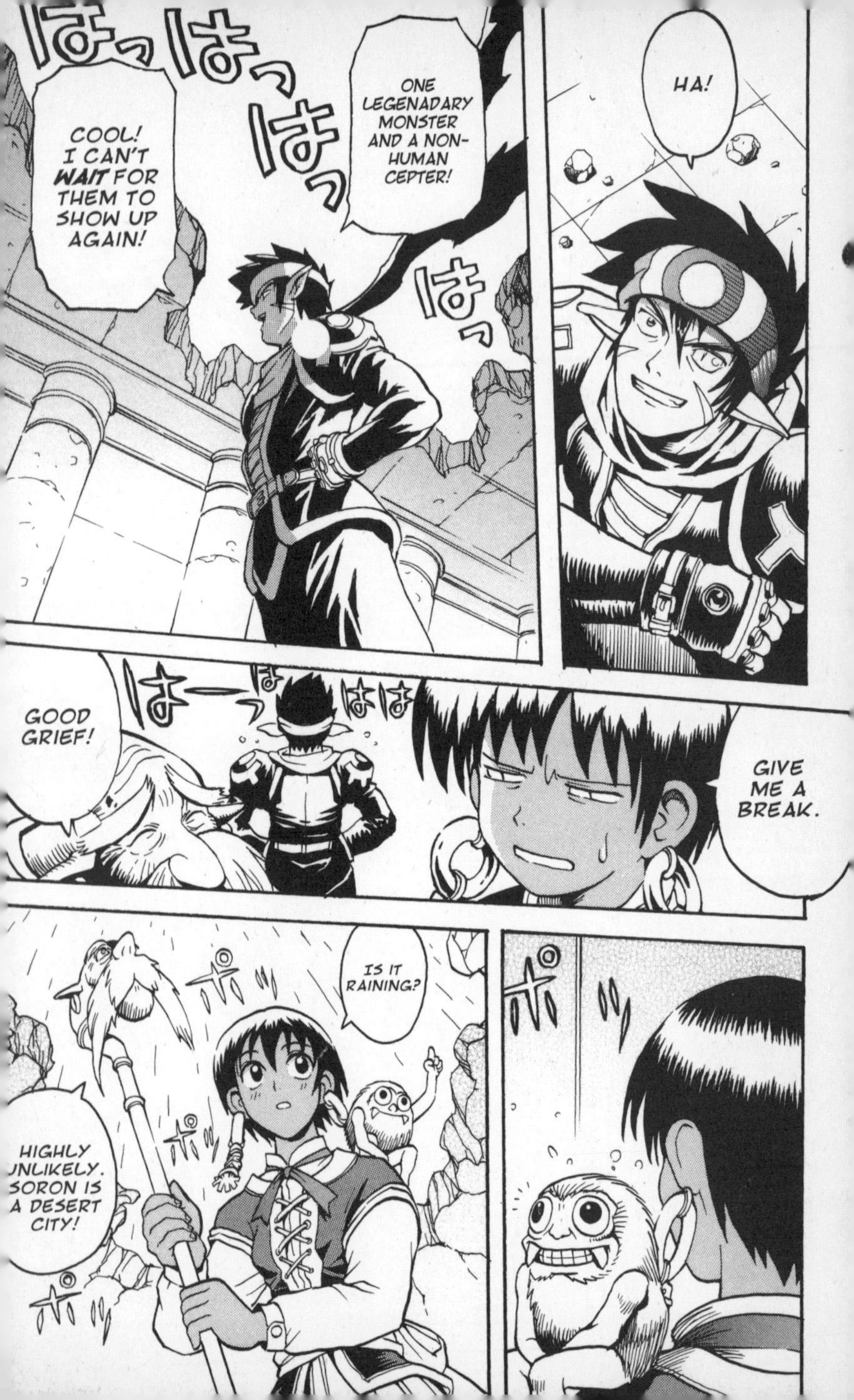
HA!
はっ
ONE LEGENADARY MONSTER AND A NON-HUMAN CEPTER!
はっはっはっ
COOL! I CAN'T WAIT FOR THEM TO SHOW UP AGAIN!
GIVE ME A BREAK.
はーっははは
GOOD GRIEF!
ポ
IS IT RAINING?
ポ
HIGHLY UNLIKELY. SORON IS A DESERT CITY!
ポ

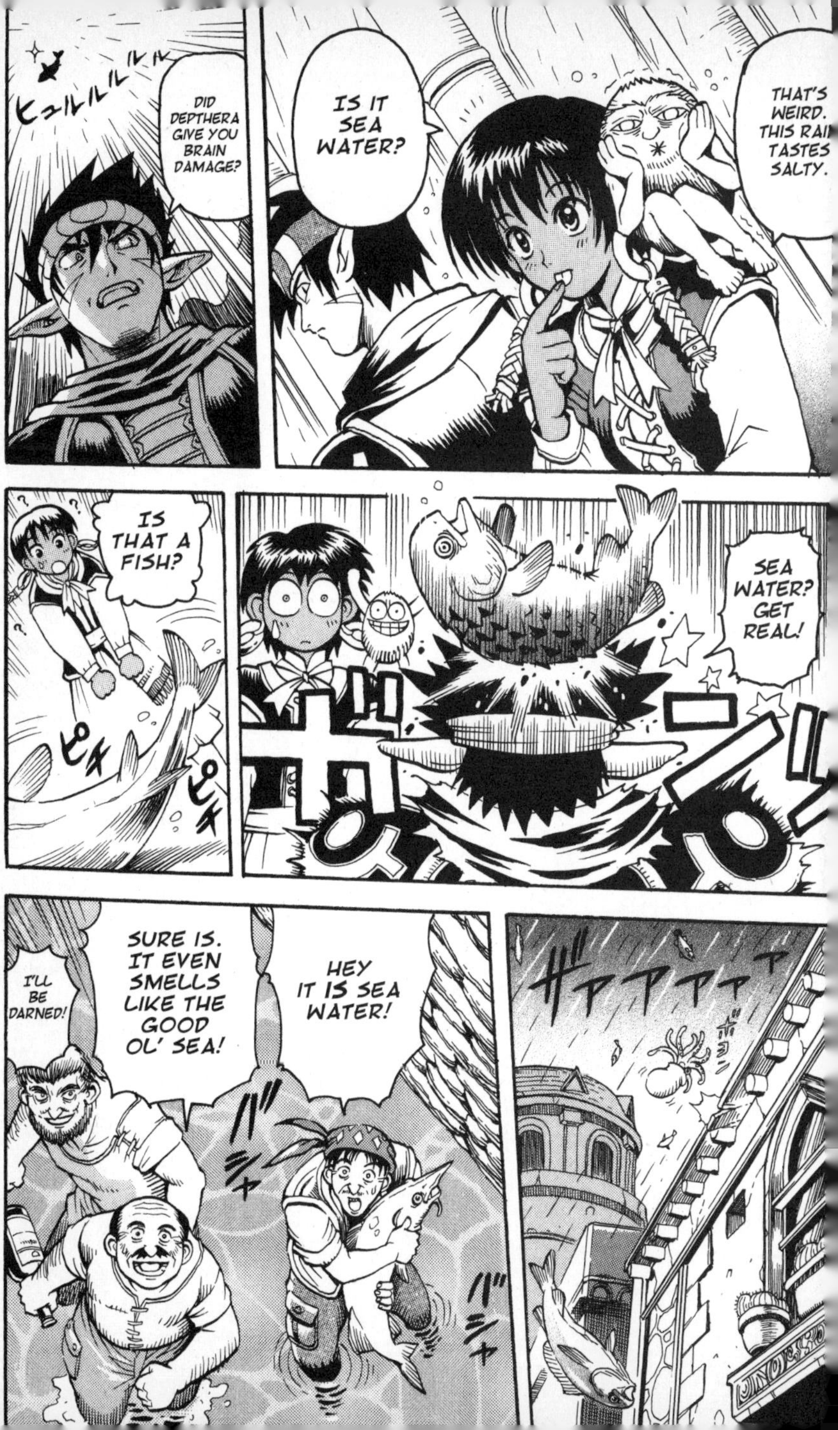
THAT'S WEIRD. THIS RAI TASTES SALTY.
IS IT SEA WATER?
ヒュルルルルル
DID DEPTHERA GIVE YOU BRAIN DAMAGE?
SEA WATER? GET REAL!
IS THAT A FISH?
ピチ
ピチ
ザァァァァァ
HEY IT IS SEA WATER!
SURE IS. IT EVEN SMELLS LIKE THE GOOD OL' SEA!
I'LL BE DARNED!
バシャ
バシャ

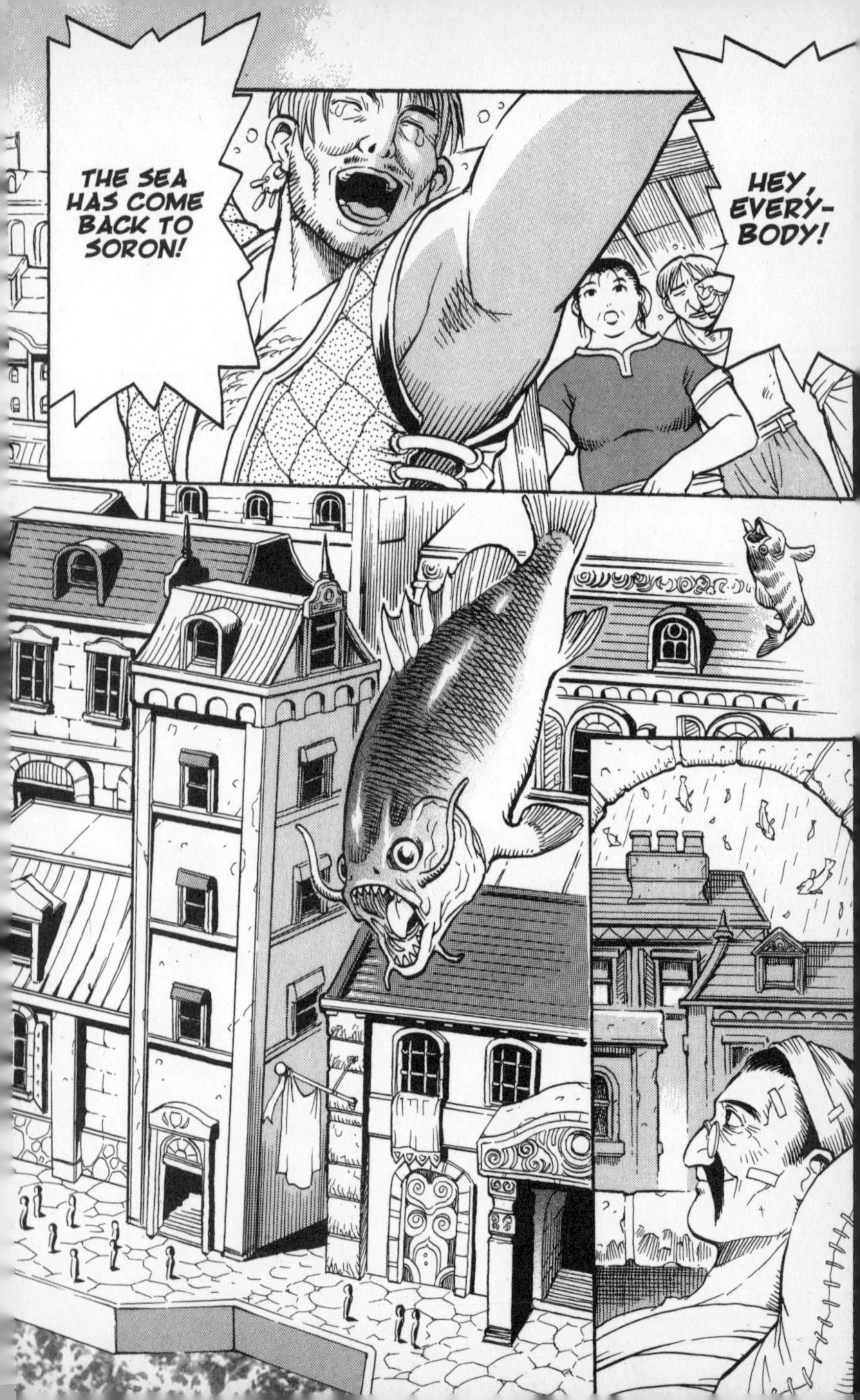
HEY, EVERY-BODY!
THE SEA HAS COME BACK TO SORON!

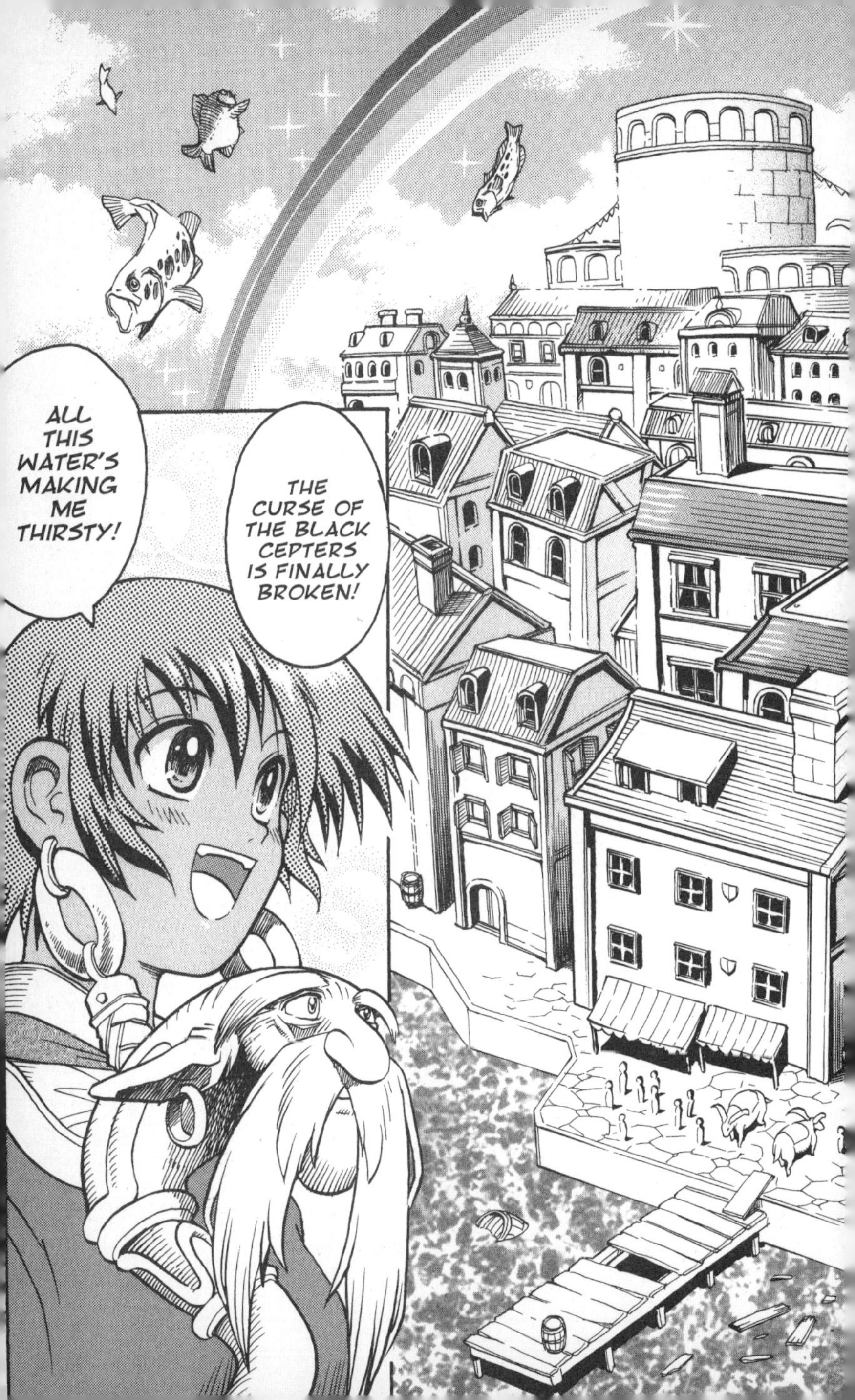
THE CURSE OF THE BLACK CEPTERS IS FINALLY BROKEN!
ALL THIS WATER'S MAKING ME THIRSTY!

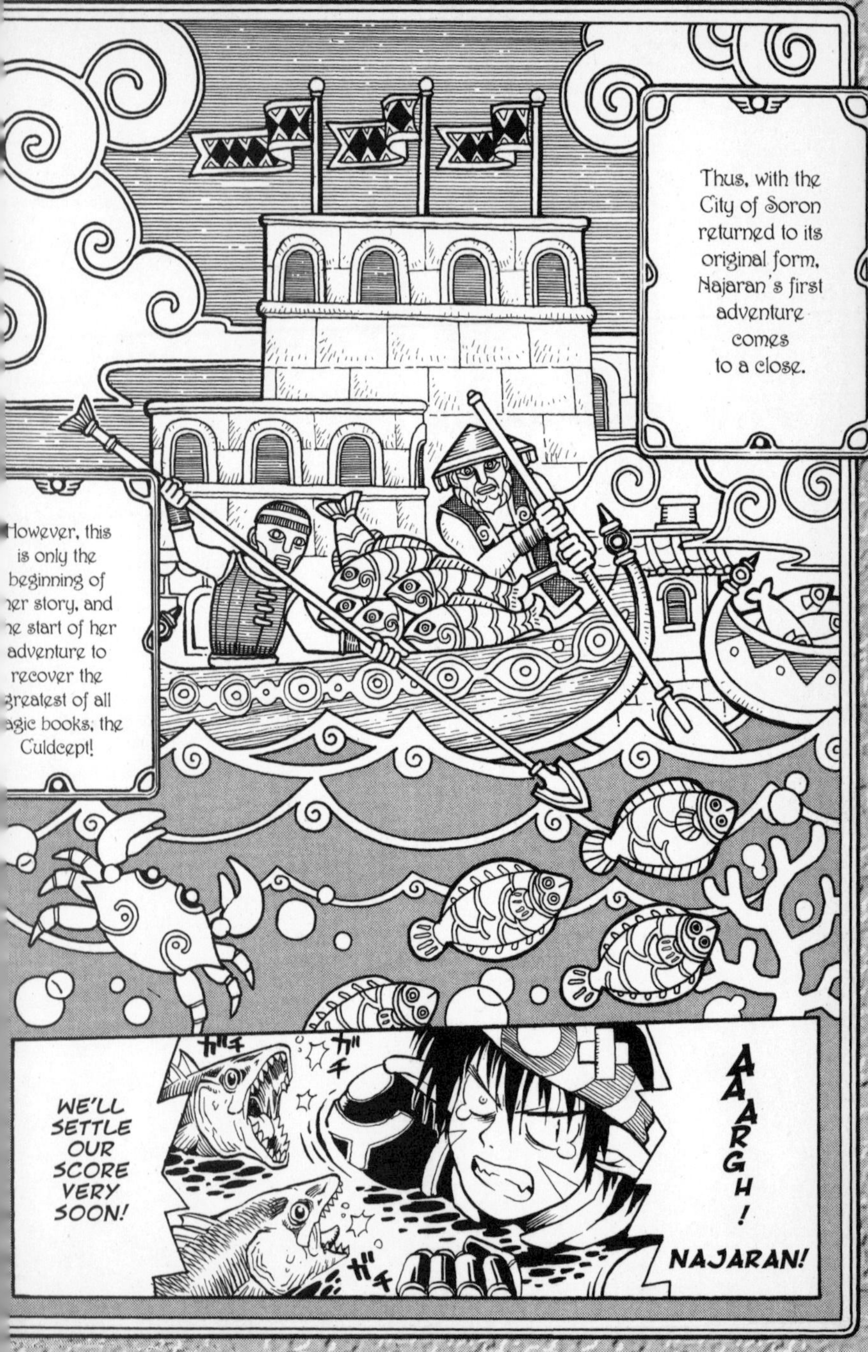

Thus, with the City of Soron returned to its original form, Najaran's first adventure comes to a close.
Iowever, this is only the beginning of ner story, and ne start of her adventure to recover the greatest of all agic books, the Culdcept!
AAARGH!
NAJARAN!
ガチ
ガチ
ガチ
WE'LL SETTLE OUR SCORE VERY SOON!

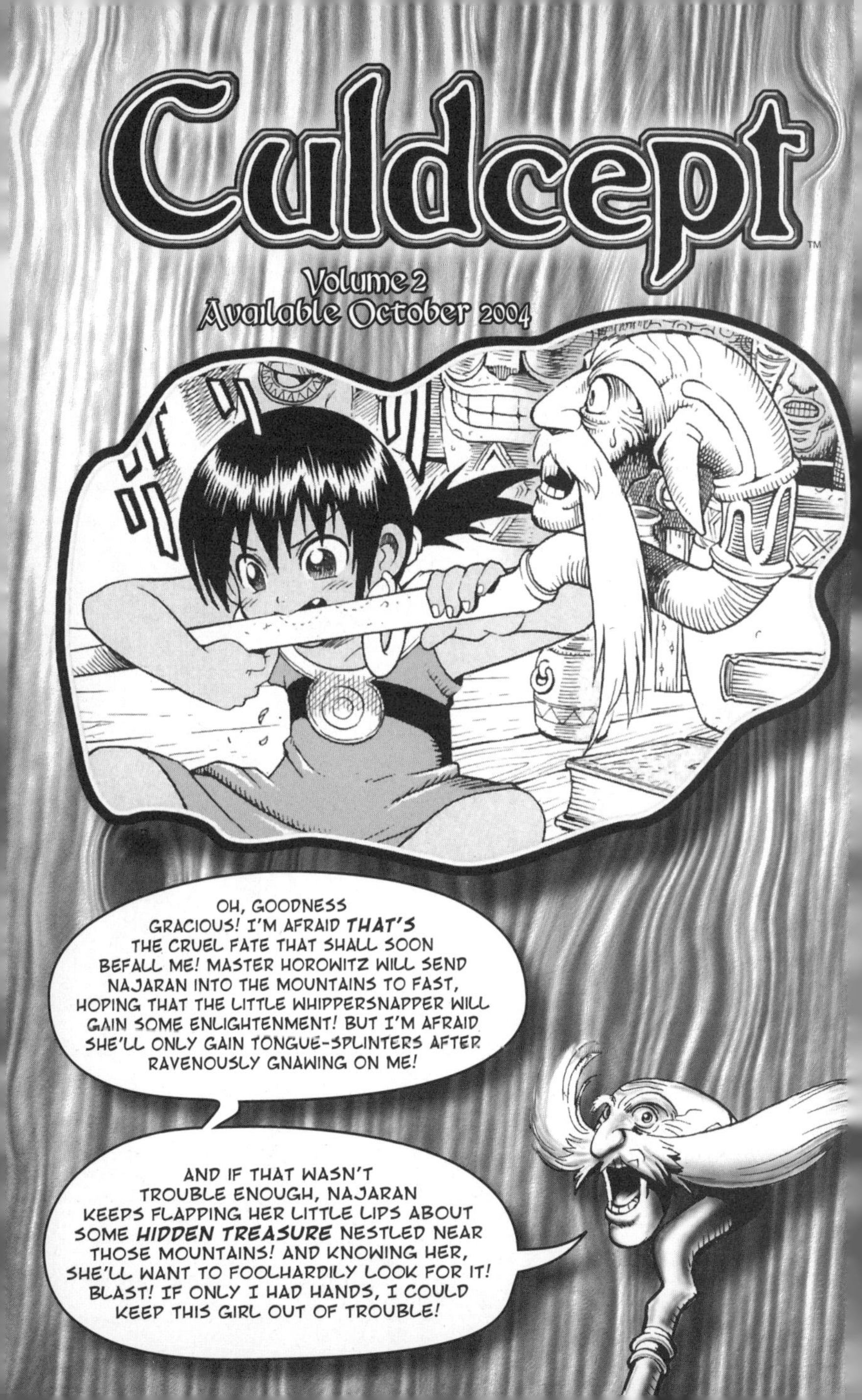
Culdcept™
Volume 2
Available October 2004
OH, GOODNESS GRACIOUS! I'M AFRAID THAT'S THE CRUEL FATE THAT SHALL SOON BEFALL ME! MASTER HOROWITZ WILL SEND NAJARAN INTO THE MOUNTAINS TO FAST, HOPING THAT THE LITTLE WHIPPERSNAPPER WILL GAIN SOME ENLIGHTENMENT! BUT I'M AFRAID SHE'LL ONLY GAIN TONGUE-SPLINTERS AFTER RAVENOUSLY GNAWING ON ME!
AND IF THAT WASN'T TROUBLE ENOUGH, NAJARAN KEEPS FLAPPING HER LITTLE LIPS ABOUT SOME HIDDEN TREASURE NESTLED NEAR THOSE MOUNTAINS! AND KNOWING HER, SHE'LL WANT TO FOOLHARDILY LOOK FOR IT! BLAST! IF ONLY I HAD HANDS, I COULD KEEP THIS GIRL OUT OF TROUBLE!

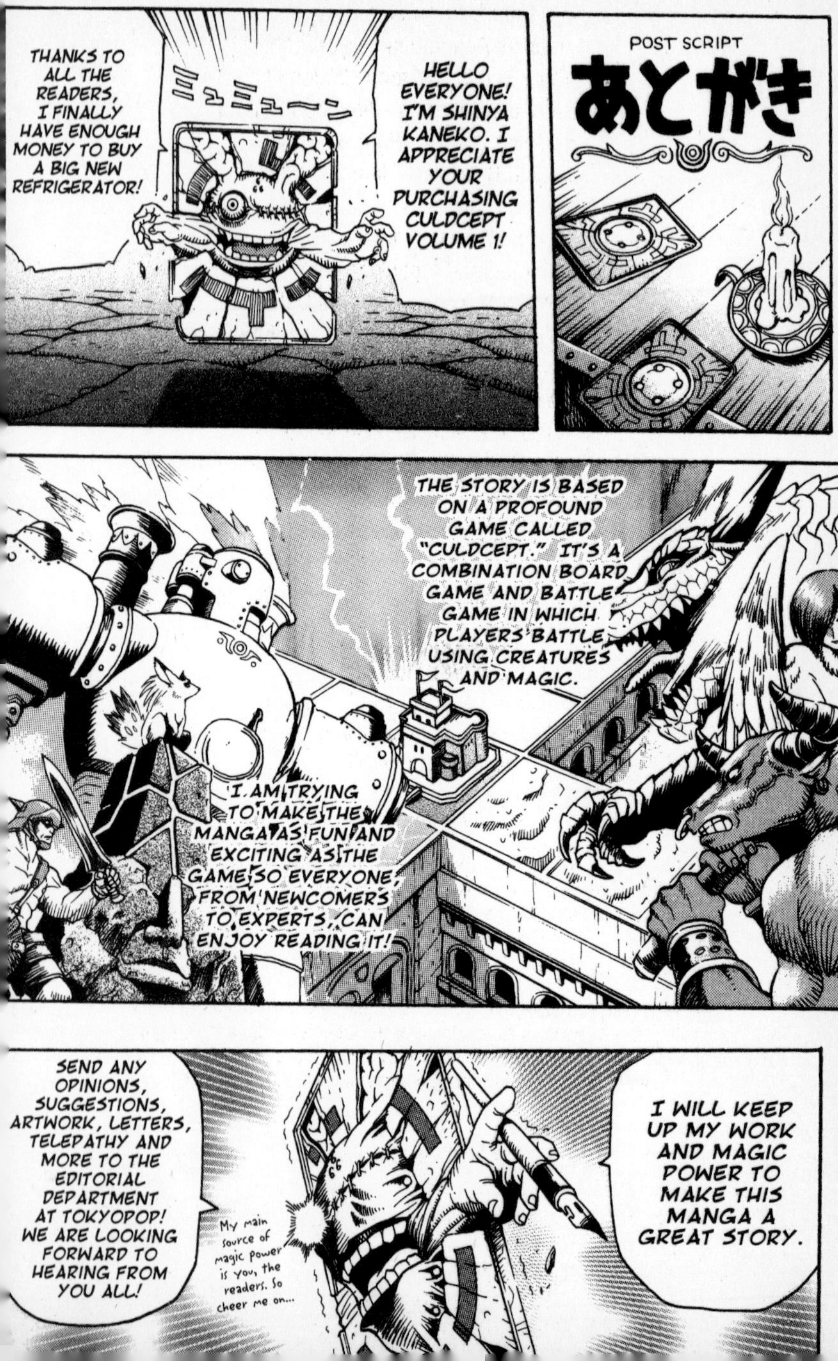
POST SCRIPT
あとがき
HELLO EVERYONE! I'M SHINYA KANEKO. I APPRECIATE YOUR PURCHASING CULDCEPT VOLUME 1!
ミュミューン
THANKS TO ALL THE READERS, I FINALLY HAVE ENOUGH MONEY TO BUY A BIG NEW REFRIGERATOR!
THE STORY IS BASED ON A PROFOUND GAME CALLED "CULDCEPT." IT'S A COMBINATION BOARD GAME AND BATTLE GAME IN WHICH PLAYERS BATTLE USING CREATURES AND MAGIC.
I AM TRYING TO MAKE THE MANGA AS FUN AND EXCITING AS THE GAME SO EVERYONE, FROM NEWCOMERS TO EXPERTS, CAN ENJOY READING IT!
I WILL KEEP UP MY WORK AND MAGIC POWER TO MAKE THIS MANGA A GREAT STORY.
SEND ANY OPINIONS, SUGGESTIONS, ARTWORK, LETTERS, TELEPATHY AND MORE TO THE EDITORIAL DEPARTMENT AT TOKYOPOP! WE ARE LOOKING FORWARD TO HEARING FROM YOU ALL!
My main source of magic power is you, the readers. So cheer me on...

Translator - Takae Brewer
English Adaptation - Jay Antani
Copy Editor - Suzanne Waldman
Retouch and Lettering - Abelardo Bigting
Cover Layout - Patrick Hook
Graphic Designer - James Dashiell

Editor - Paul Morrissey
Digital Imaging Manager - Chris Buford
Pre-Press Manager - Antonio DePietro
Production Managers - Jennifer Miller and Mutsumi Miyazaki
Art Director - Matt Alford
Managing Editor - Jill Freshney
VP of Production - Ron Klamert
President & C.O.O. - John Parker
Publisher & C.E.O. - Stuart Levy

Email: info@TOKYOPOP.com
Come visit us online at www.TOKYOPOP.com

TOKYOPOP Inc.
5900 Wilshire Blvd. Suite 2000
Los Angeles, CA 90036

Culdcept Vol. 1

©2000 Shina Kaneko. ©1997, 1999 Omiya Soft.
All Rights Reserved. First Published in Japan in 2000 by Kodansha Ltd., Tokyo.
English publication rights arranged through Kodansha Ltd.

English text copyright ©2004 TOKYOPOP Inc.

All rights reserved. No portion of this book may be reproduced or transmitted
in any form or by any means without written permission from the copyright
holders. This manga is a work of fiction. Any resemblance to actual events
or locales or persons, living or dead, is entirely coincidental.

ISBN: 1-59182-782-5

First TOKYOPOP printing: July 2004

10 9 8 7 6 5 4 3 2 1

Printed in the USA

ALSO AVAILABLE FROM TOKYOPOP®

You want it? We got it!
A full range of TOKYOPOP
products are available now at:
www.TOKYOPOP.com/shop

04.23.04T

ALSO AVAILABLE FROM

MANGA

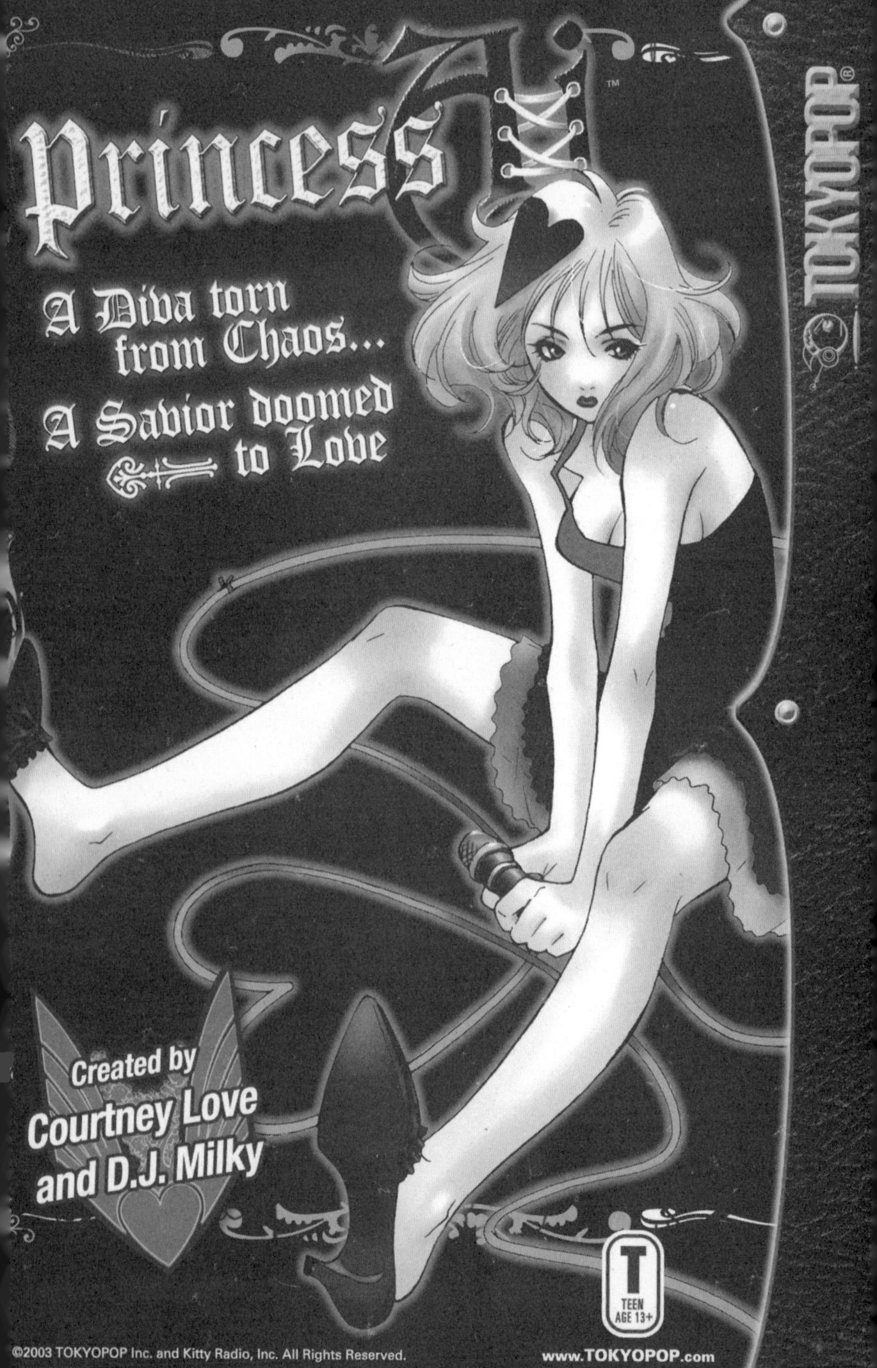

©2003 TOKYOPOP Inc. and Kitty Radio, Inc. All Rights Reserved.

www.TOKYOPOP.com

TOKYOPOP

MANGA ALSO AVAILABLE

RAVE MASTER

TIME FOR THE RAVE-OLUTION

ALL NEW ANIMATED SERIES NOW ON

CARTOON NETWORK

Rave Master TM & © Hiro Mashima • Kodansha / "Rave" Partnership.
All rights reserved. Licensed by Kodansha through TOKYOPOP®.

BASED ON THE HIT VIDEO GAME SERIES!

TOKYOPOP®

Suikoden™

幻想水滸伝

A legendary hero.
A war with no future.
An epic for today.

YOUTH AGE 10+

www.TOKYOPOP.com

©2002 Aki Shimizu. ©1995, 2004 Konami Computer Entertainment. ©2004 TOKYOPOP Inc.

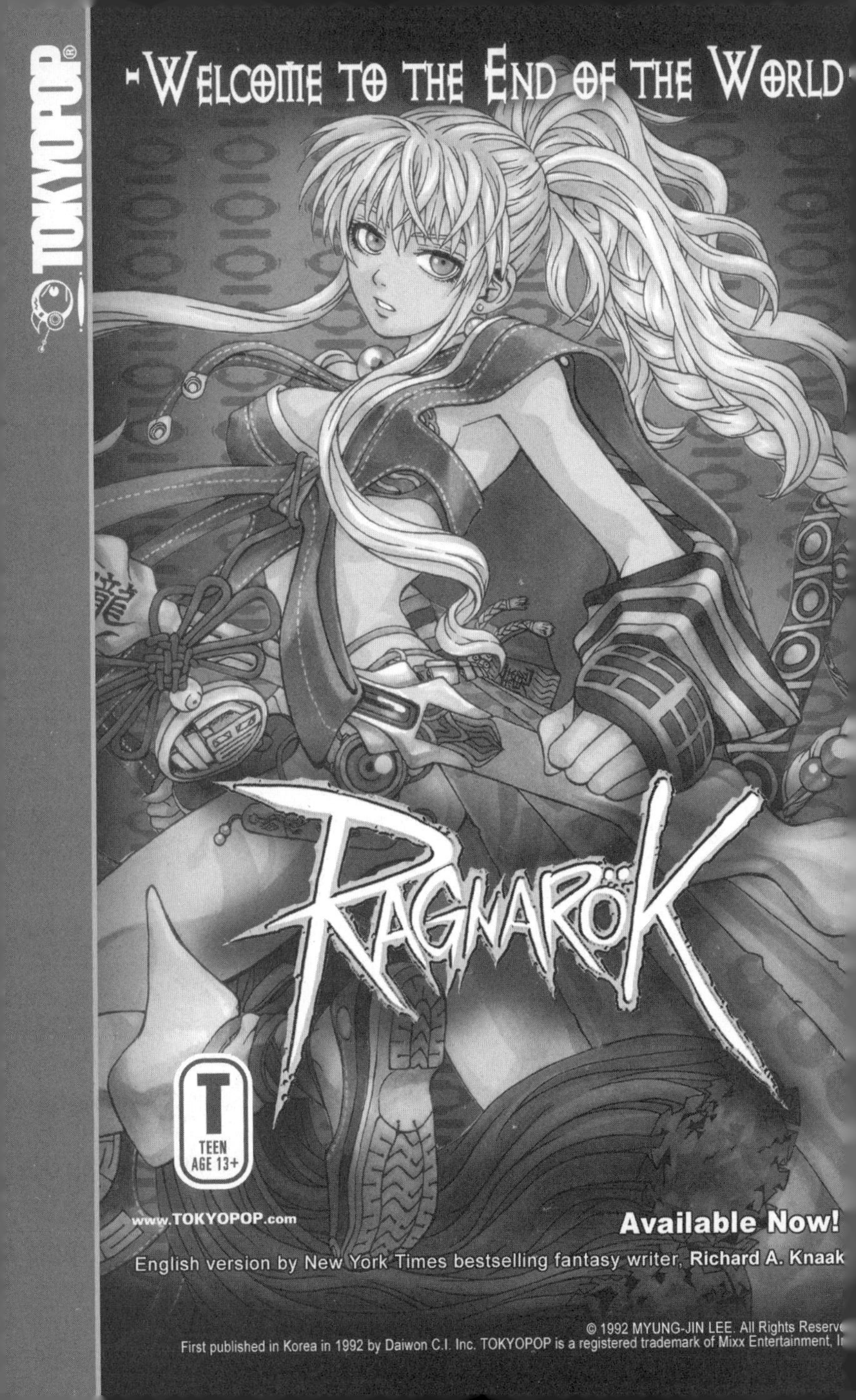
TOKYOPOP
-WELCOME TO THE END OF THE WORLD-
RAGNARÖK
T TEEN AGE 13+
www.TOKYOPOP.com
Available Now!
English version by New York Times bestselling fantasy writer, Richard A. Knaak
© 1992 MYUNG-JIN LEE. All Rights Reserve
First published in Korea in 1992 by Daiwon C.I. Inc. TOKYOPOP is a registered trademark of Mixx Entertainment, I

STOP!

This is the back of the book.
You wouldn't want to spoil a great ending!

This book is printed "manga-style," in the authentic Japanese right-to-left format. Since none of the artwork has been flipped or altered, readers get to experience the story just as the creator intended. You've been asking for it, so TOKYOPOP® delivered: authentic, hot-off-the-press, and far more fun!

DIRECTIONS

If this is your first time reading manga-style, here's a quick guide to help you understand how it works.

It's easy... just start in the top right panel and follow the numbers. Have fun, and look for more 100% authentic manga from TOKYOPOP®!